Loose Theatre

In and out of my memory

by

Margaretta D'Arcy

for Sarah Hipperson

The Cover design is from a photograph by Frank Miller for the Irish Press, 1986, laid out by Peadar de Burca.
Co-Published by Women's Pirate Press.
Visit the author's website at www.margarettadarcy.com

Printed in Victoria, BC, Canada

Note for Librarians: a cataloguing record for this book that includes Dewey Decimal Classification and US Library of Congress numbers is available from the Library and Archives of Canada. The complete cataloguing record can be obtained from their online database at:
www.collectionscanada.ca/amicus/index-e.html
ISBN 1-4120-3376-4

TRAFFORD

This book was published *on-demand* in cooperation with Trafford Publishing. On-demand publishing is a unique process and service of making a book available for retail sale to the public taking advantage of on-demand manufacturing and Internet marketing. On-demand publishing includes promotions, retail sales, manufacturing, order fulfilment, accounting and collecting royalties on behalf of the author.

Offices in Canada, USA, UK, Ireland, and Spain
book sales for North America and international:
Trafford Publishing, 6E–2333 Government St.
Victoria, BC V8T 4P4 CANADA
phone 250 383 6864 toll-free 1 888 232 4444
fax 250 383 6804 email to orders@trafford.com

book sales in Europe:
Trafford Publishing (UK) Ltd., Enterprise House, Wistaston Road Business Centre
Crewe, Cheshire CW2 7RP UNITED KINGDOM
phone 01270 251 396 local rate 0845 230 9601
facsimile 01270 254 983 orders.uk@trafford.com

order online at:
www.trafford.com/robots/04-1203.html

10 9 8 7 6 5 4 3 2

Loose Theatre

In and out of my memory

INTRODUCTION

The printing and publishing of books has become much more flexible in recent years. In consequence, I think of these dips in-and-out of my memory as more of a scrapbook than a book in the traditional sense. The publishers hold my original typescript on disc, and every copy I issue can be individually amended, to put memories in or pull them out. Intending readers can thus order their own personal selection. If they have their own memories of events that I have recorded, or if they think I have misremembered anything or been unfair to them, they can consult with me; I can write it up to their requirements and click it in to their own exclusive copy; or, for that matter, make of it a permanent feature of future editions. This may be necessary, because at times of tension it is remarkable how jaundiced one's feelings toward other people can be, and this sourness has inevitably here and there got into the diaries (from which much of this "scrapbook" is made up) because it is what I was feeling at the time. Paradoxically, because one has written it down, it has acted as a kind of purge and has cleared the emotions so that one can carry on once again with life and with love where the flow of love had been blocked. I have called the book **Loose Theatre**, because it covers many aspects of the diverse theatrical and *loosely* theatrical activities I have been mixed up with throughout my life, rather a series of samples than a complete chronology.

Part One (Chapters 1 -- 6) *is* quite chronological; it contains vignettes of my childhood, and my adolescence in the theatre in Ireland and England.

Part Two (Chapters 7 -- 17) shows how from mainstream theatre I moved away down a number of alternative paths. It includes the Royal Court and the beginning of my partnership with John Arden; then, by way of fragments of old diaries, I flick through a variety of episodes from the dark 1970s, Galway, London (my involvement with the Theatre Writers' Union), and Belfast, all overshadowed by the war in the north of Ireland. Also brief notes of visits to Madrid and to a drama festival in France.

Part Three (Chapters 18 -- Epilogue) might not at first sight be thought to deal with theatre at all; but I see its material as a valid extension of public theatre, where the Protagonists issue a challenge to the greatest Antagonist of all, the State. I begin with my own struggle in Aosdána (the Irish Artists' Parliament) against the Arts Council, which led in turn to my appropriating an airwave for Radio Pirate-Woman and challenging the censorship regulations. Out of that, my experience at Greenham Common. People often said we were wasting our lives at Greenham; did we not understand the gross improbability of the Women's Peace Camp ever getting rid of the cruise missiles and restoring the common to its natural state in the hands of the people? But this has now happened. If such a thing happens once it can happen again; such struggle contains all the *ingredients* for changing the values of the world -- e.g. persistence, commitment to the orginal vision, flexibility. It is no accident that it was women who did it, and a extraordinarily diverse gathering of women: christians, goddess-worshippers, rationalists, mothers, artists, pensioners, -- may I instance Katrina Howse, Jean Hutchinson, Georgina Smith, and above all Sarah Hipperson, midwife and magistrate? I like to think of the two threads in Sarah's life, the midwife the helper of birth, the magistrate the arbiter of justice, as so determinedly she followed the vision through to its fruition. Whether or no the Newbury people are aware of the significance of those *ingredients* makes little difference to the result: the memorial stone circle now stands there to proclaim the value of life over the futility of war. Certainly Greenham (Yellow Gate) proved in the end that the slogan of the Kings Cross Women, WELFARE NOT WARFARE, can in fact be realized. At a crucial point, Selma James and Wilmette Brown of the Kings Cross Collective came to Greenham with a core value that took the struggle out of the category of mere protest and gave it a political and global coherence. Regardless of the splits, the confusions, the pain, rejection and betrayal, the injuries and deaths, each woman through the long years of the Greenham struggle against the Warfare State had made her significant contribution. A spin-off from Greenham was the Women's Pit-stop Camp at Armthorpe, West Yorkshire (Chapter 21). I finish the book with some snapshots of Gateshead in mid-winter at the outset of the first Gulf War, followed by a string of evocative bus journeys round London in 2003.

ACKNOWLEDGMENTS

My thanks

to my sister Rosemary & to my late sister Judith
and to J.A.'s aunt & godmother, the late Mrs Joyce Feather,
for the loan of photographs

to Eileen Murray of Bray
for press cuttings about Ronnie Ibbs

to Barry Cassin
for reminiscences of Maurice Meldon

to Vera O'Donovan
for reminiscences of John O'Donovan
to Beth Junor and women of Yellow Gate
for their Greenham Common newsletters

to Esta Carter
for Greenham Common photographs

to my aunt Rossi Billig & to Miss Edith Spivak
for information about Grandmother Billig

to Martyn Turner
for his *Irish Times* cartoon

to Frank Miller
for the cover photograph

to John Arden
for his help in preparing the typescript for the printers

and to the Irish Taxpayers who provide me with the Aosdana grant
which has made this book possible

Margaretta D'Arcy
Galway, September 2004

SCHEDULE OF CHAPTERS

Introduction

PART ONE

1 LOOSE THEATRE What is it?

2 MY INHERITANCE Politics of a mixed marriage (my mother a Russian Jew, my father an Irish republican) and its bearings upon me.

3 EARLY TURMOIL AND CONFUSIONS 1934 - 42. Childhood in Dublin and Co. Wicklow.

4 THE HOUNDS OF GOD 1942 - 47. Schooldays in an enclosed Dominican convent.

5 OUT OF THE FRYING PAN INTO THE FIRE 1947 - 51. Apprenticeship in the theatre in Ireland: theatre school in London.

6 THE FURIES 1951 - 53. Dublin: alternative theatre and new voices in the arts.

PART TWO

7 HORNCHURCH 1953 - 55. Professional theatre in an English repertory company.

8 UPS AND DOWNS: & J.A. 1955 - 57. In and out of work: the reality of theatre life in England. Finding my soul-mate.

9 MOTHERS Marriage.

10 PAIN Birth and Death.

11 COLLABORATION AND PITFALLS 1958 - 69. The Royal Court Theatre. Rejection of conventional theatre. The search for a "connected" alternative.

12 CORRANDULLA & GALWAY 1975/76

a] **Diary Excerpts (from the first days of the Galway Theatre Workshop)**

b] **Neighbours' Voices**

13 LONDON 1978 & Diary Excerpts Theatre Writers' Union. British theatre's fear of Irish Republican politics. "Troops Out" agitations.

14 BELFAST 1978 Diary Excerpts

15 LONDON 1981 Diary Excerpt

16 MADRID 1987 Diary Excerpts

17 FRANCE 1992 Diary Excerpts

PART THREE

18 CORRANDULLA & GALWAY 1982 Diary Excerpts Economic independence c/o the Irish Arts Council.

19 AOSDANA Challenging the Irish Arts Establishment.

20 GREENHAM COMMON WOMEN'S PEACE CAMP narrative, diaries, letters, etc.

a] 1986

b] 1987. INF Agreement and consequences: splits

c] 1988, '91, '92. The Work of Yellow Gate peace camp.

Non-violent direct action, law cases, gaolings. The death of Helen Thomas. Departure of Cruise missiles and USAF: victory.

21 LAST STAND AT THE PIT-HEAD: ARMTHORPE 1993 Women against Pit-Closures.

22 A MAFIA OF MAGGOTS: GATESHEAD 1991 Community Arts on Tyneside at the time of the Gulf War.

23 LONDON 2003 Diary (29 August - 4 September) Bus journeys, picking up bits of the past.

Epilogue

PART ONE

1

"LOOSE THEATRE"?

Sometimes a remark is thrown out which pulls us up sharply and makes us question who we are, what are we are doing, and how other people perceive us. One such comment came at me, a year or two ago, from a young American woman, one of many from that country fired by idealism to do good, to educate, to organize the disadvantaged; she pursues her solemn task by going on lots of courses to upgrade her skills.

We were standing on a traffic island on the approach-road to Shannon Airport, protesting against the Irish government for its breach of neutrality in allowing US war planes to refuel at Shannon on their way to the military zones of Afghanistan or the Gulf. A bit of participation was requested from the public by our placard "Bleep for Peace"; many bleeped, some did not. Across the road a 24-hour Women's Peace Camp had been set up; women had arrived in their cars or their campers or by hitching lifts; they set about erecting tents and making placards, and, as night fell, building a camp fire. During the night we had some callers from Shannon satellite-town, giving us money, newspapers to read, and thanking us for expressing their own disquiet over the impending war against Iraq and the slaughter that had been going on in Afghanistan. Earlier, some of us had been in the town, looking for signatures to a peace petition addressed "to all governments". One of the women thought of the "Bleep" placard after I suggested that we should stand on the roundabout for an hour. In fact the whole experience was so enlivening that we took it in turns to stand out there most of the night -- nothing formally organized: we just took our places when the spirit moved. As each car bleeped we all let out a roar of approval and delight, saluting them. It soon became a cacophonic musical show, shouts and car-horns, exuberance, vitality; cars that had hurried past turned round and came back to join in. We had created a loose and spontaneous form of theatre: so much so, that as dawn broke the Garda patrol ending their shift finally picked up the spirit and bleeped in their turn.

My young American friend had retired to bed exhausted from all her different assignments and appointments she had to keep, so she only experienced a moment on the roundabout. Nor would she stay for the finale, a midday rally outside the airport concourse; she was going to catch a morning bus to Galway. To rationalize her premature departure, she turned to me and said that she thought what we were doing was futile; such activities nearly always were.

I realized that this was how quite a few people saw me. Constantly popping up at street corners with petitions for people to sign! what a cop-out, when I could have been going on courses, setting up drama workshops and so on. There was no way she could see "loose theatre" or anything even resembling theatre at seven o'clock in the morning, she was unable to put herself into the imagination of drivers who had just picked up tired relatives coming in on their flights from all over the world and who suddenly saw this unexpected dawn vision of a bunch of dancing women on a traffic island. How can one judge such a thing? How can one know what the effect will be, how can one measure it or evaluate it or properly assess it it in its full context?

Grandmother D'Arcy (seated) with eight children.

London School of Economics, group ramble. My mother (seated, at extreme left), my father (under hankerchief at extreme right).

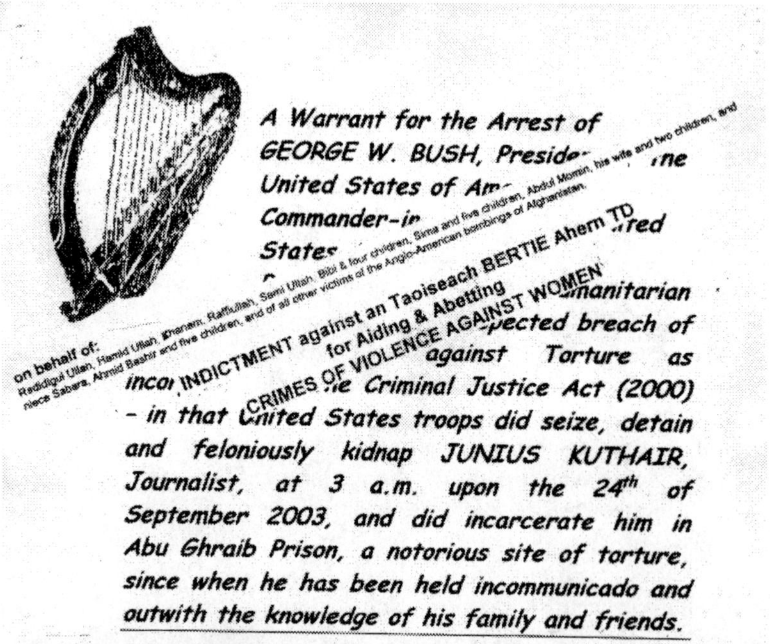

A Warrant for the Arrest of
GEORGE W. BUSH, Preside... ...ne
United States of Am...
Commander-in... ...ited
States...
...manitarian
...pected breach of
against Torture as
inco... ...e Criminal Justice Act (2000)
- in that United States troops did seize, detain and feloniously kidnap JUNIUS KUTHAIR, Journalist, at 3 a.m. upon the 24th of September 2003, and did incarcerate him in Abu Ghraib Prison, a notorious site of torture, since when he has been held incommunicado and outwith the knowledge of his family and friends.
INDICTMENT against an Taoiseach BERTIE Ahern TD
for Aiding & Abetting
CRIMES OF VIOLENCE AGAINST WOMEN
on behalf of:
Radidgul Ullah, Hamid Ullah, Ghanam, Raffiullah, Sami Ullah, Bibi & four children, Sima and five children, Abdul Momin, his wife and two children, and niece Sabara, Ahmid Bashir and five children, and of all other victims of the Anglo-American bombings of Afghanistan.
NO WAR
IT'S O.K... THE GULF IS A RUSE...
...THEY ARE ACTUALLY HERE TO SORT OUT THE KERRY GAA SUPPORTERS...
USAF
WELCOME TO NEUTRAL SHANNON

Collage; Shannon.

2

MY INHERITANCE

I was born on June 14, 1934, in the east end of London, the London Hospital, Whitechapel, the third daughter of Joseph Noel D'Arcy and Miriam (known as Marie) Billig. He was an Irishman, a catholic, he had been a freedom-fighter for Irish independence and was now incorporated into the new Irish Free State (not yet a republic) as part of its new civil service, working in London in the agricultural section of the Department of External Affairs. My mother was the daughter of émigré Russian Jews who had fled from Russia and Austria and settled in the East End. No sooner was I born than I developed pyloric-stenosis, a blockage in my gut which prevented me from digestion - the symptom was violent projectile vomiting. I had to have an operation to clear the blockage. Whether that experience altered the course of my life I cannot say. But it did have one traumatic consequence: it seems to have caused my baptism to be forgotten about, a circumstance only discovered years later by the Dominican nuns in Dublin when I was preparing for my confirmation. I'll go into this horror-story later on. And maybe the subconscious memory of all those first weeks of my life, the continuous and vehement rejection of my mother's milk, was one of the reasons for the habitual feeling of unhappiness that burdened me for so many years.

I only found release when I began to understand that much of my unhappiness was a sense of confused identity, or rather the battle over my identity among other people. As a consequence my behaviour seemed always at odds with the outside world once I ventured into it; for to me the outside world brought only discomfort, a prickly feeling of never fitting in and never getting anything right. I remember being at ease only when I was with my mother and under her protection. I could not imagine a time when I would not cry every day. The day would begin, sunshine and a clear slate, wonderful optimism! and then, as the day progressed, its incidents grew ever more muddy and disjointed, each minute bringing me a new hurdle to jump, and every time I jumped I would flounder among puddles in chaos and bewilderment. The cultural differences were too great between our own lives in our own home and the lives of everybody else outside.

I was not the only one in the family to feel like this - my sisters as well, my mother, my father - we were each of us striving in our own separate ways to work through the labyrinth. Today I can look back and lay the blame four-square on Adolf Hitler, World War 2, the Cold War; capitalism, race, class and gender; and our semi-detached Irish republic. For good measure I might as well throw in the Czar of Russia, the Emperor of Austria and John Charles McQuaid Archbishop of Dublin. Phew.

My parents rarely spoke about their childhood, save for a few anecdotes (how my father would collect jam jars to exchange for a ticket to the cinema, how my mother once dropped her new pair of red shoes into a red-painted pillar-box so that the postman might bring them to her in an exciting parcel). Both of them had given up their places in their respective tribes, and they fought hard to prevent me and my sisters from becoming infected by tribalism. As a result there was a great deal of turmoil in our family and I am now just beginning to understand the full depth of it and the full depth of my own chronic painful unease. Now that the government archives of the period are being released, I am able to make political and historical sense of the context within which I grew up.

~~~o~~~

Which parent shall I begin with, mother or father? Whichever, they would both be scornful and dismissive of my attempts to explain them: they'd say it was "rubbish". My father, the Irishman of a literary persuasion, or my mother with her turbulent Russian-Jewish temperament?

A few years before my mother's death I wrote to her asking if she would jot down some memories for her grandchildren and great-grandchildren, her feelings upon arriving in Ireland, her feelings about becoming a doctor (she finally qualified when I was fifteen) and having to leave us behind in Ireland so that she could take locum-jobs in England in order to earn enough to keep us - had we, her children, any inkling of how she felt when we all waved goodbye to her after her sporadic visits? The sub-text of my letter to her was to find
~~~

out if she felt we had appreciated the sacrifices she had made for us. Her reply was ambiguous. She never wrote intimate letters; her correspondence was as formal and brief as "duty-letters" written home from boarding-school. But this time there was a slightly different tone: it was the last letter she ever wrote to me, and it had something of a warm feeling, as though she was surprised I had been thinking of her in that way and was touched by my asking the questions. But she did not want to reminisce. She invariably reacted with instant paranoia to any mention of her in print; she never commented on anything I wrote; particularly not upon *Tell Them Everything,* my book about my experiences in Armagh Gaol. She and I never discussed those gaol-experiences - too raw for her, she had after all been a prison doctor for more than a decade - except for one time. On that occasion she was annoyed with me. My son Neuss had rung me up to say that he and his wife Karen did not want my mother coming hotfoot from Ireland to attend the birth of Karen's expected triplets - they were afraid she would be completely taking them over and throwing her professional status around in the hospital. No sooner had he put the phone down when my mother rang me to say she was in fact making plans to travel to the birth, stay in Karen's house and look after them all. When I hinted to her that perhaps she shouldn't, she spat down the phone at me, a sudden burst of venom, her voice biting into my ears: if she had ever been a magistrate (she informed me), and I had been brought up before her, she'd have sentenced me to life... One of her less endearing aspects.

I was surprised, when talking about this intended book with my two elder sisters Claire and Judith, to discover how *they* perceived her. I asked Claire, who I thought might have been on more intimate terms with her, if they'd ever had an easy reminiscent conversation. No, said Claire, our mother had never talked about her feelings, just blow-by-blow accounts of the various battles she was engaged in, with the bank, the gas-board, her other children, and so on. "You've got to remember," Claire insisted, "she never really looked after us; she always had nannies; she simply enjoyed herself." Judith was more bitter, saying mother never wanted responsibility and always fled from it. She messed up her own life and wanted to mess up ours. The way Judith saw her, she was a monster; indeed I too saw her as the two heads of Kali, the killer, the rampager, whirling like a typhoon, attempting to destroy everything in her path - until suddenly the tempest died down and it seemed as if nothing had happened, no discussion, gone, it had been no more than a "brainstorm", and all was charm and sociability once again. Judith commented, "Of course, Margaretta, *you* just evaded her." To a certain extent that was true; but also in later years my mother had learned to be wary of me because of what she perceived to be my involvement in the Republican Movement.

Once, in the early days of my marriage, she descended on me without warning in the middle of the night (when J.A. was away and my first child was due to be delivered in a week or two); it was clear she intended to make a bloody great scene - about a chamois-leather of hers which I had misused - I told her that if she didn't leave I would call the police and have her thrown out. Pretty callous behaviour from a dutiful daughter - I had really adored my mother when I was young, and indeed was a clinging child - and indeed I always loved her (from a distance!) for all her complexities - I could continue to love her so long as I never asked her for anything or took anything from her. Recently talking with one of my cousins, I found his recollections of his father (my mother's brother David) didn't seem very much different.

~~~o~~~

The Billigs could be ferocious.

My aunt Hannah (my mother's elder sister) used to say, "Billigs might forgive but we never forget." When pitted against Hannah and David, her two sibling doctors, my mother appeared fragile and vulnerable.

The Billigs came from Russia: my grandmother, Millie, from a village outside Odessa where her parents had an apothecary-shop which also sold soap and candles; my grandfather, Barnet, from Odessa itself, where his family, so my grandmother told me, owned flour-mills. My grandmother was one of three sisters. One of them was beautiful blonde Mina who ended up in California. The other one went to Switzerland: it is said that one day in 1902 she left her house to do the morning shopping and was shot dead by a stray bullet, the solitary casualty of a small local "Uprising" - I don't where I got hold of that story or even if it is true. She had married a man called Woolf; they had one son who eventually went to live in Israel. A story I heard about my grandmother, from a daughter of her great friend, Mrs Spivack: - when they were girls in the village near Odessa, she and her sisters used to swim naked in the river; per-
~~~

haps that is how she met my grandfather? - a serious young man, religious and scholarly. Perhaps he spied on them, courted and won one of them? All three girls seem to have left Russia at the same time, possibly because of a pogrom in the village. My grandfather joined them later. The story goes that he was in flight from the Czar's military conscription, which deliberately targeted Jews as a method of controlling and persecuting them. He had to smuggle himself out of Russia into Austria under a false passport, using my grandmother's name Billig, pretending to be her cousin. I do not know what happened to the rest of his family. Was he the only one to emigrate at that time? If they were mill-owners, I suppose they would have been fairly prosperous; so how was it he was so poor when he finally reached London?

With my grandmother he began a new, married, life in Austria, losing his old surname for ever. But the Emperor of Austria didn't treat him any better than the Czar. Once again he was marked for conscription; once again he refused to submit; once again he went on his travels. They arrived in the east end of London some time before 1898. They shared an upstairs flat at 41 Hanbury Street, near the corner of Brick Lane, over a newsagent's shop. Brick Lane today is associated with Asian immigrants and pitched battles between the National Front and the Anti-Nazi League. In the thirties it was Mosley's anti-semitic fascists who had to be confronted in the same part of town. 1898 was the year of Eleanor Marx's suicide. Not long before, she had reasserted her Jewish ancestry, learned Yiddish, and campaigned in the east end to unionise the Jewish tailors from the sweatshops.

Grandma was 96 when she died in 1963. Grandpa must have been in his seventies when he died in 1942. If they arrived in London (having lived some time in Austria) in the late 1890s, they must have been at least 30 when they started their family. I would have thought, by Jewish standards, this was a bit old. So what was Grandpa doing, in Russia, before he left for Austria (date unknown)? He does not seem to have learned any trade or put aside any money. And if the story is true, that he emigrated on a false passport, *in order to avoid conscription,* when did he do it? The usual age for conscripts is around 18, which would leave him at least ten or a dozen years in Austria before setting out for England. How did he earn his living in Austria; and was he already married? (We were told that his reason for leaving Austria was also *to avoid conscription:* the same difficulty applies, his age.) My guess is that he tried to avoid conscription but failed; that he was in the Russian army for some length of time, where he learned, as soldiers do learn, how to roll cigarettes swiftly and deftly; that he deserted from the army (like James Connolly from the British army in the same era), and was smuggled to Vienna. Austria at that time was very anti-semitic, with strong anti-immigration laws. To a young Jew with falsified papers it would not have been a safe place at all.

I can just hear my mother snorting, to one of my sisters, "Oh there's Margaretta once again making up her facts to suit her story." I might add, she would not say it to me face-to-face, lest I began to question her and ask her for *her* version of the facts. Instead, the sneers, the undermining, as though she were the only one in the family with a right to the story. Anne Karpf, daughter of a Holocaust survivor, has a pertinent passage in her book *Surviving the Holocaust*:

> [Holocaust-survivor] parents and [their] children often develop extreme symbiotic ties; the parents don't encourage the child's autonomy, and experience the normal process of separation and individuation in their offspring as a threat and an acute narcissistic injury to the family.

Even though I am the third generation from the pogroms (which, as Karpf points out, were *not* the same as the Holocaust), I know the syndrome. In our case the "separation and individuation" were made more complex by the circumstance that my mother's offspring were not brought-up or recognized as Jewish. Any prying on our part into her territory set up immediate barriers. In any case, she herself was something of an family outsider - partly of her own choice, partly because of the age-gap between herself and her elder siblings, partly because her father does not seem to have thought that she had the same high qualities as the other three.

Another aspect of the inbred secrecy of this family was Grandpa's refusal to allow any of them, even his wife, to speak Yiddish. Was it no more than an act of cultural assimilation; or was it a form of protection? a means of making sure that nothing came out in gossip among other immigrants about an irregular passport and - maybe - desertion from the army of a foreign power which might, who could say? become suddenly an *allied* power? Moreover, in 1905 parliament passed the Aliens Act, specifically brought in to restrict

Jewish immigrants because of increasing anti-semitism and outbreaks of overt hostility. It demanded that immigrants prove their ability to "decently" support themselves and their dependants. Can you imagine the psychological pressure on struggling families, having to hide the extent of their poverty in order to produce a sufficient appearance of *decency* to satisfy the government? Miss Spivack remembered noticing that the Billigs in those days were poorer than the Spivacks. My cousin Michael has a story of how Levi and David, as children, once went out begging, and how furious their father was. Not only was it degrading and undermining his authority as breadwinner, but it could also have got the whole family deported, had some snoopy neighbour informed on them.

~~~o~~~

Grandfather had brought no craft skills with him, so he would have had to look around to discover a small niche for himself to survive, making things that were easy to make, and finding a market for them. Some of his children had rickets, most unusual in Jewish families where a lot of fish was normally eaten; it means my grandmother could not even afford the odd herring. Mrs Spivack and herself lived beside each other in the early days; they became lifelong friends. Even after Grandmother moved house, she would spend a whole day every week with Mrs Spivack. They had babies alternate years. Mrs Spivack's children were born in "Mother Levy's" maternity home, but grandmother had hers in her own home. Mr Spivack was a tailor who made caps for the police. Grandfather began making hand-rolled cigarettes, bringing them round for sale on a little handcart, while Grandma made toffee. Later on he made his cigarettes for a small factory, piece-work, cottage-industry; and others would also supply the factory in the same way. He was beadle to the local synagogue; he gave Hebrew lessons. Even while giving the lessons he would continue to roll cigarettes.

Once again from Miss Spivack: "Your grandmother was very religious, she was also very deaf all her life and used a hearing horn, later on she got a modern hearing-aid but because it was battery-run she wouldn't use it on the Sabbath, and instead used her horn, she also followed the Jewish custom for married women and wore a brown wig. Your grandfather was much less approachable." They had nine children. It seems to have been a very introverted and claus-
~~~

trophic family. A strange thing which may explain my mother's inability to talk freely about her childhood: neither of her parents had any English when they arrived; my grandfather learned Latin in order to learn English, which was certainly an odd thing to do... Even on her weekly visits to Mrs Spivack, my grandmother would speak English - they would gossip in that language all day, but when they parted for the evening, they always ended with a little Yiddish phrase: "We have spoken all day but we have spoken no evil of any one."

It seems as though my grandfather allowed her only this one friendship; the rest of the time she was isolated. According to my mother she was unintellectual and frivolous. The children were guided and influenced by their father. They were not allowed to play with other children. Education (he must have thought) was the only way forward for those trapped in grinding poverty, education to be free from the womb-like complacency and acceptance of death and disease that so often derives from poverty. Without education the easiest and most cunning way to survive would be to prey upon one's own brethren, with a little bit of money-lending here and there, and the offering of favours to be ruthlessly called-in, the whole under-layer of lumpen proletariat... as denounced by Marx. Unlike Marx, my grandfather insisted on the full education of his daughters as well as his sons. He looked around him at the fate of so many Jewish women, reared to be good Jewish wives, to have babies every year, to struggle endlessly to keep the family together. But his emphasis on education and achievement did mean that there was no lightness in the household, no encounter with popular culture: the children, boys and girls, went to school, came home and studied. They never played outside. According to my cousin, they seem to have lived in their own world with their own made-up language which outsiders could not penetrate.

My grandmother told me once, that after the birth of her first child Esther, she travelled alone with her back to Odessa for a visit. Was that because she was so homesick that she couldn't take it anymore? And where did she find the money to pay for that long journey all on her own with a new-born baby? When I heard this at the age of sixteen it did not occur to me that the episode was remarkable; I never questioned her, for her anecdote was primarily intended to tell me what a modern city Odessa had been, even before she first left it; it was lit by electricity; when she arrived in London she was surprised to find gas-lamps still in use.

In any case how would my grandfather be content to let his children roam streets that were open to all the furious ideological groups emerging from every cranny at that time in the east end: mensheviks, bolsheviks, anarchists - every possible brand of immigrant revolutionism, under the eye of the police and infiltrated by police agents? - of course he would make sure that the children avoided temptation by receiving their intellectual stimulus inside their own home.

~~~o~~~

When I first met Jewish writers of my generation from the east end - playwrights Arnold Wesker, Bernard Kops, Harold Pinter, Michael Horovitz the poet - I suppose I had half-hoped for some undercurrent of empathy - "Oh, your grandmother lived in Cable Street? What number? Did you ever know the Goldbergs at 23?" - the sort of identification and searching for a shared memory that happens if I meet an Irish person somewhere outside Ireland. But it could never have happened. Their families had been assimilated into English life long before; I was now the alien, coming from Ireland. Also, unlike the Irish diaspora, all these families originated in different parts of Europe - Russia, Lithuania, Hungary, Czechoslovakia, and so forth... yet arriving in London to be labelled simply "Jewish". In fact I don't know if the Russian Jews were really Jews at all - Arthur Koestler has claimed they began as a tribe of some sort of Turk, galloping across the steppe, sword in hand, yearning for book-learning and a respectable religion. They discussed the question with Christians, Muslims and Jews; and eventually chose the Jewish book, perhaps because it was the source of the other two...

~~~o~~~

My mother - Miriam - was born in 1907.

She had three elder brothers (one of them, Arthur, died at the age of 13 in a football-pitch accident) and two elder sisters. Then there was a baby who died. Then a gap of a few years; then my mother, and then after her, another baby who died, followed by the last child, Rebecca. I suspect these three dead children were a reason for medicine to bulk so large in the subsequent lives of the other children: four became doctors and one a nurse. It is hard to say what would have been the chief influences on my mother in those turbulent days. I know that at the outbreak of the first World War there were virulent anti-foreigner outbreaks. The police came to the house once, after an anonymous report that my grandmother was hoarding white flour. A neighbour had informed on her. My aunt told me how the police came to arrest Grandma, and how she calmly showed them how she sifted the coarse flour to make her bread until it looked as though it was white. This was told as a family joke to show what a clever cook she was; but to my mother (as a little girl) it must have been very frightening. Let alone the feeling of insecurity as to who had reported it, spying eyes keeping them under surveillance, the sinister east end of the anti-semitic imaginings of the likes of John Buchan or Sapper - no wonder my grandfather was so against the children reading any sort of popular literature and comics; he kept them firmly to the classic novelists.

All the children won scholarships to second-level and then third-level education, except for Esther, the eldest, who had to forgo her scholarship and earn her own living because of the family's poverty at that time; she was first a nurse; and then a governess in Greece; and then a governess in the royal household of Morocco, where she was stranded in the second World War.

The eldest son Levi went to Cambridge to study Hebrew and Arabic.

When Hannah qualified as a doctor she found a job at the Jewish Maternity Hospital, before setting up a mother-and-child clinic of her own to create trust in the neighbourhood; I doubt if the patients had any money to pay her... Then, most courageously, and having built something of a reputation, she established a general practice in Cable Street, round the corner from where she lived. Miss Spivack told me the story: "Your mother and Hannah, carrying paint-cans, went and painted this old shed that Hannah had rented for her first surgery. It was opposite number 98 where she eventually lived, with the surgery on the ground floor." Hannah's work was publicly recognized in 1997 when a plaque was erected on the outside of that house. An exhibition was assembled about her life, and a children's book was written, *The Angel of Cable Street,* presenting her as a role model for the girls from Bangladesh, the latest phase of east-end immigrants. David followed in her footsteps, also working as a doctor in a deprived area, in Wandsworth. No doubt he was influenced by his sister who had shown him how to do it without any money to speak of.

Later on, the youngest sister, Rebecca (known as Bimms), followed into the profession.

But not, at that time, my mother. Instead, in the late 1920s, she won a scholarship to the London School of Economics, where she took a B.Sc.

I have a feeling that Levi encouraged her, in the hope that she would be able to join him in Palestine after she graduated, and apply her knowledge of science to the affairs of a kibbutz. For Levi, after Cambridge, had made his home in Palestine; he worked at the newly-founded Hebrew University, translating the Bible into Arabic; he was shot dead by an Arab sniper one night in the early 1930s. The family held him in the highest esteem for his idealism and his intellectual brilliance. Hannah, who was next to him in age, worshipped him; she told me how, before the second World War, she smuggled guns into Palestine in her car for the Jewish militias. (I believe in fact that when my eldest sister was born there was some talk about Levi adopting her and bringing her out to Tel Aviv.) He became part of the liberal wing hoping to make Palestine an independent socialist state, for Jews and Arabs equally, based on the kibbutz principle.

A sad comment caught my eye in *The Sunday Times,* the week of the 50th Anniversary of the founding of the State of Israel: --

> For Meir Shalev, a left-wing opponent of Netanyahu, the true cause of Zionism has been betrayed. A century ago the early Zionists wrote of a 'state of the Jews', a socialist utopia. But in the hands of the right and the religious this has become a 'Jewish state', a fatally significant change of emphasis that, for the left, stresses the tribal aspect of the place. Now, he feels, Israel is embarked on a potentially dangerous course, and he has nothing but contempt for the people responsible.

Conor Cruise O'Brien, in his book on the history of Israel, offers a number of historical facts that cast a new (and more dramatic) light on why Grandfather left Russia, and provide a possible alternative explanation of why he would not allow Yiddish in the family once he was settled in London. They give a plausible context for Levi, the eldest son, studying Hebrew and Arabic, leaving his parents behind and making his home in Palestine, an unusual destiny for the eldest son.

They also suggest how the Billigs became so ferocious. I calculate that Grandpa was born some time in the late 1860s, when the government of Czar Alexander II had brought some relief to the Jews in the Russian empire. But in 1881 the Czar was murdered. One of the assassins was a Jewish woman.

> The pogroms came back on a scale not known since the 17th century. It became horrifyingly apparent that what most united the Russian people, peasant, middle class and Czar, was a hatred of Jews... The phenomenon was not just shocking. It was terrifying, in an intimate and existential way, as the diagnosis of a grave and terminal disease is to an individual.
> Conor Cruise O'Brien (*The Siege, the Story of Israel and Zionism*)

Imagine the effect on two children, my grandfather and grandmother, of this terror and shock among the grown-ups.

> [For Russian Jews after 1881] there were only three courses that held any promise... The first... was to go to a Western country... The second was to stay in Russia and work for the Revolution... The third course, Zionism.
> *Ibid*

~~~o~~~

I am now going to take a leap, from the ascertainable into the imagined. My grandfather's birthplace, Odessa, was the most secular and cosmopolitan city in Russia. It was there where the concept was most strongly developed of the Jewish homeland in Palestine and the eventual Jewish nation-state. Three leading Zionist ideologues were either natives of Odessa, or went to live there: Moshe Leib Lilienblum, Peretz Smolenskin and Leon Pinsker. Pinsker belonged to the "Haskala" tradition, the Jewish expression of the European Enlightenment. He encouraged Russian Jews to speak Russian rather than Yiddish, originally in the hope that they would be able to assimilate more easily. But the idea of the homeland brought about the notion that Hebrew should be developed as a modern vernacular language. Now my grandmother seems to have been a very orthodox Jew from a small town; but shall I assume that her husband was a representative of the Pinsker-type Enlightenment? When Lilienblum declared in the 1880s that orthodox and secular Jews should make common cause to base a new Jewish state on the shtetl (Jewish village), thus opening
~~~

the way to the kibbutz, the collective village, I feel sure that my grandfather had some inkling of this new movement. If he had been compelled to join the Czar's army, did he meet with some barrackroom Zionist? And then, later, did he come into closer contact with Zionists in Vienna?

I feel now that the dream of the Homeland, of the perfect idealistic community, must have had a strong grip upon the Billigs, because they made such a point of rejecting the crass materialism of so many other Jews around them who aspired to assimilation in British commercial life. When they arrived in London, Zionism was still in its embryo stage and would not have been a generally accepted concept amongst their fellow-immigrants. England, on the other hand, was comparatively tolerant of immigrants, and had a geopolitical interest in Palestine as being close to the Suez Canal. Theodor Herzl, the great Zionist, came to London in 1896 and addressed an audience of poor immigrant Jews in Whitechapel. "As I sat on the platform of the working-men's stage on Sunday," he wrote, "I experienced strange sensations. I saw and heard my legend being born." Were the Billigs already in Whitechapel, and was my grandfather in that audience?

By 1917, when the Balfour Declaration was issued, promising the Jews a national home in Palestine, Levi was of an age to go to university. He had won a scholarship to grammar school, now he won another to Cambridge. I believe his course of studies, Hebrew and Arabic, was deliberately chosen to prepare him for Palestine. And when he was in Palestine, at university there, he became a member of a group known as Berit Shalom ("The Covenant of Peace") which sought peace with the Arabs and a Jewish/Arab bi-national state. Cruise O'Brien writes, "Berit Shalom remained a small and rather unpopular minority… (A quote from a letter sent to Berit Shalom's own magazine): 'You are in favour of a democratically elected legislative assembly. But how do you know that this assembly, with a clear Arab majority, will not spell the doom of Zionism?'"

Once again I interpret facts to suit my own story and my own experience. The tale goes that Levi was shot by an Arab while sitting in his study, translating the Bible into Arabic. It was this kind of Arab outrage which apparently proved that a bi-national state was impossible. Now, more than one of my friends and acquaintances in the north of Ireland have been assassinated in the course of the conflict there; the killers have never been found, their provenance and motivation in each case enigmatic. Such murders are never quite as straightforward as they seem… How convenient then for out-and-out Zionism, that a Jewish intellectual, who claimed that a bi-national state was *possible,* should thus be eliminated…

~~~o~~~

Levi, with his post at the Hebrew University, was able to help Hannah and David in their medical careers. Hannah was not yet established; David had only recently qualified; and now mother was at the LSE. The LSE was a think-tank for all kinds of new post-war ideas, planning, economics, sociology, unfettered by old-fashioned British Establishment traditions. There was also the intellectual upheaval caused by the Russian Revolution and the demands for independence from so many small nations. It must have been very exciting for a young Russian Jew to leave the ghetto-like familiarity of the east end and mix with the mainstream of the intelligentsia at the other end of town. Hannah, after all, never moved much more than a block away from her birthplace. And when Hannah set up her practice in Cable Street, my mother had been there as very much the younger sister helping the older one, but excluded from the professional life of both older sister and brother. There was in any case an intense competition and rivalry between Hannah and David; and I fancy that mother did not want to be part of it.

She was naive, romantic, idealistic, enthusiastic and very impressionable, and free at last from comparisons with her brilliant elder sister. Now she could shine in her own right. So it is not surprising that she soon fell in love with an Irish revolutionary freedom-fighter, Joseph Noel D'Arcy, nine years older than herself, blond with blue eyes. No doubt he cut a glamorous figure amongst the socialists and anti-imperialists at the college; Ireland, after all, was the first country of the Empire since the days of George Washington to secure independence (however limited); and its recent history of revolt would have carried a sanguine and inspiring message. Similarly, my father must have been bowled over by this dark slim dynamic exotic girl with a such a "sympathetic" background of racial and national dispossession. They both belonged to a hiking group; they strode over the South Downs, descending to refresh themselves at Chestertonian village pubs, and then walking all night under the
~~~

moon; photographs snapped among their fellow-students in the Great Outdoors show them glowing with health and Zeitgeist; they sang all the appropriate communal songs - "My Darling Clementine", "Drink to me Only", "What shall we do with the Drunken Sailor?", "There is a Tavern in the Town"...

They were married in June 1929 in the Catholic church of St. Anne in Soho.

~~~o~~~

My mother at the time was living with Hannah in Cable Street. She told her she was just going to the library; instead she went off to her secret wedding. The first daughter, Claire Naomi, was born in early February 1930, eight months after the wedding, so it seems likely that Mother got married because she was pregnant. (It must have been then that Levi offered to adopt the baby and bring her up in Palestine.) Anyway the whole transaction was highly irregular: I assume they chose Soho for the wedding because of its cosmopolitan congregation. No doubt the priest in such a parish would not have been too strict about the Papal "Ne Temere" which expressly forbade Jews and Catholics to marry. But my mother would have had to sign a document promising that the children would be baptised; and the first two of us were. Despite the strict orthodoxy of her family, Father was accepted by them. He did have to become a Jew, however; and then there was a Jewish wedding. But I suspect they were made conscious - via Levi - of similarities between the Irish struggle and the search for a Jewish Homeland. My father was a civil servant as well as a student (the Irish government had "seconded" him to the LSE) and belonged to the Department of Agriculture, and this would have aroused Levi's interest in connection with the development of land-ownership and co-operatives in Palestine. According to my grandmother, Father promised to bring all of us up as Jews. Each of us was given one Jewish name. Anyway it would not have mattered very much to my parents what they were promising because neither of them practised either religion. They obviously never gave a thought to any possible consequences of their perjury and to the effect it might have on their children in future years.

Their first home was in Hampstead Garden Suburb, a new model of "green" urban planning deriving from the ideas of Ebenezer Howard, Utopian Socialism
~~~

of the late 19th century. Childrens' playgrounds, nursery schools, Montessori schools (Claire was put into a Montessori school), swimming pools -above all, grass and trees... I have no memories of Hampstead Garden Suburb but I do remember all the funny little stories Mother would tell us about the place - like the time when Claire was brought to a childrens' swimming pool and there was a chute to slide down into the water. She failed to come up and they found her sitting patiently under the water waiting to find out what to do next. Mother would also tell us the names of the wonderful London furniture shops, Heal's, Maple's, Liberty's.

She was not the only Billig to make an Irish connection: Hannah's greatest friends were the Lipmans, a married couple, both doctors; their practice was in the London dockland, not far from Hannah's. Eddie Lipman was a Jew from Dublin who had been in the Citizens' Army and fought in the 1916 rising. Eva Lipman was a Catholic from (I think) the west of Ireland. There were two women working for Hannah for many years: Mrs Corbett, an Irish Catholic who looked after the surgery and Ada, an Irish Jew, the housekeeper. Also, the vast majority of her early patients at the mother-and-child clinic were Irish women and their children who suffered from terrible malnutrition.

~~~o~~~

I'm turning myself into a magpie. Picking my way through history finding my non-European connections, the map of the world spread out in front of me, as I point out all the places and countries I can claim. I remind myself of *Forrest Gump* and why it was such a popular film: the ordinary man popping up at all the great moments of American history. I remind myself of a sneering comment by the notorious Judge Melford Stevenson in 1977; J.A. and I were being sued for libel in the Law Courts on the London Strand, over our play *The Ballygombeen Bequest* (about a west-of-Ireland eviction). When our counsel put forward our proposed list of witnesses, the judge threw up his hands and played, as he so often did, to the gallery: "Do we really have to dredge over acres and acres of soggy Irish bog, in the hope of picking up the odd Irishman here and there?" The only bit of an ancestral link that J.A. and I have in common is a forebear of his who went to Russia during the Napoleonic wars, as a doctor to Czar Alexander I; he left behind him a very boring diary; I am sure he was a key figure in history, the original creator of the Stiff Upper Lip; I am
~~~

sure the only reason why Alexander wanted a doctor from England was that an Englishman would not have the imagination to poison him. And indeed he was quite right: he was one of the few Czars to die peacefully in his bed.

To continue my trawl, and fit together the various journeyings of my family with aspects of Zionism.

> The Foreign Secretary, Lord Lansdowne, told the Zionists, on August 14, 1903, that if a suitable site could be found (in East Africa), he would 'be prepared to entertain favourably proposals for the establishment of a Jewish colony or settlement... ' Lansdowne invited the Zionists to send a delegation to East Africa to look at the possibilities for themselves.
>
> *Ibid*

My aunt Esther would have been about six or seven in 1903. Think of the excitement and the imaginative leap in her mind, if she heard the adults talking about this project. To think about Africa! to look at picture books about Africa! to remember the story of Joseph and the Land of Goshen! in the midst of the grime and poverty of London, no trees, no green grass. I am not surprised that later on she spent so many years in Morocco; she must have jumped at the chance of joining the royal household just as Joseph had been co-opted into the household of Pharaoh. Morocco, in any case, has had a large Jewish population ever since the days of the Romans and the fall of Jerusalem...

I have always felt quite at home outside Europe. I was invited to Algeria in 1990 and upon my arrival I had a strong (subjective) sense of déja-vu. Also in 1969, when John and I drove with our children out of Europe through the Middle East to India... These semi-psychic intuitions may appear laughable, but in fact they are the wellspring of my theatrical imagination, my recurrent compensation for being always some sort of outsider. Of course there could be more down-to-earth reasons: for instance, until after World War Two, Ireland's standards of living and development were on a par with the third world. The countryside was not electrified until a mere fifty years ago, while piped water and indoor toilets are even today by no means universal. In the mid-seventies in Corrandulla in County Galway we were making and presenting a community agitprop play about the advantages of piped water, for women were still having to carry their heavy buckets from the village pump.

I remember, a few years ago, a lunch-time performance of M.J.Molloy's play, *The Paddy Pedlar,* at the Peacock Theatre, Dublin. It was based on an Irish folk legend: a traveller calls at a house looking for a night's shelter; he is carrying an enormous sack; the young woman of the house is naturally intrigued and opens it; in it she finds the dead body of a woman. The man explains it is his mother: he has made a solemn promise, he will carry her from one end of Ireland to the other to bury her in the place of her choice.

There is a sack upon *my* back. Even though I was prevented from looking inside it, I always knew it was there. Of course I *have* looked inside it; but I've never yet fully laid out its contents to examine them. Now is the time to do so. We now live in what purports to be an Information Era. We all being exhorted to look into our sacks and to face the facts; but what will we do with the facts? In my sack I carry three burdens: one of them is racism, anti-semitic and anti-Irish. The second is the nationalism and religious intolerance reflected in extreme Zionism and strands of Irish republicanism. And the third: I am a woman. How, as a woman, do I resolve my relationship with the other two? Can I discard them? Do I want to discard them? First I must understand them and how the pain of carrying them has affected me throughout my life. I can now recognize the baggage that my mother and father carried. They lived as though they had successfully got rid of it. But this was an illusion: their baggage was still there upon their backs; they never mentioned it; we all had to pretend we could not see it.

How has all this affected me? To begin with: languages. If I had had Hebrew or Yiddish or Irish as part of my family heritage, I might have felt more "authentic", or at any rate, people would have perceived me as being more "authentic". I was of course taught Irish at school in Dublin, and I do retain the *cupla focla... "Conas tha tu?" "Tha me go mait."* ("How are you?" "I'm grand"...). When I speak those words, it is possible for me to fool myself for an instant that Irish is my native tongue. Likewise *"Shalom",* which can make me feel Jewish; but no more deeply than an actor might feel when playing an "ethnic" role. Had my linguistic identities mattered so much to me, I could have taken the trouble to learn the languages. Hannah, after all, learnt Hebrew: indeed she had to, when she went to Israel to work in a mothers-and-babies clinic for Jews and Arabs at Baka-el-Garbiya near Caesarea. When I was in Armagh Gaol, we were forbidden to write letters home in Irish. So I wrote a few letters in basic Irish as an act of resistance to the suppression of language. Those letters, of course, were stopped. I was also in gaol, briefly, in Assam, where I had to pick up enough of the Kashi tongue to chat with my fellow-prisoners. Language, for me, is only important when I need it to do a job of work. English, whether I like it or not, is my de facto mother-tongue, and obviously useful; for (whether I like it or not) the American-dominated "One World Order" is an Anglophone empire. Wherever one goes, to conferences or seminars and so forth, there's always a version of the proceedings in English.

~~~o~~~

My father was born in Dublin in 1898, his background, I suppose, pretty conventional (of the sort so well documented by such writers as Seán O'Casey). He was brought up in a tenement flat in Henrietta Street, behind the Law Courts. The overcrowded slums of Dublin at the turn of the century were said to be the worst in Europe and worse even than Calcutta. Even by the squalid standards of the time, Henrietta Street was notorious. Today it is being restored to its original eighteenth-century elegance. His father was a craftworker for Guinness's brewery, making the bungs for the stout-casks. The brewery was just a short walk from where he lived, across the River Liffey. He died young, leaving a young family of about nine children and a widow who had to bring them up single-handed. His early death might have been a blessing; he is said to have drunk most of his wages away. Guinness, as an employer, had two faces: it gave stable employment, but also easy access to the alcohol which was very bad for any worker with a "weakness". My grandmother must have been a strong and resourceful woman. I believe she kept the family together by taking in lodgers, and she too seems to have died relatively young, for my father never mentioned her. The three youngest boys (himself including) were brought up by their elder brother Eddie. Eddie came top of all the country in the Civil Service entrance exam; he went into the Land Commission, and stayed there, modestly, for the rest of his working life. He used to live in Griffith Avenue on the Northside; he had a piano in the parlour with a piano-stool full of old songbooks; outside was a little greenhouse where he tended his tomatoes; he cycled into the city centre every day to the office; he could have been a kindly quiet character from James Joyce's *Dubliners*.
~~~

The D'Arcys, as a whole, were reserved and self-effacing. My father was an exception, and treated as such by the rest of the family. I think his sisters made a pet of him and spoiled him. He certainly never had much sense of responsibility either as a husband or a father... He was said to be a brilliant and conscientious civil servant; he was also your archetypical loquacious Dubliner, living convivially beyond his means, a type ever dear to British journalists. I don't know where this "jackeen" character originated, but I suspect the eighteenth century, the days of Peg Woffington, Goldsmith, Sheridan, when Dublin was a capital city with lofty ideas of itself, gambling, duels, high fashion, debauchery, government corruption. The story goes that the D'Arcys lost all their fortune at the gaming tables in the Hellfire Club. They were originally a well-established family; one of them was Lord Mayor; his coat of arms may still be seen in the Mansion House. Another one was Sir Patrick D'Arcy the scientist and mathematician who left Ireland for France at the time of the Act of Union, and is buried in Père Lachaise cemetery. When we were young, we lived near a country club at Kilcronie in County Wicklow. My father was a member and played golf there. The rural people used to maintain that there was a ghost at Kilcronie (the house was said to have once belonged to the D'Arcys), and that my father was the living image of this spectre. I know no way of finding out the truth of the connection between my father's D'Arcys and the old aristo D'Arcys, because so many records were lost when the Dublin Custom House was burned down during the war of Independence.

My father hated any indulgence in speculation about the glories of the D'Arcys. In the new Ireland there was great pride in families, a favourite pastime was the recollection of aristocratic lineage - the last high king of Ireland, or some other king or chieftain - which tribe? how much land? and so forth. When I was small, I would have liked to have been descended from an ancient Gaelic family but alas, the name of D'Arcy was a give-away: Norman! As a Norman I could not claim to be truly Irish; we were the usurpers, the land grabbers, part of the clique that prevented the Os and Macs from entering cities, part of the great betrayal of Dermot MacMurrough who stole someone else's wife, ran away out of the country, brought in the Norman invaders and married his daughter Eva to their leader, Strongbow Earl of Pembroke. Of course all this happened 800 years ago but it didn't matter: at school in Dublin it was if it had happened yesterday. The name was sufficent to mark the inheritance. What happened in between was irrelevant to the authenticity of the identity.

There wasn't a sausage of an O or a Mac I could lay claim to. I did have an aunt married to a MacAllinden; but that was dubious, it sounded more Scots than Irish. Had I been able to refer to a book I now possess, Brian de Breffny's *Irish Family Names* (not published until 1982), I could have put in a claim by pointing out that "descendants of two O Dorchaidhe septs... adopted Darcy as well as Dorcey as their surname" - but this would have led me into more hot water - why the hell would we have wanted to elevate ourselves into Normans? - "Some of these Darcys then fancifully adopted the form d'Arcy... " Believe it or not the whole subject of the removal or addition of O to one's name is still a hot subject with political ramifications, particularly in the north, as I found recently in Derry - one evening I sat beside a long convoluted conversation about who had or had not the right to call themselves O'Doherty as opposed to Doherty; to anglicise the name was to betray an entire heritage.

The irony is that in my youth in the south of Ireland nobody talked about what their fathers or mothers had done in the fight for national freedom: we were still in the aftermath of a horrendous civil war; internment was introduced by De Valera in 1939 while I was at school and executions of Republican prisoners were still taking place (26 of them put to death by the State between 1939 and 1946). Who fought whom, and when and where, was not part of the chattering of small girls. It was easier to stick to 1169 and the Norman invasion...

~~~o~~~

Why is it, when I start out in a jolly mood, having fun, playing with the fancies of memory, real flash-backs suddenly come zooming up as though the sky is going dark and the black storm clouds are catching me unawares: I was looking in the wrong direction, I had failed to turn my head round. In the early 1990s the American spiritual guru and activist Starhawk was in Dublin to promote her new book; she had been invited to speak at gatherings of women. I went to hear her in Liberty Hall, the historic home of Irish social revolution, which was packed with the feminist clan; a celebrated feminist poet gave the introductory speech. "Our heritage of Celtic spiritual feminism"... how proud she was that, unlike other Northern European countries, Ireland had had no witch-hunts... then she paused and added, "Except of course for Alice Kyteler, the 14th-century Kilkenny case." She then said, "Of course that one didn't count: they were all Normans!" The audience burst into rapturous applause, their feet
~~~

and voices thundering like a stampede of starving heifers. I couldn't believe what I heard, as I looked around and saw my "sisters'" ecstatic faces. Had they not heard? or was it now the right-on trendy acceptance to be up-front in one's tribalism and racism? I sat there paralysed. The noise was so great that if I had attempted to stand up and make an intervention, it would have been interpreted as the beginning of a standing ovation. These women themselves wouldn't burn women but they would stand by whilst others did.

~~~o~~~

My father followed his brother Eddie into the Civil Service, which was of course the British Civil Service at that time. After the Easter Rising (1916) he joined the IRA, in a unit commanded by Oscar Traynor. The British authorities shut him up for a while in Mountjoy Gaol. In the subsequent Civil War, Traynor's anti-treaty volunteers were swiftly outmanoeuvred in Dublin and were out of the conflict; the personnel returned to their civilian occupations. My father rejoined what was now the Irish Free State Civil Service, ending up in the Department of Agriculture.

> The best-known Department inherited in 1922 was Agriculture and Technical Instruction, then thought to be functioning so effectively that its admirers claimed it would be a mistake to dismember it.
> J.J.Lee (*Ireland 1912 - 1985, politics & society*)

He went to evening classes at the National University, and gained a BA. When the Free State set up a small Department of External Affairs with a resident High Commissioner in England, my father was posted to London to look after agricultural matters and attend classes at the LSE.

> The price paid by the Free State for its fidelity to British administrative models is difficult to determine. Adherence to the model dominated mentalities as well as institutional structures. At one level, it contributed significantly to establishing standards of personal integrity among senior civil servants that did not self-evidently derive from the values of Irish society. At another level, it enshrined the cult of the amateur in administration... Ireland was in no position to afford the intellectual style of the amateur, but she insisted on living beyond her means in this respect.
> *Ibid*
~~~

This split-personality of the civil service was reflected in the personal lives of my parents, causing my mother much unhappiness. She was never able to reconcile the dream of marriage to an official of a new, apparently high-principled, emergent nation with the reality of that nation, the searing tubercular poverty, the narrow-minded catholicism, the backbiting and begrudgery. Neither could my father cope.

He never discussed the Civil War with us, nor the War of Independence. I think he assumed that if we wanted to find out, we could read the books on his shelves. But J.A. has a story to tell. On our honeymoon we had to spend a couple of nights with my father in Dublin. Naturally enough he dragged J.A. out to the pub: --

> Somewhere in Baggot Street, a dark dingy crowded old-fashioned den of a place, where I was blurringly introduced to an indeterminate throng of Civil Service colleagues, all looking and talking like characters out of Myles na gCopaleen. Conversation was continuous and impossibly meandering as the glasses were filled and emptied. At one point my father-in-law emerged from an inconclusive argument with someone about the schooldays at the Christian Brothers, and about someone else's old-IRA background, to include me (as an English visitor) into the discussion. He carefully explained how before a dangerous guerrilla-operation "we'd all make a point of going to confession, so that if anything happened we'd die confident, know what I mean? I can tell you I was glad of it, the time at the Custom House. We were all inside the building, setting the fire here and there, 'get out of it, we're surrounded!', dodge for the exits, out into the street, Forces of the Crown everywhere, Black-and-Tans, the regular soldiers, armoured cars, machine-guns, the lot. I don't know how many men we lost. I kept saying my prayers over and over till I was sure I'd got clear away, into a little street behind Store Street, and there he was! round the corner, an armoured car, dead in front of me, face-to-face, and your man with his Vickers gun staring out of his turret straight at me. Now, the important thing, the only important thing, was to show them you couldn't for the life of you imagine who these fellows were or why they were there. Armoured car? British army? No such a thing at all… I was able to take one short look at him, give him a shrug of the shoulders, flick of the fingers like a friendly salute, walk past him, just like that; d'you know he never even tried to ask me who I was, let alone to fire a shot… "

Brian O'Nolan, alias Flann O Brien alias Myles na gCopaleen (himself an officer of the Department of Local Government), imprinted on the nation the image of "th'authentic civil sarvant", in the midst of the giant useless bureaucracy, the desperate little man, his only solace the quiet snug with the black stuff or the long and the short. When I was growing up I didn't think it was very grand to say my father was a civil servant. I was amused the other day: talking to a friend about this book and telling her how I was getting bogged down in writing about what my father actually did in the Civil Service, to my surprise she said that when she was seventeen she joined the Civil Service and survived one year of it; she was in the Housing Grants section of the Department of the Environment. This was in the 1980s. She was solely in charge of giving out the grants. I couldn't believe it! John and I had applied for a window-replacement grant at the very time she was working there; our health and wellbeing had been solely in her hands. She said the whole experience made a nutcase out of her, what with the volumes of paperwork and then "having to deal with the three methods - " "What do you mean, three methods?" She said, "Yes, really three, the old method, the new method and the one in practice." She would have to cross-check each application, using all the three forms, one for each method. In those days there was still the embargo on women working after they got married. So those in the office were either very young, or older single women unlikely to progress any further up the ladder. The men, at least the older men, would be dashing off to the pub where they were allowed to *run up the slate,* the women never. The pubs knew that when the men died there would be a Civil Service annuity for their widows, so the money would be certain. Indeed, at my father's death, his small annuity disappeared into his drinking debts. There was nothing the wives could do about this - the bar with its slate was a sacrosanct male preserve. I know that my mother broke all taboos by going to the pub once and trying to put an end to my father's slate, but the landlord just laughed at her.

J. J. Lee's comment on the British model for the Irish Civil Service was comically illustrated by the ritual that my father ensured at our County Wicklow family dinner-table when I was a young teenager and my mother was working in England. He conducted the meal with all the solemn and hierarchical procedure of his government department where the size and quality of everything from filing-cabinets to carpets to tea-cups was jealousy guarded and had to be just so. He and my mother had brought from England - from the early heady days of their marriage - a number of trophies of the liberal-enlightenment décor of their first home in Hampstead Garden Suburb: a black-glass coffee table with chromium-plated tubular legs, a matching standard-lamp, a green glass fruit bowl, a tall vase of mottled yellow glass, a cutlery cabinet, two silver-plated sauce-boats, a silver cigarette box, two silver candlesticks (the silver required constant high-polishing), and the pièce-de-résistance - the oak dining-table, always laid with mats and never a table-cloth. Father would preside at the top of the table. (J. N. D'Arcy, Esquire: never, if you please, Mr Joseph N. D'Arcy.) The ritual looked solemn enough; but somehow there was an inevitable element of grotesque anti-climax, Dickensian parody. For instance, we would all be seated there, Father well-oiled with his pre-dinner whiskies and his face glowing, while we waited for ten minutes for the potatoes to be nicely roasted and for my sisters to dish them up; then suddenly the electricity would be cut off. Father had been "watching the bill", in preference to paying it on time. The conversation would then become an enormous joke about how Father's philosophy and that of the electricity board were somehow never able to coincide. Significantly, one of his favourite characters in literature was Mr Micawber. Dickens and Joyce were his two great literary delights; he was always quoting from them. He would regularly wax eloquent about the importance of gracious living, the correct way to use the cutlery and the correct order of laying it out, the necessity of drinking soup from the side of the spoon. Otherwise, he feared we would fall into the lifestyle of *gurriers* - other dreaded gurrier-habits were his daughters wearing headscarfs in the street, or shouting to friends out of open windows when we were living in a city-centre flat. Dinner-table conversation had to have a certain quality: we were never (for example) allowed to use the word "nice", nor to introduce the question of the unpaid butcher's bill. All this, he must have learned in London when mixing with British civil servants - it could not possibly have derived from Henrietta Street.

The other endearing ritual he practised was the Sunday afternoon picnic. I think this must have been based on his guerrilla-manoeuvres in the Dublin Brigade. We always had to light a practicable fire, rather than carrying tea to the site in a thermos. We had to bring a frying pan. Our knapsacks had to be full of uncooked food - ready-prepared sandwiches were out of the question - off we went with our sticks while Father "orienteered" the expedition to whatever destination he had determined. We never took an easy walk, never just straight down the road - always over walls, through hedges, among cows and bulls, over bits of bog, through nettles and brambles, stopping at intervals to admire the view while Father recited snatches from Wordsworth. Even when we met potentially irate farmers about to complain of trespassing, he would dispel their anger with an easy charm until they began to think it was actually a privilege to have us on their land.

~~~o~~~

What kind of values did my father hope for in the new State?

The Irish Renaissance of the late-19th/early-20th centuries may be said to have been woven from three principal strands: the Anglo-Irish Revival, the Gaelic Revival and the Catholic Revival, strong cultural ideologies, each promoting its own vision of an independent nation. These visions sometimes merged and sometimes clashed with one another. From 1923 (the foundation of the State) until the 1960s it seemed as though the Catholic Revival would prevail unassailably over the other two. My father hated it; and its effect on him and on my mother and on their children was catatonic. I now understand why he would rail at us over the dinner-table for saying "nice", it was a red rag to a bull, he associated it with the self-effacing Catholic gentility which he abhorred.

The archives of John Charles McQuaid, Archbishop of Dublin for thirty years, have lately been opened up. It is clear that he had his finger in every possible pie, political, social, artistic; his spies were infiltrated into clubs and societies all over the place; he kept little dossiers on all people prominent in public life, noting how far they were authentically Irish and whether they were Catholic, Protestant, Jewish, Atheist or Communist.

I have been looking through a few papers which my father carefully preserved and left behind at his death in 1962; I assume they are documents by which he wished to be remembered.

1) The Park of the Fionn Misge, by J. N. D'Arcy. A radio documentary about the history of Phoenix Park, broadcast by RTE in 1937. Typescript and handwritten MS.
2) A letter from the director of that broadcast - "Dear D'Arcy, many thanks for your letter - I am glad you were not ill-pleased with the broadcast. Personally I felt that I was as you say 'not up to form' and we might have been 'more connected'. I think, in future cases, we (you & I) will have to have long consultations on the script before
~~~

it goes into rehearsal. As regards the 'lady compère' I think that experiment was not a success!!... Referring to the 'Dublin Castle' and your suggestion - I think the station would prefer a single broadcast of one hour even at the risk of cutting out many items. I have suggested using two broadcasts before, but the idea has not met with their approval... "

3) Handwritten MS. of another radio documentary, Return to 1913, a scrapbook of the year, by J. N. D'Arcy.
4) Typescript: The Problems of National Minorities in Europe. Paper read in the Royal Irish Academy, 8th February 1939, by J. N. D'Arcy.
5) Typescript: A Statistical Study of How We Live in the Irish Free State. I'm assuming it's by my father, but it is unsigned and undated. (One sentence reads: "I have mentioned that women are relatively less employed in the Irish Free State than in England or Scotland, but after the age of 55 we have in the Irish Free State a greater proportion of women earning incomes than in Northern Ireland, Scotland, England or Wales." It is ironical that my father died two months before he was due to be paid a pension, so that my mother had nothing and at the age of 55 she was compelled to carry on working - in fact, she took a job in a hospital at Derry in the north of Ireland. If she had paid any heed to the criticisms of my father's family and friends, she would never have gone ahead and studied medicine, and thus would have been absolutely penniless; my father always lived in rented property and his annuity was owned by the pub.)
6) A sheaf of Father's MS. notes about the United Irishmen, the Act of Union and other historical items of the same period: they seem to be the preliminaries of another radio piece.
7) Crow Street Theatre. The typescript of a historical paper; I think I wrote it at school (Alexandra College, Dublin) when I was fifteen; the first piece I ever wrote. In the history class we were all asked to produce a paper about some aspect of Dublin, and I chose the theatre in the 18th century. Father must have typed it out for me.
8) A letter to my father (when he was in London) from the Fabian Society, inviting him to the Inaugural Meeting of the Fabian International Bureau, on 24th January 1942.
9) An official letter from the Dept. of Industry and Commerce, Dublin, telling my father that in furtherance of his claim (under the Children's Allowances Act, 1944) he has been awarded an allowance at the rate of 5 shillings per week for me and my three sisters ("2s.6d for each qualified child in excess of two"). The date on the envelope is 28 April 1945; he must have just returned from England.
10) EIRE / IRELAND: Weekly Bulletin of the Department of External Affairs. June 25th 1956. This edition of the Bulletin is entirely taken up with an illustrated bio-

graphical article about George Bernard Shaw with particular emphasis on his Dublin background, his Irishness and his socialism. The cover illustration is a photograph of Shaw presenting the MSS. of his five novels to the Irish High Commissioner in London (Father's ex-boss) for the National Library of Ireland in 1946.

11) The remaining items, all in one file, relate to The Irish Association for Cultural, Economic and Social Relations, of which my father was a member from its inauguration in 1939.

A shocking thought, as I go through these papers: am I just a clone of my father? - especially as I have implied that he was an irresponsible father and a bad husband... When my children look through *my* papers, what are they going to find? A few Irish historical plays for stage and radio, odd letters and newspaper cuttings and boxes full of files of the various social, literary and political organizations I have belonged to, minutes of meetings, announcements of dates of meetings, the odd document with a muffled threat of scandal - (from a letter to my father in section 11 of his papers: "... when next I see you I will tell you the *truth* about the Prof. S -- discovery. In the meantime, suffice it to say, that, unless you want to have explosions all round, don't mention his name, least of all to Mr P -- !!!"). I am sure that a couple at least of my children could say that I was a neglectful mother, irresponsible about money, failing to put their welfare first in the choice of where we lived, the type of house, the selection of schools... I could also say, of course, that *I* am a civil servant (sort of). When Aosdána, the Irish Artists' Parliament, was set up in 1980, with a pension for impecunious artists such as myself, I am sure that whoever advised the Taoiseach Charles J. Haughey on the matter must have muttered into his ear something like - "Oh for God's sake, Charlie, we've been subsidising them for years: most of the civil servants spend half of their time writing novels, plays, poetry - so why not come clean, get rid of the dossers, put them into their own Department with a fancy Gaelic name?" I do know that in the 1970s when I was involved with the Galway Theatre Workshop, the group got a small grant from the Arts Council. We then felt we were officially endorsed and thoroughly entitled to poke our nose in everywhere, intervening on social issues, denouncing injustices. We were, as it were, paid by the State to be the conscience of those who had veered away from the principles of the 1916 Proclamation.

Of course I am not a clone of my father. But the issues contained in his file with the dreary name *Proceedings of the Irish Association* are still the issues we are wrestling with today, none of them solved, and all of them of interest to me.

~~~o~~~

There is a Constitution for the Association, dated 13th April 1951: -

> General Objects: to promote goodwill, mutual respect and co-operation between all sections of the Irish people... *etcetera.*

Then there is an agenda for some meeting, perhaps suggestions or arrangements for members to prepare papers. These are the main headings: --

1) The Crown. What is it in Ireland? in Northern Ireland today?
2) Human Rights and their security: their relative positions in 26 and 6 counties.
   a) Habeas Corpus.
   b) Divorce.
   c) Mixed Marriages.
   d) Right of Assembly.
3) Taxation and Currency.
4) Administration.
5) Consideration of Common Ground (between 26 & 6 counties) in relation to 3 & 4.
6) Irish Language.

Solutions: given common agreement followed by suitable State action:

i) Merging of local authorities into Provincial Councils with view to foundation of a 'United Irish Province'.
   Consider example of Benelux Countries.
   Review position of 'Council of Ireland' recommended to be set up in 1921 for consideration of common problems. Consider legal opinion taken on this by Irish Association.
   A National Economic Council?
ii) A Regent of Ireland? (Consideration at a later stage.)
   Consider in relation to (a) possible use of the Crown. (b) present and future relations with U.K. and Imperial Parliament, the Commonwealth, the U.S.A., the United Nations. (c) Guarantees by the Great Powers.
~~~

This could - a half-century later - have been a model discussion-document for the Good Friday Agreement of 1998.

My own direct link with the Irish Association. In mid-1951 I was a young apprentice actress, a snobbish and immature 17, believing that anyone who wasn't 100% dedicated to, and starving for, their art was not worth knowing. One day my father invited me to a cultural weekend in Armagh. North of the border! I had never been to the North and I thought it would be "good for my art". Next day I rather regretted saying yes, because as I was strolling through Stephen's Green I was hailed by a handsome young Norwegian writer called Felix Thorson and invited to a bottle-party his mother was giving on the Saturday night.

In Dublin at that time there were all sorts of exciting houses and basement flats full of exciting artists and writers. Most of these houses were "closed shops", so to speak. You would only be invited if some one thought *you* were exciting, so a strict vetting had to take place beforehand. My friend Colette Delaney, who was obviously an exciting person because she was always being invited to exciting parties, had already brought me, once, to the Thorsons'. She had told me all about the fantastic people you could meet there; she had drilled me into form to make me acceptable; I was to praise Mrs Thorson for her magnificent performance in *Little Eyolf* (which I hadn't seen) and generally be full of the right kind of discreet obsequiousness. So when Felix invited me it was obvious that I had indeed passed the test and I was about to find all doors open to me into the bohemian life of free love and starving artists who would all be bowled over and worship me…

But the opportunity was lost for ever: I could never tell my father I was going to *that* sort of party. Instead it must be Armagh, gloomy and grey. A respectable, narrow hotel, the Charlemont Arms, in the Mall in the middle of the town. A room full of serious middle-aged men and women, all very polite, papers being read, a little display of Irish dancing, a woman singing and accompanying herself on the harp. Little did I know that in twenty-eight years' time, I would be a convicted political prisoner in the gaol facing down that very Mall… And then, the next day, the Association left Armagh on a visit to Roe Park, Limavady, Co. Derry, the country estate of Mr and the Hon. Mrs George Buchanan. I was impressed with him: he read a paper about Ulster literature and the writer's situation in the partitioned North, criticising "the Éire censorship as it affected the exchange of books between the two parts of Ireland." He was a real writer whose novels had been published and he gave us all tea. I thought this was extremely grand and gracious, but then - to his amusement - I attacked his whole way of life, telling him how wrong it was for a writer to live in such luxury.

(By the way, in the 1970s, at a conference of writers in Norway, I met Felix Thorson once again, charming and handsome as ever. He was on to his third, and wealthy, wife; *all* his wives were very wealthy. He had become famous as an extreme nationalist/mystical novelist. He remembered me very well and I still had to pretend I had seen his mother in *Little Eyolf.* This wasn't really a lie, because at my first meeting with her, when I told her I had seen her performance and liked it, she became so excited that she actually renacted for me selected portions of the role of the Rat-Wife; it became so embedded in my mind that I actually could have sworn I did see her performance. In a way, that whole episode - my deceit, her generosity, the fact that she herself had put on the production of the play with her family, her pride in what she had done, and her delightful playfulness, opened up my eyes to the possibility of a quite different kind of theatre: if theatre is what you want, you don't wait for some one else, you carry on and put it on yourself. This was one of my first lessons in the artistic independence of woman.)

It is only now, looking through the Association's papers, that I realise how these people were carrying on the tradition of the first meetings of the United Irishmen in 1791, hoping to ignite once again that spirit. A portentous emphasis to place upon a little-known intellectual club? but it's just the sort of thing that kindles my imagination. In so many of my plays I have attempted to dramatise small bits of history that somehow have been written-out of the mainstream - *The Non-Stop Connolly Show, A Pinprick of History, Vandaleur's Folly, Whose Is The Kingdom?*. I am also anxious to counteract the conventional image of Ireland as a totally conservative religion-ridden backwater which only "sprang to life" with the industrialisation of the 60s and the Common Market of the 70s.

The Irish Association was set up in 1939, and reactivated after the war. Seven people from its Southern Committee travelled to Armagh in July 1950 to meet northern members to discuss the revival of activities. Amongst the seven were my father, Louie Bennett and Hubert Butler. A year later these latter two were enmeshed in controversy with the novelist Seán O'Faoláin:

> I feel inclined to tag both [Hubert Butler and Louie Bennett] as Fellow Travellers in the sense that Lanty Hanlon's ould dog who went a bit o' the road with everybody might be called a Fellow Traveller... Miss Bennett's Sword of the Spirit has the same sort of Made in Oxford (Group) look about it. I confess that as she waved it so splendidly in the firelight, where she saw visions and dreamed dreams, I felt frightfully vulgar and Philistinish, as if, in mentioning Joe Stalin, I had introduced an unpleasant subject into a gracious home... The fact is, you can batter people about in an argument: they will come up smiling with another argument. In the long run men judge by their emotions, not by their brains. In my heart I hate Communism. That is the beginning and end of it. Mr Butler and Miss Bennett hate nobody, good souls, and the Editor has his own views too.
>
> Seán O'Faoláin (letter, in *The Bell,* June 1951)

Louie Bennett was a veteran suffragist, pacifist, leading spirit of the Irish Women Workers' Union since 1916. Her reply to an earlier piece by O'Faoláin is very pertinent exactly fifty years later, in relation to the growing movement of anti-capitalist Global Resistance, as well as the rejection of the EU Treaty of Nice by the Irish electorate. We were cajoled to say "Yes" to this treaty by the main political parties, Fianna Fáil, Fine Gael and Labour. We were told that if we insisted it was the beginning of the end of Irish neutrality, we are scaremongering hysterics.

> A Third Force is now definitely emerging, a force not dependent on armaments, free of imperialism, not yet adequately co-ordinated... Fine thinkers and fine patriots are moving into that force. They have a message for the world. They believe that the great movements which release creative life are most often inspired by a minority, by small nations, oppressed peoples, the lone prophet, obscure groups of thinkers, poets, artists...
>
> And what, after all, can Ireland contribute to a creative civilisation?
>
> I think of Muintir na Tíre, the Young Farmers, the Countrywomen, the Co-operative idea slowly growing and fructifying, the theory of Vocational Organisation whose value for our economic life has yet to be fully understood. I think of the new spirit moving our younger generation in field, factory and office, in the studio and the study...

> And so thinking, I am satisfied that the Irish people, *left free to follow their own way of life,* may make a valuable contribution to civilisation. But Seán O'Faoláin and his like must be tolerant of poor doubting Thomas and auto-antis.
> Louie Bennett (on "Autoantiamericanism", in *The Bell,* May 1951)

Hubert Butler was an anti-imperialist and an anti-fascist whose work in exposing the pro-Nazi activities of certain Croat Catholic clergy brought upon his head savage denunciations from the Catholic Church in Ireland. He too wrote for *The Bell* - in itself an organ of the Irish "Third Force", edited in 1951 by Peadar O'Donnell. Here he is upon Seán O'Faoláin: -

> [He] rightly resents the hypocrisy of selling our assistance in 'the defence of Christendom' for the six counties. But does he really think we should become less, rather than more, pleased with our 'lily-white hands', our 'pure souls', if we joined the Atlantic Pact?
> Hubert Butler (on "Autoantiamericanism", in *The Bell,* May 1951)

I think Louie Bennett, at some time during the 1930s, must have recruited my parents into a forerunner of her "Third Force", a kind of Irish Fabian secularism. I always thought of her as something of a mentor to my father. As was her friend and co-worker in the IWWU, Helen Chenevix, a Quaker and a member of the Irish Association.

To return to the meeting of July 1950: there were eight northern members present. A mixed bunch. Dr Eileen Hickey, MP. Miss MacNeill, who had been sent by a General Montgomery (the founder of the Association). Major Proctor. The only names I recognise are Mr and Mrs O'Malley - that was Mary O'Malley who established the famous Lyric Theatre in Belfast.

> *Points that were discussed: -*
> The northerners complained that they were putting much more energy into making contact with the south than the southerners were with them. It was asserted that the northern civil servants had a vested interest in partition. A long list of discriminations against Catholics. A claim that both sides were guilty of discrimination and must face facts: "We Ulstermen like to govern ourselves." A suggestion that the Republic should not only join NATO but also rejoin the Commonwealth. The one thing they all seem to have had in common was the view that both governments, Belfast and Dublin, tended to stifle independent expression of opinion from intellectual circles.

Father's papers from the Irish Association finish in 1956 (the year Louie Bennett died). But I believe the Association still lives.

~~~o~~~

I must now close my father's file, for after all this is supposed to be *my* story. But I would like to add that one incident of his part in the independence struggle - I mean the action of the Dublin Brigade at the Custom House - was far more decisive in ending British rule than he ever claimed. It is clear that it was the first (and indeed only) *full-scale* military action of the campaign, and prompted an immediate British rethink of their entire policy. If he had been a different kind of man my father could have spent his life sitting back bragging about the fight, rather than joking about his escape from it; but he was too much of a realist, and with a naturally self-effacing personality, always modest and quiet about his achievements. I can well understand why my mother fell in love with him; I am glad that when he died he died in her arms.
~~~

3

EARLY TURMOIL AND CONFUSIONS

I watched both my parents dying. I might appear callous, using that coldly objective "watched", but when it is what is called a Reasonable Death, that is to say death in a bed with the family all prepared for it, I think it is reasonable to write that we watch by the bedside the last intimate moment of our parent. We have not been able to witness the other two major intimacies, birth and copulation. With death, however, there is an unprecedented opportunity for the role of parenthood to be lifted and the person revealed. Because I was privileged to watch both my parents dying I was able to observe how differently each of them handled the imminence of death.

Father died of a heart attack in 1962, when he was 64. He'd had a previous attack in 1947 shortly after coming back from London, when I was still at school, shut up behind convent walls. He had recovered from this, but he had to give up cycling. Our home was in County Wicklow, sixteen miles from Dublin, a house called "Garry Ard", a mile-and-a-half from the bus route. He would ride his bike every morning to catch the bus, which brought him to the railway for the Dublin train. "Garry Ard" was on a height, so it was downhill all the way out but a very steep upward slope coming home... After the heart attack my mother bought a car, and my eldest sister Claire would drive Father direct to the railway station.

In October 1962 J.A. and I lived on an island in Loch Corrib. We had three children; I was breast-feeding Jacob who was three-and-a-half months old. We had no phone, no electricity, no car, no engine on the boat. We used to row the half-mile to the mainland. A neighbouring farmer who had cattle on the adjoining island would give us any message from the mainland. One day word came for me to telephone Dublin urgently. I well remember that morning: a fog so thick you couldn't see across to the shore where our bicycles were left. I thought if I rowed over, cycled to the post office a couple of miles away, made the phone-call and returned, I would be in time for Jacob's next feed. It was easy enough for me to reach the mainland, but I might miss the island on the way back and find myself way out in the open lake. Sound can be very clear in thick fog, so to direct me in the boat I would keep shouting out to J.A. and I would follow his voice to our shore. Anyway I reached the telephone safely: Father was in hospital after a heart attack; I must go to Dublin at once. My mother or my sister would drive down to pick me up with the children. J.A. would follow by train a couple of days later, after securing everything on the island against storms and turning the boat upside down on the mainland shore. So I cycled back in a state of distress and called out, as arranged, to J.A. I heard a reply, got into the boat and began rowing. I realised the fog was much denser: I could see neither the mainland nor the island. I was calling all the time and hearing a reply; but the answering voice never got closer. I began to panic. I could hear panic and distress in the answering voice. I couldn't see a thing. I didn't know what was going wrong; I didn't know how I was going to get out of the situation. And the baby to be fed? We didn't have any baby-milk on the island, and what about J.A? What was he thinking? I stopped rowing; I just kept calling and listening to the other voice. Suddenly I realized it was the echo of my own voice bouncing off the mainland. I'd been rowing round in circles. Because of some freak of the acoustics, J.A. had been unable to hear me.

At that moment when I was lost in the middle of the second largest lake in Ireland, I had a clear vision of what my father must be going through, struggling to breathe - the emptiness and loneliness of death.

In both our cases the fog (at least for a time) lifted. I saw the island; I was saved.

When we arrived in Dublin my father in his hospital bed was weak but cheerful, cracking jokes about what a wonderful little heart he had. He asked us to bring him a pear. I remember him holding the pear in his hand, marve' ling at its shape, smell and color, and asking us to share his experience of t pear, the full intensity of his sensous pleasure in the pear. I had to bring children back to the flat to put them to bed; my mother remained in the pital. Half an hour later she came in and told us he was dead, he had d her arms. I opened *my* arms to my mother and held her, the only time lives such a thing had ever happened. We wept together.

His absolute intensity and awareness of the physical just before the end, was as though he had been given an ultimate experience of the NOW. I think that his capacity for feeling alive, and for sharing that feeling, was born at the time of his escape from the Custom House and his sudden realisation then that in the midst of the death of his comrades, he lived. And his gratitude for that moment never left him. The morning after his death, my mother tentatively whispered to me - not to my sisters - that Father had appeared to her, in the night, smiling

~~~o~~~

There have always been jokes about Jewish mothers and how many doctors they have given birth to. The sub-text of such humour, in the context of anti-semitism, is that the power to heal has a tangible physical reality which transcends the vicious divisions caused by class, race, religion or gender. Mother's way of fighting for her own space in the world was to be both a mother and a doctor.

To her this was the highest of all callings: the giving of life, the preservation of life. And it affected her attitude to death. Whereas my father accepted death as inevitable, she resisted it with single-minded concentration. When she was eighty-nine she came to Dublin from her home in Barleycove, County Cork, right at the root of Mizzen Head, the farthest south-westerly tip of Ireland (where she lived alone); she had to be looked after by my sister Rosemary after treatment for a recurring heart-condition. As she lay in bed in Rosemary's house, she scientifically measured her breathing, conserving her strength as though she were guarding a battery that was running down, hoping that it would recharge itself. She told me that I must excuse her if she seemed to be ignoring me: she was too busy with her own self. That was the last conversation I ever had with her.

The irony of her final defeat was that she had to go back into hospital to have a check on a cancer in her colon; they gave her prozac; when she returned to Rosemary she said she felt so much better she would travel down to Cork again the very next week; she was so full of bounce that within twenty-four ours it had bounced her right out of her life.

Reflecting on the last statement that my mother made to me, I realise it in fact the only natural bit of dialogue I had with her in the whole course
~~~

of my life - apart from that other strange intimacy the morning after Father's death. Among Father's papers I did discover a letter that she had written to him years before; it was the only letter he had kept and it gave me some inkling of their relationship. She had wanted to buy a car when we lived in Laragh, and she wrote to him about it (he was in London at the time) pleading with him like a flirtatious young girl asking a favour from her father. She had never revealed that side of her to us, and I never knew it existed. She could be only the mother-in-charge or the vulnerable girl, nothing in between; she could not treat us as equals; she could never drop her guard. There was some sort of void in her emotional development that I suspect must have been there since her youth. Her early years were completely different from those of her older siblings: she was not part of that history of poverty, secrecy, childrens' private language within the home; she was aware of it but cut off from it; so much of her family remained impenetrable to her.

I am reminded of my friend C-- in Galway. She is 34 years younger than me; she told me once about the problems of communication she had with her mother. The latter would not recognise her choice of a lifestyle (not married, no respectable job) and her sexual preferences, and was putting pressure on her to return home to help look after her sick father. The mother seemed to view her daughter as being still an extension of the household and was expecting her to carry on in the unmarried daughter's traditional role of a permanent unwaged skivvy. The more C-- had done when she was young to gain the approval of her mother, the more the mother expected from her. We were trying to work out why the mother treated her in this way. C-- then told me that her maternal grandparents had both been volunteers in the old IRA; they had taken part in the guerrilla campaign in the mountains, attacking (and hiding from) the Black-and-Tans. At one particularly dangerous stage in the campaign, the grandmother was eight months pregnant; also she had had to leave two other children behind in the care of relatives. After the war C--'s grandparents settled down in Dublin in a council housing estate. They had another daughter, C--'s mother. The grandfather became a postman; he had become very violent to his children. As the youngest, C--'s mother was treated differently and psychologically excluded from the family's experience. She had neither suffered in the war, nor been deprived, like the other three toward whom the grandmother over-compensated. C--'s mother was expected to be the family carer and the parent of *her* mother. In her own turn, C-- was allowed to slip into exactly the same role, surrogate parent and worrier on behalf of her mother's anxieties: so similar to the symptoms Anne Karpf has described in *Surviving the Holocaust*, even though C-- was the third generation from the trauma of the war. She believes that in many Irish families, where there is a high incidence of inherited domestic violence together with a "culture of guilt", there is likely to be a connection with the War of Independence (and its horrific mutation, the even more savage Civil War). She believes that this has never been acknowledged in the public discussion of Irish domestic violence.

Discussing the 150th anniversary of the Great Famine, the *Irish Times* columnist John Waters has argued that the whole country for a century-and-a-half has been in a traumatised state of denial which has grievously distorted our sense of national identity. It may well be so; but there is another state of denial which the Irish have not yet faced - the one created by the wars of 1916-23. At an anecdotal level it does come into conversation in rural areas. In Corrandulla where I have lived for the past thirty years, the War of Independence was as much against the big landlords as the British. A direct lineage is perceived, back into history, from the war, through the late 19th-century land agitation, to the famine. There are all sorts of memories and stories about all three. Any unusual behaviour, drinking, violence, mental disorder, by the older generation, described as "suffering from the nerves", used to be attributed, loosely, to the war. But the second and third generations make no connection between the war and their own distresses. The "culture of guilt" so frequently reflected in Irish literature, is usually blamed upon the teachings of the Catholic Church; but surely some of the priests were themselves traumatised and in denial, after the famine, after the war, and fastened onto points of doctrine that would help them to transfer their feeling of guilt - guilt for what? Guilt for not suffering as deeply as someone else at the time of the national calamities.

To end this diversion with a story about Kate Millett, the American feminist writer; she was invited to Ireland on a speaking tour in 1980. She was horrified to find no memorial anywhere to the Great Famine. Her identification with Ireland was her anger that "her people" had been driven out by starvation and hunger. She talked as though "her people" meant herself. She told me, "Goddammit, I'm still hungry!"

~~~o~~~
~~~

It was all very 1930-ish and modern: marriage to a promising and brilliant civil servant, with all the excitement of the intense negotiations going on in London with the new politicians from Ireland, changes of government in Dublin, de Valera and the Economic War, arguments about coal and agriculture, the whole dispute over the land annuity, and the growing achievement of Ireland on the international scene - the first Irish ambassador to Washington won a seat for the country on the council of the League of Nations. My mother was always very involved in Father's work, even during the last few months before his death. I remember visiting them at that time and there were the two of them poring over Father's papers from the office. He was preparing some report. Given any problem, my mother would throw herself into it wholeheartedly, but - there is always a *but*... When my first child was born with spina bifida, my mother was extremely distressed: the way she expressed it was to go on and on obsessively about how my father had not come to see her when Claire was born. I expect, in his usual way, a typically Irish male way, he just ambled in in his own time carrying flowers. My mother of course was used to the overtly emotional presentation of the joy that greeted a baby in her own family - Hannah and David, after all, specialised in child-care - all of them must have come to visit her before Father did. She felt truly abandoned; and ashamed for the loss of face, that her new husband should have her let her down so carelessly. Other people's marriages are always hard to understand, most of all the marriage of one's own parents. But I do know that my mother had very ambiguous feelings about each of her daughters, in turn, as we got married (apart from Rosemary, the youngest, who qualified as a doctor before marriage). The ambiguity was revealed in awful rows and scenes, quite out of the blue.

When my father returned, with his new family, to his own Department in Dublin in 1934 or '35, he rented an attractive house in Killiney - a picturesque suburb overlooking the expanse of Dublin Bay, about twenty minutes by train from the city centre, and considered a liberal "West Brit" enclave, the closest thing in the area to Hampstead Garden Suburb. Their nearest neighbours were Helen Chenevix and Louie Bennett. After all her imaginings about the enlightened New Ireland, to actually find herself living there must have been an intense cultural shock for my mother. The society that had developed in little over a decade was dominated by a doctrine of self-sufficency and self-conscious traditional values, particularly in regard to the mythology of Irish womanhood. The country had so long been dominated by foreigners that it regarded with suspicion and distaste any sort of foreign influence whatever (except for the papacy). There was, for instance, a strong prejudice against married women working outside the home. Catholic social doctrine had an absolute hegemony, and virulent anti-communism and anti-liberalism were widespread. In 1929 the existing Censorship Board was amended and given increased powers in line with Catholic dogma, forbidding all literature advocating birth-control. The most notable new repression against women was the The Conditions of Employment Bill which allowed the government to "prohibit the employment of female workers in industry, fix the proportion of female workers to the number of other workers and forbade employers to employ more women than men in any cases where a ministerial decision on a specific industry had been made." A Nazi-type policy of *"Kinder, Kueche, Kirche"* was now put into effect. In consequence, the International Labour Organisation in Geneva placed Ireland on a black list. From abroad it looked as though the country was becoming yet another Fascist enclave. The biggest shock of all for my mother was when she realized that Catholic doctrine on childbirth - the life of the baby taking precedence over the life of the mother - was upheld in all the maternity hospitals.

~~~o~~~

Anecdotes from the thirties: keeping faith with de Valera's Ireland.
In the summer of 1937 we all set off to Carraroe in Connemara. We were to learn Irish and become proper Irish children. I was three; I can remember the excitement of being packed in an old Morris car, my father a somewhat erratic driver at the wheel, my sister Rosemary in a Moses-basket with Claire, Judith and me looking after her in the back seat. I remember we stopped in Galway; the dazzle of the whitewashed cottages on the road into the city had given me motion-sickness. Getting back into the car I managed to crush my finger in the door, my first war-wound from the West... Later on we stopped for a picnic, sitting at the edge of the road, not a soul in sight - emptiness, quiet, green grass, big bunches of white daisies and the whiteness of the air - and then we all got in again and drove on - until we realised that we had left Rosemary behind.
~~~

The basket was there in the car, but no baby inside it.

Rosemary was one of the prettiest babies imaginable, always smiling, with dark blue eyes, a beautiful round little belly, a rosebud mouth and dark hair. I don't remember any panic at her loss; my mother was driving at the time; she just swung the car around and we returned to the picnic-stop. I do remember wondering, had Rosemary fallen out of the car as we all scrambled in? had I pushed her out accidentally just as we were setting off?

There at the picnic-stop were three little girls. They had blonde hair in ringlets. They were sitting in a row and holding Rosemary on the lap of the biggest one who sat in the middle. It was so still, this tableau: the three solemn little girls with the beautiful naked baby, all as though it were the most natural situation in the world. They looked as though somehow the baby had miraculously dropped from the skies. Rosemary was staring up at them, gurgling, kicking her legs. They seemed to be so small and Rosemary so healthy, each of them helping to support her weight. They seemed to be astonished at the nakedness of the baby; I felt they couldn't quite believe she wasn't a miracle; she was so like the Infant Jesus in a holy picture… When Mother and Father got out of the car, they never spoke; as Mother took the baby from them they just remained seated and silent - their impassive faces, their huge eyes - they never turned their heads as we drove off - they just remained seated there as if their function in life was to sit at the roadside and wait for babies to fall out of heaven.

The holiday was beginning to take on a magic dimension. We arrived in Carraroe at the house where we to stay. Upstairs we found beds with eiderdowns shaped like butterflies; there were china washbowls on the wash-stands with painted flowers and matching water-jugs set in the middle. I had never seen anything like it. The woman of the house had a plump and motherly appearance, but seemed strangely detached and distant. She had the same watchful look that the three little girls had had. We were exuberant, looking at everything and commenting on everything, racing up and down the stairs and in and out of the bedrooms. The less notice she took of us us, the more we wanted to engage her, but she held off. My father did no more than deliver us and drive back to Dublin; but I do remember noticing that she responded more to him than she did to Mother. Mother was slim and tanned, in a simple summer dress and no bra; as soon as she was in the house, she sat down and began breast-feeding Rosemary, talking and laughing with us. The woman never smiled or looked at Rosemary: she had made as it were an invisible circle around us and kept herself outside it. We were all trapped in the middle of her circle.

I only remember that first day. I don't remember how long we were there - maybe only a few days. I learned about the rest of our time in Carraroe from the story my mother told of it. We were supposed to be there for the whole summer but the stay was cut short for a number of reasons: the breast-feeding, our nakedness, my mother wearing shorts, my mother playing tennis on a Sunday. The priest came out of church after Mass to find her on the road hitting a ball with her tennis-racket, together with the teenage sons of the woman of the house. He must have had a word with the woman of the house, telling her to get rid of us; and no doubt she was glad to do so. Had we been Dublin Protestants she would have understood us and dealt with us in a proper category; but as it was she saw this alien pagan woman with her pagan female children and of course she had to tell us to go. This was after all the year of Dev's new Constitution, composed under the influence of his friend John Charles McQuaid; already Dev was developing his famous vision of a countryside "bright with cosy homesteads" and villages "joyous with… the laughter of comely maidens." Which sounds as though he might have meant us… but we were too brown, too naked, too full of life, and Mother was too full of the enjoyment of her sexuality and fecundity… "forbidden! not allowed! go back where you came from!"

Mother would often tell this story in a humorous way; it was part of our family folklore. But she had another story from about the same time which she kept to herself for years - in fact until her eightieth birthday.

~~~o~~~

She was sitting up in bed eating her birthday breakfast. It was in Longueville House at Mallow. We had all gathered there for the weekend to celebrate the occasion. I wanted her to say something on my camcorder as a personal record of her eighty years. So there she was, with her face half-paralysed from an accident she had had a couple of years previously. (She had tripped on the gangway of the Holyhead boat, fallen on her face and severed a nerve; this was
~~~

the first time since then that she felt confident enough to see us all together.) The weekend was a very emotional one: Mother had wept because it was such a surprise for her. Her bedroom was full of flowers, which we had all sent in advance. She was queen for a day and we were her loving subjects. Longueville House was just the sort of setting she enjoyed, an early nineteenth-century Anglo-Irish gracious home, turned into a high-class guesthouse, well reputed for its good food, its wine and its unobtrusive service.

I had arrived direct from Greenham Common, where I had been arrested. And then, on the way to Mallow on Messrs. Slatterys' cross-channel bus, a shattering experience. Two con-men called-in the Thames Valley police at Chippenham, claiming that a passenger had stolen their money: the scam was to have everyone on the bus take part in a whip-round for them - apparently with the collusion of the cops, who told us we would all be arrested and strip-searched, not to be released until the money was found or returned and they didn't care how...

What has this story to do with my mother's story? It was my hidden life, and I didn't tell it to anyone in the party. I tell it now to show how I came to her birthday in a receptive mood for the tale she was to tell me.

My mother sitting up in bed, the breakfast tray in front of her, her skilful way of buttering her toast, putting marmalade on it, biting through it with her sharp teeth - my camera pointed at her as I sat on the bed beside her - every now and then she looked into the camera as she talked and ate. Here she was secure and safe... She had a curious way of telling us anything about herself: she never started at the beginning but slipped inconsequentially into it as though engaged in a permanent stream-of-consciousness monologue. She suddenly said, "My one regret was that Father never allowed us to know about popular culture." And then her train of thought by some strange internal logic ran into the Women's Movement and how careful I had to be if I found myself trusting women. I think she was recognising - for the first time - *my* involvement in the Women's Movement, not only at Greenham but also in the Irish umbrella-group, the National Women's Council. She too had been involved in her early days in Ireland - I guess in 1936 or 37 - she was invited (she explained) to speak at a meeting held by the Women Graduates Association to protest against the draft Constitution. The main issue was social and economic equality for women, with the slogan "Equal Pay for Equal Work"; there was a campaign to amend the draft to that effect, because otherwise it looked as though women were to be removed from all spheres of public life. Mother's speech was to deal with the importance of publicly-funded creches and child-care if women were to go out to work. But no sooner had she got going than a section of the audience, to her appalled astonishment, exploded in fury. At which point she was abandoned and isolated by Louie Bennett, who she thought was her friend, and by the other women who had called the meeting and invited her. She felt she had been used, a catspaw, a flying kite, a patsy, to put forward an non-Irish notion (non-catholic, crypto-communist), and that if she failed it didn't matter, she was expendable, unaccountable, foreign in appearance, speaking with an English accent. She did not embroider the story; merely told it to let me know that women betray women. But I can well imagine how deeply it would have affected her, her whole attitude toward living in Ireland, toward her marriage, toward her children.

The background to this campaign of women against the 1937 Constitution was very fraught; they saw it as the last chance for the recognition of their work in the Irish freedom struggle. Women had taken up arms, had gone to gaol, had been on hunger-strike - with their propaganda they had energized the whole country after 1916 when the leaders of the Rising had nearly all been executed and the foot-soldiers interned. And now de Valera was determined to keep them in purdah.

Mother had enrolled at Trinity College to study medicine. As an example of a mother of four children going back to university and asserting her right to have a career, she must have seemed to many women an attractive proposition as a speaker at one of their rallies. But she obviously did not realise that there were innumerable contradictions within what appeared to be a united feminist front. Louie Bennett, as an executive of the Irish Women Workers Union and a member of the Labour Party, was not going to split the labour movement and isolate and endanger her union by supporting *married* women's right to work when it was already opposed by the party and by the Irish Congress of Trade Unions. She agreed with Congress that *married* women in the workforce would not raise the standard of living but would be used as a way of lowering wages for men and women alike. She saw the total exhaustion of married working-class women compelled to go out to work to make ends meet, while at the same time having to look after the house and the children. Louie Bennett perceived the Women Graduates Association, with its unqualified support for all women's right to work, as a divisively middle-class phenomenon. In fact the Irish Women Workers Union was to withdraw from the campaign against the Constitution, once de Valera agreed to amend Article 16 by restoring the phrase "without distinction of sex" which had been dropped from a definition of the civil rights of Irish citizens.

The real hurt for Mother, however, was that when she decided to study medicine, Louie Bennett tried to influence Father to stop her.

~~~o~~~

She slowly began to understand how isolated she was in Ireland. All the people she knew tended to be situated in well-knit and supportive extended families. They also tended to be of Father's generation, about ten years older than herself; their friendship with Father and their involvement in the struggle spanned two or three decades. Louie Bennett and her sister, Susan Manning, for example, belonged to a whole rake of women's social and political groups which dated back to the earliest days of the women's suffrage campaign in the 1870s. They were both members of the Irish Women Citizens Association, founded in 1919 to encourage women to use the vote. After the 1916 Rising, Louie edited *The Irish Citizen,* the newspaper of the Irish Women's Franchise League - part of the International Women's Suffrage Alliance, which had delivered a manifesto to all governments in 1914, calling on them to avert the threatened hostilities and pointing out that "women had no direct power to control whether they lived in peace or war". And then there was Mary Manning, Susan's sister-in-law, who belonged to the Hilton Edwards/Micheal McLiammoir set at the Gate Theatre. As well as being a playwright, she edited the Gate Theatre's magazine, *Motley.* Susan's son, John Manning, was a founder-member of the Irish Association and a well-known liberal intellectual. He helped to set up the Irish Film Society. These were all connected - by membership of societies, by family and marital ties - to the Sheehy Skeffingtons, the Childerses, the Bartons.

Most of this liberal bloc derived from enlightened Protestant or Quaker business dynasties. Helen Chenevix, for instance, who lived next door to Louie
~~~

Bennett; she was a member of the Labour Party, and the only one to support my mother's right to her medical studies.

It is interesting to see, when I read the histories of those times, how frequently the same small list of names keeps cropping up, right to the mid-sixties. In the late sixties the Irish Women's Liberation Movement was formed, which later evolved into Irish Women United, an organisation set up to challenge and radicalise the earlier groupings through direct action and spectaculars such as the "Contraceptive Train", running banned condoms into Dublin from the north. One of Irish Women United's demands was for state child-care - my mother would have felt at home with them thirty-five years after her ill-fated speech! Their impetus came mainly from a whole new bloc: young women journalists, lesbians and working-class women.

~~~o~~~

I am sure Louie Bennett was totally unware how great an influence she was to have in my parents' life and subsequently in mine. I wrote earlier that my father had been petted and spoiled by his sisters. I now think that in his more mature years Louie Bennett and the Manning women to some extent took their place and guided his development. I believe Louie Bennett was instrumental in bringing my father into the national resistance movement after 1916; her union played a very important part in the opposition to wartime conscription, organizing for instance a one-day general strike. Later she headed a union deputation to Oscar Traynor (IRA Dublin Brigade commander and my father's immediate superior), endeavouring to stop the surge toward civil war. She seems to have been one of the most sophisticated and ubiquitous figures in Irish radical life. I do not know how she would have regarded Joseph D'Arcy, her golden-headed boy from the slums of Dublin, coming back from his stay in London with such an independent and exotic bride. I am sure there was a great deal of tension; and a great desire on her part to protect my father; she saw it all from his point of view rather than his wife's.

It is simplistic to suggest that this was Louie Bennett's only reason for not supporting Mother's desire to study medicine. Louie's energies were devoted to large public issues, particularly the organisation of cooperatives; and Father in the Department of Agriculture was very useful to her in her desire to influence
~~~

the direction of national farming policy. She must have feared that his career would be adversely affected by an unconventional marriage. An Irish man in his position could marry a foreign wife, so long as the wife subordinated herself and immersed herself completely in the husband's interest. Louie saw this as a matter of ideology. The husband's interest was the national interest, as she perceived it; and mother's running off to become a doctor - at Trinity, of all places, described at the time (by a Mayo county councillor) as "not the culture of the Gael, rather it is poison gas to the kindly Celtic people," - could only have been a means of putting her own whim in front of her duties to Ireland. A notably foolish whim, because there wouldn't be any hope of my mother getting any sort of local authority medical job in the country, in view of the ban on married women obtaining public employment. Nor would she have any standing in Ireland, financial or family-connected, to enable her to set up her own practice or to be taken on in somebody else's practice. It would look to the right-wing catholic faction inside the civil service as though Father was colluding with a foolish and wilful act of defiance of the new Constitution.

But Mother had her own agenda, her safety valve. I think she realized that marriage while living in Ireland was impossible, and she was preparing her contingency plans, first to try and get Father transferred to London again, then she would continue her studies in London and qualify, and then maybe join Hannah or David in their practice. So long as she was dependent upon Father's erratic financial quirks she could not feel that we or she could ever be secure. She could not accept the acceptibility of the drinking-habits of the Irish family male. She refused to regard it as an inevitable part of the fabric of Irish society where the woman slaved at home to cover up the truth of her existence and the hidden poverty. The normal middle-class practice was for the man to buy a house. Once this home was paid for, his responsibility ended. Mother went against the conventions; she was not going to be trapped by home-ownership; we lived always in rented accomodation. She put sound economic reasons to Father, which he accepted, that we should move from Killiney into Dublin city; renting a flat there would much cheaper than a house; there would be a saving on train fares and lunches, and most of all (not expressed to him) she would be able to keep an eye on his drinking after work - there would no excuse, such as a missed train, for him not to come straight home. She made all her own clothes and ours; in fact she was a most innovative manager of money. Trinity's fees in those days were not large; her biggest expense would have been her books, which she could have got from Hannah or David. The argument was won. She went ahead.

~~~o~~~

We moved to an upstairs flat in Wilton Place, just five minutes' walk from Trinity College, and five minutes from the Government Buildings where Father worked. I think Claire, Judith and myself were shunted off to a Montessori school in Hatch Street, nearby; while Mother brought Rosemary with her to her lectures, where, discreetly, she would breast-feed her. She had no ideology; just her own intuition. She would have dismissed any crudely feminist analysis of her motives; and yet she did anticipate the incontrovertibly feminist slogan, "The Personal is Political", and this is what she handed down to me. It was an incredibly brave act to sit in the middle of a lecture-room full of young men, exposing her breast to give nourishment to a baby. That act, in itself, proclaimed both her belief in life, and her professional commitment to the Hippocratic Oath. It personified her whole human existence. And it was noticed and remembered as much as forty years later, when Alfred Bradley was producing an Arden play in Manchester for the BBC: his production assistant Glenys Miles turned to J.A. and told him that her father remembered, with admiration, giving lectures to medical students in Trinity, while this beautiful woman sat there in front of him feeding her baby and efficiently taking her notes. Women even today are still not free to open their dresses and feed their babies anywhere they want.

My mother was fully aware of the *theatrical* impact of her lecture-room breast-feeding; and she was proud of it; it became part of our family legend, reinforcing for all of her children the value of mother's milk, and ensuring that we did not feel a need to go into purdah for the purpose. I suspect that when she was barracked at Louie Bennett's meeting, she might have raised this very question, telling women that such a natural function should not impede their right to work.

~~~o~~~

My last memories of really feeling comfortable and at ease date from around 1937 and 1938, that's to say between the ages of two-and-a-half and four. We lived in three successive Dublin addresses, Killiney, Wilton Place, and Greenville Road (Blackrock); but each summer we went to London to stay with the Billig grandparents. My first memory of Grandma was when she brought me to the synagogue, up into the women's gallery looking down into the men's space. I remember running down the stairs when Grandma was talking to the beadle. This must have been at the beginning of 1937, when Mother and I had travelled alone on the mailboat from Dun Laoghaire; she was going to London for the birth of Rosemary. My grandparents must have been looking after me while she was in the nursing home. I loved London; I don't remember whether the grandparents were living in Wandsworth or the East End at that time; but I found the whole place warm and exciting. Grandpa would leave early in the morning to go to the market to buy plums for us to eat, black-purple plums, so sweet and full of juice. London, for me, *was* plums; even today, I still associate the city with the fruit. While Grandpa would be showing me the plums, Grandma bustled around, bringing in the porridge. I don't know exactly how she made this porridge, but I still remember its particular warm, rich smell, mixed with the tang of the salt and pepper that Grandpa sprinkled on his helping. I had brown sugar and cream on mine. Then I would have to be quiet while Grandpa went into a corner to say his prayers, putting on his special shawl and cap and draping a long strip of cloth over his left arm. I shared a bed with Grandma and Grandpa. There was a fireplace in the bedroom, and when I got into the bed I would burrow down to the bottom of it, where I imagined I lived in the bend of the chimney and was looked after by an old man with one leg. My mother found me there once; years later, she told me it was because I wanted to return to her womb.

Down in the bottom of the bed was where I made my first discovery of self-pleasure... I was so delighted by this discovery that when I returned to my sisters in Dublin I demonstrated the act to them - my first bit of public theatre. Later, when I was five and went to school for the first time (Avoca School at Blackrock), I made a conscious decision to perform my "bit of theatre" during one of the more tedious school episodes - waiting to be called into line to be marched off somewhere. I assumed that my act was met with approval, because nobody told me to stop it. But it looked as though I was going to be so totally ignored that the teacher would not call me into line. I was the last one left out of all the children, and something was obviously wrong. As the teacher didn't say anything, I kept on with my masturbating; it seemed to be too late to stop. In the end she did call me, and I stopped. She was a young woman and must have been too embarrassed to know quite what to do about me. But at end of the day, when I had come home and was playing in the garden with my sisters, I saw her coming down the road. She walked up our garden path without greeting any of us; she knocked on the door and was brought into the drawing-room by Mother. The door was closed behind her. I knew I was in trouble. I could hear quiet voices... Then she left, still without looking at any of us. My mother never mentioned it to me; but I did not repeat my act at school.

There followed what I take to be a psychological consequence. The school put on an end-of-term show with all of us enacting nursery rhymes. Judith was to be a Grandfather Clock, and I was cast as Little Bo-Peep; Mother made me a lovely shepherdess dress with a crook. I knew all my lines. The great day dawned. During the dress rehearsal I was struck with a terrible stutter; I could not get a single word out; my part was given to someone else, and instead I had to play a *silent* Mouse running up the Grandfather Clock.

You might think I had learned my lesson; that I would not bring my bright ideas of home activities into the school. But one day there were school sports; my sisters with Mother and baby Rosemary had all gone off to them; I had decided to stay at home and play in the garden in my swimsuit, which is what we always did in hot weather. I then thought I would after all go to see the sports. I decided I would not bother to put on a dress as it was so hot. Off I went (the school grounds were just around the corner from our house in Greenville Road) and at the entrance I bumped into my eldest sister Claire: horror on her face at the very sight of me. I looked around and realised that everyone else was fully and elaborately dressed-up in hats and flowery dresses. And everyone was looking at me. Claire grabbed my hand without a word and brought me home. Why were there two standards of behaviour, I would ask myself? Things I could do at home, that I couldn't do at school? I could not understand. And this is where my journey of discomfort and confusion about life seems to have begun.

It is odd, bearing in mind the various public humiliations I suffered before reaching my teens, that it should have been the theatre to which I was attracted for a career, and to which I fastened on as my great objective in life. It is usual for a child who enters the theatre to have a few natural talents, or at least one: beauty, musical ability, a singing voice maybe.

Even my singing was to be brought to an ignominious end. There was a sudden shift of direction when I was about eight. Instead of being a nice little West Brit brought up in the suburbs of the Dublin Southside, I had landed up as a boarder in an enclosed Dominican convent at Cabra on the Northside, where once again I participated in an end-of-term concert. I was the pet of an elderly nun who taught us music. She was rather deaf. In the planning of the concert, which was to include the whole school, junior and senior, a couple of solos were allocated to us juniors. Mother Mary Raymond would select. She had us lined up to sing "Away in a Manger." She thumped out the tune on an ancient piano and we followed her. I was chosen. Mother Mary Scholastica, the seniors' music-mistress was in charge of the whole concert, and there she sat at the final rehearsal, in front of her beautifully-tuned grand piano, softly playing the accompaniment. No doubt there was some quality in my rendition of the carol; but keeping in tune was not part of it. If was as if there were two independent musical events taking place. But there was only room for one interpretation; and it was not mine. Out I had to go. Not only did I not sing my solo but I was forbidden even to sing in the choir.

One might think I would have been crushed for all time.

On the contrary. The more public failures that were heaped on me, the more I realised how arbitrary and nonsensical was the world. Instead, I would reject the world's values. I would suffer in silence. I would doggedly go forward following my own ideals. I would change the world.

~~~o~~~

Before I go any further into my schooldays I will put down their sequence: the schools themselves and the different places where we lived.

Home No. 1: - Killiney, at the south end of Dublin Bay. 1935 - 1937. A detached house with a large garden. I was not yet going to school.

Home No. 2: - Wilton Place, Dublin. 1937 - 1938. An upstairs flat. I was not yet going to school.
~~~

Home No. 3: - Greenville Road, Blackrock, just outside Dublin city. 1938 -1939. Two successive semi-detached houses in a newly-built cul-de-sac, with gardens in front and behind.

School No. 1: - Avoca School, Blackrock. 1938 - 1939. A non-sectarian (but predominantly Protestant) establishment, set up by C. P. Parker who had been a teacher at the well-known Sandford House School. Such interdenominational schools were very rare in Ireland at this time.

Home No. 4: - Laragh, near Glendalough, Co. Wicklow. 1939 - 1941. A rented gate-lodge in the grounds of a country hotel. No school.

Home No. 5: - Pembroke Road, Dublin. 1941 - 1942. A ground-floor flat.

School No. 2: - Miss Merediths. The famous Catholic girls' day-school, run by the Meredith sisters, in Pembroke Road.

Home No. 6: - Garry Ard, Kilmacanoge, Co. Wicklow. 1942 - 1950. A rented Indian-style wooden bungalow with verandahs.

School No. 3: - Cabra, North Dublin. 1942 - 1947. I was a boarder in an enclosed Dominican convent.

School No. 4: - Loreto Convent, Bray, Co. Wicklow. 1947 - 1948. A different order of nuns; I was a day-pupil.

School No. 5: - Alexandra College, Dublin. 1948 - 1950. A Protestant day-school.

~~~o~~~

Our stay in Wilton Place was very short. The tenants on the ground floor were disturbed by our noise and complained to the landlord.

No sooner had we moved to Greenville Road than we were all whisked off to London. Permanently, we thought, because Father had been transferred there again. But then came the Munich crisis and all of us except Father had to go straight back to Dublin. When it seemed as though there wasn't going to be a war after all, everything was packed up, including the furniture, to be put into store, and we made our next attempt at a move to London. We had scarcely arrived before we all had to dash to Euston for the last train to Holyhead: Hitler had marched into Poland. I vividly remember the panic: the giant barrage balloons, the constant letting-off of practice sirens, the gas-masks with which we were all fitted (except for Rosemary who was too young and would have to share Mother's), lots of huddled conversation between Mother and her brothers and sisters, the hysterical crush at Euston in the dark, rumours
~~~

of a little child falling under a train and being killed (I thought it was one of us), and a man sitting down on his suitcase - somebody kicked the suitcase, there he was on the ground with his hat fallen off, crying... We travelled with another family, with children of the same age: the Brennans, who were going to America. I rather wished that we were being evacuated to America as well. (One of the Brennan children, Maeve, became an acclaimed writer, only to end her days as a bag-lady in New York.) Anyway, we managed to get all of us safely on the train, except for a valise full of shoes. When we arrived in Dublin we stayed temporarily in a small hotel. The other guests looked upon us with pity because apparently we were refugees - the first refugees to arrive in Ireland. My two elder sisters were thrilled with this new status. Back we went to Greenville Road (into another rented house there), my mother and her four little girls.

~~~o~~~

Instead of Father, we had a new addition to our family, Kitty Spain from Nenagh, Tipperary, and she had come to look after us. She was a stout young country-woman with a florid complexion, her face smothered, on her days off, in Outdoor Girl pink powder. To us children she had a remarkable and astonishing characteristic: she enjoyed eating the fat with the meat. She had black straight hair and false teeth. Before we saw Kitty dressing-up for her day off, we never knew that women could equip themselves with such garments. She was well upholstered inside her black suit. My mother wore the minimum, just a pair of home-made cami-knickers with a home-made dress over them. But all Kitty's clothes came from the shops. It was her pink boned corset that we couldn't take our eyes off. It had seemingly hundreds of hooks and eyes which she had to squash herself into. Under the corset were heavy serge bloomers and a vest. She would clip up her stocking-tops to apparatus beneath the hem of the corset. On top of the whole thing would be a slip. Then - instead of a blouse - the modesty-vest, the piece-de-resistance, made of some sort of starched lace, a kind of bib or "dickey". Then she would struggle to get into the black skirt and hook-and-eye it up. Then she would put on her high heels, then the great flurry of her powder with its very strong cheap-sweet smell, then the lipstick (she would make an artificial bow of her lips), then the black jacket, and finally the beret. Off she would go, transformed, to have a rare old time on the town with her innumerable friends - all of them from Nenagh or thereabouts.
~~~

There is always an assumption by Dubliners that if you come from up the country you are alone and lost in the big city. But this is to ignore the vast and continual exodus from the rural to the urban. In the 1930s there was devastating poverty in the countryside in consequence of the "Economic War": de Valera had withheld payment of Land Annuities claimed by the British; "In justice," he said, "Ireland is under no debt to Great Britain... [because of] the manifold injuries and losses suffered by our country under British rule"; the British retaliated by imposing special duties on Irish imports; Irish cattle could not be exported to Britain and the Irish agricultural economy was on the verge of collapse. (I remember my father frequently disappearing on something called "Trade Missions" - on one of them he went to Germany in search of some cattle-export deal - when he came home he and my mother were whispering together about Hitler as though they didn't want us to hear.) Kitty's coming from Tipperary to take up service in Dublin was typical of the time.

Her name itself conjured up romance -

> The King of Spain's daughter
> Came to visit me
> And all for the sake
> Of my little nut tree.

Her home-county, Tipperary, was in those days a part of the country as foreign to us as Spain itself, she used to promise to take us there on a holiday. In the end Rosemary was the only one to go. She came back with a present for all of us, a tiny delicate tea-cup and saucer of translucent china, with gold round the rim. Even though Kitty stayed with us for seven years, from 1939 until Mother returned in 1946, she remains a shadowy presence in my memory; I find it difficult to pin down anything definite about my personal relationship with her. She first came when Rosemary was a little over two years old, so naturally Rosemary was her pet; my other two sisters were nine and seven, by Kitty's standards practically adult. I was five, which is awkward; I suppose we had an awkward relationship. I was a bit of a blabber and inclined to blurt out the first thing that entered my head. I couldn't keep a secret to save my life. I got onto a wrong footing with her in the first couple of weeks of her stay: each afternoon she would take us for a walk, and my mother, as she waved us goodbye, would call out, "Remember, Kitty, don't buy them sweets." There was a corner sweetshop a little distance from Greenville Road, where we would stop to gaze in at the window; it was prettily arranged with boxes of chocolates in all shapes and sizes, shiny ribbons, pictures of soft fluffy white kittens with blue eyes, and Kitty (of course) would always take us in and buy us a pennyworth of sweets. Now one day when she let each of us choose something, I chose a fizzy sherbert bag with a straw to suck at - I had never tasted anything so remarkable - all it was was lemon crystals and yet they *fizzed* inside your mouth. Even though Kitty had previously sworn us to secrecy, and I had solemnly promised that not a word would pass my lips, as soon as I was going up the garden path I began to shout, "Kitty bought us a fizzbag, Kitty bought us a fizzbag!" Mother in fact didn't say anything; but Kitty shot me a dark look, and from then on she never trusted me with any of the secrets. Claire and Judith remained part of her conspiracy; I would see them huddled together; I would beg to be told what was going on and one of them would say, "Go away, you can't keep secrets, you're just a blabbermouth."

I used to beg Kitty to take me with her when she went to visit her friends. On one occasion she told me that I could accompany her to a friend who worked for a doctor. My idea of a doctor's way of life came from my mother having taken us all to consult Dr Robert Collis, the leading Dublin paediatrician and social reformer. We were thrilled when we went up the steps to his front door in Merrion Square, with its brightly-polished doorknob and brass plate. In his hall were great bunches of roses in bowls. He bounced out to greet us in his white coat, and led us all into his consulting room where he had toys for us to play with and shiny coloured picture-books. I naturally expected Kitty to bring me into the same sort of place.

The house was in Fitzwilliam Street, with the steps and the doorknob and the brass plate; I immediately ran ahead to climb up the steps, only to be grabbed by Kitty and steered down the narrow entrance to the basement, dark and mildewed. Inside was a dark sitting-room and a very quiet little upright woman, rather older than Kitty. There was an iron grill on the window and the room was full of statues, holy pictures, little candles and lamps. She talked non-stop in a breathless genteel voice about the doctor and his family, how wonderful they were, how they were at present away on their holidays, it was as though she were on the holidays with them - she gave us every single detail of their lives, what they wore, what they ate, how they talked. I asked Kitty if we could not go upstairs and look at the consulting-room, but Kitty's friend said, "No, little girl, no: no-one is allowed to go upstairs when the doctor and his family are away." She was a kind woman, however: she gave me a tiny holy statue of the Christ-child, the Little King, which I gave to Kitty to look after for me.

I couldn't understand why a doctor would keep Kitty's friend in such a dungeon, and not let her use the whole of the house.

Kitty had another friend whom she met sometimes in the street when Rosemary and I were with her. We had to wait for what seemed to be hours while this woman would corner Kitty and then talk and talk and talk. I could not imagine how anyone could have so much to say. The structure of her monologues was always the same - "And I said to her… and she said to me… ", on and on like a partially-blocked tap spluttering. Just as I was beginning to understand what it was all about, she would lower her voice dramatically, whisper something into Kitty's ear, and carry on again with increased emphasis - "*And* I said to *her*… *and* she said to *me*… " When we got home, I would spend hours with Rosemary doing interminable imitations, playing at "I said and she said," until we drove everyone mad.

Kitty once brought me to visit a family in a part of the city altogether different from the comfortable and sheltered surroundings of our home. It was one of the new corporation housing estates to the south-west, Kimmage, or Drimnagh, or Crumlin, rapidly thrown up to rehouse the city-centre slum-dwellers; it was also a district to which rural families would gravitate; they lived there like refugees, isolated in little box-houses spread out along unfinished roads where you had to step over builders' rubble and through desolate puddles of mud; indoors I saw neither paint nor wallpaper on the starkly plastered walls. I was unhappily aware of a house full of children all staring at me, wondering who I might be. I understood I was supposed to play with them, but there was nowhere to play, they just wandered about outside kicking stones in a bored fashion. My little problem was that I was extremely fastidious about going to the "lav," and I was inclined to get a runny-tummy in any new surroundings. So I suddenly was aware I had to go; I whispered to Kitty; one of the children pointed the way. I was shocked. There was no toilet paper, only newspaper cut in squares on a nail on the wall, and brown smears of shit were streaking the walls. I came out at once and again tugged at Kitty to tell her. So now all the adults were alerted to my problem. I remember their insulted faces, looking upon me as at some little creature of unmitigated snootiness. That was the last time Kitty brought me to any of her friends. Later on, when she took Rosemary for a visit to her family in Nenagh, she made it very clear she did not want me along or any of my loudmouth comments.

It was Kitty who first brought me to Mass. (I think Judith and Claire at this time went to a Sunday School attached to Avoca.) I didn't like it very much. The church was absolutely packed. Kitty said that when we went in, I was to kneel down. We found a bench and we both knelt. But when it was the time for us to sit, I discovered that an old woman had crept in behind me and had taken my seat; so I had to stay on my knees the whole length of the Mass.

I don't think we made much of an impression on Greenville Road. One little anecdote I heard a good few years afterwards, from Leslie MacWeeney, the artist. She was a child at the time, living beside us with her mother and three brothers and sisters. She said she always remembered the way *my* mother would come out of the house and call, "Minadex time, darlings!" (Minadex was a childrens' tonic; we used to have Emulsion and Minadex, because Mother was terrified of our contracting TB, which was rife in Ireland in those days.)

~~~o~~~

At Laragh we returned to semi-innocence and paganism. The gate lodge was part of the hotel-farm complex owned by the Somerville-Large family. It was what is known as a "Parnell House". These were built all over the country as cheap housing for labourers; they were named after the great nationalist politician, champion of the Land League, who had always insisted that landlords and farmers had a responsibility to house their dependants decently. His sisters Anna and Fanny excelled him in militancy, and set up the Ladies' Land League. Anna's view of landlords was that if they "had not deserved extinction for anything else, they would have deserved it for the treatment of their own women." The Parnells were a family of relatively impoverished protestant gentry whose home at Avondale was not very far from Laragh. (Another well-known protestant family, also not very far from Laragh, were the Bartons; Robert Barton was a co-signatory of the Treaty of 1921; he was related by marriage to Erskine Childers, novelist and republican activist, who was shot for his opposition to the treaty.)
~~~

The lodge was called "Honeymoon Cottage"; it had two stories with rambling roses round the porch; as was the norm in those days, no electricity or running water (rural electricity didn't arrive until after the war, and piped water in many places not until the 1970s); an outside earth-closet; the water-supply from our own well. The first thing Mother did was to drop the "honeymoon" name. She bought an Aladdin Lamp, which was pretty elegant and gave a far better light than the cruder type of paraffin lamp that was already there. The Aladdin had a long narrow glass chimney and a delicate gauze mantle over the wick. If you pumped too much paraffin in the initial lighting, the whole flame would flare up quickly and burn out the gauze, causing black smoke to stain the chimney. So the lighting-up each evening had to be done with caution. Mother was very efficient at all these intricate workings which she had to learn from first principles. She would stand back and contemplate the apparatus until she understood it and then she would go ahead. Kitty would follow her example. It was amusing to us to observe these two women - one who had never lived in the country and the other who had lived there all her life.

The next task was to make sure the well was always clean, and the water filtered. And then we had to make sure there was a plentiful supply of dry sticks to light the turf fire; every day we would go off collecting the sticks from the hedgerows, removing the nettles and brambles as we pulled the sticks clear of the undergrowth. Mother was very good at coaxing even the wetter sticks to take fire, tightly rolling-up bits of paper and (if all else failed) a spoonful of sugar, which used to horrify Kitty - sugar was very scarce in those days. Other people used paraffin to get a blaze going, but she refused to do this because it was too dangerous. We had to bring in turf every day from the stack outside the house - we were warned to be careful about which section we got it from - it had to be dry. Our clothes were washed in a tin bath with a scrubbing-board, outside the back door. We children had a task when sheets were washed; we would twist them between us in opposite directions until the loose water was wrung out, and then we would throw them across a nearby hawthorn bush for the thorns to hold them fast while they dried. Ironing: the iron was a heavy metal block with heating-slabs which could be inserted into the end of it after they had been warmed up on the range. If it was too hot it left scorch marks. Bread was cooked in a pot-oven, a heavy iron pot with a lid; sods of red-hot turf were laid underneath and on top of it with the tongs. The use of both iron and pot-oven involved a carefully-calculated balance of heat.

Kitty explained to Mother how to use the pot-oven. When Mother said that it could be used for other things than bread (such as roasting meat, making stews, apple-tarts or cakes) Kitty was astonished. So that our living-standards should not go down, we children became a tribe of gatherers - every day in summer and autumn we had to go out to find fruits and berries, crab-apples, blackberries, elderberries, to make jams and jellies, and rose-hips for syrup (we hated gathering rose-hips because of the unpleasantness of removing the hairy pips). Even though we didn't go to school at this time we developed a good educational grasp of the resources of the countryside and what could be done with them. In summer, at dawn or after rain, out we would go to pick mushrooms. If we were stung by nettles, we would pluck a dock-leaf and rub it over the sting.

To the local people we were a bit of a puzzle. Living in rented accomodation gave us no status; and picking food from the hedges was abhorrent, both shameful and shameless, a public advertisement of one's poverty. There were two historical reasons for this: the traumatic expedients of the famine, and the fear of the landlords who claimed exclusive ownership of every hedgerow.

With foresight for the coming shortages, Mother brought with her a tea-chest filled with small square boxes packed with tea - this was for Kitty, the great tea-drinker in our family - together with sacks of flour and sugar. Rationing came in a few months later -

> Bless 'em all bless 'em all bless 'em all
> The long and the short and the tall,
> Bless de Valera and Seán MacEntee
> For giving us shell cocoa and half an ounce of tea!

The tea-chest was our barter exchange. Kitty was in charge of it, and sure enough, all doors were opened to her for any help that was required. Farm produce from the hotel farm, such as butter, milk, eggs and vegetables, was part of the deal when the cottage was rented.

Mother continued her studies at Trinity, travelling regularly the 30 miles or so into Dublin. Kitty taught her to ride a bike; she would cycle to the main road and catch the St. Kevin's bus which ran once a day each way between

Glendalough and Dublin. When petrol-rationing put an end to the daily service, she would cycle all the way to Dublin, sometimes staying the night there. We were always nervous when she cycled to Dublin, we thought her brakes might give way as she freewheeled down the long hill. In the end she acquired a rather shy, beefy student with a car and his own source of petrol; he would bring her back for the week-end. He was *her* friend; we never had anything do with him: the fact that he shared her bed didn't cause any problems. There would be some slight tension when he was around, with us expecting the same attention from her as when he wasn't there, but we quickly understood that he had the first claim.

Kitty's love life was a public affair in which we all became involved. I can't remember when we all started to say our bedtime prayers (but I do remember my prayers always finishing with, "And let Jimmy Timmons love Kitty and Larry love me!"). Nor do I remember how many Sundays Kitty took us to Mass. The chapel was in Laragh village, a couple of miles away. It was always a surprise to me to see all those other children all dressed-up and streeling along the road. I don't remember any chat or salutations as we passed; there would have been an assortment of traps, horses and carts, donkeys and carts. As we came closer to the chapel, there was a sprinkling of cars with better-dressed people. I remember a very strange family: we used to pass a derelict mill and there, hanging out of the glassless windows, were all these wild-looking flaxen-haired children watching us as we passed.

~~~o~~~

We spent two years in Laragh; our first summer there was one of those classic summers of childhood memories, the haymaking and cutting of the harvest in August. Kitty brought us all down to help with the haymaking. Irish summers only have a few short spells of unbroken sunshine: the good weather brought a tremendous surge of energy and excitement as the hay had to be cut by hand quickly, tossed and made into cocks without any delay. All hands were used, so Kitty naturally helped. It was one of the few occasions where there was a natural harmony. Each man would have his own horse and empty dray; we would sit on the edge of one of the drays, legs dangling, going down to the long meadow. If there was to be any match-making or mating, that is when it took place, because it was one of the few times that men and women worked
~~~

together, the men moving forward in a rhythmical movement, swinging the scythe from side to side, their shirts off, their backs turning pink, then red, then a golden brown; the women following, tossing the hay into little piles. Then the break for the cold tea, brought out in cans, and the soda bread wrapped in towels. It was during the tea break that the initial flirtations commenced. I announced to the world, blather-mouthed, six-years-old, that Kitty was in love with Jimmy Timmons, and then I went up to Jimmy's cousin Larry, and told him that I was choosing him to love. I remember the roar of laughter when I made this solemn announcement. For the rest of the haymaking I attached myself to Larry, riding with him on his dray.

After the hay, there was the wheat and the oats. The men with the scythes kept cutting in a circle until the very last bit, and then we could see the rabbits all running away. The love I had for Larry remained with me: his gentleness, his acceptance of my love without embarrassment or questioning. He never teased me, or commented on how I looked. This was unusual, because any time one was introduced one's appearance was openly commented on, like, "She is not going to be the beauty of the family, she's not as pretty as her sister, her mouth is too large, she's very dark." It was as though nobody knew that children had ears. Years later, at the Hornchurch Rep., when I played the young girl in *The Summer of the Seventeenth Doll* (an Australian play about migrant workers), I thought of Larry. It was his maleness that attracted me, the combination of the harvesting of the wheat and oats, the sun and dust, the fresh spicey smell, the colour of his hair and skin, so like the wheat and oats. The idea has crossed my mind that our outspokeness of matters of the heart made it easer for Kitty to break the barrier of shyness and find a mate. There were troubled times ahead for Kitty, and for us, because every time she had a tiff with Jimmy there was a complete stand-off between the farm and Kitty which meant that we no longer went there. I would then pray harder and harder to God to "let Kitty be happy with Jimmy Timmons!" When they made up I too was filled with happiness. But I had my own struggles in trying to be happy: the contrast between heaven and earth was beginning to be apparent; I would lie on my back looking up at the sky with the white clouds gently floating without a care in the world - why couldn't I be like that? - but the next moment the unexpected - a thistle to prick my bare foot; a soft mushy cowpat which looked to be hard-baked but when I stepped on it my foot would fall through to be stuck in foul-smelling yellow goo; if I had a wee, a hidden nettle would surely sting my bottom; if I ran down the lane I'd be sure to fall, grazing my hands and knees, or else fierce hens, alarmed, would suddenly rush at me, their beaks open and squawking, screaming in rage; the final indignity of country life was the weekly de-worming that my mother carried out, poking her finger up our anuses one after the other. Successfully to get through one perfect day was an impossibility.

Even my own feelings of tenderness were fatally flawed. One day we were out collecting sticks; we heard a crying inside the hedge; there we saw a ginger cat caught by the barbed wire, the sharp serrated edges stuck firmly in its fur. I didn't want to see or hear its misery; I fled. My elder sisters, more practical, returned to the house for Mother. She came back with them, myself tailing along at a good distance; she carefully extracted the cat from the wire, carried it home, cut away the fur and washed its wounds. I couldn't face the terrible open lacerations along its back. My mother nursed the cat back to health and it became a pet - not mine, because every time I looked at it, I remembered my own cowardice.

~~~o~~~

Death.

At the other end of the avenue lived the Staceys, in a smaller gate-lodge than ours. Mr Stacey was a casual labourer, not employed by the estate. Kitty used to visit there. It was a kind of subversive household, full of disrespectful gossip about the goings-on on the estate. The house was always full of Mrs Stacey's relations, whose exact connections I could never fathom - the Staceys' baby turned out to be the uncle of an eleven-year old boy! Rosemary and I used to play happily for hours there, while Kitty was in the house. We made cakes in the mud and held tea-parties with an an old broken tea-pot. Mrs Stacey was expecting a baby; and one day we were brought down to see the baby. There was Mrs Stacey sitting up in a settle-bed in the kitchen, the usual (year-old) baby at her breast, while her husband knocked nails into a white wooden box. Mrs Stacey was laughing her head off. When I asked to see the new baby, she replied, "Oh the doctor brought it in his bag and took it away again." I couldn't understand why a doctor would go to all that trouble bringing a baby and taking it away again. The more insistent that I was the more the roomful of people laughed.
~~~

At Christmas it was time for killing the pig, and the farmyard was filled with a strange intensity. Normally every one was friendly to me, but now, as I passed one of the outhouse doors, a shovelful of little pink mice in a heap of soft flour was suddenly thrown out the door and nearly hit me as I passed. The men roared with laughter at my dismay, their white teeth flashing from the darkness of the outhouse. That night there was a terrible thunderstorm with lighting and rain. The men were running around with their tilly-lamps, shouting and bellowing. In the middle of it all came the piercing screams of the butchered pig, they went on and on - Kitty came and fetched us home and explained how the pig had to be bled for the black pudding - in my imagination the pig was hoisted up and they were all sticking hay-forks into it, letting the blood out through a multitude of small holes.

~~~o~~~

The war and how it impinged on our life.
There was a rumour that a government inspector was to go round all the houses to see if anyone had enough room to take in evacuees. (There had been a German air-raid on Dublin, which we didn't know anything about, of course; but the authorities must have been worried that Ireland's neutrality was about to be seriously violated.) My elder sisters were quite excited by the idea of other children coming. They were already 8 and 10, the age of making friends; they played with the Somerville-Large boys when they came for their holidays from their boarding schools, whereas I only played with Rosemary or hung round Kitty. The idea appalled me. I imagined myself completely shunted out by these hordes of strange children who would take over the whole house.

There was a lot of excitement about German spies. One day we went down to the post office at Annamoe, which was also a little shop, run by an old lady. Claire saw a poster on the wall and read it out to us. It said there was a German spy in the Wicklow hills and a reward was offered for his capture. We were thrilled and were determined to win the reward; we spent hours on the golf-course looking for this spy. Little did we realise that even as we looked for him, the spy (a Lt. Herman Goertz) had already walked along the very same road, in the opposite direction towards Laragh Castle, where he was by now safely ensconced with his hostess Iseult Stuart, a fiercely anti-British republican, the daughter of Maud Gonne MacBride.
~~~

Laragh was a curious enclave inside conventional catholic Ireland, a kind of alternative-lifestyle haven: individuals or couples escaping from Dublin, setting-up smallholdings, chicken-farms, beehives. Francis Stuart, husband of Iseult, had originated a chicken-farm at Laragh Castle. The castle was owned by Maud Gonne; it had been built as an army blockhouse during the 1798 rebellion. The chicken farm was not successful and Francis had gone off to Germany with an academic appointment. There were two children, Kay and Ian, in the same age-bracket as my sister Claire. I felt an empathy with them, because they were just like us, looked after by the mother while their father was away. Claire must have met them down by the lake and brought them home for tea. They asked us back for tea. I was longing to go, but Mother did not encourage this friendship. I had sensed an unhappiness within Kay, and, sadly, in her mid-thirties, she was to take her own life. I think it was about this time that my mother became wary of us going down to the hotel to swim in the lake when other guests were around.

The hotel was on a terrace where the guests sat on garden chairs as they sipped their afternoon tea. On our way to the lake, we passed below this terrace. One day I noticed an old lady dressed in lots of black chiffon. She sat with her legs apart as old people often do; I looked straight up and saw she was not wearing any knickers - I was quite shocked, but it didn't seem to bother her at all. Somebody told us she was French, and said that French women never wore knickers ... We always wanted mother to put on one of her pretty frocks, sit on the terrace and join the guests. She never would, and was always a bit distant in that regard.

In the spring of 1941 Laragh began to change. A new manager took over the hotel and the estate. Our first encounter with him as we were strolling along the avenue picking daffodils: a man on a horse suddenly stopped beside us and roared at us, what the hell we were doing, stealing his flowers? A tight cruel face jerking out the words - we were not allowed to walk up his avenue, we were not to go and help the men on the farm any more. Kitty's love affair with Jimmy Timmons petered out. And there was only one small tea-box remaining in the chest, with a little bit of tea left at the bottom. I fancy my mother must have felt that Laragh was no longer safe, with all the talk of spies and the Nazi sympathisers down the road. The hotel had obviously been warned to tighten up its relationships. And when Mother negotiated for the renewal of her rental, she was told we would not be entitled to any more food from the farm.

That summer we did not help in the harvest.

~~~o~~~

Mother came in one evening and told us that we would be going to boarding-school: which one would we like to go to? We had a choice. She showed us the prospectuses: Newtown, the Quaker co-ed school at Waterford; or the enclosed Dominican convent at Cabra on the northern edge of Dublin. I chose Cabra, where the nuns owned a farm; I imagined it would be just another version of Laragh, except that I would be running around in a blue uniform with a white veil, like the Virgin Mary. My sisters also chose Cabra, but I don't know what their reasons were. A convent education in Ireland at that time was comparatively cheap, much cheaper than a secular private school like Newtown, because the teachers and the servants were all nuns: unwaged labour for the love of God.

Looking back it is easy to understand why mother decided to pack us off to boarding-school and herself to return to England to help in the war effort. 1941 was the bleak period of the war when it looked as if the Nazis might use an invasion of Ireland to help them defeat Britain. If they did this they would seek the help of the IRA, and would have supported them in another Rising. In fact Iseult Stuart had been secretly finding contacts for Lt. Goertz with the IRA in Dublin. Shortly after his stay in Laragh, 400 IRA suspects were interned by de Valera in the Curragh camp. There was very heavy censorship in Ireland during the war, but some of this would have been known to my mother, or if she didn't know it she surely suspected it. Could the Irish Jews trust de Valera if the Nazis took over the country? We now know that he would have been willing (like the Vichy government in France) to give the Jews up to the Nazis if the worst came to the worst. He had been reluctant to assist Jewish refugees coming into the country lest they became a "destabilising" factor. The Catholic Church in its prayers at Mass still blamed the Jews for the Crucifixion. At this time Hannah, David and Bimms had all joined up in the Medical Corps in the Indian Army. Bimms went to Malaya and Hannah and David stayed in India. My mother must have felt that somehow she too had to do her bit. She got a job in the laboratory of a plastic-factory at Ipswich, carrying out research for wartime production.
~~~

I realize today that so long as she remained with us she endangered our lives: we would have a better chance of survival in a boarding-school; the safest place of all would be an enclosed order like the Dominicans. She must have been relieved when we chose Cabra. Our uncle Eddie, Father's brother, was to be our guardian while both our parents were in England. All this is my interpretation of her motives for leaving us. She never discussed it, nor did we question her about it. I know she was prepared to put our lives in front of hers. I remember one day before I could swim, a hearty young woman offered to carry me on her back while she swam in the lake. I clung so tightly to her throat that she was in danger of drowning us both. When Mother saw what was happening she tore off her clothes to jump in and save us - she was a weak swimmer who could barely keep afloat - fortunately this alerted others to rescue us. The progress of the war and the bombing in England did not alarm us: we had neither radio nor newspapers, and in any case there was the censorship. We saw our father only once at Laragh - he came over for one short visit. So it seemed perfectly natural that Mother should go away. Kitty was to stay and look after us in the holidays.

From now on there was always an ambiguity and always tensions about whose authority we would accept. Early in the war, Mother would come for short stays in the summer. And then travel between England and Ireland was forbidden. After the war she continued her medical studies, qualifying in 1951. She never adjusted to the fact that during her absence our lives had become quite different from what she remembered. Nor did we understand what she had been going through. Our relationship became a battleground that was never resolved. Perhaps she was never clear on just why she had left us.

~~~o~~~

Before I leave my memories of Laragh I must mention the huge and wonderful Mrs Cohen who ran the small shop. A year later, we were on the beach at Bray, the seaside resort not far from Kilmacanoge where we living at that time, and there we saw an amazing sight - Fatty Cohen (as people called her) strolling along in great style, a two-piece bathing-suit, high-heeled peekabo sandles a la Betty Grable, bright red lipstick, hair dyed blond; she was followed adoringly by her tiny lover holding in one hand a parasol to protect her from the sun and in the other a brightly-coloured beach towel. In her great rolls of
~~~

fat she walked every inch as though she were the most desirable golden-haired beauty that ever existed, a figure straight out of Fellini. I gazed at her with awe: it was my first glimpse of the joyous illusion of theatre.

On the other hand, when Mother took us to see *Peter Pan* in the Gaiety Theatre in Dublin, I found the experience altogether too real and painful. I identified entirely with Mr Darling, who had to live in the dog's kennel until the children were home again. If my memory serves me, there was no big scene of him returning to the house; but perhaps because Father was away, I could not get him out of my mind, stuck there in the kennel neatly dressed in his suit and hat (which is how I always remembered Father). I was also upset by the business of Tinkerbell and the task given to us to keep her alive - we all had to chorus that we *did* believe in fairies or else she would fade away and die. I saw her as a real person; when I left the theatre I resolved I would never let her die, but would always repeat the mantra. After a time, though, I kept forgetting, and in the end I gave up. Although I believed in Tinkerbell, I never really believed in fairies.

(J.A. has told me that *Peter Pan* had a similar effect on him; he too was distressed about Mr Darling, identifying the character with his own father.)

~~~o~~~

Before going to Cabra we spent some time in Dublin, the "emergency" Dublin of the '40s, where, at least for the middle classes, the violent upheavals of the nearly immediate past might never have taken place. Manners and modes were typically British, pre-war British, there was very little sign that a war was going on over the water. On the surface it was a tight, controlled society, everyone knowing their place and knowing how to behave. Patrick Pearse's "Commandments of Respectable Society" were much to the point: "Thou shalt not be extreme in anything... Thou shalt not give away thy substance... Thou shalt not carry a brown paper parcel lest thou shock Rathgar... Thou shalt not have any enthusiasm..."

The main difference from England was the sectarian division. The protestant middle classes or West Brits lived south of the Liffey, the catholics to the North. Where you shopped gave away your allegiance, There were protestant
~~~

(often Quaker) shops and cafés, and certainly at that time the staff would be chosen accordingly. The northside had tea in the evening, the southside dinner; northside dinner-tables were set with table-cloths over oilcloth, on the southside table-mats were laid directly on the polished wood. Both protestant and catholic middle-classes had maids; but the southside maids were better trained, inclined to wear uniform and to call the children Master or Miss. Although we lived on the southside, we still retained some of Father's northside attitudes. (All his brothers and sisters still lived on the northside.) A little bit of me wished that Kitty would wear a white cap and a black dress and call us Miss. Kitty in fact was somewhat set apart and not in an ordinary "maid category". She did call my mother Ma'am.

Dublin shop assistants were conscious of their roles in a formal buying-and-selling play. The customer, the shop-boy, the assistant, the cashier, the manager or owner, were all well rehearsed - the protestants had been playing their parts longer and so were more at ease in their parts. I suppose the difference between protestant and catholic shopping was like the contrast between a West End production and the touring version. Protestants felt that if they shopped in a catholic establishment, they would probably be cheated and the goods would be inferior. Catholics felt that they were being patriotic by supporting national industry in national businesses and keeping the money inside the country - unlike the West Brits, whose shopping habits kept the British Empire going. Also they knew that many protestant shops refused to employ catholics. Because we were new players on the scene with new parts, we seemed to act in a play that didn't quite fit the stage. Mother presented herself as something of an anomaly, the emancipated new woman, classless and husbandless, a mature student with four children and a future career.

Whenever we went out, she experimented with her performance for the benefit of the shop assistants or waitresses, who duly played their part in cooing over us. Maybe she was playing a more positive role than appeared to be the case - in a sense, any time she went into a public place she was subverting the theocratic state by flaunting her independence, demonstrating by her dress and behaviour that there was another way for women to live - certainly it is amazing how many women were affected by her, even though they didn't know her personally, and remembered her as an active propagandists, doing what other propagandists only preached. She was a perpetual agit-prop play, but she had no entrance into either protestant or catholic middle-class circles of young mothers and children. Mother was as wary of them as they of her, we never met or mixed with other families. Young wives in those days had a very restricted life, totally dependent upon their husband's status and finances, with no possibility of divorce. Love affairs were inhibited by fear of a "Crim. Con." prosecution of the lover - this was an item still remaining on the Irish statute book that had long been abolished across the water. My own feeling is that there was very little mixing except through family connections. We had no past to share with anyone, we lived only in the present, as soon as the past was gone it disappeared out of our memory.

Once again we had moved into a flat, a ground floor with garden at the back, in Pembroke road, a few minute's walk from Pembroke School (run by two sisters, the Miss Merediths), where we spent a few months before our places were ready at Cabra. This was the only catholic school in Dublin in the hands of lay people, it was and is well-loved and remembered by hundreds of grown women. While I was writing this, J.A. told me how in the 1950s he and a young Irish engaged couple were in a restaurant in Knightsbridge, London, and the fiancée was in full flow with a funny story of her schooldays. Suddenly a woman at the next table leaned over excitedly and said, "Oh you were at Miss Merediths - so was I!" The English people, dining with her, were astonished by the immediate warmth and intimacy this revelation produced... In Dublin, it would not have been astonishing. I met a woman recently who told me she remembered me and my sisters at the school, where we were known as "the D'Arcy girls". Before we arrived, the school was gathered together (the autumn term having already started), and given a little talk to the effect that four children were coming who had spent two years in the wilds of Wicklow and had not been to school for all of that time. The impression was given that we were some sort of savages.

The Miss Merediths began their task of civilizing us by ensuring that my two elder sisters made their First Communion; this was done privately, the school arranged everything and provided a wonderful breakfast afterwards with real white bread. They whipped the bread out from behind their backs and held it up like a conjuring trick - we all clapped at their delight in being so clever as to outmanoeuvre the restrictions on the flour-supply. Before the summer was out, I too had made my Communion along with all the other children.

Until we left Laragh I was always known as Gretta, but when I was preparing for the Communion, I discovered there was no Saint Gretta and no Saint Margaretta, so I announced that I wanted to be Margaret. When I stopped being a catholic (at the age of sixteen) I reclaimed my full name, Margaretta. On the whole my nine months at Miss Merediths were pretty uneventful. At last I learned to read - in Laragh all I could do was to pore over books, aching to find out what was inside them - and now at last I knew.

I do remember one small and rather disturbing incident from Miss Merediths. There was great excitement one day because some men's old clothes had been thrown over the wall of the school yard. The Garda Siochána were called and we all went crowding after them in an ecstatic mob out into the back lane. After the guards had completed their enquiries and departed, we were sharply called in and scolded for being so vulgar as to rush out. Those who had joined in the rush were asked to put their hands up. I put up my hand. The teacher looked at me with a doleful face and said she was extremely disappointed that some one like me should have behaved in this way. I was mortified: I was the only one singled out, and what did she mean by "someone like me"? Why shouldn't we have gone out to see what was going on? Our freedom to use our eyes was being curtailed by some obscure rule I couldn't understand. All I wanted to be was a normal schoolgirl like everyone else, well-behaved, well-thought-of by my teachers, going off every morning in my white blouse and my royal blue tunic with its three long pleats carefully held in line by a cord, and on my back my little leather schoolbag.

~~~o~~~

Dublin was wonderful, at least the area where we lived, off Baggot Street. The Monument Dairy was like a palace of gleaming white tiles, the clean slabs of butter waiting to be cut on their greaseproof paper, the smiling assistants behind the counter in white coats and caps, the polished white or brown eggs in racks and - most delicious of all, the rows of milk bottles with their various-coloured tops. Our bottle-top was gold because we bought the jersey milk, thick and creamy - there was a picture on the wall of a jersey cow all golden like the bottle-top. Also on the counter were fresh vienna loaves. Because we lived beside the school, we used to come home for lunch. I remember one day Mother gave us finely-mashed potato soup and a vienna loaf, a real luxury for
~~~

us after our regular and mundane bread from Johnstone, Mooney and O'Brien. (Incidentally, the Johnstone, Mooney and O'Brien bakery in Ballsbridge, just at the top of the road, burned down while we were living in Pembroke Road. The blaze lasted for days; I think the whole of Dublin came to see it.) In contrast with Laragh, where fresh food tended to have bits of grass or manure attached to it, all this was heaven. And everything so clean: the pavements, the gardens, it was autumn and leaves were raked up for the little garden bonfires. The library beside Herbert Park where we could go in the afternoons and choose books, the polished wooden counter, the wicker chairs with chintz cushions to sit on, the librarians always so cheerful, warm and welcoming. The pond in Herbert Park where we went catching tadpoles, bringing them home to watch them turn into frogs. Everything was exciting.

And then we all had to be fitted out for the boarding school. Going down Grafton Street to Bradleys' and having our feet measured in a sliding wooden ruler: the assistant would bring the rod down exactly onto our big toe and mark off the size of shoe we needed. The shoes were given to us in a white cardboard box tied with string with a little loop to carry it with. In our other hand we were given a balloon on a string: a balloon marked *Bradleys' Shoes.* The four of us shepherded by Mother would then go to Roberts' Coffee-house, where Trinity students went for their coffee, to be shown off to the waitresses. Mother used to brag there about her four little darlings; so when they saw us in the flesh, all the waitresses crowded round us, while we stood there grinning, and on our best behaviour. And then on to South Great Georges Street for new coats from Pimm's (a shop owned by Quakers). Three little girls in three little princess-blue coats; each of us could choose the hat; I chose a bonnet - wrong choice! as soon as I got home I swapped it for Judith's. Claire, being the eldest, got a gaberdine coat and a black hat. Much talk between Mother and the assistant about feeling the quality of the cloth - making sure it was first-class *English* cloth… Then the buying of the Chilprufe vests and the navy-blue knickers. After the purchases, the climax of the buying-and-selling drama, the mysterious disappearance of Mother into the shop's inner sanctum - people never paid cash over the counter in those days, she would have had go into the office to open an account. These accounts were very flexible: you didn't have to pay for years. And then off to Kellett's next door, to choose Vyella material for our new nightdresses, the big rolls put out on the counter for us to make our choice. In the end we selected a pretty little floral design. And then the choosing of the pattern for the nightdresses themselves, which Mother was going to make. We settled for short puffed sleeves, which turned out to be completely the wrong choice, because at Cabra everyone else had nightdresses with long sleeves. (We held our breath in case we saw Iris Kellett, the famous show-jumping horsewoman, daughter of the Kellett who owned the shop. The Horse Show at the RDS was just up the road from where we lived; we did see Iris Kellett there, splendid in her black and white gear. She never looked at us or noticed that we were wearing coats bought at her father's emporium.)

Then on to St Stephen's Green to the Country Shop, set up by the Irish Countrywomen's Association to sell its produce - jams, cakes, honey, knitwear - there was a restaurant attached where they served afternoon tea, and (an innovation for Dublin) potato cakes, thin, triangular and hot, with a pat of butter on top. The Irish Housewives' Association used to hold its meetings on the premises. Once again the names of Louie Bennett and Susan Manning appear, as founders of the IHA, along with Hilda Tweedy. Hilda Tweedy was a founder-member and first chair of the Council for the Status of Women, where I met her in the late 1980s. (The Council became the National Women's Council of Ireland; I was to serve a term on its executive.)

When we finished our historic shopping-day - never again repeated; from then on we wore hand-me-downs and Claire as the eldest was the only one who ever got new clothes - we went back to Kitty, to show her everything. It was from her sidelong comments that we knew all the shops we had been to were protestant. Kitty was an expert at who-owned-what in Dublin.

~~~o~~~

Mother moved us out of Dublin to a bungalow called "Garry Ard", in the Rocky Valley, Kilmacanoge, a house with electricity but no drinking water, in another "alternative" enclave, a refuge for loners all getting on with their lives. The Rocky Valley was in many ways reminiscent of Laragh. Paul Henry the landscape painter lived not far away with Gladys Young, another painter, to whom he was not married. Behind us, further up the hill, was Arthur Power, novelist and painter, he lived with his partner Doris and his only son. We all knew who lived where but there was no socialising. There were also the hill
~~~

farmers, who lived their lives and tolerated ours. A mile away was Kilcronie, where there was a hotel, swimming-pool, golf-course and the River Dargle. Bray was four miles away. We were overlooked by the Sugarloaf mountain. Our landlord, Oliver, was a young dark good-looking man from Bray, a protestant; he would pay us a visit just once a year for the rent. As at Laragh, we had to get our drinking water from a well about 200 yards from the house down a steep hill, so we were back again to being hunter-gatherers, going down every day to bring up the buckets. The tap water was rainwater collected in a tank on the roof, which on the whole caused no problems except in the summer. We had a magnificent view of Dublin Bay and could see the Holyhead boat arriving in Dun Laoghaire.

And now all the bustle of getting our clothes ready for boarding-school, the lists, the name tags, the new uniforms, we were so busy that the fact Mother was leaving us never dawned on us. The whole turnover in our lives was dealt with very cleverly by Mother; she brought us to the convent at Cabra, the home of the Dominicans, the heresy-hunters of the Inquisition, the "Hounds of God" (*Domini Canes*, a mediaeval pun as old as the order), with its high walls and its massive Latin motto carved over the great gate, *Laudare Benedicere Predicare* ("to Praise, to Bless, to Preach"); she handed us in to the nuns and then departed, not only from the convent but from Ireland altogether. Because I had only a sense of the present, I did not feel sad or homesick; she was gone, Kitty was still there, staying in "Garry Ard" to look after us in the holidays.

Louie Bennett, with (left to right) Claire, Judith, Rosemary, me; at Killiney.

Kitty and Jimmy Timmons, with (left to right) Judith, Claire, Rosemary, me; at Laragh.

(Left to right) me, Rosemary, Judith, Claire (standing) and my mother.

My father at table, Garry Ard.

4

THE HOUNDS OF GOD

Let us say, that up to the time of Cabra I had been indoctrinated with two forms of conditioning, the first was health, by my mother: eating raw carrots for strong teeth, drinking milk for one's bones, lots of fresh air and nakedness, gathering food from the countryside, berries, mushrooms, crab-apples, to prevent colds in the winter, being sociable and open, finding ways to keep oneself busy, books - and do not do something just because other people are doing it! The philosophy was simple and logical. Second, outside the home, from the two secular schools: rules of social behaviour, which I could on the whole understand. But now at Cabra (at the age of 8) came the total transformation. The control of the essence of the whole person, no space left at all for any deviation.

The Dominican nuns were founded in the 13th Century by St Dominic Guzman to counteract the Cathar heresy; they were to lead lives no less devoted and austere than those of the highest type of heretic - the *perfecti.* They were an enclosed order, which meant that once they became nuns they never again went out into the world. If they had to change convents, they travelled swiftly and directly from door to door by car. To me it was a more glorious version of the Never Never Land of *Peter Pan.* Within their walls all our senses were impregnated, beginning with the sense of sight. Public art everywhere, statues of saints in every nook and cranny, life-size statues, totally realistic, indoors and out, in corridors, on stair-landings, in every corner of the gardens. The chapel, magnificent, gold, silver, marble, and fresco on wall and ceiling around the sanctuary. The altar-cloths and the priests' vestments. The gleaming monstrance, and the canopy over it, the thurible with the smoking incense. The year, divided into the liturgical seasons, a different colour for each one, green, purple, white, gold. I used to read in my missal all the wonderful instructions for observing the liturgy - "Division of the Ecclesiastical Year... The Temporal Cycle... The Sanctoral Cycle... " and then the explanation and analysis, "The liturgy has also for its aim the sanctification of mankind. It is the most fruitful source of divine graces which, spreading from the Father through Christ into the Mystical Members of His Body, assure to them the divine life of grace." The missal itself, with its pictures of particular vestments and particular rites, and then our personal holy pictures, which we gave one another as presents and swaps, and would keep between the missal's pages. The rosary beads, the habits of the nuns, natural fine white linen held in by a brown leather belt, with stiff starched scapulars hanging down back and front, the white starched wimples, the black veils, the wonderful sweeping black cloaks of the softest-woven wool. And then, ourselves on Sundays, with our own net veils put on for Mass. Our faces would be covered as we went into the chapel, and then, as we sat down, we would toss the veils back over our heads, so that only the Lord on the altar could see our faces.

The hierarchical structure of Dominican Catholicism was as formal and intricate in its formality as the imperial palace of Byzantium or the Forbidden City in Beijing, a landscape which slowly began to fill up with a multitude of people, saints, angels, the whole court of heaven with the Virgin Mary presiding. Their sole purpose was to help us to prepare ourselves to be part of this wonderful court. Our purpose on earth was to get all the other people to understand the joyousness of the possibility that they too could be part of the court. We must intercede with the saints who interceded with the Virgin Mary who interceded with Her Son who interceded with His Father, God Himself. We had free will to choose or not to choose to be part of the court, and even if we stumbled on the way there, we had all these outstretched hands to guide us and help us. And most important of all, each of us was given our own two personal guardian angels.

General Mulcahy, Minister for Education in the late 1940s and 50s, declared that educationalists in Ireland must accept that --

> The proper subject of education is man whole and entire, soul united to body in unity of nature, with all his faculties, natural and supernatural... the foundation and crown of youth's entire training is religion.

This is the philosophy upon which the Dominican schools based their reputation, and I became an eager participant.

Cabra was a completely self-contained self-governing women's community. The nuns ran a farm, a national school, a junior boys' boarding school, a junior and senior boarding school for girls, and a school for what were known then as "deaf mutes", the only such establishment in the country. The deaf-mute girls from poor families would then stay on as servants for the nuns. (We picked up sufficient of their sign-language to be able to chat a little.) From a back window of the junior school we could see every day a line of Dublin's poor, queuing for their food outside the convent kitchen in a yard which never saw the sun.

The nuns themselves fell into two categories, the teaching nuns, and the lay nuns who wore a different quality of clothing. The lay nuns came from families who couldn't pay the substantial dowry. They dressed in heavy coarse yellowish linen, their scapulars inferior cotton, likewise their wimples and veils, they always smelt of the kitchen and the farm, and their black shoes were usually broken down.

The nuns had their own democratic election every four years for the post of Mother Prioress, who would then choose the various heads of the educational sections of the establishment, the junior school, the senior school, and so forth. Within the girls' school there was an art department, and a musical department with a school orchestra. We were also taught singing, including Gregorian chant for the various religious ceremonies, the Sung Mass for feast days, the High Mass, the concelebrated Mass on rare occasions, Benediction every Sunday, and the May Procession.

The nuns had their own choir separated from us behind a grill at the side of the altar. Once a nun was elected Mother Prioress, she was known as Mother, even after she had relinquished her post, for the rest of her life. The lives of nuns must have been a hotbed of politics because of the often quite radical changes that took place after elections. They lived in their own section of the school, where we had no access to them. The only men allowed on the premises were an ancient doctor and a young priest, our chaplain (he was destined eventually to work in the Vatican); there was also an old man who helped on the farm. These three did not live in the convent. There was a parlour where we entertained our visitors; as a rule only relatives were allowed to visit. We had no newspapers or access to radio, and magazines were forbidden. There were two libraries, one for the seniors, one for the juniors. There were a few day pupils allowed. At Mass on Sundays there were always two or three unaccountable lay people sitting at the back. There was also daily Mass.

~~~o~~~

The model order of behaviour.

- The body: to be covered at all times. Undressing: use the dressing gown to cover ourselves as we took our garments off or on.
- Hands crossed over the chest as we slept.
- A chemise to be worn in the weekly bath.
- Eyes cast down when walking along corridors.
- When speaking to a nun never look directly into her face but avert the eyes.
- Never run but glide, looking up to salute the statues of the saints as you passed them.
- Never put your hand up first when "volunteers" were asked for: a sign of forwardness. Wait for the nun to pick you.
- At all times, when alone, use the occasion to say prayers to obtain indulgences for the souls in purgatory.
- Talking during the meals only allowed for a limited time.
- Immodest behaviour, like whistling or crossing your legs, caused the Virgin Mary to blush. (This explanation was pretty clever, as blushing was something that most of us suffered at some time, the horror of the face filling with that red hot flush, the jeers of the onlookers when one was observed.)
- Prepare yourself all night long for the taking of communion the following morning, by concentrating your thoughts and trying to make yourself as pure as possible for this miraculous visitation.
- Never forget the endless suffering of Christ, as vividly illustrated by the Stations of the Cross; every offence we made, every illicit thought we had, caused the actual events to take place over and over again, the Crown of Thorns pressing into His head.

~~~o~~~

I was certainly provided with enough imagery to keep me busy. I selected from Jesus's suffering items with which I could identify. Like the thorns: did I not know about thorns? how they assumed a life of their own while I was pulling the dead sticks out of the hedges - the way they would disguise themselves, there would be a perfectly innocuous-looking dead stick, and suddenly that dead stick would have a vicious thorn on the underside pricking one's finger, beads of the red blood slowly dropping, the sorenesss of the wound, and then - if it happened again and again? - the thorns pressing in further and further... I hadn't experienced nails hammered into me, but I did know about rejection and humiliation, the internal wounds all children have experienced.

Everything combined to refine our sensibilities. Whoever has not sung the Gregorian chant has not fully tasted life. The early church certainly knew what it was doing with its use and control of liturgical music. Consider the opening of the Kyrie, the holding of the notes, the humming, the vibrations when it is sung by a whole choir of women in a building with the right sort of acoustics where it echoes and reechoes in the vaults. Grotowski, years later, developed a similar technique, which is now part of the voice-exercises and company-bonding for any ensemble of actors.

Preparation for holy communion: the more preparation, the more joy and ecstasy, ecstasy combined with recollection of Christ's pain kept me pretty busy recreating the repetition of the feeling over and over again. I could say that preparing for communion is very like preparing for a role in the theatre - the perfect Stanislavsky training.

Our own pain and humilation was "offered up", it was given to Jesus on the Cross as our own personal empathy. In fact it was a pretty good ecological recycling bin, nothing was wasted. Not one human experience was redundant provided you kept to the guidelines.

Many little hiccups were to afflict me during the five years I spent at Cabra: I did not think of them as examples of cruel or unacceptable behaviour or psychological abuse, because the nuns did not finally have power over me.

~~~o~~~

While my soul soared upwards like a rocket exploring space I still had to deal with my fellow beings, pupils and nuns, a very mixed bunch. The older nuns
~~~

had brought into the convent inevitable vestiges of their families' background and politics during the early days of the national struggle and the period of the Gaelic revival, which is to say, before 1916 - there were therefore historic tensions manifesting themselves as favouritism. I was taken up by two nuns who were sisters, Mother Mary Raymond the elder, head of the juniors, and the younger, Sister Mary Cecilia, who later replaced her in this post. They were what in the pre-independence politics were known as Redmondites, they came from Waterford, and they took me and my sisters to be more English than Irish - which appealed to them. You could imagine them (as young girls) walking through the pages of George Moore's novel *A Drama in Muslin*, the two sisters, tall with striking deportment, especially Mary Cecilia swanlike with her imperious accent, rejecting any suitor of inferior status, and in the end joining the Dominicans because of the superiority of the order and its elegant habit. (In fact many of the nuns were very good-looking with fine figures set off to advantage by the leather belt, and the natural flow of the folds of the garment, as they swept down the corridors.) They targeted me as a child with potential, a possible future Dominican, putting me forward to do special things - like the disastrous solo-singing in the school concert - and it was always me who would be chosen for any little task like fetching a skipping rope left outside in the playground, a great honour because it meant that I was trusted to go outside into the garden on my own. I would be chosen to give reading lessons to a girl who was slow, to read out a story to the class doing needlework, to play parts in the school plays (when the senior girls needed juniors to make up the cast), and, supremely, to be the girl who led all the juniors into the chapel for Sunday Mass, where I would sit in the front row and be the first up to communion. The boys' junior school sat at the other side, and the head boy and I would walk up and kneel at the altar both at the same time, our eyes devoutly closed, our tongue hanging out for the host.

By contrast, there was another nun who taught us history and was very anti-British; she could hardly speak to me, so offended was she with what she believed was my "English" accent. The more Sister Mary Cecilia built me up, the more this other nun put me down. She emphasised my name as being Norman, during the lesson on the Norman invasion, and later, in the playground, those of us with English connections divided ourselves in overt rivalry against those bearing Gaelic names. The "English" side were other evacuees, their parents being Irish who lived and worked in England; during the holidays they were looked after by relatives in Dublin. The Righteous Gaels were strong-minded girls from various parts of rural Ireland; after parental visits they would proudly show off large boxes of chocolate and hold sway over who was to be admitted into their "set". We all had to be in a set of about five or six, because we were not encouraged to walk in couples. The girl with the largest box of chocolates naturally had the pick of candidates to join her set. About twice a week there was a distribution of sweets in the afternoon to those girls whose visitors had left a packet for them. For the ones without such generous visitors, a twopenny bar of chocolate was available, already paid for at the beginning of term. One term, the spring term, just before St Patrick's Day, I queued for my bar only to be told I couldn't have it: no money had been paid in. It was the history-nun who was on duty that day, she announced to the whole junior school queuing for its sweets, that the D'Arcy girls had no money and if other children cared to, they could share some of their sweets with us. Her triumphant air as she announced this, a history lesson in itself, see how the conqueror was now at the mercy of the conquered! - it didn't matter how many battles you had won, if you couldn't even afford a Cadbury's twopenny bar. The lowest of the low....

It always seemed to be this anti-British nun who found satisfaction in showing up our poverty and the associated anomalies. When we first arrived, not only did our nighties not have the correct sleeves, but she discovered that we only had one dressing-gown between the four of us, and that went to Claire in the senior section, another part of the building. Likewise, one comb and one hair-brush between the four of us, no slippers, no nightdress case, no eiderdown to be folded like a butterfly on the bed, just the white counterpane. No best coat either; and our uniforms were all slightly wrong, having been previously worn at Miss Merediths. When I think of the amount of extras that the other girls brought to school, no wonder they did not feel the need to embrace the model order as ardently as I did! At least I could be holy. It was possible to be holy without earthly riches. Encouraged by the two sisters, I could one day attain sainthood.

And then the bombshell.

~~~o~~~
~~~

Quite efficiently and quietly and discreetly it happened. My class was being prepared for confirmation; this was the one sacrament that only a bishop could give, the laying-on of the hands, the ultimate authority handed down unbroken by Jesus to Peter and from then to each successive head of the church, Christ's Vicar, the Pope in Rome, by whom all bishops and archbishops are made. We had to undergo careful preparation for this final ceremony to bring us into full membership of the church; there was an oral examination on our knowledge of the Catechism, the bishop would be asking us questions himself, and a priest from the Dublin archdiocese came to instruct us. The archdiocese was McQuaid's. This was 1944, the year in which he was tightening the screw on an already severely regulated system of catholic education - Ireland seemed well on the way to becoming an absolute theocratic state. The archbishop's directives to every priest in his populous diocese were bound through mere strength of numbers to influence the country as a whole. Separation and isolation between catholic and protestant children was to be complete. He brought into play his ultimate weapon, the sanction of Mortal Sin for any catholic parent or guardian sending a child to a protestant school. "Those schools alone," he wrote, "which the Church approves are capable of providing a fully Catholic education." It was the unequivocal duty of all catholic parents to make sure that all their children were baptised.

My sister Rosemary was to make her first communion at the same time as our confirmation; all this was to take place in Phibsborough parish church, in north Dublin.

You could not be confirmed until your baptismal certificate had been checked: the equivalent of a passport, to verify your citizenship. And now the nuns discovered I did not seem to have one; and neither did Rosemary! I can imagine the panic and fear amongst the nuns when this was revealed. In their eyes it was not just Cabra that was involved, the ramifications could become a stain on the whole order, we had been there for two years without anyone knowing we were not in fact Christian. Nor could it be covered up. Because of the impending confirmation by one of his bishops, the archbishop was directly involved and must be informed. Why, the school could be closed down, Rome itself could be brought into the debacle, and what about the young priest with his eye on the Vatican? - he was meant to be our chaplain and had been giving me confession and communion for that entire length of time! - surely the end of all his ambitions! And again, if it got out, what about its effect on all the right-wing catholic extremists, whom even the archbishop was trying to tone down? - there were many of them in Dublin, philosophising and propagandising, enthusiasts for the 13th century (the era of St Thomas Aquinas, the Angelic Doctor, the greatest glory of the Dominicans) as the age when the social order most nearly achieved the fulfilment of God's plan, only to be frustrated by the Protestant Reformation, the French Revolution and the Russian Revolution. The last two, at least, were believed by the extremist element to be the fruit of deep-laid conspiracy: the ultimate author of this conspiracy was Satan, but its immediate agents were the Freemasons, while both Freemasons and Communists were instruments of the Jews. The extremist element, if it felt like it, could use the situation to thoroughly discredit the Dominicans - Satan, in the guise of a Russian Jew, had infiltrated the order by leaving an apparently innocent child within the bounds of the enclosed convent to do the devil's work unobserved. (Rosemary's case was different from mine: no blasphemy was involved; she had not yet received Holy Communion; the whole burden was upon me.) And how terrible a falling-off! for, after all, the Dominicans, as instigators of the Inquisition, were well aware of the implications: Lucifer like a roaring lion lunging for his final revenge upon not only St Thomas Aquinas but also St. Catherine of Siena, Dominican nun, international diplomat, to be declared (in 1970) a Doctor of the Church. All this could topple. Everyone knew, God's Hounds especially, how the devil could come in so many guises: why not an eleven-year old girl with all her pretensions to sanctity?

Exaggeration? histrionics? - maybe, but consider what happened to me next.

I was fetched out of class by Sister Mary Cecilia in an unusual manner: instead of slipping into the classroom and whispering to the teacher who would then call my name and tell me to go, she hissed at me from the doorway and beckoned with her finger that I was to follow her. Of course I thought of only one thing: one of my parents must be dead, this was the only reason for a girl to be called so dramatically out of class. I went with her in silence and was brought to an empty classroom where Rosemary was sitting. Mother Mary Raymond came in and the two sisters told us that we had to stay in this room, we could not mix with the other children, at bedtime we would not sleep in our regular dormitory, and we must not tell anyone that we had *never been baptised.* Arrangements were being made for Kitty and my uncle to come and be godparents; we would, very soon, be baptised in private in the Phibsborough parish church and until then we were virtually Untouchable. After that, I could be confirmed with all the others.

On the morning of my baptism, I went to the library, also used as a classroom, for a book; my old enemy, the history-nun, was there talking to some of the girls. I opened the door and was just about to enter the room, when she looked up and saw me. Her face contorted with rage. She shouted at me, "Get out, you are filled with the devil!"

~~~o~~~

There were deep long-term repercussions. When my mother returned to Ireland after the war, in 1946, she told us that we *had* been previously baptized, in London, but because the church was bombed, all the records were lost and it was impossible to get hold of the registration. I brooded over this, sometimes believing her, other times not, chewing over her remarks and finding different connotations each time I heard her voice in my head. When Father came back after the war, I never questioned *him.* He would arrive in from work, tired, he'd settle down with his whiskey and the music on the radio, waiting for his dinner; if I were to interrupt him it might precipitate one of the explosive rows between him and my mother. I feel now that the blame must have been put on him by the clergy; as the catholic in the marriage it would have been up to him to ensure that our baptisms took place in the proper fashion; and it would surely have been entered against him in McQuaid's little black notebook.

The archbishop kept a massive pile of files, dossiers on thousands of people within the diocese. When John Cooney was writing his book about him, a documentary was shown on television, with shots of rows and rows of archives, containing every small detail of every meeting that was held in Dublin (so it seemed): who attended, what they said, and what was their general attitude to the church and to politics. McQuaid's operation was conducted as thoroughly as the work of the East German Stasi; he had hundreds of devout and devoted agents. In 1945, when Father returned to Dublin, he naturally assumed he was in line for promotion, because of the highly successful negotiations his department
~~~

had completed seven years earlier, ending the "economic war", and eliminating the special restrictions on Irish agricultural exports to Britain. But he did not get the promotion, and the disappointment ate into him. Whiskey seemed to be the only thing that soothed his pain. Years later my brother-in-law, an artist, was painting the portrait of James Dillon TD, a prominent conservative catholic who had been Minister of Agriculture in the late 40s: he turned to my brother-in-law and said, "Your wife's mother is a Russian Jew, is she not?" An astonishing remark from a comparative stranger that explained a great deal. In those years the fear of any sort of socialism was intense; it was bound to lead, so they said, to atheistical communism; anyone tainted by any such assocation, no matter how far removed, was instantly under suspicion.

A curious by-product of my baptism: immediately after the ceremony, instead of being liberated from my sins, I felt sharply that the devil had in fact crept in. I never felt holy again and I gradually became quite disruptive. (It could have been the natural change in my hormones as I was approaching puberty; even though I didn't menstruate until I was fourteen and had by then left Cabra.)

Even though no one was supposed to know about my lack of baptism, it did become known; the information came back to me in a rather oblique way. There was a girl whom I will call Siobhán Fitzsean, a very pretty girl (and she knew it) from Downpatrick in the north. Dark curly hair in a tangle of ringlets, violet blue eyes, her skin smelt so sweetly - she would allow us to smell her face when she put on Nivea cream, sometimes she would open her tin and let us smell the cream itself - Nivea was quite unobtainable south of the border in the war years. Her father was a big cattle dealer. Cattle dealers had the same magic aura of wealth in those days that property speculators have now. He was a fleshy genial prosperous-looking man, he always arrived in a big shiny new car, he had four children at the school. Siobhán was very proud of her mother because of her fashionable clothes; we once saw her pulling at the mother to get her to take off her coat when she climbed out of the car; she feared it wasn't smart enough. Siobhán was a very manipulative little girl, and like all manipulators she had a following who hated themselves for allowing themselves to be led by her, and allowing her charm to work on them. Shortly after the confirmation, Siobhan's parents (who of course were the only ones with a camera) had taken a group-photo of us. Later on she was showing the photograph around; she said to me, "My daddy says you must be Jewish because you're terribly Jewish-looking." This was the first time that any one had referred to my looks as being Jewish. But why did it make me feel that a guilty secret had been let out?

~~~o~~~

As children often do, I had, without being aware of it, totally buried the past; my memories of Grandma and Grandpa and the Jewishness of the family gatherings were utterly hidden. Even when Siobhán seemed to tell me I was Jewish I was unable to make any connection. Because her father had only referred to *me*, I began to think I was set apart from my sisters, I became very self-conscious about my looks, I also began to think that I must have been adopted. I now realise that my mother always called herself British and never Jewish - she kept her origins well concealed - and would certainly never have told the nuns. But you cannot keep anything secret in Dublin; they obviously suspected. The casual laughing way in which Siobhán tossed the words out, as though she knew something that others didn't know, suggests that one or other of the nuns must have said something to Mr Fitzsean. He was the nuns' most honoured parent; whenever he came down to visit, in his huge car, they would come running out the convent down the steps with cries of welcome and delight. He would be beaming away in his sheepskin coat, all of a glow after his journey from County Down. I suspect he had not only come to see his children but also to buy cattle from the nuns. Ireland was the larder for Britain at that time.

Soon after that, I began to notice in the playground that Siobhán would be huddled with others around her; when I approached they would all move off. Then one day a girl came to me and told me she was sick of the way that Siobhán was treating everyone, deciding who was to be in her set and who was not. I said, "Let's make our own set, and she can't be in it." We did so, and all the girls in the class joined; they had all suffered at some time from Siobhan's whims. Then I would see Siobhán walking forlornly alone, or with the nun on duty. (Girls who had no-one to walk with would walk with the nun, a confession of social failure.) I decided that we were being negative and unkind; we should not be just a Keep-Siobhán-Out clique; instead we should transform ourselves into a revolutionary religious group and go forth like the
~~~

early saints, St Francis of Assisi or St Teresa of Avila (who set off at the age of nine to convert the Moors), giving up sweets, giving all our money to the poor. And we should ask Siobhán to join... The girl who had first approached me looked doubtful at that, but I ignored her and went ahead; I went to Siobhán, I explained the situation, I invited her to join, and she joined.

But behind our backs she went to Sister Mary Cecilia, and told her how we had originally ganged up against her. That evening, in the assembly before we went to bed, Sister Mary Cecilia announced that a very shocking thing had happened; she hauled me out in front of everyone and denounced me for my mistreatment of Siobhán, who was standing there smirking. I had expected some understanding of my motives - after all, the nun would have known nothing about it if I hadn't had second thoughts and owned up to Siobhán - but no explanation was asked of me. I was made directly to lie down at full length upon the floor, while Siobhán was the first to lead the whole junior school to walk over me. Also no-one was to speak to me or play with me for the rest of the term. I can't say that I felt any great shame as I lay there, I just realized I'd done the wrong thing by asking Siobhán to join. The recollection of my misplaced politics in this affair still gives me the occasional sharp nip; and every time there is anything about Chile on the television, my heart goes out to the late President Allende and *his* misplaced politics when he invited Pinochet to look after his army for him.

And moreover, it still festers in me that Sister Mary Cecilia, with whom I had once got on so well, should have taken the matter so badly and given me so severe a punishment. Autobiography necessarily discovers a lot of loose ends, and one of the reasons for writing it in the first place is to look back with hindsight and try to tidy them up and to worry out how and why certain things happened. I guess in this case there must have been some outside pressure: Siobhán had told her father (or the nuns were afraid that she would tell her father) and the father was the sort of man who could make a lot of trouble for them - what! his daughter persuaded by a girl, who was only baptised last week and was clearly a species of infidel, to give up all her money and run away from school, was she not being influenced in a way he had never dreamed of when he put her in the care of the Dominicans? And again, the one thing the church feared above all was the sin of pride, which is to say disobedience or challenging the proper authority; which was what I had done by attempting to set up my own order of saints; for such an offence there can be no mercy. And so, at recreation for the rest of that term, I walked alone.

Only one girl broke the ban on me, Isobel Hartley. Her father was a widower with two daughters, one of them a deaf mute who lived in the other school. Every Sunday he cycled to visit them.

Isobel was always falling foul of the nuns and was punished by having to isolate herself; I began to notice that if you didn't have parents who had pull, some of the nuns felt free to take it out of you. There were parents who paid the full fees and others who couldn't pay the fees at all. In our case, the fees were always late and I don't know if they were ever completely paid. I remember one very sad girl who had lost her father; she was left in the convent by her mother (who was related to one of the lay sisters), a country woman dressed in shabby black, practically walking on her knees to the nuns out of respect and gratitude.

~~~o~~~

It is fashionable to hark back to the days of an innocent Ireland where "material things did not count," but in my experience there was always great consciousness of material things - I remember the bragging amongst some of the girls - I now suspect there wasn't much to brag about, but they found plenty - those who ate fresh salmon compared to those who ate canned salmon, how many windows you had in your house, how many wrist-watches (golden, of course) that their mothers threw out of the windows (a legendary extravagance remotely derived from the antics of 18th-century bucks?), the critical examinations of our legs and our eyebrows to look for high breeding - this was not so noticable amongst the city girls as the country girls. Some of the latter lived in large gaunt houses discarded by vanished landlords. I can well imagine that only a couple of rooms would be furnished. Such bragging well illustrates the very sparse kind of life that was lived in the countryside at that time. Our own bungalow with electric light and electric cooker counted for nothing; it was semi-suburban and outside their experience. Moreover, it was rented, a fact we had to hide; if you did not own your own house you were beyond the pale in an Ireland of second-generation "peasant proprietorship." When we came home for the holidays, and our mother
~~~

was there, she would go berserk to think that we were so naive as to believe all the brags of these girls.

The nuns taught us how to love God, in an abstract way; but as they showed no ability to love or even to feel intimate with one another, they passed on no such ability to us; they had no social ease with us; of course, the babies in the school were *petted,* which is not quite the same thing - when Rosemary first arrived, she was only four-and-a-half - a motherly nun would look after them, gathering them like a clutch of chickens inside her cloak. This general lack of domestic warmth was exacerbated in our case, because when we went home for the holidays, our father was not to be seen until the end of the war, our mother only came intermittently, we had no-one but Kitty and Kitty herself had no experience of family intimacy. Ireland was a harsh place and cold, which is why it was good place for the imagination, the feel for literature and music; certainly at Cabra we had great opportunities to sublimate our feelings through the arts. However, the poems we were given to read spoke not so much of human emotions as the symbolism of trees and flowers expressing God's love for us through His creation. We never did any "creative writing" of our own. The essays we turned in had all to follow a regular formula full of high-minded quotations. I suppose our education was a throwback to a type of mediaeval communal consciousness rather than any modern system of individualism and self-expression. Irish writers who did express themselves (one thinks of Kate O'Brien, James Joyce, Liam O'Flaherty or Seán O'Faoláin) were either officially banned or simply not available. The nuns themselves had only a limited knowledge of literature, because they would not read anything that did not have the catholic Imprimatur. My happiest times in Cabra were playing the cello for the school string-orchestra, Mozart and Bach, contributing my own part to the soaring strength of the violins, the viola, the double-bass.

~~~o~~~

The two school plays that I was in were superbly presented. They were "big productions" put on for bishops and other dignitaries, upon important centenaries or anniversaries, I forget exactly what. The first was *Hiawatha* (which I think must have been a staged version of Coleridge Taylor's cantata) with a complete set of hired scenery and hired costumes; flats, wings, backcloths, sky-borders and makeup for all the cast (the nuns didn't do the makeup; a lay
~~~

person was brought in from the outside). Judith played the young Hiawatha in a short leather skirt, bouncing on with a bow-and-arrow and paddling away in a cut-out canoe. Claire was the lovely Minnehaha's father, and Maeve Dillon played the lovely Minnehaha herself. We juniors were fire-flies dancing in the forest; our costumes were adorned with phosphorescent paint, which I only discovered once we were on the stage and dancing in the dark; when we were first dressed our getup had looked so drab, with mere streaks of dark blue and silver; nothing prepared us for the wonderful transformation. I also took part in a dance of daffodils; but rather spoiled my performance, for the audience saw me earnestly counting out the beat to myself: "*One* two three, *one* two three, *one* two three *one*." The hypnotic sweep of Longfellow's rhythms put us into a mini-frenzy; all barriers, for once, were broken down backstage as the Dionysiac spirit swept over us. The church and all its teachings went into abeyance as nature and human beings were as one - my spirit was momentarily released while the rivers, the birds, the trees came alive; without being aware of it, I was reverting to my old self at Laragh when we freely ran around naked among the trees and the bushes and into the water. This was the first time I saw the nuns as human beings; they were as excited as the rest of us and very much part of the theatrical collective. Of course, by the end of the play, we were all harnessed once again into the correct order of things: the Dominicans being a proselytising order would never have chosen a play about pantheistic Native Americans if the European missionaries had not arrived in triumph just before the fall of the curtain. Hiawatha listened to the gospel but refused to commit himself; instead, he climbed into his canoe and -

> Sailed into the fiery sunset
> Sailed into the purple vapours,
> Sailed into the dusk of evening...
> Thus departed Hiawatha!

I was torn: on the one hand I longed to sail away with Hiawatha, but on the other hand I knew that the *truth* was with the missionaries. And the missionaries were all there, in front of the stage as well as on it, bishops and dignatories of the order, home in Ireland on leave. Before they arrived, we had all had to help get the hall ready, carrying in the big red velvet chairs with arm-rests, to be placed in the front row for the bishops, the red leather upright chairs for the monsignors and priests, the black leather chairs for the nuns and the plain wooden chairs for the pupils - the boys bringing their own chairs and the deaf mutes likewise.

Years later, in 1970, J.A. and I and our four children were travelling through Bihar in northern India: we found a touring theatre company playing the sacred epic *Ramayana* (in Hindi) in a fitup proscenium in the market-place of a village. We only saw one night of it, in fact it went on for a whole week. Most of the action was mime and dance, with a vigorous verse-narration delivered from the corner of the stage, accompanied by drums and an electronic keyboard. The rhythm of the verse was exactly the trochaic metre of *Hiawatha.* Ever since Cabra these rhythms had lain buried within me. We discussed using them for our *Non-Stop Connolly Show,* which was in any case based on the long episodic structure of *Ramayana.* But in the end we decided that once you get into *Hiawatha*-type verse, it's impossible to get out of it, and we needed much more variety for the very varied career of James Connolly...

The other Cabra play had been written to celebrate the canonisation of St Thérèse of Lisieux, the Little Flower, the young Carmelite nun who never did anything extraordinary, but gained sainthood through simple "self-forgetful but complete obedience"; she died of tuberculosis at the age of twenty-four. In Ireland in particular there was an identification with her, and widespread devotion, for so many young girls died young of TB. It was as though people thought that an early tubercular death meant the sufferer was so precious to God that He could not bear not to have her in heaven. There was a young nun who supervised our music practice; she was very pale and gentle, she was rumoured to be dying of TB. We constantly watched her for signs of intense holiness, we wanted to be close to her: and then we believed she *had* died, because she suddenly wasn't there any more.

TB has very largely been brought under control nowadays, nevertheless in 2001 a reliquary containing some bones of the Little Flower was toured throughout the country from diocese to diocese. Three million people are said to have gone to see it and doubtless to pray before it.

In the play I was cast as an altar-boy carrying a lantern to show an elderly priest the way to where the saint lay dying, upstairs in her attic cell. Unfortunately a little misdemeanour took place - I think I was caught talking

- so my costume and lantern were taken away from me and I was replaced for the opening night; but I had been there for the dress-rehearsal and had seen from the wings Thérèse's transfiguration and translation into an icon only a moment after her death. It impressed me enormously. The play was probably French; this culminating vision belonged to a whole European tradition of baroque mystical drama going back at least to the Jesuit plays of the counter-reformation era. In the 1970s, in Cracow, I saw something very similar in style, but adapted to the theme of National Liberation - Wajda's production of a 19th-century play by Adam Mickiewicz. I had been taken to pantomime, which also had spectacular transformation-scenes; but I had not enjoyed it very much, it was insufficiently serious for me at that age, I was alienated by the raucous comedy and random cruelty. But being in a play was completely different - through the process of rehearsals you slowly moved into a different world and were part of its creation, so that it wasn't too strange and in the end it all made sense.

~~~o~~~

Cinema didn't excite me; we did very occasionally have films, but if an *unsuitable* sequence was seen to be about to take place, the projector would be stopped, the lights switched on, and the film fast-forwarded in some way to leapfrog over the suggestive bit. This was not an efficient method, because all I can remember of the films are the shots immediately before the interruptions. The nun working the projector would not have had an opportunity to see the film in advance, so she would have to watch quite a lot of the unsuitable sequence before she could be sure there was something wrong with it; in fact, what she was doing was highlighting the supposed pornography and inflaming our imaginations. Greer Garson in *Pride and Prejudice* is for ever frozen in my mind in the act of standing there in her pantaloons waiting to have her stays tightened. In another film (I think it was *Blossom Time,* a biography of Schubert), there was an episode at a frontier-post somewhere in central Europe, where a beautiful lady, desperate to get through, was barred from doing so by an oily cad of an official because she did not have the correct papers. She sat down on a chair, crossed her legs (in itself enough to make the Blessed Virgin blush), and slowly lifted the hem of her skirt, all the time pretending she did not know the official was watching her. Her ankle was revealed, the projector was stopped, the lights went on; I can remember nothing more about that film.
~~~

~~~o~~~

Altogether these experiences made for a very confused little girl straining to keep within the confines of righteousness, and yet at the same time wishing to find ways of circumventing them. I had no contact with the opposite sex at all, I was never allowed to see a man and woman kissing in a film, I never heard popular music (let alone crooners like Crosby or Sinatra), and yet I had began to feel a strong attraction for one of the altar-boys, he was so serious and solemn with his blue eyes and fair hair, so correct in everything he did on the altar, so oblivious of me in the front row of the girls' section. How I yearned to be close to him. The only way I could be close to him, in my imagination, was for me to be a nun (I really did want to be a nun at that age) and become head of the boys' school - I then would have total access to him, calling him out of his class into my office, going to the dormitory at night where this innocent angel lay sleeping, and waking him up - but what for? I had no idea, although I did know that there was something wrong, impure, about my feelings for him. This was where the film-censorship came in; just as I was approaching his bedside, the projector in my mind would be stopped. I had all the anticipation but none of the consummation. It is just as well I did not become a nun, I'd have ended up in the courts as a paedophile...

Over the last few years in Ireland a lid has been lifted from the hidden history of paedophilia in catholic-run schools. In nearly every case, the clerical authorities have excused themselves by saying, "We didn't know anything about this in those days." Compulsory celibacy has been blamed, or the fact that erring priests were themselves abused as children, but to my knowledge there has been no examination of child-abuse as a consequence of censorship in the seminaries. Because the church forbade its seminarians to read any books about sexuality unapproved by Imprimatur or written by non-catholics, factual or fiction, the young men were given no understanding of the sexual undercurrents in the minds of children - their own minds indeed - and the way these can carry over into adult life. (It is interesting that my fantasy at the age of eleven or twelve had to place me in the role of a nun, where I acted with God's permission and had unquestioned authority over the object of my desire.) All that the moral theology textbooks seem to have been concerned about was sex between adults (or adolescents); what was permitted or forbidden was all set down in print and very considerable physiological detail, together with guide-
~~~

lines as to the gravity of any particular sin. In the confessional we were taught to examine our conscience with legalistic particularity; "impure thoughts" were very exactly defined, which encouraged us to be as a devious as a lawyer in a court-room. For example: one day during the holidays we took out one of Mother's anatomy books, and there we saw an engraving of a man's penis. We giggled and sniggered at this unwonted phenomenon. Now, I knew that there was something wrong here. But what category would I put it in when I went to confession? Indeed, how would I explain it at all? So I told the priest I had been "rude." He said, "In what way?" I said, "I laughed at someone." He gave me absolution. Afterwards I began to worry: I had not really told the whole story. So the next time I confessed to "impure thoughts." He did not ask me *what* thoughts. He gave me absolution and I was off the hook without having had to talk about penises. I certainly never confessed my fantasy about the altar-boy. I knew my feelings were in some way taboo, but they seemed to belong to no particular category of sin. I could not call them "impurity," for impurity had to mean doing something physical like crossing your legs, or thinking about something physical like another person's nakedness.

~~~o~~~

The end of world war, the beginning of cold war. Zealots were on the prowl.

We were the zealots, scrutinising the laity outside Cabra. The only recognition that the war was over was a half-day holiday for the school but no extra giving-out of sweets. In the summer of 1945, Father came home; we really didn't know him. But we soon found out one thing about him: he didn't go to Mass on Sundays. I don't know which of my sisters alerted me to the fact that on his bookshelves there were immoral books - I think it was Judith - she too was "going to be a nun", a medical missionary. We began to look at our home in a different way. I became conscious of the non-catholic nature of the house - not one holy picture on the wall, except some dark prints of cathedrals, and they turned out to be English and protestant. I obsessively searched the drawers for some evidence of catholicism, a document, a photograph, even the remains of a broken rosary bead. Father's not going to Mass meant that every Sunday upon which he failed to go he was accumulating mortal sin, and if he died without repentance he would go straight to hell. But if there was the slightest indication of faith he could be saved: I had to find it. There were two
~~~

big bibles; I took them out of the shelves with a great feeling of relief. Claire said, "They're not catholic bibles." We gathered round like secret police and scrutinized every page to try and find the Imprimatur; it was not there. This must mean that Mother (whose books they were) was a protestant, which at least was one degree better than being a Jew - thank goodness we were not Jews! - *we* had not crucified Christ! Looking back fifty-five years, I cannot for the life of me recall how we got ourselves into such an inquisitorial state of mind - it was not as though we had been given any specific instruction about this kind of investigation, although we had been notified that protestants were not saved and if we played with them or swam with them we would be in grave danger - our one function was to be a true catholic and openly to manifest our faith; a great deal of time was spent all over the country by people secretly observing the conduct of other people to check were they protestant or catholic, and if catholic, were they *true* catholics?

I do not know how we knew which books were immoral or banned. But there on the shelves was Liam O'Flaherty's *The Puritan;* I opened it at random. A scene in a bedroom: a young man and a young woman, the girl was taking off her skirt, the man was watching her. Adrenalin rushed up in me, I was transfixed with inexplicable emotions. (If the nuns had not censored *Pride and Prejudice* and the Schubert film, I might not have been quite so inflamed.) I showed the passage to Judith. Her reaction at once: "We must tear all these pages out and burn them." She was busy making a pile of all the books she had found that lacked the Imprimatur. In fact she did not find one book that *had* the Imprimatur. Claire intervened: the pages were not to be torn, the books were put into the back of the shelves and "we just won't look at them." But of course I did. I found *Sister Teresa* by George Moore; I thought it must be all right, because it began, "As soon as Mother Philippa came into the parlour Evelyn guessed there must be serious trouble in the convent." And then there was Dostoievsky's *Crime and Punishment,* Tolstoy's *War and Peace* - these were filled with remorse and unhappiness, but they had no women undressing in front of men, so I guessed they need not be condemned. I skimmed in great haste through all these books looking for sins of impurity, and hoping for evidence of repentance and redemption. The whole house appeared to me to be shrouded in dark shadows; every night I would be on my knees praying for Father and crying bitterly, willing for his sake to take upon my shoulders all the suffering of Christ on the Cross. I looked at him and I couldn't believe that he could be so carefree.

~~~o~~~

I did not realise that my prayers would be answered with such directness. When Mother came home a year later, I did indeed take on the sufferings, and with a vengeance. War broke out between her and all four of us; I do not know how things got so out of hand. Of course we had become institutionalised, with our rosary beads, the holy pictures in our missals, our little statues in our bedrooms set up as shrines with fresh flowers every day (I had my old statue of the Little King), round our necks we wore dirty scapulars which we never took off, grimy bits of relics or blessed bits of gauze inside them, our constant crossing of ourselves, and then Judith and I announcing that we were going to be nuns to save the souls of both our parents. Faced with this impenetrable wall of alienation between herself and her daughters, our mother could see hardly a trace of the little girls she had left behind. Incomprehensible our obsession with modesty, the prudish way we shuffled off our clothes at night, the sanctimonious way we fell on our knees at our bedsides - she must have wanted to tear us apart and obliterate us - she saw us laden down with superstition, idols, graven images, anathema not only to her secular freedom but also to her Jewish upbringing. She reacted by going on rampages - we called them "blitzes", after the bombing-raids on London - we never knew when they were going to come or which of us caused them. They would be on us in a flash. We would be preparing for Mass on a Sunday; just when we were nearly ready in our clean white socks with our prayer books to hand, the storm would burst. We were not to go to Mass! - now, she knew (because we had told her) that we *had* to go to Mass; if we didn't go we would be in mortal sin; if we died in that state, hell was awaiting us to keep us for ever in everlasting flames - we begged, we cried - her response was to show us what hypocrites we were - my bedroom was untidy, the house was in a mess, the dining-table had not been polished, the breakfast dishes had not been washed up - our frantic beseeching wails could have been those of Early Christian maidens, when their pagan fathers discovered them at their prayers, and tried to force them to offer incense to false gods and to desecrate the cross. At last she would relent, exhausted; we would promise to mend our ways; and off we would go running like hares to Kilmacanoge church, a mile and a half away, in a panic lest we should be late.

~~~o~~~

I was not only torn between the two opposed cultures of the nuns and my mother; there was the third element, Kitty Spain. Kitty and Mother were in many ways well suited for one another; they did not encroach on each other's space, they never gossiped about each other outside; they kept their own counsel on each other's private lives. When we were with Kitty she never mentioned Mother, there was no, "I'll tell your mother," or, "Your mother will be pleased;" likewise Mother never mentioned Kitty in any disparaging way. What they thought of one another or what kind of relationship they had when we were in bed, I do not know. Neither of them spoke to us of their lives when they were children. The fact that they were so separate meant that we related to them separately; we led different lives, according to which one we were with at any given time. Kitty felt much more at ease with Father. She enjoyed servicing him, ironing his shirts, giving him breakfast, bringing in the freshly-baked loaf of soda-bread for him to smell, and he of course would always compliment her on her bread-making; there was always a little ceremony about the new loaf. I remember how Father once had a friend come to stay, who had been ill and was with us to recuperate; when he sat at the table and took a slice of Kitty's bread he got up and began walking round the room holding the slice in his hand, lifting it up and down in wonderment at how light it was, "Marvellous," he said, "marvellous!", while Kitty stood and grinned from ear to ear. (The one thing Mother could not do was to make bread, pies or tarts.)

Kitty's background would have given her a bit more in common with Father at a subconscious level because of their innate attitudes towards Irish history and rebellion. Tipperary, and indeed all the south-west of Ireland, had been in constant rebellion ever since 1798, whole counties intermittently under martial law, right up until 1921. And then in the Civil War the area had supported the anti-treaty Republicans. There was also a history of anti-clerical catholicism. The 19th-century novelist Charles J. Kickham, a Tipperary man and a secret-society Fenian, wrote --

> When priests turn the altar into a platform: when it is pronounced a "mortal sin" to read the Irish People, a "mortal sin" to even wish that Ireland should be free, when priests call upon the people to turn informers... we believe it is our duty to tell the people that bishops and priests may be bad politicians and worse Irishmen.

Kitty's catholicism rested easily on her, she made up her own codes as it suited her, but she was above all a daughter of the revolution, feeling comfortable only with the plain people of Ireland (which is to say, the plain and *catholic* people). When she visited us at Cabra, she never fawned upon the nuns or was overwhelmed by them. I never remember her talking to a priest, nor do I remember any nuns hovering in the background. The only time we had anything at all to do with a priest was when a concert was organised in the village hall at Kilmacanoge; Claire gave a recitation of a poem by A. A. Milne (I think), her party piece, about a bold bad baron who gets his come-uppance; Kitty took her into Bray to buy her a "shop-dress" for the occasion, dark green cotton with white spots and a belt - we were all thrilled, and the parish priest was in charge of the whole event.

Kitty was always ambiguous about Mother's friends. She was not happy with social formality and demarcations, such as when we visited Louie Bennett in her Killiney home with its casual but gracious atmosphere; we were delighted because Louie treated us as adults, we would sit in the garden for tea and she never minded us trying out all her different garden furniture. She had a faithful housekeeper who would carry the tea out, a silver teapot on a tray and triangular crustless sandwiches, and this housekeeper of course would be dressed in a black dress with a freshly-starched frilly white apron. Louie would suggest that Kitty might like to take her tea with the housekeeper indoors. On the way home we would all be chattering excitedly about the visit; but Kitty would stay silent. I just knew that between herself and Louie Bennett's housekeeper there was nothing whatever in common. I suppose you could say that Kitty was a silent emblem of the free spirit that the Irish had fought for; no matter what Louie Bennett's reputation might have been in trade union circles, Kitty still saw her as a West Brit, a remnant of the old ascendancy. It was people like Kitty who had deceived the old landlords into thinking that on the whole they had an excellent relationship with their Irish servants and that their Irish servants really saw things exactly as the landlords saw them. As for me, I began, without knowing it, to see life through Kitty's eyes. Even though to look at her you would think that butter wouldn't melt in her mouth, she never gave anything away through her facial expression; only when she stopped talking did you begin to wonder why.

~~~o~~~
~~~

Kitty had a high old time during the three years she looked after us while our parents were away.

The one thing mother had been very careful about, was that we should never go into cheap cinemas. TB was rampant at that time; she was terrified of our catching it; she thought that small badly-ventilated auditoriums were hotbeds of infection, not only TB and other diseases but also from lice and fleas. The cinema was one of the few warm places poor people could afford to frequent, and of course they brought with them their coughing, and their spitting, and the pungent smell of damp clothes, tobacco smoke and the smoke of cheap coal fires. But Father had somehow acquired for Kitty a permanent free ticket to the Green Cinema on St Stephen's Green. I think he got it for her when we lived in Greenville Road, so that she could use it on her day off. When we were at Kilmacanoge during the Cabra school holidays we rarely went into Dublin and Kitty never had a day off. There was no money for the crowd of us to go by bus or train into the city. There must have been some pressure on Kitty by one of my elder sisters to bring us to the cinema; days beforehand the three of them were all huddled together planning something; I overheard mention of money and the counting-out of money. And then Kitty announced that we were all off to the pictures the next day.

Well, she had made plans that would have done justice to the Fenians themselves in regard to the logisitics of getting us there. The transport involved two gravel-lorries and one bread-van. I have already referred to her ability to organize everyone around her. Well, here was living proof. The lads who drove the gravel-lorries (how she became friends with them I do not know) came out from Dublin twice a day to load up at a quarry along the Enniskerry road; then they would return to Dublin, passing close to the bottom of Rocky Valley about a mile from our house. We were to meet them at a bend in the road, well-concealed so that no-one could see us being picked up. Kitty, Rosemary and me would be dropped off near the cinema and picked up there after the show. There wasn't room for Claire and Judith, so the driver of the Johnstone Mooney and O'Brien bread-van, a Mr Burke, would be responsible for their delivery into town (Kitty had become great friends with him when he delivered the fresh pans of bread; he always came in for a chat and a cup of tea). The organisation of the bread-van was not quite so easy, because it meant Mr Burke would have to come earlier than usual with all his consignments of bread, then he would have carry Claire and Judith into Dublin, and then he would have to make some excuse for returning to Kilmacanoge when he fetched them home again. I couldn't go in the bread-van because Mr Burke had the bread-boy in the front as well; which is why two gravel-lorries had to be requisitioned. The unexpected hitch in all this would be if any of our parents' friends happened to see us and tell Father what they had seen (Mother was still in England).

The pictures in those days had three showings, one in the late morning, one in the afternoon, and then the evening one. We all had to be safely back before Father returned from work. The film was *The Invisible Woman* with a B-feature afterwards which we missed the end of, so I will never know if the young couple were crushed to death by the falling building or saved. The only scene of *The Invisible Woman* that I can remember (thanks to the Cabra censor at work in my head) was when she came into a man's room from out of the rain and began to take her wet clothes off - first her hat, then her coat, then she put her leg forward and began peeling off a stocking from an invisible thigh - in my opinion, one of the most erotic scenes in the history of the cinema.

The transport plan worked beautifully but no sooner were we standing outside the picture-house after the show, with Kitty gathering us up into an orderly group, when a woman on the other side of the street spotted us - a Mrs Flynn, her chiffon scarf floating in the wind. She was just getting ready to cross over to intercept us when Kitty with one hand pushed us into an almighty trot along the pavement in the opposite direction. I was sorry about that: Mrs Flynn, after all, might have brought us all to tea at Mitchell's. She was a theosophist and vegetarian who was most anxious to recruit Mother into her movement, and Mother always tried to avoid her. When she knew that Mother had gone to England, she began dropping little notes to Kitty, saying that if she ever took us into Dublin, we should visit her. She was a childless middle-aged woman who lived with her husband in a large first-floor flat in Wilton Place; Mother must have got to know her when we were living nearby. I remember visiting her once and I was fascinated by her, especially when she showed us her wonderful collection of glass paperweights. Kitty couldn't stand her because of her gushing. We wondered what would happen if she bumped into Father and told him she had seen us in St Stephen's Green... But she didn't. In the end we returned safely, all demure to greet Father in the evening, four little lambs who had not shifted or roamed all day.

~~~o~~~

The reader might well be perplexed at this stage of my story - what about my scrupulous conscience? and here I was deceiving my father? did that not rankle, whilst every night I was on my knees praying for his redemption? What about my own immortal soul in peril? Somehow, because it had been a collective action rather than an individual one, and other people were helping us out of the goodness of their hearts, morality didn't seem to come into the equation at all - if I had sneaked off on my own and told a lie about it, that would without doubt have been a sin. Certainly Kitty didn't think it odd at all. All we had been doing was to break out of the norm and take an initiative. Father was always encouraging us to take initiatives, so long as they were initiatives that fitted into his romantic notions, such as finding new places in the river to swim, or exploring new routes through the countryside. He wanted us to live to the full; Mother wanted us to live to the full, provided she was in control of our living and the centre of it; Kitty didn't mind what we did provided *she* was living. (In fact she was to die from TB when she was only forty-six; years later TB scars showed up on an X-ray of my own lungs; 50% of my age-group were infected to some degree). Neither colonialism nor the catholic church had proved able to impose their authority upon the Irish beyond a certain point: always there sprang up from under the repression hidden springs of bubbling energy, enjoyment, improvisation, the delight of the unexpected, the veering away from routine, always the hope of adventure.

~~~o~~~

One summer when both parents were still in England, Kitty and my elder sisters decided to plan a party for Judith's birthday. Kitty had become friends with two of the footmen from Powerscourt House. The Earl and Countess of Powerscourt always seemed to be away; their estate was a popular spot for day-trippers with its famous waterfall. We used to walk through the estate to the waterfall. It would have been rather rare in those days to see four children, all girls, wandering on their own. If we were local we would have been at home helping around the farm, running messages, looking after animals, walking behind a cow or tapping a donkey down the lane. Even the way we dressed was out of the ordinary, in our sun-suits and sandals, brown as berries, running and leaping along - after Iris Kellett we imagined we were on beautiful show-jumping ponies or racing or galloping across wide pastures. Boys played and wandered like this, but not girls; so I suppose we soon attracted the notice of the two young footmen bored out of their minds in that vast silent grey mausoleum of Powerscourt, where all the furniture lay shrouded under white dust-cloths. Then they would have encountered Kitty. As a result, when we came past the house, they would bring us in, and we raced around wildly, sliding on the polished floors, lifting up the cloths, sitting on the sofas - of course we had to be careful in case anyone saw us from outside and *told on* Oliver and John. *Don't tell* was Kitty's potent mantra; we never heard her say *I 'll tell on you.* Oliver was a handsome dark young man training to be a professional singer in the style of John McCormack. He had a very pleasant light tenor voice but he had to be really careful with it; to get that liquidity of sound he would swallow raw eggs with a dash of cream and honey. We were fascinated by this egg-swallowing; he would show us how he cracked the egg deftly in one hand while holding the glass in the other; he would swiftly toss the egg into the glass, then the cream and honey; then he would swallow the lot down; and he would sing. We would be sitting on the vast covered armchairs in the middle of the empty mansion; his voice would soar... John was fair and slighter than Oliver; he was Oliver's encourager, and anxious for his success; he explained to us that the slightest cold or strain would produce an uneveness in the voice. They both became quite excited by the idea of the birthday party and said they would help: Oliver would make a sherry trifle and bring it along with trifle dishes, real cut-glass Waterford. Our eyes opened wide as he showed us in a locked glass cabinet all the ware that he would bring.

The great day dawned: we all helped to decorate the birthday cake, the house was full, Mr Burke of the bread-van, the bread-boy, Séamus and Pádraig the gravel-lorry drivers, and Oliver of course, and John. John brought a gramophone, the music was blaring, there was dancing and Oliver singing in the kitchen - in the middle of it all, the door opened and Mother was standing amongst us, holding her suitcase. She hadn't told us she was coming, she too was being spontaneous. Judith's birthday was also her birthday and she came all the way from England for it. I'll never forget the look on Kitty's face: she must have felt sure she would be told to pack her bags and leave immediately - but Mother, being Mother, loved parties and she loved young men. The only flaw in the evening was the beeline she made for Oliver who was not interested in women, no matter how vivacious, and was solely concerned with his voice.

~~~o~~~

By 1946 both our parents were back from the war. Kitty left us to return to her family in Nenagh, despite my mother's begging her to stay and warning her that her TB might be reactivated.

Claire left Cabra and was enrolled once again at Miss Merediths, travelling into Dublin every day, with Father on his way to work, and Mother, who was completing her medicine, no longer at Trinity but at the College of Surgeons. Before she left the nuns, Claire had been chosen to be a member of the Legion of Mary; she wore a medal round her neck on a blue ribbon over her uniform. I discovered only recently the reason for her asking to leave. It seems that she felt she had suffered an injustice. Jewelry was not allowed to be worn; on her birthday she had been sent a small brooch and she wore it; it was confiscated, to be given back at the end of the term. But at the end of term it was not returned to her.

Adjustments had to be made in all of our lives. I was moved up to the senior school, and I was getting out of hand, giggling, tearing around the place; the senior school head was Sister Mary Louis who had previously been head of the boys' school. She was very free with the belt, even though she didn't look it. She was small and dark with a sweet triangle-face and a tiny waist, but when she got swinging with that belt onto our hands she turned demonic like a dervish-dancer, her scapular took on a life of its own, her white robes swirling, as faster and faster she laid into us. She belted us to break us down. I remember standing there once, facing her, my hand outstretched, looking her in the eye and smiling. And then, when she swung the belt I was so fascinated by the motions of her body under her robe, and of the robes and the scapular, that I had no time to feel the sting. After 25 slaps she gave it up; instead she poured more punishments over me, taking away all my privileges - no sweets, no films and so forth... The next day I caught the measles epidemic, and went off to the cool and relaxed sick bay where they gave me hot blackcurrant drinks.
~~~

My religious intensity had quietened down. Perhaps because my mother (on one of her fleeting visits from England) had discovered that we were suffering from malnutrition. She must have passed this on to the nuns; in any event an ice-cream machine was installed so we had ice-cream most days. In all probability the religiosity was as much due to faulty diet as to anything else. But before we all left Cabra we had worn Mother down so ruthlessly, that one night in the holidays she actually *broke* down and cried and promised us she would become a catholic. But this was a turning point: afterwards she seems to have made up her mind never to lose control over us again, and never to allow our mob-pressure to control *her.*

Father seemed, on his return, to have positively enjoyed the war, standing on the roof of the Free State's London offices amid the blitz and all its fireworks, drink in hand, conscious of Ireland's neutrality, yet excited at sharing England's danger. He also enjoyed telling us that, as a result of new legislation, he was now able to claim two-and-sixpence each for Rosemary and me as Childrens' Allowance. It was not pocket-money for us, he said, which naturally we thought it would have been.

Goodness knows, though, how much lasting damage was done by these wartime separations, in the way of permanently stunted relationships between parents and children, and what was the real cost to women who saw the war-effort, rather than motherhood, to be their first priority? Of course the war-work did make them economically independent; the money earned was often given back in one way or another to the children; Mother used to save all her food coupons and travel permits so that she could come back to Ireland once a year to see us, with money for our clothes and to pay the bills, and with a suitcase packed full of food which she had saved from her weekly rations, food unobtainable in Ireland, such as raisins, cocoa, sardines and some peculiar nutritional bars of compressed vitamin-food (it was said they were issued to the troops on active service), as well as samples from the plastics factory, bakelite dishes, mugs, and indestructible scarves printed with maps of Europe - the latter were manufactured for RAF aircrew to aid their escape if they were shot down. She never told us of the great difficulties she must have had, securing her permits and making these wartime journeys across the sea; she always made light of it as though she could defeat any sort of obstacle. Of course we were excited by the goodies, but in the end it always came back to whether her soul was saved or not.

I don't regret those horrendous years of religious distortion and covert sado-masochism; if they didn't make me a permanent catholic, they certainly prepared me for the theatre and also for gaol. Later on, through the anti-nuclear Committee of 100, I met Michael Randle (who had been at Cabra when I was there) who was to spend the 1960s in and out of gaol in England for his pacifist convictions. He had already been part of a direct-action group, breaking official secrecy by publicising the location of the cabinet's personal nuclear-proof bunker. He was imprisoned for demonstrating in the Greek embassy against the colonels' coup. In gaol he met the spy George Blake and then assisted his escape for reasons of high principle; years and years afterwards he wrote a book about it; he and his accomplice Pat Pottle were thereupon hauled into court, an historic case: they were both found Not Guilty. Another ex-Cabra was Leo McCabe; with his theatre partner Stanley Illsley he ran acting-companies in the 1950s, putting on contemporary drama. They were the first to present Tennessee Williams (*The Glass Menagerie*) in Dublin. In their day they were as famous, if not so flamboyant, as that other famous partnership, Hilton Edwards and Micheál MacLiammóir.

5

OUT OF THE FRYING PAN INTO THE FIRE

In 1947 I turned thirteen. Mother was taking her final exams, Claire at Miss Merediths was taking Matric, and Rosemary, Judith and I were going to the Loreto convent in Bray as day pupils. I was in the school orchestra, along with Judith and another pupil from Cabra, Eileen Mulligan. Because we had played in the Cabra orchestra and knew how to sight-read, our arrival meant the elevation of the Loreto orchestra one grade in the national music examinations, and all the nuns made a great fuss of us in consequence. Incidentally, Eileen Mulligan and I planned to write an opera together after I saw a Gilbert and Sullivan performance at the Gaiety Theatre in Dublin. I came home inspired: I was going to do the libretto and Eileen would compose the music. My plot was highly melodramatic: a king was murdered by a rival king who also kidnapped the first king's daughter and kept her in a dungeon. Her father's ghost appeared in the guise of an enormous eye, following the murderer everywhere until the nerves of the villain broke down and the daughter was liberated. I did in fact write some of the arias (for the daughter) but I don't think any of the music was ever completed. It was all a bit beyond our skills: I wanted a huge orchestra with gigantic sound effects and visual effects.

I remember most days cycling into Bray from "Garry Ard" to go to school, about four miles. If it was wet we would ride in Father's car and come home on the bus. My mother for some odd reason had me put into classes higher than I should have been, with the result that I found it difficult to follow the lessons and appeared to be a bit of a dunce, with the further result that for some time I did not have any friends, for who wants to befriend a dunce? And then, as we were sitting the end of term exam, a bit of paper was passed to me: it was a doggerel poem using my name as a rhyme. I replied by sending another doggerel back; and that is how I got my first real buddy, Dorothea Coughlan, who lived in Bray itself. She and her family had been in the States for the duration of the war and had recently returned to Ireland. (I had had a couple of friends whilst at Cabra, but only during term time; they too were children who had been sent there because their parents lived in England.

One of them was Margaret, sister of Michael Randle.) Dorothea was a year older than I was; she had a younger sister Maureen, so the three of us would go off cycling in the Wicklow Mountains. We went to Dublin once because Woolworth's had opened a cafteria in the American style; we then went down to the docks and the captain of a German ship invited us on board to show us around. This last exploit somewhat alarmed my mother.

After a short time at Loreto I was transferred to the famous Alexandra College ("Alex"), a protestant day-school on the southside of Dublin city; once again I was moved up a class. I stayed there for five terms, until shortly before I reached sixteen, and then I went off to London to learn how to be an actress.

~~~o~~~

It was all a bit unbalanced, and out of the regular sequence of schooling. We were being pushed along like an over-speedy conveyor-belt to get us finished as soon as possible at the end of the line, so that when Mother qualified we would be off her hands. Rosemary went back to Miss Merediths and then had a final year at Alex before going to Trinity to study medicine. Judith was put into a crammer's to prepare for *her* entrance to Trinity, where she too was to study medicine - a profession she didn't want at all. Claire took her matric at sixteen and then went to the school of architecture at UCD (University College, Dublin). She would have preferred domestic science; and Judith was determined to work on the land. But Mother ignored these little drawbacks and saw only the prestige to be reaped by telling her sisters and brother that now she had two daughters at university. Rosemary, in the end, was the only one of us to come up to scratch (according to Mother's professional standards!). She did study medicine and has had a highly successful career, becoming the first consultant clinical microbiologist in the country.

From this time on my sisters and I had very little to do with each other. We were all living our separate lives. Once Mother qualified, she was constantly going off to England to take locum-jobs all over the country. Left alone with Father, we had as much freedom as we wanted, so long as he found his dinner on the table in the evening and his clean shirt in the morning. The clean shirt was Claire's responsibility. Claire was the driver of the Morris Minor car,
~~~

collecting Father when he had had a few. Apart from the parties, organized in Mother's absence by Claire for her college friends (mostly young men), we were pretty much left to our own devices. As Claire had the use of a car, a rarity for a student in those days, she was pretty popular. The memory of us, I have discovered, still lingers on, as "The Four Wild D'Arcy Girls", to be resurrected at embarrassing moments.

While I was at Alex, Dorothea saw an advertisement in the local paper for actors in an amateur company in Bray, and we decided to apply. The play was American, by John Van Druten, *I Remember Mama,* about Norwegian immigrants in San Francisco: Dorothea had an American accent and thought it would be a bit of fun, so we went along.

My first steps into the amorphous world of the amateur theatre. At the age of fourteen.

~~~o~~~

For the next six years of my life, until 1953, it was as though I was wandering in a treacherous forest, sometimes in England, sometimes in Ireland, only in the end to be unofficially and ignominiously deported from Dublin for bringing shame upon my sisters by what was perceived as a spectacular self-destructive act of mayhem. I was shipped off across the water into the care of my mother... One of the reasons why I am trying to sort out the pattern of my life is to make positive connections between events and their consequences - events which might have crushed my spirit but somehow did not, for the spirit can slip sideways and gallivant in quite another direction away from the accepted course, taking its own independent line out of the forest and into the light.

Looking up the past in literary magazines of the period, such as *Envoy* and *The Bell,* I am not surprised at the shame and the mayhem. The only reason why there was not mass-suicide among the contributors to the magazines was the incessant consumption of booze. The vitriolic spleen that emanated from the pens of Paddy Kavanagh and others contained clues to an analysis of the malaise but there seemed to be nobody out there listening and noticing. Here we were, the new post-colonial republic (proclaimed in September 1948, the first independent republic to be separated from the British Empire since 1776), still faint with
~~~

fatigue after one great burst of energy, sunk in self-loathing, filled to bursting with the sense of an entire artistic community trapped in fish-bowls exhaustingly swimming around lost, and London too busy building up its own post-war culture to come like the fairy prince to put the slipper on the Irish Cinderella and whisk her off. (Which had happened at the time of the Gaelic Renaissance as personified in the Abbey Theatre, discovered and hailed in England before ever it was recognised at home; but that was before Independence.)

> London with its intellectual life, its enquiring minds, its adventurous publishers, its aristocratic belief in the importance of the poet... The Catholic intellectual's problem is the problem of freedom of expression. This is particularly a problem in Ireland where some members of the Hierarchy exercise or attempt to exercise control over the written word. But more so than bishops in this censorship is the Catholic conscience which makes cowards of us all. It also makes cowards of us in the political and social fields.
> Patrick Kavanagh ("Diary", in *Envoy,* December 1950)

I was mixing with the generation described by another poet, John Montague, as typically "arrogant and precious", also defensive and ignorant, and plunging around. The fashionable cult was one of hoplessness - we were prisoners locked in and our only key to open the door was emigration.

Of course when I was avidly reading *Envoy* I read only for my immediate concern, theatre. I was blind to the words of warning, I was blowing hither and thither, attracted by the idea of becoming a leaf in the wind fleetingly landing on a wet pavement, creating a momentary pattern there to catch the eye of some discerning poet or painter who might marvel at its beauty in the moonlight. I was an unattached idealistic female in a scene controlled by the frisky rams, where indeed there were women working and creating, but women who usually gravitated to men.

I wanted something, but I didn't know what. Because I hadn't finished school and gone to university in the regular way, I had no peer group to be bonded to. Could I perhaps have found myself in the Dublin Theatre? As it was, my mind was only opened to what the theatre ought to be when I went to England in 1950 for a year. Two years later when once again I left Dublin, I did so with a feeling of betrayal and dismissiveness: I was getting out. Most of us did in the end get out.

~~~o~~~

Diatribe against the theatre and actors. Diatribe against women.
There was a negative and spiteful lashing-out by certain Irish writers which caused theatre-people to close their minds to anything new, to distrust anything intellectual, to distrust any enthusiasm, to keep hidden any real emotions or purpose in life. These writers had set themselves up as spiritual gurus, taking on the worst aspects of the authoritarian church hierarchy which they attacked, while the hierarchy itself had taken on the worst aspects of the old oppressive landlords, controlling the people's souls in the same way that the landlords used to control their daily lives. Control was the keynote: the savage mockery of all those who stepped out of line by daring to be themselves.

> Is the actor an artist? No .... I do not wish to appear over-earnest or a disliker of actors and their kind as persons, but only because this is a glittering veneer which brings out the feminine in society. It appeals to women as all lurid flashing colours do, the colours of jockeys equally so... Women, as no doubt many others as well as myself have said many times before, are amoral.
> Patrick Kavanagh ("Diary", in *Envoy,* September 1950)

The ones who stayed and endured all this, keeping their craft alive in amateur companies and small basement theatres, are the real heroes and heroines of the Irish drama, and largely unrecorded. In later years John O'Donovan set up the Society of Irish Playwrights, to protect for the first time the interests of playwrights, securing decent contracts, giving them a place on the board of the Abbey, publishing scripts. It was this society that saved J.A. and me from total artistic collapse when it supported our strike against the Royal Shakespeare Company in 1972. We are thus deeply beholden to the commitment of certain Irish playwrights who were able to stay in the country during the era of emigration, and I feel eternally grateful - the more so when I remember the glibness and callowness of my youth and how dismissive I was of the playwrights of the day.

~~~o~~~-

To get back to the amateurs in Bray. The company was called the Thespian Players; it had just been founded by a man called Colbert Martin, an electrician who had broken away from another group of amateurs in the same town. (Hugh Leonard in his memoirs gives a hilarious account of him in this other group, how he fell off a roof fixing some wires and Leonard was brought in to replace him at short notice as the vicar in Ronald Millar's *Frieda,* a play that had been substituted for a piece by Paul O'Carroll when the local priest made moral objections.) Dorothea and I arrived at a shabby draughty room above a pub to find that the Thespian Players consisted of Colbert Martin and a young fellow who worked in a butcher's shop; there was also the latter's girl friend (from the butcher's cash-cubicle) who didn't take part in the productions but just sat there. Add Dorothea's younger sister, Maureen, aged thirteen, who always had to come along with her, and that seemed to be all. We sat round and began to read *I Remember Mama.* Maureen was cast as the little girl in the play. Throughout the reading Colbert was anxiously shooting glances at the door in the hope that more people might split away from the other company and turn up to be in his cast. But nobody did turn up, and Colbert finally realised *I Remember Mama* was not practical. Instead he would revive *Frieda*, by bringing in Annelisa Fuchs and her father, Austrian refugees living in Bray; Mr Fuchs played the violin and gave music lessons. They had both been in the earlier production with Hugh Leonard. Annelisa was so authentic in her role of the young German bride of a British officer, fetched into the bosom of his typically home-counties family, that every time the play emerged at a drama competition, her performance always won a prize for it. Alas, this time, Bray had seen *Frieda* once too often; despite the fact that Dorothea and I (as newcomers) were sent out along the Promenade to distribute fliers, the audience for our sole performance was very small. This didn't dishearten Colbert, and we went on to give another performance at the TB hospital in Newtownkennedy; we met Dr Noel Browne there, it was still his place of work even though he had become Minister for Health in the new coalition government; his vital research for the eradication of TB had been carried out on its premises. I was thrilled to encounter this charismatic young radical in the flesh: we had had a mock election at school and I had voted for him and Seán McBride as representatives of the new left-wing party Clann na Poblachta.

In *Frieda* I played the officer's middle-aged mother who was so beastly to the German girl - Colbert, I suppose, cast me because my accent was thought to be English, thanks to my mother's insistence that we should not pick up Irish intonations; at Cabra we had had elocution classes, enunciating carefully

"A pound of raspberry jam, I walk on the grass, I spread butter on the bread." Butter must not be pronounced *boother,* raspberry must not be *razbry,* and grahss can never be *grasss*. I don't know at exactly what point it was decided that I was definitely going to choose acting as my career. But it was Colbert Martin who initiated the process. I think it was because at the performance in the hospital he gave me a wrong cue, a whole act in advance of itself, and without stirring a feather I was able to bring the text back to its proper place. He was so impressed by my coolness and stage-instinct that he wrote to my mother to say that I should become a professional, and that he would train me; I somehow picked up the erroneous notion that he would do this in a caravan at the bottom of his small suburban garden and that the caravan was to be my new home. My mother took his offer seriously. She was in Ireland on one of her quick visits; having just qualified as a doctor, she was travelling in and out of England on her locum-jobs. She had not had a chance to meet Colbert, and was obviously relieved that somebody had discerned some sort of talent in me. I can't say I was overjoyed by the thought of his caravan, he was a taciturn withdrawn character and I had never had a conversation with him. He had thin ginger hair and was extremely earnest; his very earnestness made comedy out of his otherwise alarming fall from the Town Hall roof. In the event nothing came of his idea. (I do not know whether he thought that Mother would pay him? I don't know whether *she* thought that he would pay *her*?) Instead, my aunt Hannah offered to pay: a year's training in London for me, at the Pre-RADA theatre school, beginning that autumn, 1950; it was decided I should leave Alex in the summer. I was only fifteen; but how old was Peg Woffington when she first trod the boards?

~~~o~~~

A short word about Alex. It was the sort of school which produced distinguished women in the arts and in public life in general. Although it was officially a protestant establishment, many catholics sent their daughters there, and the teachers were a mixed lot, conservatives and progressives. I remember how our history teacher (whose brother was in South Africa) explained to us in glowing terms the virtues of apartheid. On the other hand, our French teacher, very socially-orientated, got us to volunteer ourselves as helpers at the Mount Street Club, a co-operative for unemployed men, with garden allotments and craft workshops - there was a youth-club attached for boys; I went there once to do
~~~

my duty but found it a bit embarrassing. I had no brothers of my own and had never mixed with boys; I wasn't at all adequate for it, and by no means sure just what I was supposed do. Alex encouraged initiatives and projects. One of these proved very influential: we were instructed to find a historic building in Dublin and write about it.

Father was always picking up secondhand volumes about the city as he browsed among the bookstalls along the Quays. One day he found the story of the 18th-century Smock Alley Theatre; I was absolutely fascinated and went down to the Temple Bar district to look at it. In fact it had long ago disappeared and there was nothing there but ruinous old warehouses. Nevertheless I wrote about it, quoting great chunks out of Father's book - I had had no idea the theatre could be so exciting, all the politics, the feuds, the riots, the uproarious behaviour, Peg Woffington in mens' clothes, the love-affairs and duels - here indeed was life that I could identify with. After this, I began on my own to visit the bookstalls. I was able to do so because in order to go to Alex I had a weekly train ticket to Dublin. I used to cycle into Bray to catch the train. On Saturday mornings I played hockey, which I very much enjoyed. My position was Wing, because I was a fairly fast runner; which was just as well, as often the game would finish slightly after time and I would see the train for the city-centre coming while I was still on the hockey field and would have to run for it to the station and hoist myself into the very last carriage just as it pulled out. In my short red playing-skirt, white blouse and white cable-knit sweater with my hockey stick and my two plaits of hair, I would ramble through the town looking at books. One day I found Micheál MacLiammóir's *All for Hecuba,* which I still have, price exactly one shilling. I had a shilling a week pocket money. In that book he tells all about the Gate Theatre, and also the Longford Players. I discovered that Lord and Lady Longford and their Players were still there at the Gate, and gave a matinée every Saturday: the cheapest ticket was one shilling! I never went to the Abbey - I suppose there was no matinée.

The Gate today has become very upmarket and has had a face-lift; but half-a-century ago there was no portico and hardly anything to announce a theatre - just a narrow side door straight in from the street (so as not to disturb the classical architecture of the old Rotunda building), while inside there was a cramped box office and, up a narrow staircase with photos all along it, the foyer with more photos and a tea-and-coffee bar against one side wall. The theatre itself was a long rectangular auditorium with a narrow proscenium stage. At one corner below the stage sat the music, a string trio of three elderly ladies who played as we took our seats and again during the interval when the usherette brought the orders of teas-and-biscuits to patrons in their seats. Just before the interval we would hear the rattle of the tea cups and smell a marvellous aroma of freshly-brewed coffee wafting in through the curtained door. There was never a large audience for matinées, maybe twenty or so genteel retired couples or clusters of hatted ladies, conversing whilst the music played. The shilling places at the back were slightly elevated; we sat on black padded benches. Usually there were only three or four of us; we were very solemn and self-conscious, never so much as exchanging a glance.

During the interval we would wander out to look at the photographs, taking care neither to catch people's eyes nor to bump into them, a slow-moving somnolent ballet as we created our own ritualistic patterns. None of us had money for coffee. The silence and air of reverence gave a religious atmosphere, pretty much Church of Ireland, certainly not catholic, assisted by the devotional style of the female staff and the musicians. I remember there was always a young Trinity student who sat like myself on the front row of the benches; he had a rollneck black sweater, a dark beard and brown corduroy trousers; someone told me he was very wild and wanted to be a painter. I suppose I always hoped he would glance my way and we would have a poetical tête-à-tête, but it never happened. Like myself, he always stared straight ahead, leaving a chaste gap between us on the bench. The near proximity of him heightened the tension and expectancy as we waited for the curtain to open. There is nothing like suppressed sexuality to sharpen the senses. We always sat in the same places, me with my hockey stick firmly clasped between my sturdy thighs in case I left it behind. If he had any poetical imagination surely it should have been kindled by the contradictory picture I presented. I sat there like a frozen block and waited for the play to begin. How could he not have realised how fiercely my heart was beating?

The plays I saw at the Gate gave me a fair panorama of good classical theatre from the eighteenth and nineteenth centuries, with some modern plays by Christine Lady Longford herself. The Longford Players were a repertory company where much the same group of actors played the same characters in every play; our familarity with them produced a sense of relaxation and trust that nothing was going to be really bad, but on the other hand there would be nothing exceptionally good. All the plays, whether Farquhar, Shaw or Chekhov, were played in the same rhythm, like recitations from the printed texts, those red-bound standard editions; the very journeyman quality of the acting-style made it possible totally to concentrate on the content of the play. Once again I bring in the religious analogy: it never mattered how badly a Mass was said, for it did not distract from one's own relationship with the divine. *Mrs Warren's Profession... The Seagull... The Recruiting Officer...* Dublin theatre of this era has been compared to a museum or a mausoleum, and in fact the sameness of the ceremony every time we went there offered a certain peace of mind, no deviation from any of us as we left the theatre, blinking into the daylight, quickly dispersing, only to meet again (and once again without acknowledging each other) at another production. And it was this to which I proposed to dedicate my life?

> If circumstances permit, nothing satisfies the narcissist so profoundly as to dedicate herself publicly to the theatre ... For lack of action, woman invents substitutes for action: to some the theatre represents a favoured substitute.
> Simone de Beauvoir (*The Second Sex,* 1949)

~~~o~~~

At Alex several of the girls talked openly about their ambitions to do various artistic things like writing novels or going into the theatre. I think particularly of Moira Stoddart, and also Verena Sladen who had signed up for Pre-RADA - which is how I knew about the place and how my mother was able to talk to Hannah about it.

It never fails to amaze J.A. how often ghosts from the past turn up in my life. In 1971, returning from India (fired with revolutionary zeal), we found the Tories in control and Mrs Thatcher the new Minister of Education. One of her first initiatives was to cut the school-childrens' milk. "Maggie Thatcher Milk Snatcher". We had moved to Muswell Hill, north London, because the Haringey Council (Labour) had given a 100% mortgage to any family who bought a house there. The whole area had been built at the end of the 19th-century, the original owners were dying off and the houses going into disrepair. The council's generous offer was intended to revitalise the area by filling it
~~~

with young families like ourselves - full of progressive notions about health and education for our children. We put up a card in the local post office, asking if there was anyone out there who wanted to stop the Tory cuts. We got a little group going; we organised a march and put on a couple of small agitprop plays, *Little Red Riding Hood and Granny Welfare* and *My Old Man's a Tory,* in the streets and in a school. (Maggie Thatcher would have had a fit if she had known about the school performance; but the government hadn't properly got into its stride.) After the play a rather glamorous slim young mum approached me saying, "Don't you remember me? I'm Moira Stoddart; I've somewhat changed my shape," and indeed she had. I remembered her as a very stout, even bullish girl, although the manner was the same, the way she came up to me once at Alex during the lunch break with her abrupt opening sentence, "I'm Moira Stoddart and I poked my brother's eyes out when he was six," and indeed she had: he was one of the first blind students at Trinity and the first to become a blind social worker. Her father was a retired British Army general. I had never met a general's daughter; she obviously modelled her booming voice on his, probably to overcome her shyness, and as I was shy too, I decided to pick up her tactic of getting attention by a startling first line. In later years Moyra had a novel published and became part of the support group for the Greenham Common women's peace camp. She was crippled with arthritis; she had married a composer, Peter Hope; they were separated and she lived alone, bringing up her children on the slope of Muswell Hill.

I also met Verena Sladen in London; she had had a short theatrical career with Caryl Jenner's childrens' theatre, she too had had a novel published; she too was separated and bringing up her children on her own.

I much admired the style of some of the girls at Alex: there was one from Dublin's Jewish community; she was connected to the Elliman family which ran the Gaiety Theatre. She used to come sweeping in, talking non-stop to no-one in particular, yesterday it would be tantalising glimpses of her exotic life - she gave off the atmosphere of a femme fatale in embryo, always at home in bohemian/theatrical locales, drinking in Davy Byrne's or the Bailey or eating in Jammet's - "and today, I was just in the shop there trying on some clothes, the assistant said to me you should be a model, you look so good in those clothes, would you ever stay on and just walk up and down for a while wearing them?"

In complete contrast there was a girl who never spoke to anyone. Her father was reputed to be an eccentric professor who believed in dressing his intellectual daughter as a pre-world-war-one suffragette, in big heavy black boots, hair severely tied back, thick spectacles, a long black dress and her head always in a book, even when she was walking. Her father seems to have been terrified lest she be tainted by any modernity or frivolity.

I was in what was known as the College Section of Alex where girls finished their last two years before taking the Trinity Entrance or the Matric. In those days you could go to university as young as sixteen. I took the Trinity Entrance but failed English. Unfortunately I had chosen a subject for the essay which made me too passionate - "Should Shakespeare be taught in schools?" I got carried away with my denunciations of teachers who hogged the best parts when we were all supposed to be reading the play together and sharing the lines. I wrote in an "expressionist" mode which was totally incomprehensible to anyone trying to mark it for an exam. On the other hand I passed in French, a subject I wasn't good at, I had only recently taken it up and was lagging behind the others, but we had a teacher with a real love for both France and its language; she was very good at getting us to pronounce the accent correctly and to get the feel of it by gesticulating, shrugging our shoulders and altogether becoming French. For this exam we had an oral (in those days called a "Viva", an exotic piece of Latin) for which we went into Trinity itself into the great exam hall to be tested by one of the lecturers. He was young and dishy. My mother had made me a well-fitting wine-coloured dress with a v-neck which showed a bit of the cleavage of my newly budding breasts. I rather liked looking down and seeing these two pearly eggs nestling there. I decided to wear this dress for the Viva. As I sat across the highly-polished table from the examiner, and leaned slightly forward (I am short-sighted, but I had taken off my glasses before going in), he could not help being engaged by what was laid out before him. I passed. My first successful bit of whoring.

~~~o~~~

It was a relief for me to go to the quiet Gate Theatre alone: to take my mind off all the drama that would be going on in "Garry Ard" when I got home. For instance: Father having to crawl round the outside of the house so that his brother Eddie, paying an unexpected visit, would not see him drunk; but
~~~

Eddie, looking out of the window, did see him; and there were our three geese following after. Eddie called out, "Joe, what on earth are you doing?" Father had set himself up as a smallholder and was fattening the geese for Christmas; they wandered freely around the premises. There were also a few hens which Rosemary looked after, and a dog, Scylla, a bull terrier bitch, which my mother's lover gave her as a present - his wife used to breed them. I had my own cat, Mother Cat, whom I'd had since she was a kitten; she looked after me. I used to lie beside her and her kittens and cry: she treated me as one of her own, licking my face alongside the kittens' faces. She also tried to instruct me in killing. One night she woke me up by jumping through the window with a large rat. I screamed so much she withdrew it and gave me up as a bad job. Rosemary, when *she* was miserable, would curl up in the dog basket. "Being happily miserable" was a habit we all indulged in; the phrase was coined by my mother.

Mother and her lover was not a furtive affair: she could never hide her feelings when the *grá* took her over. Father didn't mind or else he kept his eyes shut. So long as there were no spoken definitions nobody minded. Mother quite enjoyed the drama and ambiguity of the situation, telling us all the rumours that were going around Dublin, how women said they had seen her flashing about in a big car - in fact the lover had an ancient Bentley - he was Anglo-Irish, a bit of a waster, the wife had the money and he dealt in old cars, the wife came from one of the leading medical families and dedicated her life to her dog-breeding - they lived in a ramshackle ascendancy-type house somewhere up the long hill near Roundwood. They occupied only the kitchen; it was full of doggy stuff, constantly foul-smelling, with pans of cows' lights for the dogs bubbling away on an ancient stove. One aspect of their shabby-gentility which I observed: they did have a drawing room and a dining room full of antique furniture, with tarnished silver candle-sticks and tea-things lying hickelty-pickelty all over the place. It didn't matter how unkempt these rooms were, the fact they were there gave the owners their class distinction. The wife, a tiny little tomboy, went round in an old tweed skirt full of dog hairs and puke, pinned together with several safety-pins. When she went with her bull-terriers to the famous St. Stephen's Day dog-show, she was totally transformed with a fur coat, lipstick on her little gamine face, and casually-brushed blond hair. I used to look at her and wonder, did she mind that my mother had stolen her husband? She never looked as though she did mind. (She killed herself a few years later, but I do not think that had anything to do with Mother.) Mother couldn't stop herself stealing men if she wanted them; if she didn't want them, she would declare that they were no good - which caused quite a bit of drama when my sisters and I were choosing our own mates. She really had the temperament of a a feudal Grande Madame entitled to sample her daughter's lovers before she could approve them. Nor was she averse to machiavellian tricks to nip in the bud any of our relationships that did not meet her standards.

All these bits of gossip are here to illustrate how I built up defence mechanisms against my general pain and insecurity; to see my family as an *eccentric family* was some comfort to me, and I was able to put it into a theatrical context - I used to read all about the chaotic lives of the great tragedians, Sarah Bernhardt, Eleanor Duse, Ellen Terry, and so forth, and how they were able to use their inner distresses for their art.

I was influenced in the same direction by A.P.Herbert's *The Water Gypsies*; also by the life of Augustus John. Indeed, some of our neighbours did refer to us as "gypsies", particularly the man next door who claimed a narrow strip of land from the "Garry Ard" property - it ran in front of our gate, and he blocked the gate by putting in a gate of his own. His quarrel was with the landlord rather than us, and the odd way he expressed it made a funny story in the local newspaper.

Having discovered *All for Hecuba* I was all on fire to join the Edwards/MacLiammóir Company; but in those years they were out of the country while the Longford company occupied the Gate. Even before I went to Alex, I had written to Lord Longford, assuming that his actors toured, and saying I wanted to join them because I enjoyed the gipsy life. I received a formal reply: "The Longford company does not tour," and that was it. I was always writing away for jobs to try and change my life. I wrote to Jacobs' biscuit factory but was turned down. I didn't realise that to get a job in such an old-established firm in Dublin, you had to have someone whom they knew, and was working (or had worked) in the factory, to vouch for you. It was not strange for a fourteen-year-old to be looking for work because free secondary education did not come in until ten years later; most children left school at that age and one of mother's little dramas during her blitzes was to threaten to remove us from school and throw us out to fend for ourselves. I guess I began to get into the habit of preparing to leave home early. And what about father? - so long as we were reading good books, he thought, education didn't matter.

While I was at Alex, Mother was studying for her finals and doing her pre-med work in hospitals, so we got the brunt of her tensions - she was also trying to screw money out of father to pay for the exams - one could attend lectures without too much pressure about the fees but the exams had to be paid for, no fee, no exam. Add to which she needed to buy a professionally-tailored suit for interviews: she could not possibly go in the only one she had, she had made it herself and it looked like it.

~~~o~~~

My elder sisters were both independent by now with their own lives and their own sets of friends. Claire was full of the college gossip about the glamour-men of UCD. One of them was Paddy Loftus, the star of the drama society. I had known his sister slightly at Loreto. They were a characterful family, notably outspoken. The father was a doctor in Sligo, and one of the children went into politics as an environmental independent on the Save-Dublin-Bay ticket - he changed his name by deed-poll and became Seán Dublin Bay Loftus. He is still going strong on the environment, but he remains very conservative on sexual issues. Alex was just across the street from UCD; we would hang out of the window at lunch time, ogling and teasing the students. My one famous moment of upmanship there was in connection with Dorothea's birthday party. She had not invited me; I assumed she had forgotten and I sent her a big birthday card. She arrived at "Garry Ard" with an invitation. It was the only teenage party I ever went to; a mixture of Dorothea's friends and the friends of her older brother who was at UCD studying law; it was arranged in the American style; Judith lent me her turquoise-blue fine-cord dress; I went along and found I was supposed to have brought an escort. In default of this necessity, I had to sit along the wall waiting for some spare boy to invite me to dance. None of them did. My heart sank lower and lower when I realised that without an escort I couldn't go into the next room to have supper. I also realised why I hadn't been invited. Dorothea had not forgotten: it was her mother who had arranged all the business of escorts with other mothers, and she did not know *my* mother. Her life-style was not my mother's style, and my mother had rejected her initial overtures which might have led to such events
~~~

as all-female bridge parties and coffee mornings, which in any case did not interest her.

Suddenly, out of the blue, Paddy Loftus (who had not brought an escort either), came over to me and gallantly escorted me into the supper-room with all the others. Here was my chance to try out my Moira Stoddard opening line: "Have you read Strindberg?" He was astonished that a schoolgirl should know about Strindberg. Dorothea and I used to get passions on certain romantic-looking poets; we would go up onto the top of a Wicklow mountain, chanting their names, yelling out their verse and throwing ourselves around in an abandoned fashion. I had seen Strindberg's photograph in the *Radio Times* - a play of his was being broadcast - tortured, sullen and mysogynistical - the man of my dreams - he had been married to an actress for whom he wrote parts. Mother bought me a volume of his plays, *Miss Julie, The Father, The Ghost Sonata,* and this was now my only idea of What Theatre Ought To Be. In many respects, I took after my mother: if a man was not impressed with me I wasn't interested in him. This was the first time I had ever had a conversation with a young man. I asked him to wave when he passed into college: which he did. We were all waiting for him at the school window and we were thrilled.

~~~o~~~

One day, during the summer after I left Alex, Judith, Claire and I were on the train returning to Bray. At Dalkey the most romantic man one could ever imagine leapt on board. He wore a black beret, a red kerchief round his neck, he had brown unruly hair, a French porter's blue blouse and cord trousers - all-in-all what we imagined French artists to wear. He had yellow tiger eyes and a sensual mouth. He got off at Bray and we followed him to where he was going: the Little Flower Hall. He looked as though he belonged to the Ronald Ibbs Players who had just arrived for their summer season, and indeed he was their scenic designer, and there they all were. Ronald Ibbs himself, and his wife Maureen Halligan in an enormous white fur coat with her blond hair piled on top of her head. Ronald, with his matinée good looks, also blond, had a corduroy green velvet jacket and a cravat. They were getting out of a vast movie-style car, a white and battered Chevrolet. Claire decided to go home; but Judith who was much spunkier than I was, went up to Ronald and asked for a job. He said we could help out in the box office,
~~~

but he couldn't pay us anything. At last I was with people straight out of my books on the theatre.

The company was typical "summer stock", putting on two plays a week, West End comedies, *Blithe Spirit, Rookery Nook, French Without Tears.* There was a stage-set of basic flats, one only had to change the windows, doors, curtains, pictures on the wall and furniture - hey presto! it was transformed. Rehearsals: the cast spent one morning doing the moves, next morning a run-through, the final day a lighting rehearsal and dress rehearsal. They had to learn their lines whenever they could find time, and then, every evening six days a week, the performances. The characters were all out of stock and the actors supplied their own wardrobe - unless there was any unusual requirement, such as a clergyman or policeman outfit. Actors today might think this impossibly gruelling, but in fact it was all very relaxed, the company were well-practised and treated it as a matter of routine. None of them had heavy roles in every play and the plays were well chosen so as not to exhaust them. Sometimes an actor would be brought in for one particular play. They tended to see the summer season at the seaside as a bit of a holiday. Several of them rented cottages.

What was my attitude to being part of summer stock, after all my attentive attendance at the serious classics of the Gate Theatre, plays which laid out and analysed such important social themes as living off immoral earnings, living amidst dangerous delusions of intellectual grandeur (with the actors spilling their guts out in long anguished speeches about the human condition), or - in the case of Farquhar's comedy - living in an eloquent world of civil and military corruption? In the 1950s intellectuals and would-be intellectuals in the theatre wanted drama to ask and answer intellectual questions - the great scripture of the time was Eric Bentley's *The Playwright as Thinker.* And yet here in Bray were these slick fast-moving plays with virtually no reflective content, and purely functional speeches which were in fact little more than the immediate motivators of urgent physical movement, and not only of actors' movement (bouncing on and off like puppets) but of technical effects such as knocks upon doors, the opening and shutting of doors, the clang of the telephone bell, the musical inserts, the flicking on and off of the lights... Of course I was bound to slightly despise it, to feel that although this was acceptable experience it was not really my idea of what I wanted to do in the theatre. I think most of the others in the company felt the same and I picked up an *ambience* from them.

~~~o~~~

It was only when I went to the Hornchurch Repertory Theatre three years later (in 1953) and acted alongside brilliant and experienced comedians, that I understood what amazing feats of energy (physical and mental) are required of them. I also came to realize how much comedy and farce depended on the whole-hearted co-operation of a collective - unlike "serious" or classical theatre, where teamwork of course is desirable but not essential: the company's work is normally centred upon one or two leading performances which carry the play through, in other words an individualist/capitalist way of doing things. In those days it was accepted that a great actor-manager like Donald Wolfit or Anew McMaster could succeed even when the rest of the company was second-rate.

A comedy-collective is not simply the acting-company; it includes the audience as well. The accumulation of the laughs determines the pace of the show. Any gap or faltering in this accumulation can let out all the air from the play; it needs desperately hard work to pump it up again, which cannot be done by the director but only by the intuitive skill and awareness of experienced comedians. In a well-cast farcical comedy everyone is looking after everyone else; there is no glory for a single performer; if one of them fails, the whole thing fails. Oddly enough, although light-comedy actors are often perceived in the profession as tending towards conservative opinions, if not downright reactionary prejudices, their attitude to work is fundamentally egalitarian - "United We Stand, Divided We Fall!"

From a feminist point of view there is also, in modern comedy, a like egalitarianism between male and female roles; and often a crossing-over of the expected stereotypes. The word "stereotype" needs looking at rather carefully; it has had a bad press in recent years, but since the days of Aristophanes it has been the basis of all good comedy, often because the stereotype is only built up in order to be subverted and deconstructed. Thus, a pompous clergyman will suddenly lose his trousers, a snobbish woman will sit down on a squeaky cushion and everybody thinks she has farted. If the pomposity or the snobbishness is insufficiently glaring (i.e. not stereotyped enough) the joke will be insufficiently funny. And, from the actor's point of view, the men and women on the stage had to be of equal importance in the mechanics of the play, because
~~~

the West End comedy of the 1950s was always about personal relationships - admittedly within a very narrow stratum of society - and about the power-struggles within those relations, between men and women, between women and women, between men and men. I don't know whether I am shooting this arrow quite accurately, but the most popular playwrights of the era, Noel Coward and Terence Rattigan (whose plays were performed at Bray), were homosexuals and therefore criminals in the eyes of the then law. The Lord Chamberlain's censorship made sure that any overt sexuality in their plays had to be heterosexual; they took a delight in observing the absurdities of hetero-sexual behaviour with a cool sardonic gaze, very much from the outside.

I was always torn between a yearning for the serious and a delight in the farcical. The more I was to learn about the politics of money (which dictate art), the more I thought of farce and comedy as reactionary - because it originated in the commercial West End and was subsequently used by any company to pull in a crowd to make money - and the more I believed that serious theatre was essentially progressive and had nothing to do with money or the size of its audiences. It was years before it became clear to me that the techniques of comedy and farce derive from a very ancient tradition of populist subversive art; whereas modern serious theatre belongs in the same world as (and competes with) church sermons and patriarchal educational polemics. Comedy/farce is basically amoral; if its plots revert at the end to a safe status-quo where anarchy is sorted-out, Jack and Jill go off together to make babies on the top of the hill, and debagged parsons return to their parishes, humbler and better men, but no less dignified, this is solely because of the financial dictates of management and the need for playwrights to earn a living. The anarchy has been displayed, the threat is still there, but the immediate danger has passed... "Peace in Our Time."

At the beginning of the revived Women's Movement, in the 1960s, I found it hard in a theatrical context to see myself as oppressed or discriminated against by reason of my gender. And indeed, in *The Second Sex,* Simone de Beauvoir excludes theatre women from her argument - they enjoyed, she thought, a sexual and economic freedom not available to the petty-bourgeois female. At Ronnie Ibbs women ran the show. I remember Josie McAvin, the stage-manager, hauling in the flats, putting them up and organising everything backstage - she was the real boss and she wore dungarees long before they became the symbolic gear of Women's Lib. In the '80s she won an Oscar for her film designs; she was truly an independent woman. I remember Mary Brady, electrician and PRO, climbing ladders, fixing the huge lights, tearing round in her little car with posters and paste-bucket, whisking up the posters and sticking them in a single deft movement before careering on to the next lamp-post or electricity pole. It is only now, when I am in my seventies, that I can fully appreciate the richness of those early days in the theatre; how fortunate I was, and still am, that I worked among such people and am able, even today, to meet many of them and talk to them yet again.

A woman and her sixteen-year-old son were officially in charge of the box-office, and they did not mind at all that Judith and I were there to help them with the summer trippers. On the last night of the season - the night before I was due to depart for Pre-RADA, the company held a party. Ronnie gave Judith and me a copy each of Harold Hobson's collected reviews, *Theatre* and *Theatre 2,* signed, "with my love and thanks, Ronnie." Inside the first volume was a mention of Ronnie himself when he played in London with the Gate company in MacLiammoir's *Ill Met by Moonlight*, directed by Hilton Edwards. "Mr Ronald Ibbs as the family's guest agreeably shows that the jokes the Irish make about the English are much the same as the English make about themselves." My glamorous artist with the yellow tiger-eyes - for whom my heart every evening had throbbed with longing, if only just once he would take notice of me! - was there at the party; and he did take notice. I spent a chaste but tender night wrapped in his arms. I really can't remember how it all happened, but I do know that five of us (myself and two sisters and his married brother) had all ended up in his big bed in a cottage in the mountains. It turned out that he and his brother had a penchant for young girls…

~~~o~~~

Before going to London I had to undertake another momentous act of independence, choosing and registering my nationality at the local garda station to enable me to get an identity card to travel to England. As I had been born in England, I could, now that Ireland was a republic, travel under either the Crown or the Harp. Off I went on my bike to the Kilmacanoge garda station, expecting some kind of congratulation from the Gardaí when they were to realise the importance of the mission of this new Irish citizen, leaving the country to
~~~

become a great actress. They told me it wasn't necessary to put down on the form the exact purpose of my visit - "student" would do... So now it was my turn to be driven to Dun Laoghaire and waved off on the boat, waving back as I leaned over the side with all the other emigrants, the car waiting until the boat turned round out of the harbour and finally disappeared with me on the prow, my face toward England as the engine gathered speed, cutting through the Irish Sea amid a screech of whirling gulls. I looked back now and again to see Carriguna hill, and the Sugarloaf behind it, recede and finally vanish, while I clutched my memory of my night of passion as though it were a piece of wedding cake concealed in its little white box and put under the pillow so that I might dream of my tiger and go over and over every little morsel of that night and early morning - early morning on his motor-bike, as we swept up to see the sunrise on top of the hill. Hand in hand in silence, looking out at a glorious burst of colour, the sun blazing strong as my passion, or that is how it seemed, how it is constantly enshrined in the movies; in fact in real life there are always a fatal flaw - in this case the sudden knowledge that I had got my new brown suede party-shoes wet on the grass as we stood there. I looked down and saw them, damp and spoiled, with bits of grass sticking onto them. I should have been more poetical and philosophical, and accepted them as the everlasting proof of that moment - the wet patch on the toe as the coming together of nature's disorderly freedom and the artificial conformity of urban life.

In all plays about love there has to be a lovelorn-swain character loitering palely in the wings; and indeed one suddenly intruded into mine. Just before the party, the sixteen-year-old schoolboy, the other box-office helper, had unexpectedly fastened his mouth onto mine with a clammy fish-like kiss. He saw it as *his* night of passion; he too had his little piece of cake under his pillow, and waiting for me in London was his love letter. I wrote back as gently as I could that we would both be too busy to write any more to each other. He wrote back agreeing with me. But as for my tiger, I held *him* in my heart and couldn't wait to return to "Garry Ard" to see him once again.

~~~o~~~

When I arrived at Hannah's house in Cable Street, in the east end, the first thing I had to do was to go with her to get my food ration-book. Wartime rationing was still in force in England for some commodities - butter and sweets, for
~~~

example. Mother gave me five pounds a month allowance, out of which I had to pay for a season ticket on the tube to Highgate, the station for Pre-RADA. I cannot say that my stay at my aunt's was a great sucess. I naturally thought that after my time with the summer players I was already an independent woman; but Hannah treated me as a very inexperienced young girl of sixteen who had to be carefully watched-over amid the perils of the docklands - of course I was avid to experience all these perils, the Chinese drug smugglers, the prostitutes, the gangsters, the sleazy cafes. At the other end of town the bohemians were parading around with their free love in the King's Road. I wanted to be in on everything; I didn't want the restrictions which were placed on me only because I was the doctor's niece whose every movement would be watched and reported back to Hannah. It was Cabra all over again.

Hannah thought I did not have enough clothes, so she brought me off to a large store to buy some. In the changing-room I took off my sweater and she discovered, to her embarrassment and that of the shop assistant, that I did not wear a bra. My mother had not equipped me with one; she took great pride in never wearing one herself and never discommoding the freedom of her body with corsets and slips and suspender-belts. Her regular underwear was a set of chenille cami-knickers. My own knickers were still the old schoolgirl bloomers. Hannah bought me a bra and new knickers; I felt that this bra was a symbol of the new conformity that was being pressed upon me, and I felt that if I *did* go down the King's Road the bra would prevent anyone thinking I was a truly natural free spirit.

~~~o~~~

Hannah was a real Londoner: she loved and was proud of the city; she wanted me to appreciate and take delight in all its marvels. Her London had undergone great changes from the war. There were vast devastated areas of bomb-damage infested with purple weed and wild cats. Near Hannah's house there was the shattered skeleton of a church with only the apse left standing; an elderly woman would come here every day; I would look down and see her in the ruined crypt feeding the cats. The other side of Cable Street had all been flattened; huge blocks of council flats had sprung up to replace the little terrace-houses. The old east end that Hannah had known when she was called the Angel of Cable Street and honoured with the MBE for her work during
~~~

the blitz, had practically vanished. In fact, 90% of the district had been razed. I had not thought about any of this, had not been made aware that 70,000 tons of bombs were dropped upon London during the war, that more than 60,000 civilians were killed and more than 3,700,000 homes were damaged or destroyed... It astounds me to think back and realise that it didn't mean anything to me, even though both of my parents had been there when all this bombing was taking place.

Hannah's house was one of the few to have survived the bombing, a narrow, gloomy, three-story late-Georgian building, facing north. The sun never came into its windows. At the back was a narrow, dusty garden. It was at the "near-end" of Cable Street, not far from the Tower of London and the Royal Mint, and separated from the docks by the Highway - Ratcliffe Highway, as it used to be called, once notorious for the criminality of a great international seaport, squalor, violence and depravity. People outside the east end still thought of it like that, a darkly separate entity, alien to the rest of London.

Many of Hannah's original patients in the district had moved out to the rapidly-built housing schemes in the Isle of Dogs, which meant she had a very wide area to cover on her rounds. She never talked to me about the past, or about my mother or herself as girls, even though she had been born and bred in the east end and had never moved out except for her service in India. One might have expected her to indicate to me that after all I was coming home - had I not been born just half a mile away in Whitechapel? But there was no point in her showing me the routes and places that she and Mother knew, because most of the landmarks were gone and most of the people gone too. In any case, why talk about the past? - the only thing to do after such a cataclysm was to adjust to the present and carry on. The whole tradition of the Billig family had been never to look back. Her own house had been hit by a bomb - she did tell me about that - and Grandma had had to be rescued when the roof nearly fell in.

Hannah's one link with the pre-war past was her faithful adherence to certain shops which she had always known and which, remarkably, were still in place. She was very much a "character", and knew it. She was a chain-smoker - though not in the surgery - at any spare moment she would pant upstairs to light up. She never opened the surgery on time. She took pride in, and often told me about, her independent attitude toward the Indian Army, a woman in a male world, how she refused to acknowledge regular army time but would lie in bed until she was ready to get up. The colonel could never persuade her to obey this rule. She also told me about her gun-running days in Palestine. She never sat down and chatted with me, but on her way out of the room she would casually slip-in these tit-bits. She was brusque, with a sense of humour about herself, chuckling away at the memories; but very quick to turn on you if you said the wrong thing.

~~~o~~~

The first thing she did for me was to give me a map of the bus-routes and underground, and send me out every day on my own on a specified journey to find my way to the various landmarks of London, St Paul's, the National Gallery, Westminster Abbey, the Tower, the Tate Gallery... In the galleries I could scarcely believe I was actually seeing the real pictures, so different from the dingy photogravures in our shabby old art books at home. At the Tate I gravitated to the Pre-Raphaelites and later Victorians, and stood in wonder in front of the spectacular portrait of Ellen Terry as Lady Macbeth in her peacock-green gown. When Hannah first recommended me to go to St Paul's and Westminster Abbey and the City churches, I hesitated, because every catholic knew it was a sin to enter a protestant place of worship. When I did visit them, I could not believe that they were protestant, there were so many statues in many of them and they were called after catholics - St Paul was of course a catholic and so was St Peter, to say nothing of St Mary - and some of these churches actually advertised Holy Communion (even Mass) and I did not know whether or not I should cross myself as I walked past them. Hannah had her Irish daily-woman, Mrs Corbett, and she told me where to go, locally, to Mass; she also told me about Westminster Cathedral. Westminster Cathedral proved to be my gateway *out of* catholicism: compared to the protestant churches, it was such a hive of activity and business, with money chinking into boxes in every aisle, continuous Masses and confessions buzzing away in one chapel after another, that there seemed to me to be no tranquillity or reverence there or respect for the sanctuary-lamp. The final act of my religious disillusionment took place in the cathedral in Holy Week the following year. We all went up to the altar to kiss a relic of the True Cross: the bored and dismissive expression on the priest's face as he
~~~

perfunctorily wiped away each kiss entirely put me off. And anyway, the life I had set myself to lead would soon have come into collision with catholic teaching upon matters of love.

Once a week Hannah had a night off and she would whisk me away to a play in the West End. Because it was always at short notice, we went to any play at random. Robert Morley in *The Little Hut*; or a play by Aimée Stuart; and once to the Arts Theatre, with Uncle David and his wife Auntie Rossi, to see Jean Forbes-Robertson as Hedda Gabler, which I thought magnificent - I identified with it absolutely, there was Hedda locked into marriage, cheated of greatness, pacing around like a panther in a cage desperate for a way of escape, and there was I shut up in Hannah's house... Her defiant speech about the supposed suicide of the genius she had loved -

> I only know that Ejlert Lovborg had the courage to live life in his own way. And now - this great deed, with all its beauty! That he had the strength and will to break away from the feast of life... and so early.

The problem with Hannah and David was that they were professional people and extremely opinionated. I was opinionated too. So I went on and on about how wonderful *Hedda Gabler* was; they thought it was outdated and self-indulgent morbidity. Hannah and David were very close, even more so since both of them had served in the Indian Army, David a major and Hannah a captain, they shared gruff and peppery mannerisms developed from giving orders to Indian subordinates. When I turn over my memories of them, and how they behaved towards each other, excluding anyone else - and with a certain professional competitiveness, as they talked about their practices and their patients - I can see how they were when they were children in their own private world. And now, in the luxury of the exclusive West End theatre-world, there must have been this bond of secret pride between them - how far they had come and how much they had done! Both of them were strong supporters of the new National Health system and Hannah was notably active in the Jewish Medical Association.

All of which meant that I had two intolerant heavyweights squashing my naive outbreaks of enthusiasm, although everything would have been fine had I always agreed with them. I could well understand why my mother preferred to elope with my easy-going father rather than remain in the bosom of these Billigs. But when I was quiet and behaved like Hannah's Little Sir Echo, she did take me to all sorts of interesting places - her evening visits round the Isle of Dogs, or the Yiddish Theatre (in its last days) in the Commercial Road - she always supported all the Jewish cultural events such as art exhibitions, and she would buy paintings - her house was filled with exotic eastern pictures and artefacts as well as wonderful books: there I discovered plays by Ernst Toller and Steinbeck. Hannah pointed me in the direction of Foyles', and there I bought a copy of *Two Plays for Children* by Gertrude Stein and Picasso's play *Desire Caught by the Tail.*

~~~o~~~

My grandmother, eighty-six and partially crippled, lived with Hannah, who would carry her on her back upstairs to bed. She was able to walk downstairs on her own, very slowly, to her chair in the sitting-room, where she would crochet all day. She was very deaf and spoke with a strong Yiddish accent. On Friday nights, when Hannah was in the surgery, it was my duty, as the goy, to switch on the light, because it was the beginning of the Sabbath and Grandma was not allowed to do it. Nor would she wear her hearing-aid on the Sabbath. Despite her meek and mild demeanour, she was the one who kept a fierce eye open for any ritual improprieties in the house, and a fierce eye open upon Ada (the Dublin-born Jewish housekeeper) in case she failed to prevent me from defiling the household arrangements. At the start of my stay in Cable Street I was always doing the wrong thing: hoping to be useful to Ada, I would begin drying dishes with the wrong tea-towel - Ada would shriek at me that I was using the milk-towel instead of the meat-towel and now it would have to be thrown away and everything washed again - I had made all the dishes impure. Or I would put out the butter and bread when we were going to have meat for dinner, not realising that only unbuttered matzos could be eaten with meat. The meat, of course, had to be kosher and bought at a special Jewish shop in the district; there were two types of bread, one for the Sabbath and another for ordinary days, also from a special shop. And then a different shop for the weekly seed-cake for Hannah to eat in the afternoon - sometimes a chocolate cake. Then yet another shop to buy flowers for the surgery. Hannah was known at these shops, because they too had survived the bombing. Finally, her special chocolates: for them I had to go to the Haymarket in the West End where
~~~

hand-made chocolates could be found. They would go into her wooden box of sweets on the sitting-room table. Before the war, when Claire and Judith had stayed with Hannah, they had told me about this magic box, always full of chocolates; and Hannah had promised that I could one day come and stay and get a chocolate from the box.

But now, with the food rationing, I found it hard to adjust my appetite. I felt all the time that I was starving and couldn't get enough to eat. At home we had always gone into the kitchen when we wanted and eaten what we wanted. If a cake was made, we'd scoff it all at once. I was certainly not used to the formality of Hannah's meals - such-and-such a portion for each person at table. I was only able to satisfy myself by going on my own into the kitchen and filling myself with bread-and-butter and cake. But Ada would watch the food - she knew I was a thief - we played a cat-and-mouse game against each other. I would try to creep downstairs for bread when everyone was asleep. I slept on the third floor in the attic, beside Ada's room. Her ear was always cocked to hear if I was going to get out of bed to steal food. As soon as I opened my door one of the floorboards inevitably creaked, and there at once was Ada, standing guard. I got the better of her, however, on Saturdays, her afternoon and evening off, when I was in charge of the house and Hannah was out visiting patients. That was the time I would enter the kitchen and search for the bread where Ada would have hidden it from me. As soon as I found it I would stuff myself so full that I gave myself diarrhoea. Upon Ada's return, the first thing she did was to check on the state of the bread. If she saw it was nearly all gone, she would throw me a vindictive look, and I would be standing there triumphant.

Even though both Ada and Mrs Corbett were Irish, we never talked about Ireland - they had both built up their identities upon their respective religions rather than their country of origin. Mrs Corbett was a tidy tight-lipped woman, kind, but she never gave anything away. I never found out anything about her family, although I knew that they had been bombed-out and were now living a new council flat. She took great pride in "doing for" the doctor. Ada was fat; she took a great delight in watching me blow up like a balloon, nearly as fat as her, not only with the stolen food but with all the cheap buns I used to buy on my walks round the city. She would *comment* upon this.

I was very homesick, because I had no-one to gossip with and to laugh and quarrel in a silly way, as I had always done with my sisters. Judith was working at the time for a farmer in Salisbury. She was not very happy there. She was able on one occasion to come up to London to meet me and exchange news. Father came over once, and took me out to breakfast at Lyons Corner House in the west end. My having to go back every night on the tube to Aldgate East (dangerous foreign territory to my fellow-students) reinforced my isolation at Pre-RADA. Outside of the school, I never met a young person. Sometimes I would visit David and Rossi in Wandsworth; they had two very young children, but the Jewish domesticity hemmed me in; there was always a little lecture from Rossi on how I should behave. I did not realise quite how homesick I was until one day I went to the Pathé Newsreel Cinema in Victoria and what did I see up on the screen but de Valera and the Irish tricolour, with the Irish national anthem on the soundtrack? - the tears began streaming down my cheeks.

It really came home to me at Yom Kippur (the Day of Atonement), that Hannah was always aware that I was a goy; underneath it all was her sense - and my grandmother's - that Father had betrayed them by not keeping his promise to bring us up as Jews. Yom Kippur when all the unclean utensils have to be taken out of use for the day. It would have been my grandmother, as controller of the ritual, who pointed out to Hannah that I could not stay in the house during the period of the fast; and Hannah then explained to me that I must stay away from them until sunset.

J.A. remembers that when we were first married, I took him down one Sunday to be introduced to Grandma, then over ninety years old. At this time my mother was working in Cable Street in partnership with Hannah, in expectation of Hannah's retirement to settle in Israel. Lunch was about to be served, when Grandma suddenly became mysteriously agitated, making abrupt gestures and whispering into Hannah's ear; Hannah responded with various hushing noises, muttering in J.A.'s direction something on the lines of - "Take no notice, she gets confused," and so forth. Afterwards my mother explained that the "confusion" was a misunderstanding about the plates - apparently Grandma had thought the milk plates were laid out instead of the meat plates. At any rate this sort of thing made J.A. very conscious of his status as an outsider.

To return to that day of Yom Kippur - I went to Kew Gardens and found a little bit of wilderness preserved there - I lay on the grass and studied an exercise I wanted to learn, a speech from *Saint Joan* -

> But to shut me from the light of the sky and the sight of the fields and flowers; to chain my feet so that I can never again ride with the soldiers nor climb the hills...

Words which so evoked my memories of the hills of Wicklow that I burst into tears and sobbed out my heart under the trees in my misery and homesickness for "Garry Ard".

~~~o~~~

I might as well indulge here in a bit more of my "happily-miserable" mode and recapitulate my original accusations against Hitler, the Czar, McQuaid and all the rest, specifying for good measure the British occupation of Ireland, the oppression of women, the persecution of the Jews as well as racism in general. Was not my casting-out, as unclean, symbolic of the whole history of humanity? (Casting-out for the second time: first by the catholics, now by the Jews.) The only identity and instruments of control that were left to my grandmother to cling to were her rituals: she was the only one of her family who had remained in London throughout the war, and she had kept her religion intact.

Hannah and David had returned from India to find they must make big adjustments to their own status, in particular Hannah. She had been one of the few women from the East End Jewish community who had come out of it to become a doctor and then returned to serve her people. She had been worshipped and adored. But now, with the NHS, free medical care for the poor was an entitlement, and generally accepted as part of the new Welfare State. This was what Hannah had fought for, for years, and once she saw her battle was won, she began to turn her energies to Israel. She was already learning Hebrew. It was not therefore very surprising that she and David squashed my opinions at every possible opportunity.

Ireland, after all, they must have reflected, *had proved to the world it was still living in the dark ages, where one man in a mitre can put a stop to an entire national health scheme, as was just now happening - Archbishop McQuaid giving*
~~~

orders to the government to reject the Mother and Child bill out-of-hand. What had Ireland done for progress in the last fifty years? It had remained neutral in the fight against Nazism, while the greatest holocaust of all time was taking place only a few hundred miles away and the IRA was willing to make a dirty deal with Hitler. India had at least offered a considerable degree of co-operation, to fight on the right side for the right principles, and as a result Gandhi had been allowed to prevail and the country was now independent.

If this is how my aunt and uncle were thinking, none of it was openly spoken about or even hinted at, but I am sure the feelings were there. They never talked of Ireland but did refer to India in very loving terms (which is why a visit to India became one of my great dreams, eventually fulfilled in 1969).

Their Zionism and their exclusivity did not only affect me but was also manifested in their treatment of their eldest sister, Esther. She was physically more like mother, small, wiry, dynamic and enthusiastic. She was not a "professional" woman, although my aunt Rossi and Miss Spivack both told me that she was a mathematical wizard. She had done some government work during the war; when I first met her she had just returned from Greece where she had been a governess. The occasion revealed to Hannah my utter incompetence in following directions. I was told to meet her under the clock beside the newsreel cinema in Victoria station and I went there with my mind focused solely on the cinema. There were in fact two cinemas - I chose the wrong one, having forgotten about the clock. So we very nearly missed each other. She took me out for the day - she was having a spree on the town, meeting her girl friends at the Trocadero, that glamorous eating-house in Piccadilly. Much to my surprise. Hannah and David would never have eaten in a non-kosher establishment. But Esther was very relaxed about it. Afterwards we went to Liberty's and we looked at marvellous cloths; we fantasied together about the colours and type of material I would choose to wear when I became a famous actress. For the first time since coming to London I felt at ease - it was like having a fun time with Mother - I let my imagination roam and said how I would love to have a snake as a pet. Esther went and told this to Hannah. Hannah, to my astonishment, got into a terrible state; she rang up David and Rossi, who came hurrying round - in outraged chorus they emphatically declared I could no account keep a snake. Esther tried to intervene and calm them down by explaining it was only a joke; but they totally rode over her, and treated her as if she was contaminated by my disastrous idea. I wonder now, was their horror at a snake simply a recollection of India, or did it go rather deeper - could the notion of it have hit a hidden Hebraic chord - the intrusion of evil into the paradise garden?

> And the Lord God said unto the serpent, Because thou hast done this, thou art cursed above all cattle, and above every beast of the field; upon thy belly shalt thou go and dust shalt thou eat all the days of thy life...
> *Genesis,* III, 14.

> And every creeping thing that creepeth upon the earth shall be an abomination... Ye shall not make yourself abominable with any creeping thing that creepeth, neither shall ye make yourselves unclean with them, that ye should be defiled thereby...
> *Leviticus,* XI, 41 & 43.

In the end, when she was over sixty, Esther met Arthur; he was eighty, they got married and lived in a bungalow very happily together; I never saw her again.

~~~o~~~

Pre-RADA was a rather inconsequential kind of place. It had originally been set up by Irene Vanbrugh as an offshoot of the prestigious Royal Academy of Dramatic Art in Gower Street. When I went there it was run on a shoestring by Eric Capon and his wife in what seemed to be their back garden in Shepherd's Hill, Highgate, and then expanded to include two or three detached houses along the road. They also had residential accommodation for students who needed it. Verena from Alex lived there. The school's chief and original purpose was to prepare students for the entrance-audition to RADA. Eric Capon introduced a second-year course for aspiring directors and for those who did not want to go to RADA.

Pre-RADA had a motley kind of gathering, about forty or fifty altogether: students like myself who were too young to go to RADA; overseas students who had had some experience in their own country and wanted to extend their expertise; quite a few Americans, including a married couple; a young woman from the Icelandic National Theatre; Ali, a young man from Pakistan
~~~

who wanted to train as a director; two older Englishmen who had just finished their national service; and a few youths waiting for their national service call-up. The majority of students were women: a couple of them had been to child-acting schools and were proficient in tap-dancing and now wanted to go on as serious actors. There was a sprinkling of celebrity offspring, such as Vivian Leigh's daughter by her first husband (a business-man), her name was Suzanne, she looked nothing like her famous mother but was shy, plump, and seemed to be very insecure; there was Audrey Dalton, a dimply Irish girl, whose father was something big in a big American movie company. We were divided into groups, and like boarding school if you didn't board you were a bit excluded from the life, so I can't really remember much about the others. I always had to go straight back to Hannah's after school; but maybe there *was* a lot going on.

Before my entrance-audition, I had a couple of preparatory sessions with Valerie Hovendon: she ran a charming company, which included some of the Pre-RADA pupils, doing alfresco 18th-century plays, as well as plays for children. I would like to have taken part in one of these; but no! - back to Cable Street I had to go. I first came across the curious English assumption that all Irish people must be familiar with horses when I was introduced to Valerie's husband and he questioned me on the subject. I didn't like to tell him that I didn't move in horsey circles; instead I spoofed about the fine quality of the grass on the Curragh, which seemed to satisfy him. His other great love was the Hobbit books by Tolkien, and he made me promise to read them.

The main concentration at the school was upon the voice, with breathing exercises to move it from the back of the throat to the front. We spent hours chanting "Minnie-minnie-moo," testing to see if the vibration had reached our lips. We learned to understand how the diaphragm was a tank of air that could replenish the air in the lungs. We also did tongue and lip exercises to remove any regional intonations; but very little movement and dance - only once a week - and for a short time we did have the famous movement-teacher... but then she somehow disappeared. In those days English classical actors, with the exception of Olivier, were famous for their movement; Kenneth Tynan said of John Gielgud's Hamlet, "His voice is all soul, injured and struggling; but the body is curiously ineffectual." Our next task was to choose a variety of appropriate audition pieces, which we would demonstrate at the end of the year. We also studied plays, two Shakespeares in my first term, *Twelfth Night* and *Richard II.* When I say "studied plays", I don't mean that we sat down together, read and discussed the meaning of the play. Instead, the group was divided into smaller groups, each of them allocated a particular scene, and then all the scenes were joined up and presented. I came a real cropper when I was given the part of Bolingbroke in the first scene of *Richard II,* because I had no idea what was going on and nobody told me. It killed any ambition I might have had to be a Shakespearian actor.

(J.A.'s contribution to the chapter.)
This scene is practically incomprehensible even with the best cast in the world. The action derives from a murder committed before the play begins, the circumstances of which are never explained. Either Shakespeare expected his audience to be aware of more details of Plantagenet history than we are familiar with today, or else he supposed that everyone had seen another play of about the same date, the anonymous Woodstock -- *which ought to be better known: it could usefully be retitled* Richard II, Part One.

The purpose of these Shakespeare efforts was to show how well we could boom out our vibrations and articulate our enunciations. This was the RADA style, which was to accrue much ridicule and is now defunct. There was a large fruity lady with an ample bosom who used to supervise our minnie-minnie-moos; she and her daughter seemed to be the only regular members of the staff; the daughter one day took us for solo improvisations. It only happened once and it was the only time at the school where I showed any inkling of talent at all. I brought down the house with the improvisation I thought up. I invented an awkward social worker visiting a dysfunctional family on a housing estate; seeing a pram, she presumes there is a baby in it; in order to break the ice she bends down to coo over it, only to discover it is a rat which jumps up and bites her. I could call this my first original play; it had echoes later on in J.A.'s *Live Like Pigs* .

We were given no practical theory of acting or exercises in different styles. The majority of actors gained their experience in fit-ups or repertory companies, watching their colleagues and picking up tricks from them. The correct placing of the voice was the only thing you couldn't pick up so it was vital to have training for that. A West End actor, who was resting between parts, used to take us through our audition pieces. This was the first inkling I got about sexism in the theatre. He certainly gave our confidence a great boost when he appraised the females of the group like a dealer at a cattle market, saying that none of us had any style, we would get nowhere, except for Audrey who had no talent but would get by with the dimple in her cheek and her charm. As indeed she did. In later years she turned up as the star of a Western movie. He also informed us that we were a lot of prissy virgins; we should go out and experience Life! - for example, go and sit in railway stations and observe. So I used to get up dutifully at six in the morning and sneak out to Waterloo station to watch the early mood of London waking up. His remarks, even though brutal, were true. The only way that women were able to advance their careers in the West End or in J. Arthur Rank's movie stable, was through their looks - the pretty English rose, the leggy blonde or the sexy bombshell like Diana Dors - assuming that they already were furnished with the artificially clipped, elocutionary, over-bred stage-English accent. And of course, there was always the casting-couch.

~~~o~~~

Eric Capon himself was a contradictory man. His establishment was supposed to serve RADA; but his heart was most certainly not in that kind of theatre. He rarely put in an appearance, even though we were supposed to have had a lecture from him once a week on theatrical history. He gave us only two lectures and I still remember what he told us. First of all, he said, we had to go and see as much serious theatre as we could. Avoid the trivialities of the West End, but go to the left-wing Unity Theatre. (Hannah would not let me go to Unity, she had never heard of it and it was in a dangerous slum area at the back of King's Cross.) We had to buy certain books and read them: Allardyce Nicoll's history of world theatre, Stanislavski's *My Life in the Theatre*, plays by Bertold Brecht. His final bit of advice was the most important and it gives some indication of where his ideas were really coming from - the importance of crowd work: not just a case of standing there muttering *rhubarb* but an opportunity for each of us to create our own living character, to work out why we were there and what was our response to the speeches we heard or the action we witnessed. He was a Brechtian before Brecht's company appeared in England; he was surely familiar with Brecht's theory of epic theatre, as promulgated in 1936: -
~~~

> The spectator of the *dramatic* theatre says: "Yes, I have felt the same. I am just like this. This is only natural. It will always be like this. This human being's suffering moves me because there is no way out for him. This is great art; it bears the mark of the inevitable. I am weeping with those who weep on the stage, laughing with those who laugh."
>
> The spectator of the *epic* theatre says: "I should never have thought so. That is not the way to do it. This is most surprising, hardly credible. This will have to stop. This human being's suffering moves me because there would have been a way out for him. This is great art; nothing here seems inevitable. I am laughing about those who weep on the stage, weeping about those who laugh."

A small incident will illustrate Eric Capon's artistic ideology. Each student who aimed to be a director and join the special course next year, was allowed to choose a short play, cast it and direct it. Ali decided to put on a one-act stage version of Ernest Hemingway's *The Killers,* a highly atmospheric short story, almost entirely in dialogue, which might have been written for direct transfer to the screen - except for the fact that its date was the early 1920s, several years before the talkies. It was set in a diner; a pair of gangsters come in to order supper and wait for a man called "the Swede" whom they intend to shoot. Nothing happens, the Swede does not arrive, and at length the two hitmen leave; but it is clear that they will be back. Ali knew that this play was the antithesis of everything that Eric Capon stood for in theatre, he chose it as a deliberate challenge. We, the audience, were going to have to sit and empathise with the attendant at the counter, immersed in grim tension, quivering in apprehension of a murder about to take place, and neither he nor we privileged to know why. I only heard about the production in its later stages, when a young man, a student in our group, asked me if I would help backstage, because Ali was finding problems; very few students were anxious to be involved in his play. I volunteered, and I must say he directed the piece extraordinarily well, considering the few resources there were. The lights, the music, the atmosphere, the tension building up - whatever you thought about the play, there was no doubt about his talent as a future director. When it was over, Eric Capon just walked out without a word to Ali. Ali turned to me and said, "That's the end of me at Pre-RADA." Later on he was rejected for the director's course. He told me that Eric Capon had intimated to him that as a Pakistani he should be putting his energies into anti-imperialist plays and not get caught up in mainstream Americana. A lot of people were worrying at the time about American intrusions creeping into British culture, and on the left wing there was much hostility toward American cold-war-mongering and anti-communist blacklisting. The main reason for Ali's choice of play was to show that he did not want to be stereotyped by his race or his nationality: he had as much right to work in the commercial theatre as any English director.

Eric Capon was not against American drama as such - he pointed us in the direction of Maxwell Anderson's *Winterset* as a source of audition pieces, and indeed I had chosen a passage from that work. He told us all about the importance of the politically-conscious playwrights of the 20s and 30s, Odets, Elmer Rice, Irwin Shaw, Lillian Hellman, as well as Maxwell Anderson, whose themes (to quote Kenneth Tynan) were based on -

> The conviction that modern civilisation was committing repeated acts of criminal injustice against the individual.

He must have thought *The Killers* encouraged actors to glamorize gangsters instead of properly analysing their criminality. When I went to him for my interview at the end of the year, discussing my future, he told me I wasn't ready for RADA. But he didn't invite me to stay on for another year, and he implied that he was disappointed in me for having involved myself with the Hemingway sensation-drama - coming from Ireland and being aware of the Abbey tradition, I ought to have known better. The more so as I had chosen two passages from Synge - from *Deirdre of the Sorrows* and *The Tinker's Wedding.* (The Abbey had never performed *The Tinker's Wedding;* it was thought that the audience was "not ready for it." A year or so later I was to be involved with the very first Dublin production of the play, by the 37 Theatre Club.) So that was the end of my Pre-RADA activities, and - for the time being - my life in London.

~~~o~~~

Snapshots of the London theatre in the middle of the last century.
The Gallery Door Ritual to obtain the cheap seats: every West End theatre had its *gods*, that is to say the highest gallery right on top under the roof; if you wanted to be sure of a seat you arrived a couple of hours before the curtain went up, and someone gave you a small slatted stool with a number
~~~

on it. Then you sat there outside the theatre until the gallery door opened for the sale of tickets. Next, a gigantic scramble, stools flying all over the place, as we crammed toward the box-office window, grabbed the ticket and flew up the narrow stone emergency-stairs, past the stalls, past the dress circle, past the upper circle until we arrived at the gods and threw ourselves panting onto the wooden benches. The best seats were in front, where we would hang over the rail to see the stage miles away There was a whole culture of the gods - the French call them the Children of Paradise - because we were poor we were so much nearer heaven, both literally and figuratively, as well as being segregated from the more prosperous sections of the audience by our special box-office and staircase. Theatre architecture firmly reflected 19th-century class-distinctions. We were kept far removed from the glamour of the foyers, bars, chandeliers, plush seats, obsequious uniformed attendants, and their splendidly-accoutred clientele, dinner jackets, bare shoulders, fur coats, boxes of chocolates, perfume. It was considered by management that the gods were the best and truest judges of a play, because only a genuine devotee could endure the discomfort. Actors taking their bow would acknowledge their gratitude to the gods. Some managements maintained that if the gods approved on the first night the play was bound to be a success. So it was always a lively experience to be sitting there on your little stool, enduring rain and cold, and feeling very superior because we knew that we alone were the Faithful - just as in the catholic church - *the meek shall inherit,* and so forth.

Buskers came to amuse us - two elderly men dressed like Egyptians in nightshirts and fezes would perform what they called a Sand Dance - a well-known eccentric who looked a bit like the late Sir Henry Irving would career up and down in a frock coat, holding an umbrella whether it was raining or not, his long white locks flying in the wind - it was said he was an actor who had gone mad.

Every week, off I would go alone, on Eric Capon's recommendation, to see the classics and the great actors. I never talked to anyone, but that did not matter; we would see the taxis arriving and all the glittering nobs tipping out into the main entrance of the theatre; and when we left, we would see all the taxis again, queuing up to carry them away to their exclusive late-night suppers. Apart from young students, most of the people on the stools for the gallery were working-class or lower middle-class and getting on in years; they had fallen in love with the theatre in the days of the great actor managers - Irving, Beerbohm Tree, du Maurier - they had seen every notable performer and they *knew what theatre was.*

The Old Vic, bombed during the war, had opened its doors again. The country was beginning to recover, not only from the war but also from the post-war "austerity"; the Festival of Britain had been announced; and lavish productions of Shakespeare, Jonson, Molière, Vanbrugh, Garrick, Shaw, Chekhov, and Pinero were all over the West End. The only problem about seeing these plays and fully appreciating the quality of the actors, was the distance of the gods from the stage - unlike the audience in the rest of the house, the gallery was not supplied with binoculars and what we saw looked like a show of tiny marionettes whose faces, most of the time, were invisible. Sometimes we could see only the lower half of their bodies and less than the lower half of the scenery. But we could hear them. Their voice projection was always as clear as a bell - hence the importance at school of the boring minnie-minnie-moo exercises.

The annual Theatrical Garden Party: as drama students we were all given tickets to go there, to see and perhaps to get the chance actually to talk to them. It was in fact a bit disappointing, there was such a crush, and as so many students and wannabe actors were wandering around looking like famous actors, it was difficult to find out who was who. Tents were erected for the stars to dress in or to sit with their own personal friends. I poked my head into one tent and there was Margaret Lockwood putting on her characteristic eye-liner and beauty-spot. She saw me in her mirror; she whirled round and barked at me to "fuck off!"

Sybil Thorndike: in Dublin, her son Christopher Casson had kindly given me a letter of introduction to her. She was playing at the Haymarket Theatre. I handed in the letter at the stage door. A reply came down that I could visit her after the matinée; so I duly presented myself to her in her dressing-room. There was also a young American man paying his respects. She was very gracious and relaxed, treating us as old friends and asking me how "Michael" was. She was referring to Micheál MacLiammóir: I had never met him, but had to pretend I had. Fortunately I remembered that he and his company were just coming back to Dublin to open a new season at the Gate. He was to play Hamlet. She said with a laugh, "He can be so good, but oh he is so naughty!" and we both laughed in a knowing way. I curl up when I recollect my dissembling. Afterwards I resolved that meeting celebrities for the sake of their status is not something that suits me. Not so the young American. As we stepped out onto the pavement, his eyes were shining: he was transported.

Another bit of a letdown: Kathleen Feeney, from Ronnie Ibbs, was in a play at the Lyric, Hamersmith, brought over by a company that had split away from the Belfast Group Theatre. The play was *Over the Bridge* by Sam Thompson, who based the story on his own experiences in the shipyard. It was a plea for religious tolerance, and the Group Theatre had refused to put it on because they feared it was too controversial. Kathleen had asked me to look her up when she was in London, so along I went with high expectations expecting the same easy-going friendliness as in my time in Ronnie Ibbs. I met her backstage and she said, "We're all going to be in the pub next door, why don't you go there and wait for us?" I had never been in a pub before, and anyway I was too shy: so that was that, I didn't go.

The plight of the refugees: London was getting back to normal, but not yet for all. One of our term-plays was about Polish refugees in England. I had made friends with a student whose sister was married to a Pole: she asked me if I would like to visit them and get to know the Polish accent. She brought me to their flat somewhere in Bayswater, a dark basement flat; the sister was six months pregnant; the husband was getting ready to go out to his job as a washer-up in one of the big hotels - he would work there until the early hours of the morning. He had been a college lecturer back in Poland, but there were restrictions on the kind of work he could apply for in England. A low-paid kitchen job was the best he could get at the time. Gloom and unhappiness pervaded that flat at the prospect of a life of permanent drudgery.

The Abbey Theatre burnt down: I turned up at Pre-RADA the morning it happened, to be shrieked at by one of the American students, "What a terrible thing has happened! What a tragedy!" I didn't know what she was talking about, for of course I had never been to the Abbey; I was able to put on a convincingly tragic expression and share her grief.

George Bernard Shaw died: once again it was one of the Americans who was weeping. On her first arrival in England she had gone on a pilgrimage to Ayot St Lawrence and had hung about his gate all day and all night until she actually got a glimpse of him. These Americans came to Europe by ship; there were no cheap jet flights in those days. One of them told me about a romance she had had with a steward, a grope behind a lifeboat: I had not experienced that sort of sexual passion, but at least I had slept all night with a man. (I tried to erase the memory of my pushing his hand away from under my dress, not from excessive modesty but because I was embarrassed lest he find out I was wearing a suspender-belt. I tried to erase the memory of how I had not known how to respond to or return his kisses.)

Sweet sixteen and never been kissed.
Sweet sixteen and never kissed.

1950, Christmas holiday: briefly back in Ireland. When do the rosy fingers of dawn transform into the full strength of the sun? When do the buds of the trees burst into flower? When do the flowers grow into fruit? When do the hormones of a girl pulse into sexual desire, thus entering her into the cruel world of confusion and conflict and possessive ownership? When does she change from the simple act of loving into the imperious act of demanding? One afternoon I stormed into the studio of the man with tiger-eyes and imperiously obtained my first full passionate sensuous kiss.

My holiday job: working with Ronnie Ibbs backstage in their winter Shaw season at the Rathmines Hall in Dublin. *In Good King Charles's Golden Days*; and *Pygmalion* with Paula Byrne playing Eliza Dolittle, her last role with Ronnie Ibbs, she and her actor-partner Eric were about to depart for London. Eric became an agent there, and the last I saw of Paula was playing a nurse in a hospital series on TV. The atmosphere was completely different from summer stock, longer rehearsals, Ronnie was playing both leading parts, Christopher Casson and Nora O'Mahony were in the company this season. Christopher, between the matinée and the evening performance on Sundays, would bring in his harp and play to us all in the greenroom. His music was like an extension of the play but without the arguments - an enclave of tolerance and civilisation. Ronnie said that when I returned from Pre-RADA I could join them for their summer season.

~~~o~~~

The only play that imprinted itself on my mind during this period was *Point of Departure,* a French boulevard piece at the Lyric, Hammersmith, the sort of thing Eric Capon did *not* recommend. The plot was simple: Mai Zetterling and Dirk Bogarde played a pair of young people who met on a station platform while waiting for their separate trains, they fell poignantly in love and then had to say goodbye when the trains came in and departed with them in different directions. Why did the combination of those two particular actors take hold of me so strongly and stir me to such a depth? I think it was the unusual harmony of one voice against the other. Her Swedish accent in any event carried a quality of yearning which Bogarde was able to pick up with great sensitivity. It was altogether a remarkable piece of kitsch-music, that strange minor-key once banned by church authorities lest it opened the door to licentious emotion. The play was slight, but the intensity of the two was the most evocative I had ever seen. Certainly not Brechtian; but it did have a sort of quasi-Brechtian effect upon *me.* "That is not the way to do it... This will have to stop... These human beings' suffering moves me because there would have been a way out for them." -- why couldn't they both have got into the same train?

Dirk Bogarde's part was a romantic poet; his costume was practically identical with that worn by my yellow-eyed tiger when I first saw him waiting to get onto the train at Dalkey. Memories came flooding back and with them a renewed surge of passion. I was determined that once I was home again in Ireland, by hook or by crook I would get him to repeat his kiss with me, and this time I would have no fear of kissing him back. I would give myself totally uninhibitedly up to the moment, just like Mai Zetterling.
~~~

6

THE FURIES

> There is evidently a conflict between the girl's narcissism and the experiences to which she is destined by her sexuality ... She would like to be a fascinating treasure, not a thing to be taken.
> Simone de Beauvoir (*The Second Sex*)

In the summer of 1951 I finished with Pre-RADA, returned to Ireland and joined Ronnie Ibbs' summer season in Bray. I was seventeen; I was rejecting the rules by which the catholic church would control women's sexuality, extremism and passion. But what would be the responses of those men who themselves had rejected the authority of the church, had embraced the arts as a kind of alternative authority, and yet in their own lives retained the church's implied definition of woman as either mother or whore? They still craved, for their own needs, the control over woman's image.

And as for the control over woman's fertility, the battle was being fought out that summer between Noel Browne's Mother and Child Scheme and the catholic hierarachy. Was the situation of woman-as-childbearer still to be preserved as something sacred and private, or was it to be a matter of ordinary life for which the state should take responsibility?

The failure of the Dáil to stand up to Archbishop McQuaid and carry through the Mother and Child Scheme made nonsense of any pretence that the country was a modern democracy.

> Here in the Republic, as this crisis has revealed to us, we have two parliaments: a parliament at Maynooth [the catholic seminary] and a parliament in Dublin.
> Seán O'Faoláin (Editorial in *The Bell*, June 1951)

This Mother and Child affair had its consequences in our family. Nothing was ever quite cut-and-dried with my mother: she would have stayed in Ireland and worked as a qualified doctor, if she could, for since 1948 there been various proposals put forward for some sort of national health programme on the British model. She hoped that she might be able to follow the pattern of Hannah and start up a clinic in Kilmacanoge for mothers and children. I remember her discussing it with us - we thought the idea was wonderful - she even went so far as to talk with the local priest; he was the one who had set up the concert; he was young and open-minded; but all such notions came to naught with the slamming down of Noel Browne by John Charles McQuaid. We had been very proud of Mother when she qualified as a doctor and we had been constantly making plans of how we would celebrate the day of her inauguration. In fact nothing happened on that day, she didn't even go to the final ceremony, there wasn't the money. But shortly afterwards she did drive to Dublin to pick up her certificate from the office, and we went with her. On the way back we passed through Bray. Outside the Royal Hotel is a war memorial with seats on the plinth where men would hang around drinking. We saw a man lying on the ground; a few people were standing about ignoring him; Father laughed, assuming he was drunk, but Mother sprang out of the car, rushed into the hotel and came out carrying a bowl of sugar. She leaned down and inserted some of the sugar into his mouth. In a short time he recovered; he had been a diabetic coma. Mother drove us home without waiting for any one to thank her. We couldn't get over her quick observation and immediate reaction; our own reaction when we saw her was that she must have gone mad.

Father was against the Mother and Child scheme, even though as a reader of *The Bell,* he must have been well aware of the sort of opinion I have just quoted. He didn't see why his taxes should be increased to help any one else. So much for his idealism in the fight for the New Ireland. His self-centred attitude was typical of the cynicism of the time. Mother of course was all for it, and so was Louie Bennett - who had other, international, preoccupations, about which Father was not so cynical, as he was seriously involved in the Irish Association. I remember afternoon tea with Louie one day in her garden during that summer. John Manning and Helen Chenevix were there, worrying over next year's elections in the USA. They supported Adlai Stevenson as a possibly progressive candidate for president. Seán O'Faoláin's denunciation of Louie as a fellow-traveller had appeared in the very edition of *The Bell* from which I have quoted him on the Mother and Child Scheme. I cannot say that I was able to follow all these arguments but it was fun to listen to them, and I mention them now to illustrate the way certain people were thinking in those days.

In hindsight I would say that the destruction of the Mother and Child Scheme was the beginning of the end of catholic totalitarianism in Ireland, even though it didn't look like it, even though for many years afterwards church power seemed to augment rather than decline, with such obscurantic groups as Maria Duce holding their demonstrations and proclaiming their demands - a process that continued right up to the furore over O'Casey's *The Drums of Father Ned* in 1958.

~~~o~~~

Ronnie Ibbs once again at Bray, the company looking forward to an autumn tour of America with a repertoire of Irish plays, under a new name, "The Irish Players." Milo O'Shea and Maureen Toal would join them to go to the States. Several of the company would make American contacts; in the end they would stay there - like Milo O'Shea himself or Josie MacAvin.

All summer I worked backstage. One of my jobs was going round the town borrowing props from shops (mainly second-hand bric-a-brac shops): pieces of furniture, ornaments, pictures, trays, tea-sets and so forth. They would lend the items in return for a mention in the programme. Backstage work meant a much longer day, arriving at the theatre on my bicycle at ten in the morning and not returning to "Garry Ard" till after eleven. On the prompt-book, sometimes, for rehearsals, making sure the actors remembered their moves; standing on the stage in lieu of the actors for the lighting rehearsals; dressing the stage with props, and checking the props backstage, for every performance. Backstage in the women's dressing-room listening to all the gossip, watching Diana Campbell. She was a very bubbly girl full of fun, the first really extrovert girl I'd ever met, she gave an impression of living life to the full and by some miracle not teetering over the edge. Davy Byrne's pub off Grafton Street was the place she talked about most, where all this fun was happening; it is mentioned by James Joyce in *Ulysses* and became even better known among the virtuosos when Cecil Salkeld adorned it with his famous mural depicting Dublin writers and other characters. Diana had just got engaged to a young man who was not an actor; but by some fluke he had gone to an audition for
~~~

Maura Laverty's play *Tolka Row*, which was to go on at the Gaiety - one of three she wrote at this time about the living conditions of the Dublin working class - it dealt with the rehousing of an inner-city family in a new and dreary housing estate. It was later developed into one of Ireland's longest-running radio series. Diana's fiancé gave such a brilliant audition that he was offered the part on the spot - alas it was just a fluke: he turned out to be a lousy actor, ridiculed in the press. I don't know what happened to her in the end, that potential shining star. Her mother was always hovering around her; she must have been a replica of Diana when she was young, she seemed to re-live her rapturous life through her daughter. I used to watch Diana bubbling and chatting away as she tanned her long legs for her part in *French Without Tears*; her hands rhythmically sweeping up and down to rub-in the makeup liquid. Others in the company were Ann Casson and Pat and Peter Dix (brother and sister) - all three of them had been adopted by the same elderly woman, who hoped that Ann and Peter would eventually marry, which one day they did. Ronnie had two students coming in for the smaller parts; one of them was Colette Delaney; she and I became friends.

I enjoyed being a member of a company; it was very easy-going. None of the actors had any narcissistic tendencies; they got on with their job as a way of life. Indeed I believe the reason why Irish actors do so well in the States or the UK is because in general they are so very pragmatic. The Abbey actors were the only ones in the country on permanent contracts, and they kept themselves to themselves. The rest of the profession divided their time routinely enough between the Dublin companies and the touring companies. There was no such thing as directors *stretching* actors, playing psychological tricks with them or presenting great egotistical displays. Nor was there any pretension of an ideology. Directors plotted moves and that was about all. In any case, they were usually acting in the plays themselves.

~~~o~~~

When Ronnie's season ended I had no idea how my career in the theatre was going to proceed. I had no idea of how to look for jobs, so I just stayed at home whilst everyone else went off to school or to work. I lay in bed, eating and growing fat, only getting up in time to hurry round, tidy the house and see that dinner was ready for the others when they came home in the evening.
~~~

Mother at this time was in England doing locums. Colette too was waiting until she started a drudge-job. There was another loose cannon, Anthea, daughter of a retired Church of Ireland bishop who lived in Bray; she also had been a Ronnie student hanging round the summer season; she was a girl with ample curves - as she was always telling us. She also told us how much the boys liked them, in particular the boy in the butcher's shop where they bought their meat - every week she would go along to collect the bishop's order, and the butcher's boy cast his glances on the ample curves and liked them very much, liked them better when he was able to put his arms around them - she used to stand in front of us and talk about the ample curves in the third person as if they weren't really attached to her. Colette and I visited her once in the bishop's house - an ordinary small semi-detached house in the suburbs of Bray - he was ensconced in his study so we never saw him. We crept into the sitting room and Anthea put on a display of belly dancing in her knickers and bra, twirling a gauze scarf about her face in a libidinous manner with one ear cocked toward the door in case the bishop would suddenly appear.

We decided to have a repeat performance in "Garry Ard". Anthea brought bottles of cider and a record of Ravel's Bolero. We sat on the floor and popped benzedrine, getting as high as kites. In that era benzedrine was the fashionable drug, the Ecstacy of the day; it was not as strong as Ecstasy, but it did keep you high. We had found some pharmaceutical samples, belonging to Mother, in a drawer in the house.

I think that Mother in the end (upon one of her between-jobs visits home) clued into the fact that things she didn't like were going on behind her back; so an interview was arranged by Susan Manning with Hilton and Micheal at their house in Harcourt Terrace for them to decide whether or no I had a future in the theatre. First I had to be interviewed by Mary Manning. She took one look at me and said I was too fat, too untidy, everything wrong. At all events the main interview was arranged; and by the time Mary Manning and my mother had done with me, having my hair cut, my jacket and skirt well brushed, instructions on how to behave poured by both of them into my ears, I felt like a pudding wrapped up in a boiling-cloth.

Mother: "Don't talk too much!"
Mary: "Don't smile too much, and mind your manners!"

When I arrived at Harcourt Terrace Hilton and Micheál were still having lunch; I could hear their laughter in the next room. They were entertaining the actress Coralie Carmichael. They both entered through the sliding doors and took one look at me sitting there with my knees tight together like the dumbest kind of convent girl. They did try and relax me with friendly conversation; but all I could do was sit there rigid and answer them in monosyllables. Micheál gave a sideways glance at my girth and said, in that fruity high-camp voice of his, "Well darling, whatever you do, don't grow any bigger," and that was that. Mother thereupon decided that I should not go into the theatre but retake my entrance exam and enrol myself into Trinity next term. I decided to read history.

~~~o~~~

Colette's father had died when she was young, and she lived with her widowed mother, who had a small pension, in a big house in Wellington Road. They had let the basement out to a lodger. The house was imposing from the outside, but inside it was shabby; obviously nothing had been done to it for years, an atmosphere of genteel poverty. Colette led a free life with very little interference from her mother. However, it was not possible for her to pursue a career in the theatre full-time, because day-to-day she had to earn her living, her drudge-job in Wills' tobacco factory. She never complained about this, and we never discussed her work there; but as she had passed her Leaving Exam., it must have been some kind of clerical job, something that had to be done for her and her mother to survive. Later on, she was able to leave Wills', and was one of the first students to take a Social Science degree at Trinity. Eventually she became head of the Irish Society for Prevention of Cruelty to Children.

I was shocked when her mother told me of another widow who was so passionately in love with her husband that, when he died, she cut off his pubic hairs and wore them in a locket round her neck as a memento. Colette impressed me by the cool way in which, having invited me one day for coffee at Robert's, she found the money to pay for it; she went into her mother's bedroom, opened a drawer, took out one of her mother's necklaces, and brought me to a pawnshop to watch her hock it. I had never been in a pawshop, but obviously Colette was familiar with the proceedings: such a simple transaction, she just handed the necklace over and received a ticket and money, just
~~~

enough to buy a quarter-pound of Bewley's fudge, which she was mad about; we took the fudge to Roberts' and ate it with our coffee. The next week, when she got her wage packet, she would hand in the ticket, repay the loan with interest, retrieve the necklace and put it back in her mother's drawer. Her mother never knew it had gone.

She became an agent for a high-class cultural magazine from London, which gave all the gossip and the lifestyle material; she used to sell a few copies to people she knew in Dublin.

Colette, cool, detached and ironical. Me, all hot and panting. She was a year older than me, taller than me, with a seductive cooing voice very good for verse-speaking. She was part of a verse-speaking group which the poet Austin Clarke conducted on a Sunday evening. She had an elegant dress sense and a knack of getting to know exotic people. One of them was John Gibbon, son of the writer Monk Gibbon. He and his friend Michael Frier were Trinity students and affected an Oscar-Wildeish style of dress; following the example of the Master, they drank nothing but crème-de-menthe. This was to get them into trouble: they found themselves suing the Trinity magazine for accusing them of being homosexuals. Colette procured me an introduction to John Gibbon; we were to meet him at a tiny basement theatre in Baggot Street, the 37 Theatre Club, after a performance of *The Adding Machine* by Elmer Rice. Colette had been extremely excited by a new American actor in this play, Jack Aronson. When I saw him, he reminded me of what Orson Welles must have looked like in his youth when he acted with MacLiammóir at the Gate. He had a powerful physical presence and a most flexible voice, employed with great intensity in his role as Mr Zero, the obscure clerk replaced by an adding-machine, who shoots his boss in his one moment of rebellion, is tried and executed and goes to heaven as a martyr for the alienated workforce. But in heaven he lives his life as drearily as he did on earth, refusing the love of a woman who killed herself out of sorrow at his death. So he is chucked back on earth again to relive his miserable existence.

We took a lesson from the play, that we were right to try to live *our* lives in a permanent state of revolt. And certainly John Gibbon was the antithesis of Mr Zero; we duly met after the show, and, as predicted by Colette, he took us to Davy Byrne's - *the* Davy Byrne's, which I had heard so much about - we sipped crème-de-menthe and smoked John's black sobranies - he invited us to see the new play which he and Michael Frier had written and were presenting at Trinity the following afternoon. Colette couldn't go because she was working at Wills', so I went along alone to search for this play. Trinity did not have its own theatre at that time; the performance was in an empty room without any stage or any appearance of what could be perceived as a set - except for a ladder which the two of them sat on. They were the only actors and I can remember little of the play: it must have been in some kind of free verse and was a philosophical discourse in what I think they thought was the manner of J.-P. Sartre. I couldn't understand one word of it, but it was my first experience of real avant-garde theatre.

It reminded me of a childhood experience when we living at "Garry Ard" during the war. There was this solitary little girl, Monika: she and her parents lived permanently in Kilcroney. The mother was German, a tall willowy silent blonde, tragic and haughty-looking, with a big scar down her cheek; she resembled Marlene Dietrich. The father always trailed behind her, he had been in the British army, the traditional officer-type, tall with a little moustache; presumably they had come to Ireland to avoid the wife's internment as an enemy alien. They had brought a faithful servant with them, Ella, a middle-aged woman who looked after Monika.

Monika was a very commanding little girl, much younger than any of us. One day she told us that she was going to let us into her secret: she had a magic well. There were about six or seven of us, and highly sceptical, but her personality was such that we all trooped off to see the well and stood around sneering as she demonstrated its power. She put a tiny bit of thin rubber tubing to catch a thin trickle of water coming down some rocks; she extended the trickle into a hole that she had made. This was the magic well; and we all ran away laughing at her silliness. I too laughed and ran away with the others but her disappointed face amidst her short blond hair remains with me to this day. Things we sneer at and dismiss are often the very memories that linger longest. But it *was* Monika's well; she *had* rearranged nature and captured it; she *had* created a theatrical moment. And despite our subsequent mockery, we had willingly suspended disbelief and gone with her to see her secret. In the same way, in that room in Trinity, when I saw John and Michael sitting earnestly on their ladder with no-one but myself to watch them, disbelief was suspended and I realised for the first time how much more there was to theatre than curtains drawing back and lights going on and a play taking place behind a proscenium arch in front of a formal audience seated in orderly rows.

~~~o~~~

In the space of two days a whole new world had been thrown open to me. I wrote a letter to Barry Cassin and Nora Lever, who ran the 37 Theatre Club, asking for an audition.

~~~o~~~

To return for a moment to my secret passion, the man with the tiger-eyes. That Christmas I had stormed him in his studio and got my kiss and he was there again during the summer; but by this time his interest in me had waned. He still held a proprietary control over me; in fact he had quite a harem of discarded girls. One of them, who persisted, was now his regular handmaiden, bringing him little dishes of hot food and generally looking after him. This was not a role I wanted, so in the end I ignored him, although we did have one episode of passionate reunion.

It was my first day back for the summer, having finally finished with Pre-RADA. Claire met me off the boat and drove me home. On board I had met these two sad-looking Canadian women, one of them recovering from a miscarriage; they were touring Ireland as a way of helping her recovery. I invited them to stay the night, so we all drove home together. There in the house was my passion! - he was staying the night as well, and because of the shortage of beds he was sharing a bed with Father. A bit of farce: as soon as he and I were alone we fell into a passionate clinch with a promise he would visit me in my bed later. And then of course Father was calling him to bed just as he was trying to get to me. I was waiting for him in my nightdress, he managed to slip away while Father was in the bathroom (all the walls were very thin, we could *hear* Father in the bathroom), he reached my bedside, but my body froze as he lifted up my nightdress and put his hand on my intimate parts, then Father bellowing to him, asking what he was doing, telling him to hurry up, Father all this while thinking he was in the sitting-room finishing his drink; my bedroom opened out of the sitting-room. That was the last time we ever made contact, except for the flash of his angry face when he saw me one night going off with a young man who had come to meet me after the show. He hurled a coil of chain at my back as I was going down the steps. Our relationship had been a silent one; no words had ever been uttered between us.

> Man encourages these allurements by demanding to be lured: afterwards he is annoyed and reproachful. But he feels only indifference and hostility for the artless, guileless young girl.
> Simone de Beauvoir (*The Second Sex*)

After John Gibbon's play I went off to have coffee with him and Michael Frier. They may have dressed like Wilde, but their talk was all of existentialism and Sartre and Simone de Beauvoir, who would not accept the exclusivity of the sexual relationships between men and women - "We must create values for ourselves," she wrote, "through action and by living each moment to the full." My imagination was already all of a jumble with all the books I had been reading, contradictory images of young women, Caroline Lamb, Trilby, the Constant Nymph... wild girls, bad girls, artists' devoted muse-girls, all of them outside the norms of society. I wanted to be seen as one of those *disgraceful* girls from whom respectable young men are warned-off by their mothers - the perception of the time was that the young men of course would feel an initial fascination but in the end they too become shocked and repulsed and prefer the good girl as delineated by the church. The only disgraceful girls who survive are those who are able to achieve economic independence.

I certainly had no economic independence. My work with Ronnie Ibbs had been voluntary and unpaid. In pursuance of my notions of existentialism, I was to have my virginity taken from me by an alcoholic student drop-out. He enjoyed showing me off in the long earrings and long red cigarette holder that I affected. We would go into Davy Byrne's, he would order me a Pims and then wander away to talk to his friends: that was the style in those days. He had a permanent girl friend who was studying in England, so I was his fancy woman, an object to be desired and envied. He was supposed to be training to take over his father's business; but instead he wanted to be a poet in the style of Francis Thompson, with a similarly debauched habit of life. He did a good imitation of George Sanders in *All About Eve.* He gave me two volumes of Henry Miller to read; on the strength of their raptures we were to undertake the same pleasures. He ejaculated too quickly; he himself was a virgin; there was very little pleasure for *me* (which I commented on); mortified, he fled out of my life.

I was falling into a delusion that the recognition of the moment of magic which I cast upon a man would of itself be sufficent to sustain the relationship. Bad catholic girls paradoxically derive their badness from the preparation and anticipation of the ecstasy of Holy Communion. But bad catholic girls don't understand that in this way they are putting themselves up to replace the godhead with the goddess. Of course there was no one to talk to about these matters.

I wonder how so many of us do manage to survive when we are in our teens, in spite of all our efforts not to survive. I can only speculate as to why that should be so. Not long ago in Galway I found myself walking behind some girls on a sunny summer's day; one of them said to her friend, "I would love to die, just to see what it was like." The solitary journey, the seemingly independent act... there must be a vacuum there that cries out to be filled... It is easy for the commentators to pontificate and to tell us that an attempt at suicide is an attention-seeking act, a call for help, but when you are caught in the thickets, desperately trying to free yourself, you do not think of it in those terms, you do mean to die.

~~~o~~~

A little story of **my** *attempted suicide.*
I got a reply from the 37 Theatre Club stating a date and time for an audition. My mother said she would drive me into Dublin. But on the previous evening, some row brewed-up between her and me - I can't remember what it was about - she said I was not to go for the audition, she would not drive me in. When I retorted that I would make my own way into town, she said she was expressly forbidding me. This was the first time that I had *personally* come up against her by her for a battle of wills - we had had the *collective* taking-away of treats often enough, always to find them returned to us with the happy ending - but this seemed to be different, a direct ruling on my life, a wall built up before me. I knew her determination when she met any obstacle we might put in her way: she never let go. For instance, one of my sisters wouldn't eat spinach or drink
~~~

soup; Sunday after Sunday my mother would try to force the soup between her lips while the rest of us at the dinner table sat there looking on, frozen by the fury. Even if I disregarded my mother and went for the audition on my own, she was capable of storming into the theatre and dragging me away: a theatre producer is no match for a raging mother. The family's rights would reign supreme… My only escape was death.

That night, before lying down in my bed, I took an overdose of benzedrine tablets, a handful, that was all. The fact that I didn't know how many would kill me is immaterial to my story; I thought the amount I had taken *would* kill me. I lay there waiting for death. The approach of death appeared to me in a luminous white global light; in the centre was this circular conveyor-belt crowded with shadowy figures going round and round; I was standing outside the circle trying to get on, but the speed of it kept knocking me off; hands were stretched out trying to reach my own outstretched hand, but the belt moved them on before they could grasp me. I felt a calm euphoria and no agitation as I waited patiently for my turn… but the figures began to fade away. I was not to go with them. For the rest of the night, I lay wide awake, my heart beating faster and faster and a kaleidoscope of colours whirling in my brain.

Next morning I faced the day with a new strength. The storm was over. Mother did drive me to Baggot Street and I had my audition - my usual pieces, *Deirdre of the Sorrows* and *The Tinker's Wedding.*

What had it all been about? Why did my mother so suddenly decide to put the boot in? (I do like to tidy up loose ends - for who knows, some great illumination may result on the mother-and-daughter relationship?) Status was at the root of it. I have already written that Mother was unable to separate our identity from hers. When Mary Manning and McLiammóir and Edwards dismissed me so contemptuously, it was a reflection on her. After all, she was the one who had, no doubt proudly, promoted me to Mary Manning, who had then interceded on her behalf. The result was rejection: so she had to reject me and reject my ambition - wipe it out, it was a hiccup, it must not be repeated. I must not be given the opportunity to fail again, and with another failure bring another humilation for her. She could never allow these buried insecurities to be dredged up; hence her attempt at totalitarian exercise of power.

Did she know of my attempt to end my life? She must have noticed the altered pupils of my eyes that morning - my sisters all noticed, and there was a tremor of excitement among them. They told some of their friends, and the friends reported back that that they had observed me after the audition walking down Grafton Street and my pupils were huge - the drama of seeing someone they knew in the very process of self-inflicted death! My mother wisely ignored the whole incident; I didn't die; I didn't collapse; the only ill effect was that I didn't sleep for a week. She never again pushed me to such an extent; she never took much interest in my career, either. She didn't understand that in the theatre there was a whole new movement coming up, a regular Phoenix Ascending; the 37 Theatre Club was the heart of it.

I couldn't tell whether my audition was any good or not, but the overdose had released my nerves and I felt a new confidence and strength and a purer, truer emotion as I spoke Deirdre's words of her love for Naisi which transcended death: -

> It was the choice of lives we had in the clear woods, and in the grave we're safe, surely...

The audition was held on the tiny stage in the middle of the set of the last act of *The Adding Machine*, surrounded by white tombstones painted with black crosses where Mr Zero had returned from the dead, highly symbolic for one in my state. Barry Cassin and Nora Lever said that their next play, *The Man with a Load of Mischief* by Ashley Dukes, had already been cast; but I could help with the stage-management. So I started work the following week. Then, one day, just after opening-night, Barry rang me up to call me urgently to the theatre: Gráinne O'Shannon, who played the maid, had been offered a job by Hilton and Micheal in their new season, and I was to step into her part! I felt that because I had been willing to face death rather than give up the theatre, the furies had relented, had accepted my offering, and in return had rewarded me with an offering of their own.

The 37 did indeed lay the foundations for the new post war theatre and a new generation of Irish actors: Anna Manahan; Pauline Delaney; Norman Rodway who was one of the founders of The Gaslight Theatre and later the Globe and the Gemini companies - Gemini discovered Hugh Leonard and

J.B.Keane; Jack Aronson who married Anew McMaster's daughter Mary Rose, and went off to San Fransisco to start an Irish Theatre which was still there when I visited that city in 1967. The famous Pike Theatre which first put on Brendan Behan and introduced Beckett to the Dublin stage, would never have happened without the example of the 37 and its directors - Nora Lever was also the first to bring Shakespeare to Irish schools; Barry Cassin later became one of the principal directors of the Irish Theatre Company, a touring offshoot of the Abbey.

I can say with pride that we were the embryo of the Irish theatre of today; and then again in London in 1958, at the Royal Court, I was able to contribute my own little bit to the post-war *English* Phoenix. Hilton and Micheál were the glories of the past. I did not belong to the past. I was the future - part of the new inspiration, the new ideas pushing us forward, pushing the human race forward upon its path toward the inevitable collapse of capitalism - so there! We will get around the current little hitch of the neo-liberal global free market, somehow...

~~~o~~~

In the early fifties Baggot Street was not wholly absorbed by offices, small companies, little restaurants: families still lived there. I always found something mysterious about strolling along this straight street lined with Georgian houses, a main thoroughfare, yet an intimate one, looking down into the basement windows, seeing people's lives in brief cut-off glimpses - in the morning their remains of breakfast left on the table; and then in the evening twilight, the lights on before the curtains were drawn, where people would sit unconcerned at our observing them as if in a play. One basement was different; it pulled the passer-by up sharply. A black-curtained window, an enigmatic black door, a discreet sign on the open gate: 37 Theatre Club. How many others were as intrigued, excited, delighted, as I was, when they first went down the stone steps and through that black door?

Inside the front door there was no foyer, just a black curtain to keep out the night air. As soon as you came in, as a member of the audience, you found yourself immediately in the theatre, with the slightly-raised stage to your left, at your very elbow. To your right, against the wall, was the table where you
~~~

bought your ticket. I suppose the little room held about forty for a full house. It was always warm, heated by a paraffin stove. Cecil D'Arcy was there at the ticket-table, an informal hostess, (my namesake, but no relation); with her sparky English accent, she brought with her the atmosphere of what you imagined went on in the roaring twenties, the days of the illicit night-clubs, the days of her youth, in fact. She gave the impression it was you and no-one else she had been waiting for all night, and who could say now what madcap adventures might follow? In the interval the black curtain that separated the auditorium and stage from the dressing-room area was drawn back and coffee, tea and biscuits were served; because it was a club, their price was included in the ticket. I seem to recall that the audience took its refreshments in company with the cast who were preparing for the next act, coming in and going out collecting their props, their clothes hanging up along the wall, the make-up mirror with the sticks laid out, and the intermingling smells of greasepaint, coffee and paraffin.

When preparing to write this, I rang up Barry to jog my memories: I asked him how he used to choose the plays, did he have a particular policy? He told me no. He simply read hundreds of plays, as published by Samuel French, and selected those that (a) were rarely done, and (b) could be conveniently cast. He filled a gap in Dublin theatre with lesser-known plays: some had been seen in the city before the war (as, for instance, *The Adding Machine*, produced in the 1930s by MacLiammóir and Edwards), others were put on for the first time. Barry and Nora made a strange pair; he appeared to be younger than her, in his late twenties, very tall, with a cadaverous physique; she, by contrast, was tiny and sharp-featured, when she wasn't acting she wore her blond hair tied up on top of her head, it was impossible to say how old she was, for the rest of her life she seemed the same age as when I first met her. Neither of them had any "theatrical" manners, no effusive chat, no special gatherings, no fuss for first nights. No gathering in pubs after the show. Nora lived with her mother and her collection of cats - she was deeply involved with the Society for the Prevention of Cruelty to Animals - and Barry lived there too.

We were conscious that we were professionals, even though some of the actors had to work at other jobs during the day. Norman Rodway, for instance, worked fulltime in Guinness's; and Pauline Delaney in Switzers' department-store, at a rather grand glass-enclosed cash-desk just inside the main entrance.

The younger ones like myself had no money at all. Most of us lived at home. All this helped to explain why there was no social life around the 37 Theatre Club. Some months later, we moved to bigger premises on the first floor above Cafola's ice-cream parlour at 51 Lower O'Connell Street, and Barry was able to pay us all a small wage. I got a £1 a week, which meant that I was now eligible for provisional membership of Irish Equity, the actors' trade union: proof that I was at last a professional.

I did once earn the vast sum of £3. Barry was involved in a documentary film which was being made to promote the new rural electrification scheme. I was an extra, pushing a pram along the street. The incident I remember most, and was most proud of, was that George Fleischmann, the cameraman, actually put the camera in my pram; and I had to push it until we got to where we were shooting - a vital part of the proceedings - I wasn't only an actress but a member of the film crew. The crew was just the two of us, Fleischmann and me! All these little crumbs went to build up my CV. This documentary was important from another point of view - it was one of the first made by the Irish state for propaganda and education. Film companies - mainly English - had already been coming to Ireland and using Irish actors and extras: *Henry V* was made in Powerscourt when we were living nearby at "Garry Ard"; for the battle of Agincourt practically the entire male population of the countryside was recruited, so long as they brought their own horses; then there was the comedy-thriller, *I Spy a Dark Stranger,* with Deborah Kerr and Trevor Howard; it was shot near Rocky Valley on the Long Hill. My sisters and I went along to watch some of the work. When we arrived they weren't actually shooting. Actors dressed for a funeral-scene were all sitting alongside the hearse playing cards, drinking and talking - including the "widow" in her weeds - a farmer came past them and spat on the ground, muttering how disgraceful it was - what do people get up to? - especially the women, talking and laughing like that - no respect for the dead! pointing indignantly at the widow. And of course in the 37 we got all the juicy bits of gossip about how the stars behaved. I remember one story about Ava Gardner shocking an inexperienced catholic actress with her introductory remark - "I love fucking but I can't stand all the goddamned foreplay." Diana Campbell played a young Traveller in a film called *No Resting Place*: she had to have her teeth blackened out. As soon as the director's back was turned, she would rub the blacking off. He would have to chase her and put her "under guard" until he was able to shoot the scene.

How seriously did we take our work? - I mean, those of us playing small parts. Actors at the 37 were left on their own to develop their roles. Jack Aronson impressed us all because he actually did exercises during the day to limber up for his performance, an unheard-of activity at that time. Anna Manahan and Norman Rodway had a very serious attitude to their work. I think Norman must have been able to take time off from Guinness's for rehearsals. I began to experiment in some of my small parts. I was a housemaid in a play by the 19th-century Norwegian social dramatist, Bjornsterne Bjornson. All I had to do was announce a visiting dignitary, who was played by a lovely English actor, an elderly man called Ken Huxham. We devised an unspoken relationship between us: we implied a sexual dalliance and indicated it both when he came in and when I opened the door for him to leave. To this day I cannot remember either the name or the plot of Bjornson's play; all I can remember is my own little play-within-the-play. Each production with which I was involved plunged me into a different world. Clemence Dane's *Granite,* for example, a gloomy but intensely imaginative play about a shipwrecked sailor washed ashore on Lundy Island in the Bristol Channel with a background of tide and tempest and isolated human passion. In that tiny theatre a play would so take over the space that the whole area seemed to palpitate with the emotion and atmosphere of the story. The actors themselves were thoroughly caught up in it; there could be no slackening of the concentration with the audience so close to us. It changed somewhat when we moved to the larger theatre. To prepare for the move, we younger members of the company without day-jobs were all roped-in to help with the carpentry; sawing and hammering away to get the stage built in time.

In this new theatre we now had a proper box-office, and we would take it in turns to look after it. One morning when I was selling tickets there, Barry Fitzgerald (in Ireland for his role in John Ford's *The Quiet Man*) came in to reserve a seat - such a very modest man, I couldn't believe that with his fame he should just walk up the stairs and buy his ticket for *The Tinker's Wedding* like any one else. This was in fact the first production of the play in Ireland, fifty-one years after it was written. It would have been of particular interest to Barry Fitzgerald, as an old Abbey Player, for Yeats and Lady Gregory had refused it at the Abbey when it was new - they thought that a Dublin audience was "not ready" to see a priest being tied up in a sack. For the 37, it was a prestige production, being our contribution to An Tostal, a national cultural festival inaugurated that year (1953) for the benefit of the tourist trade. This highly-publicised affair was met in Dublin with the city's usual scepticism, not least because the corporation commissioned a bowl of flames on O'Connell Bridge. This was nicknamed (by Myles na gCopaleen, I believe) The Tomb of the Unknown Gurrier and was promptly and ceremoniously thrown into the Liffey by a group of Trinity students. I remember having to address envelopes to all the foreign embassies, sending them invitations to our first night. I don't remember feeling any awe or sense of history at the time. Indeed I was not aware there was anything significant about the production, or even that it was a première, until my recent conversation with Barry Cassin. He said that the company never thought in terms of blazing any trail anywhere, they were just "putting on plays". It was not until 1957, when the Dublin Theatre Festival was inaugurated by Brendan Smyth, that the presentation of plays old or new was accompanied by PROs whipping up hype for visiting British critics - this became necessary if London was to be made aware that there was a Dublin theatre not necessarily attached to the old reputation of the Abbey.

We had a full house for the first night of *The Tinker's Wedding.* Seamus Kelly of *The Irish Times* was the doyen of the Dublin critics: he sat there with his dour face and fox-like sharpness, which can be seen in his role of Mr Flask in John Huston's *Moby Dick* film; it was unusual for him to come to a theatre-club production, and his presence heated up the excitement. Brendan Behan in the audience made *his* presence felt by calling out that he was a "better playwright than fucking Synge." He was doing his best to get into the spirit of An Tostal - he had already cheered on the pagans against St Patrick in the religiously-orientated pageant at Croke Park - "Up the Druids!" as though they were a football team - and he brought back a flavour of the rowdy old days of the stage before Yeats so firmly insisted upon respectable respectful audiences. It is true that Yeats did have serious trouble with audiences - there were orchestrated ideological riots for both *The Playboy of the Western World* and *The Plough and the Stars* - but he sought for far more than mere politeness from his public. He wanted them to undergo a religious experience, to feel a sense of the numinous, when witnessing a play. Hence the solemn strokes of a gong before the curtain went up at the Abbey, reminiscent of the Angelus or perhaps even the Sanctus Bell that signals the Miracle of the Mass.

Altogether, whether we realised it or not, with this play we were making a small contribution to Irish theatre history. There was no sort of protest. I don't know if anyone expected the rosary brigade to come demonstrating outside the theatre against the supposed blasphemy of the text, but they only seemed to display themselves on protest outside really big events - we were too small for them to notice, and they may not have known anything about the play anyway.

I don't understand why *The Tinker's Wedding* is always slighted as "not one of Synge's better works", but re-reading it today at a time when the influence of the catholic church is in decline in the south of Ireland and sectarianism on the rise in the north, I am struck with how anti-catholic it is as well as anti-clerical in its horrified observation of a village priest haggling with the tinker-woman over the price of a sacrament - Luther on the subject of indulgences could hardly have been more passionate against priestly exploitation.

PRIEST

If you want to be married, let you pay your pound. I'd do it for a pound only, and that's making it a sight cheaper than I'd make it for one of my own pairs is living here in the place... Wouldn't you easy get it with your selling asses, and making cans, and your stealing east and west in Wicklow and Wexford and the county Meath?

SARAH:

Wouldn't you have a little mercy on us, your reverence? Wouldn't you marry us for half a sovereign, and it a nice shiny one with a view on it of the living king's mamma?

PRIEST:

If it's ten shillings you have, let you get ten more the same way, and I'll marry you then... When will you have that can done, Michael Byrne?... Let you get a crown along with the ten shillings and the gallon can, Sarah Casey, and I will wed you so.

If there were such a thing as a Paisleyite drama group and they were to perform *The Tinker's Wedding* nowadays in the north of Ireland, I wonder what the reaction would be? As a play it is very strong, the harshest kind of comedy; and I can only suggest that the slighting of it is due to the (no doubt unconscious) discomfort of catholic criticism in the face of its plot. This possibility struck me in August 1999, on Inismaan in the Aran Islands, when I heard Brian Friel make the keynote speech at the restoration-ceremony of the cottage where Synge used to stay; in effect Mr Friel claimed him, with conventional wisdom, as a man who became "one of our own", having courageously rejected his imperialist/protestant/unionist background. The same sort of fudge occurred in a British TV documentary on the playwright which was broadcast by RTE in August 2000. Synge certainly rejected imperialism and unionism. And as for religion, of *any* denomination, he rejected it altogether. Neither Brian Friel nor the film-makers felt able to put their fingers on the subtle distinction between different types of atheism. People who cease to believe in the god of their fathers, nevertheless continue the ethics appertaining to that god. If Synge was an atheist, he was a protestant atheist, not a catholic one, and *The Tinker's Wedding* is a clear declaration of it.

~~~o~~~

The next play was more immediately relevant: the premiere of Maurice Meldon's *Aisling* on April the 4th, 1953. This was the first modern Irish satirical play since Denis Johnston wrote *The Old Lady Says No* in 1929. Maurice was 27 at the time, a quiet shy young man, who was to die tragically at the age of 35 when he fell off a bicycle and crashed his head against the curb. He had already had a play on at the Abbey and had won a Radio Éireann drama competition, but he deliberately offered *Aisling* to Barry Cassin. It had a very large cast; practically everyone in Dublin who could remember a line was in it. John Jordan was one of them, short-story writer and literary critic, contributor to *Envoy,* with a reputation for great integrity and astuteness. I managed to hunt down a copy of the play in my shelves. In fact I could remember very little of it because of my subsequent breakdown. I was surprised to discover what an important play it was, and still is, to anyone in search of an easy understanding of Irish history and literature in terms of parody and extravaganza. Almost everything wrong with the nation and its politics is thrown into a big bubbling cauldron. It ought to be required reading in all drama departments which offer a course of Irish studies. Seamus Kelly wrote of it -

> Meldon flashes brilliantly as a social satirist, and says all that O'Casey tries to say in *Cock-A-Doodle-Dandy* with far more incisiveness, lightness, and economy. What's more, he says it in the voices of some half-dozen of his great predecessors, in parodies so inspired that it is virtually impossible to know where their victims end and where Meldon begins.
~~~

Maurice himself, in his programme note, paid homage to -

> - the spirit of disinterested dishonesty which enabled me to filch, unblushingly, the translated genius of so many distinguished people... Any resemblance to the styles of Shaw, O'Casey, Synge, Johnston, Gregory, Chekov, Ibsen, Strindberg, O'Neill and Longford is purely intentional.

The plot, briefly. British soldiers have kidnapped Ireland in 1921, in the person of a young woman called Caithlin Ni Houlihan, and they put her up for auction. She is rescued by "dissident" republican guerrillas and goes on the run, with a poet, taking short cuts through most of the stories and plays dealing with ancient mythology as well as the modern-day independence struggle. In the end she is once again put up for auction by the Dublin county council after the establishment of the Republic in 1948; the bidding is still going on when the play ends. She is an emblem for the whole country, but she is also an individual Irishwoman; what cannot be hidden is the author's genuine anger and disgust at the way women were, and are, treated by the state. I'm not just putting this in because I'm prejudiced in favour of Maurice or because on the first night he was so nervous that he held on to my hand in the wings while we were waiting for our entry-cues, as tightly as if he was clinging to his life. The feminist subtext of his play is unmistakeable and the speeches I quote here illustrate it very well. First, from the Auctioneer about to sell Caithlin for the second time -

> Ladies and Gentlemen, we have here on offer, a really fine specimen of Irish womanhood. This is the final - and I would add - the choicest item in the entire programme of ex-Imperial effects. Bearing in mind the difficult situation in regard to the supply of cheap domestic labour, this offer must be regarded as one of unique value. Here for an initial outlay and for a small cost of maintenance is a durable human machine, capable of uses under almost any conditions of exploitation. I am offering you this wonderful mechanism, this extraordinary bargain, this symmetrical animal... Who will make the first bid?

And secondly, an argument in the county council as to whether Caithlin and her lover, the poet Padraigeen, should be allowed to get married -

Cllr. SHAUGHNESSY:
Mr Chairman, I object. I think that the whole thing is scandalous. Early marriages are the curse of the world. Early marriages, Mr Chairman, are productive of divorces and overpopulation. I, personally, refuse to consent.

A WOMAN COUNCILLOR:
Mr Chairman, the conditions of women in the home are intolerable. Young girls are plucked from the happy soils of liberty and independence and forced to drudge for the remainder of their lives under conditions of complete slavery. The low salary rates of the depressed classes - the so-called bourgeois or white-collar workers - makes it impossible for them to hope to live normal social lives. In the interests of the boy and the girl themselves, I withhold my consent.

Today, in the year 2000, there are nearly as many women in the workplace as men; and yet the gap between the poor and the better-off continues to widen and the risk of poverty has increased for women… I was playing one of the chorus of women whose voices run throughout the play and Caithlin herself was played by Colette.

Aisling has all but disappeared from theatrical memory. It ought to be revived; and not only as a historical curiosity, but for its pre-verberations of what was to come, Ireland joining the EU, the Maastricht Treaty, the Amsterdam Treaty, the Partnership for Peace - not to mention the Treaty of Nice, when the Irish people collectively rejected the whole of the establishment, church, state, labour-bureaucracy and business. The central "Gestus" of the auctioning-off of the country could also be taken as a comment on the northern Peace Process and the referendums that accompanied it, bartering Articles 2 & 3 of the Constitution of the Republic for a Stormont Assembly under continued British rule. The play must have had a far stronger influence upon me than I realized at the time, and this perhaps accounted for my strange and impulsive action during rehearsals.

I felt woefully inadequate; I couldn't get into the story, because I was only too aware that I knew little of Irish history or of Ireland itself. I had been no further than a few miles away from Dublin since I was three; and yet the script was full of all these references to the wide open countryside west of the Pale. Also, since we moved to St Stephen's Green I hadn't been out of the city at all. I felt I was a failure; I decided once again to kill myself; I went off to say goodbye to a young friend of mine, a sculptor (of whom more later), and found that he too seemed thoroughly depressed, yearning to escape. He was about to go to County Clare in the far west by a roundabout route; someone he knew was giving him a lift in a van; it was the manager of the Old Grand Hotel in Ennis, who was picking up supplies; he said why didn't I come along, at least for part of the way? I forgot about suicide and jumped in.

But I had already left a vaguely-phrased suicide-note behind me.

In those days the rural areas of the west and south had hardly changed in thirty years. There were very few cars on the road, only the odd commercial traveller, the priest, the doctor, the petrol tanker. There were donkeys and carts everywhere, and ponies and traps, and donkeys loaded with panniers led by serious little bare-foot children. In Kerry the women still had their cloaks lined with crimson, in Cork the cloaks were blue, in Galway they wore shawls, black or soft colours. We at last arrived in Ennis where our friend the hotel manager treated us to lunch, marinated steak and french-fried chips. I then hitched some lifts going north and finally was picked up by a petrol tanker delivering to the pumps all round Connemara before ending up in Galway city. The driver showed me everything: the ruined efforts of ill-thought-out government schemes for small factories and agricultural projects, seaweed-processing and tomato-growing; or the place where the young doctor had drowned herself, to be found stuck in a crevice in the cliff - the tide had left her there, fully dressed with her hat on and still holding her handbag; he kept calling out to people on the roadside, "Have they found the body yet?" - another sucide, someone had thrown himself into a lake and had maybe floated out of it down a river. It seemed that Connemara was the regular place to be if you wanted to take your own life. He delicately pointed out to me the twelve conical mountains known as the Twelve Bens - also called the Twelve Breasts. By now I was beginning to understand the inner bitterness of Maurice's play. The heartbreaking beauty of the land, and yet the neglect... And the suicides.

At that time I was what might be termed an eclectic dresser, picking up odd items of clothing in the Iveagh Market. My aunt Hannah had given me her old army waistcoat made of rabbit skin, designed to keep out the cold of the Himalayas. I wore my bright red ceramic earings (which I had come to think of as a kind of talisman), I had long hair, a black skirt over a pair of red corduroy trousers and a pair of Japanese wooden sandals which clacked as I walked. I was the first of the grungies. No-one who gave me a lift commented on what I was doing or who I was.

When the petrol tanker dropped me off in Galway the market was just in the process of dispersing; a small boy tugged at his father, pointed at me and cried in a high-pitched voice, "Will you look, da, at the wild man!" I called to see a friend of Claire's in the hope that she might offer me a bed for the night. I thought I might make my way to the Aran Islands, because now I was earning money I had three pounds in my post-office book. The friend's house was crammed with relatives. They were preparing for a wedding and I was obviously in the way; so I went to the Garda Station to enquire about the Aran boats. The Guards all looked at me. One of them said, "That's not her. She's not wearing trousers." Another one said, "Can't you see them under her skirt." They told me that my father had alerted them to look out for me. They would give me a lift to Mullingar in the morning and then I was to take the bus to Dublin. They put me up in a hotel. The Guard who brought me to the hotel took off his uniform cap and made overtures to me in the poky little lounge beside the bar. The bar was a hubbub of men smoking and roaring and drinking after the market. I had a knife in my belt which had one of those pointed spikes for making holes in harness-leather; I produced it; the Guard's shirt had come adrift revealing a fine soft belly; I pushed the point into him until he retreated.

The only other man on my journey to make sexual advances toward me was a middle-aged priest who had given me a lift along the coast road. He asked me, was I a catholic? I thought it best to tell him I was a protestant and so avoid further probing questions. His response was, "Why don't we stop and you go into the sea over there and have a swim?"

I said I had no swimsuit.

He then said, "If you're a protestant it's no sin for you to go for a swim without your clothes."

Apart from these two little incidents, I found that all over the west people treated me with great gentleness and respect.

From Mullingar to Dublin I hitched with a very sensitive young man who loved the cinema. We talked about the possibility of a cinema where you could experience everything, 3-D vision, stereo sound, smell, feeling... I had only been a couple of days away, and I was able to rejoin the cast without anyone commenting - particularly without any remark from Nora and Barry who were both extremely tactful. Later I found out that Edie Howard had seen me going off in the van to Ennis; she had at once spread the rumour I had eloped.

Not only did *Aisling* confront me with my own history but it was also the cause of my meeting IRA ex-prisoners for whom the armed struggle was by no means over, a piece of up-to-date history of which I had been totally ignorant. Because the play dealt so vividly with the politics of contemporary Ireland, it attracted a much more politically-conscious audience. If Colette and I went into Robert's for a coffee, we could be sure that somebody there would recognise us as members of the cast, would greet us and ask us to sit down and join them. Brendan Behan, sober, was frequently holding court there. He asked me once if I would like to read a play he had written, and help to persuade Barry Cassin to put it on. He pulled out of his bag a tattered pile of stout-stained pages; he couldn't find the rest of it - he said he'd give it to me later, but never did. It must have been his early work *The Twisting of Another Rope;* rejected by the Abbey, it eventually turned up at the Pike, reshaped as *The Quare Fellow.* He used to tell funny stories about his youth: how one of his teachers beat him and he ran home to tell his mother; she immediately tore off down the street to confront and "flay-into" the teacher, with little Brendan there holding onto her, hiding behind her skirt, and grinning his face off. He enacted the scene as if it had happened yesterday, his features crumpling up like a six-year-old's - "Mammy, Mammy, he's after slaughtering me!" He was telling this story as a way of making his two silent companions feel comfortable - they had just been released from gaol in England where they had served sentences for their part in the 1939 bombings - the same IRA campaign which put Brendan into Borstal. I remember one of them was called Eddie Connolly. He was very quiet and very respectful of my stage experience. This was the first time anyone had taken me seriously as part of the genuine Dublin theatrical scene.

~~~o~~~
~~~

I should say here that my memory of where I had been living before the 37 transferred to O'Connell Street is a bit blurred.

I do know that we left "Garry Ard" and moved into a first floor flat on St. Stephen's Green some time in the autumn of 1952, owing to the condition of Father's heart, and the strain of his bicycle journeys up four miles of hills from Bray. I suppose we must have given up the car by this time - because of the expense? All of us were going in and out of Dublin at odd hours, no buses, hitching in the rain and so forth. I really have no memory at all of the actual change of residence, which is a bit strange considering that we had lived in "Garry Ard" for nearly ten years. It took place, however, at the same time as the 37 flit, and probably the theatre-move engrossed me so much I never noticed the house-move. Several months before we settled in St Stephen's Green, Claire and I lived for a while in a top-floor flat in Fitzwilliam street. This had been lent to Mother for a couple of months by a colleague, newly-qualified, called Pat Pringle. But what did happen to the car? and how was Father getting to work? He stayed on in "Garry Ard"; did he have another heart attack? - it is all a distant blur in my mind. I do know that while we were in the Fitzwilliam Street flat I was supposed to be studying at Trinity, and also that it was there I lost my virginity, because the clothes in which I used to flaunt myself in Davy Byrne's were Pat Pringle's colourful garments that she had left behind in the wardrobe - I was crossing St Stephen's Green one day when we passed each other going in opposite directions - she was very thin and I was plump and the sight of me squeezed into her clothes must have caused her to wonder if she was having some sort of hallucination - neither of us spoke - she just gave me an astonished double-take and walked on.

* * * * * *

A few years ago I replied to a letter in *The Irish Times* which asked for women's recollections of Trinity, and this is what I sent in: -

> Dear Elizabeth Mayes,
> In response to your letter in *The Irish Times* (19 June 98), here is a short reminiscence of Trinity, which I hope you'll find useful. Perhaps you could check on the history lecturer I call "Miss Ottaway" - I am not sure whether I remember her name correctly?
>
> In 1951 I was seventeen. I found myself at a crossroads, undecided what sort of career I

should follow, academic or theatre, or both? I enrolled myself at Trinity to study History. (I thought it would enable me to have a good grasp of the history of the theatre.) I did not get permission from Archbishop McQuaid, even though Trinity had been made a matter of mortal sin: all Catholics would burn everlastingly in hell if we received such an education without his sayso. I turned up for my first lecture, which was given by Miss Ottaway [in fact Otway]; her subject was the Middle Ages. Unfortunately I never worked out *which* Middle Ages, Irish, British or European, as I couldn't understand a word of what she said. I found it impossible to disentangle the syllables of her exaggerated Oxford drawl. I had been given a booklist, but I couldn't get hold of the books from the library, there was such a queue for them, and I couldn't afford to buy them. If I had had the books I might have been able to have made some sense of her lectures.

At about the third lecture I suddenly realised that her introductory remarks on each occasion were in fact a statement to the effect that she would not give credit to any student who came to the lecture-room incorrectly dressed. I had to understand this because she was looking directly at me. She added that headgear or scarves were not to be worn with gowns. I was adorned with a bright red scarf which I had tied in a dashing gipsy style, together with long red earrings. I thought these set off the sombre black gown very fetchingly. We looked at one another in silence. I was too mortified to take the scarf off. So she just continued her roll-call, without including my name.

And that was the end of my academic career.

But not the end of my theatrical one.

Some time afterwards, strolling through the college, I saw an announcement on Trinity Players' notice board, asking people to turn up for an audition for the forthcoming production of *She Stoops To Conquer,* which was to open the new Players' Theatre. There was an outside director, May Carey, the well-known actress. I had a successful audition and she gave me the part of Miss Neville. The review in the college magazine said, "Miss D'Arcy in her puce and pink would have frightened off a braver lover than Mr Hastings." This notice did not surprise me very much. Already I knew that some of the cast felt I was illegitimately there, not being a properly registered student. Also, I suspected that May Carey only gave me the part because fourteen years earlier she had complained to her landlord in Wilton Place about the "very noisy small children" continually jumping about in the flat upstairs. The children were myself and my sisters; the landlord gave my mother her notice to quit; May Carey at the audition remembered my name and asked me if it had indeed been my family...

Trinity, at that time, had quite a few young people like me wandering around, with no money for the fees or for books. When we felt a bit hungry we would partake of the ample hospitality given out by the various student societies that might be organising a spread of tea and cakes. The History Society was the most hospitable.

[*I later met May Carey's son Denis at the Glasgow Citizens' Theatre, where he was directing the first production of J.A.'s play,* Armstrong's Last Goodnight, *for Iain Cuthbertson -- a story of desperate attempts to get rid of a turbulent family... The magazine that attacked me was the one sued for libel by John Gibbon and Michael Frier, as already described.*]

* * * * * *

I left out a few things from the above note, which I thought at the time of writing might be better forgotten: they were no more than what many adolescents get up to, drunken student parties and the subsequent casually promiscuous behaviour with men whom I don't even remember - all part and parcel of breaking away from the discipline of the convent combined with the fact that we had a flat of our own without parental supervision, which was quite rare in those days. Parties were the chief entertainment for students: the fashion was to find out where a party might be and then to crash it. I don't think there has been much change over the years, except that nowadays there are discos. In those days there used to be "hops" - I never went to them because I didn't have the money, and I didn't have a boy-friend to take me. There was always somebody's pad afterwards to continue the party. Crashing a party of course meant freedom to behave badly, for no-one knew who you were. I remember one party in the college itself; a group of us outsiders for some reason decided to have a bit of a class-war on the unfortunate student-host who was trying to clear us out of his rooms; we threw all his suits into a bath full of water. There was perhaps a lot of hidden anger and resentment but no actual physical violence that I can remember. Working permanently at the 37 steadied me somewhat; it gave me a focus. But the crashing of parties still carried on.

Aisling had continued its run until May. The tourist season was beginning, and what a difference was the play that came next: *George and Margaret,* a successful West End comedy of a few years earlier, the quintessence of the social snobbery of the English middle classes - I played the maid who goes off to marry the boss's son and leaves his mother servantless just before the posh friends are arriving for lunch.

There were a few of us at 37 who used to enjoy a bit of craic together. Edie Howard, for one: her mother kept students and one of them was an Egyptian, a medical student with whom Edie was having a quite heavy scene. At one time she thought she was pregnant, but it ended happily; the last we heard from her was a postcard from Egypt, she was on her honeymoon and sailing up the Nile with her newly-qualified doctor. Then there was Gilbert McIntyre, about the same age as me, an American who lived with his sister in Dublin. I was amused to read in Carolyn Swift's book *Stage by Stage* that he grew up into a very good-looking young man playing romantic roles at the Pike and even having a short fling with Carolyn; but when I knew him he had that raw uncomfortable look typical of spotty male virgins.

I can't remember which of them it was who told me about a Hallowe'en party being held in the flat of George Morrison, the film-maker who was to direct the celebrated national historical documentaries, *Mise Éire* and *Saoirse.* It might have been Cecil D'Arcy; she certainly egged us on to go to it, and Gilbert and I decided we would. Then he cried off and I went by myself, cheered on by the indomitable Cecil who behaved like a surrogate mother. This was not a student party, but a motley collection of artists, homosexuals and free spirits. I remember my entry, like a frozen frame from a movie. There was an open basement door blocked by Brendan Behan with an enormous red swollen face, a broken nose, broken teeth and thick body. His hand was outstretched ready to grope the newcomers; he attempted at once to put it under my skirt. I avoided him skilfully and got into the room. It was crowded, mostly with men. Dickie Wyeman, a tall, very camp, ageless Englishman, who had once run a notorious establishment in Fitzwilliam Street called the Catacombs, was standing by the fireplace, glass in hand, swaying precariously and singing -

Oh dear what can the matter be?
Three old ladies locked in the lavatory
There they were from Monday to Saturday -- *(etc.)*

Carolyn Swift was sitting on the lap of Dominic Behan like a naughty schoolgirl determined to have a wicked time. An exhausted inertia pervaded, now broken by the entrance of someone new - as I was female, there was a surge of men, some bearded, some not, who moved forward trying to grab me. I noticed a quieter young man who looked like a portrait by El Greco. I took his hand

Aidan and I never spoke about the painful *reality* of living. He was fascinated by relationships, however, which we would see in a thoroughly objective light, without in any way judging them. He was working on his first novel, *Langrishe Go Down,* lengthily and obsessively polishing every sentence in turn, as well as keeping a notebook for phrases he would hear or read. (He did have some encouragement from John Calder, who later became his publisher.) He introduced me to the work of Djuna Barnes and Sam Beckett. He was one of the few Beckett devotees of the time; he reckoned that only about five people in Ireland or Britain knew about Beckett and had read him.

> Beckett [in the 1940s] was the invisible writer, the Greta Garbo of modern literature. None of his work was in print, such was the intellectual isolation of our state at that time, something which had helped to drive Beckett out of the country.
> John Montague (*A Chosen Life,* 2001)

The Beckett myth was not only the idea of what Montague elsewhere calls the "aloof hermit", but it also included the readers of Beckett. Because they were small in numbers, almost a cult, they were endowed with magical qualities. An example: a Beckett devotee is walking down a road in London at midnight. A woman in a fur coat leaves her house, poring over an open copy of *Murphy.* The devotee approaches her, and says, "What, you too!" She takes him by the hand and brings him into a waiting taxi. Under the fur coat she is naked; they make uninhibited love. Aidan told me this story, and he gave me *Murphy* to read. Not until my pronouncements on the novel matched his own, did he feel me worthy of his continued company. He was very close to John Beckett, (who in turn was close to his cousin Sam Beckett in Paris, and in correspondence with him) and to Vera Slocum who lived with John and looked after him, and had some sort of small income. John Beckett was a serious musician and composer and something of a guru. I was familiar with his name because of his writings in *The Bell.*

> It is an obligation of the performer to present to his listeners that music which is to him significant; performers in this country, as elsewhere, must introduce, sometimes with diffidence, but always with consistency, significant new and unfamiliar works to their public.
> John Beckett (music review, in *The Bell,* June 1951)

In addition to my great love for the sculptor, I was having a kind of dalliance with a painter and musician called Michael Morrow; he was a haemophiliac, with a slight limp, and he had to go into hospital at intervals for blood transfusions. I used to visit him in Sandymount, where he lived with his mother and his sister Bridget. Bridget was at Alex when I was there. Brother and sister played recorders in an Early Renaissance music group set up by John Beckett. This connection led me to John Beckett's concerts.

Vera Slocum was a tiny bumble-bee with what was known as a Chelsea drawl - extraordinary distortions of vowels - she had a cutting wit to slay anyone who caught her eye unfavourably. Her public behaviour was for shock and sensational effect; she had been married to a Scottish painter called Slocum; there was a tale of her filling the Earl of Wicklow's belly-button with jam and licking it off; she was also said to have arrived at a party given by Ralph Cusack in a huge sweater and nothing else. This seems to be a spin-off from the Beckett-reader myth; I do not know which version came first. More commonly Vera dressed herself in a very tight short leopard-skin skirt; her hair was cut in a bob after the style of Louise Brooks in Pabst's *Pandora's Box.* Whenever she appeared at a party she would sit curled up like a dangerous kitten on the portly lap of John Beckett.

She could be very spiteful and at times would turn on Aidan with her whiplash tongue, accusing him of leeching off them just for a meal ticket. Aidan would retreat for a couple of days until the storm blew over and then return as if no words had ever sparked between them. Vera did like making her presence felt in quite an offensive way, especially when she had a few drinks inside her. I remember a party where there were a couple of African medical students wearing their own national dress. Vera came up to them spitting and screaming that their get-up was pretentious, and why, when they were in Ireland, did they have to dress like that? After having thoroughly embarrassed them and everybody else, she invited them to lunch the next day. She was erratic and unpredictable, but essentially good-hearted. As for her own work as a painter, that was well hidden from the world and all her energies appeared to be expended upon John.

Because he had not been to either of the two universities in Dublin and was therefore not part of the network, Aidan had to work bloody hard to insinuate himself into literary circles, where Anthony Cronin and Patrick Kavanagh held sway. One little experience of meeting those two, to illustrate the position of young women… I was walking down Grafton Street and was waylaid by the up-and-coming poet John Montague, a friend of Aidan's. He had been one of the group of writers associated with *The Bell.* I admired him, because he was less insular than some of the others, having been born in America. I was on my way to the theatre for a dress rehearsal of *George and Margaret* and I was wearing a genteel little straw hat that was to be part of my servant-girl costume in the play. It was so incongruous, taken with whatever else I had on, a long skirt, my rabbit-skin waistcoat, my Japanese clackers, that he invited me for a drink in McDaid's. Kavanagh and Cronin were there. The three men at once engaged in conversation. I was supposed to just sit there like an ornament and be silent. I felt so uncomfortable and silly, with the stage-play hat on, that I left.

~~~o~~~

Gods and Goddesses.

Young people, devotees of art, afflicted by poverty, find that their imaginations create exotic immortals out of artists whose work they admire, artists fit to be worshipped as they walk through the streets with their consorts. It is not only that they look exotic, but we know from their pictures in the exhibitions that their minds are exotic. There is a parallel with the visions of the Virgin seen by poor peasants, usually girls, in such places as Lourdes, Fatima and Knock, where the Blessed Mother (God's intermediary) passes them the doomsday message of how she weeps for the state of the world.

One such godlike couple in Dublin at that time was Neville Johnson and Pam Scott. He was an Englishman, extremely striking, tall, with a great shock of hair. He had drifted down from Belfast with other painters to take advantage of Victor Waddington's patronage. He subsidized himself by taking in a few private pupils; one of them was Anne Yeats, daughter of the poet. He was always to be seen in proverbial artist's garb, big Aran sweater, grey corduroy trousers with a wide leather belt and sandals on his bare feet. Pam acted at the 37 and was in the cast of *Aisling.* She had had a short marriage and was now separated. She wore flowing clothes with a 22-inch waist and
~~~

chestnut-brown curly hair; she looked like the allegorical portrait of Lady Lavery as "Éire" on the banknotes. When she and Neville walked down the street hand-in-hand and proudly erect, with an Irish wolfhound on a lead, I always felt the crowds should have cheered and the traffic should have stopped in homage and wonderment. For some reason or other, Pam took a fancy to me, and invited me to visit Neville at the mews-studio where they lived together. This studio was a sparse and simple loft with an oil-stove in the middle, clean and bright, beautiful stones and flowers and bones on shelves which Pam had collected. They were working on a book of photos of old Dublin. Pam produced me as a trophy to entertain him; she was like a humble servant in a temple, placating the god. I had first seen Neville when he came to Alex to give us a lecture about art. He had opened my eyes to painting and I had immediately gone to the National Gallery in Merrion Square to look at the works he recommended; also to the Victor Waddington Gallery for his one-man exhibition, which everyone was talking about. His paintings were like his studio, very sparse with a slight surrealist feeling, which was the northern Irish style at that time, seen also in the work of Dan O'Neill and Colin Middleton.

Pam's relationship with him was coming to an end; she was desperately trying to hold onto him; she was distraught. She used to have me there as a kind of buffer whilst she harangued him on his indifference to her; it was my role as a young woman to be the confidante of the usurped older woman. (Pam would have been in her late twenties but she looked about seventeen.) She would go on and on about all the help she had given him, all the services she had afforded him; she was convinced he was going off to a wealthier woman, an artist with money, who (she said) was as ugly as sin. All this raging began to enter into my mind. She was able with some success to insinuate that my relationship with my sculptor was the same as hers with Neville. Which it wasn't: it was free and non-committal. When I wanted to see the sculptor, I went to see him, at home or in his studio, or he would come to me at the theatre. Some afternoons I would sit on his studio-floor, while he chipped away at his work, and then we would make love amid his sweetly-smelling wood-shavings. He never turned me away and I never turned him away.

Contraception? It never entered my head, nor did I worry about getting pregnant. In fact I knew nothing about contraception; and even if I had known, there was nothing I could do about it because it was banned in Ireland. Responsible young men (such as my lover) practised Coitus Interruptus.

Pam's constant denigrating remarks did a lot of damage to us: I think in her hurt and fury she wanted to destroy anyone's relationship that seemed to her to have the naive starry-eyed quality that used to be there between Neville and herself. The end of the Neville-and-Pam love story was dreadful: years later he wrote his autobiography and cruelly dismissed her as his anonymous "landlady's daughter".

Another god-and-goddess pair had an equally cruel ending. The painter Patrick Swift lived with the American poet Claire McAllister, known as "Marmalade." He was tall and thin and wore black. She was also tall, tawny-haired, with tawny-coloured clothes. I first saw them in a box, with others, at the Gaiety Theatre, drinking champagne; he was sitting on the edge of the box with his leg casually dangling; he had one eye on the stage and the other on his friends in the box, a scene straight out of Du Maurier's *Trilby.* He had immortalised her in a famous exhibition which he shared with Lucien Freud. He filled the gallery with pictures of Marmalade together with a marmalade cat. Shortly afterwards, he left for London, to set up the magazine *X,* with the poet David Wright. He then a started a relationship with a woman much richer than Claire. I remember in 1963 visiting her in her basement-flat in Dublin; the painter Paddy Collins was there, and she spent the whole evening mourning Patrick Swift, and hauling painting after painting of his from under the bed. In the end she was able to pull her life together: she married a lord.

> In the cloak of the sheets we hide and seek safety in dreaming
> While morning pours a cold flame through the curtain.
> We try for a time to forget we've no answer to morning,
> In silk light dressed to pose her question.
> [from "Pantoum for Morning" by Claire McAllister, in *Envoy* (September 1950)]

A small but melancholy vignette to conclude these Dublin poignancies. One summer in the late 1970s, in a top-floor flat in Muswell Hill, I heard Aidan Higgins's ex-wife Jill and John Beckett's ex-companion Vera as they sat and drank wine and excoriated their *ex-men,* telling me of the years of devotion they had wasted upon them; as soon as John and Aidan found "something better", they obliterated the women from their lives and went off. In Aidan's case, he left a most malicious record of the marriage in print (admittedly, with Jill's name disguised).

~~~o~~~

One of the few areas of Dublin cultural life to offer any sort of exciting glimpse of the future was the annual Living Art exhibition.

> The more or less enforced isolation of the war years ... demonstrated even more strongly than involvement [in the war] that we were part of modern Europe, and not, as some would pretend, an exotic and miraculous survival from a Celtic Middle Ages. At any rate, the result was that Ireland, for the first time in her history, developed a body of painters comparable to their contemporaries in Europe and America.
> Edward Sheehy (article, "Recent Irish Painting", in *Envoy*, September 1950)

Living Art had been set up in the early forties by Evie Hone, Nano Reid, Louis le Broquy and Hilary Heron, to provide an alternative to the RHA (Royal Hibernian Academy.) The emphasis was modern and experimental; it gave young painters and sculptors a rare chance to show their work in a collective context. That summer I went to the opening of the exhibition with Colette; we had been invited either by Michael Morrow or Pam Scott. Everyone was a-buzz with the news of the surprise winner of the Unknown Political Prisoner sculpture competition, which had caused such expense of creative energy throughout the year. I remember that Irene Broe had just flown in from London, where she had attended the award ceremony as one of the competition entrants. She was practically in tears of rage that a complete outsider, an architect, not a sculptor, had won the first award. There was some consolation that William Trevor was a runner-up - at least he lived in Ireland. (He later became better known as a writer of short stories.) Delia Murphy, the singer, was there; she was the wife of the Irish ambassador to Australia, and in Dublin on a short visit; she entertained us with traditional Irish airs, including her favourite, the Spinning Song, accompanied by a harpist.

It was while I was listening to her that I found myself standing beside Alan Simpson. I knew that he and his wife Carolyn Swift were thinking of setting up their own theatre, the Pike, in a coach-house; it would be small but fully-
~~~

equipped, a *real* theatre in contrast to a room with a stage at one end like the 37. I had already seen their production of Carolyn's play *The Millstone* in the town hall at Dun Laoghaire. He invited me to look at the space he had acquired, and I went with him. He showed me the skeleton of what was to be the auditorium and he suggested that I might care to join the company when the building was finished. We then drove round in his car looking for a pub which was supposed to have an after-hours licence. We couldn't find it; and we landed up in yet another basement flat at the fag end of somebody's party. There was a young actress there whom I knew slightly, she was a drop-out UCD student and a single mother, well on her way to becoming an alcoholic. The sickly smell of recent sex pervaded the small flat. She was lolling in a half-drunken state on a man's knee, a casual pick-up. Alan made a pass at me to try and be part of the scene; I slapped his face; he took my rebuttal quite well; and we then went on to another party, the pre-nuptial celebration of Jo-Jo O'Reilly, a wealthy young luscious widow, an artist of some sort who held open house for the free spirits of Dublin. Her husband-to-be was about twenty; she was coyly squirming on the sofa, hinting that she couldn't wait for the wedding night. He was busy playing with a train set she had given him as a wedding present.

Was this to be my life? I felt a sudden surge of self-disgust. I did not want to join the Pike on these terms, inane parties one after another, being picked up by any man who wanted a night's entertainment, having as usual arrived late, after the theatre, when the first party flush had ebbed away and the atmosphere was sinking into a demoralised puddle.

~~~o~~~

It was at one such gathering that I finally flipped. Yet again in a dilapidated bottom-storey flat, in Martello Terrace in Bray, dark and crowded. I had invited Aidan to accompany me. My sculptor was there, overcome with gloom, having just come back from a funeral. Death hung in the air. Vida Lestrange, a young German musician, one of Pam Scott's lovesick swains, was playing the piano by candlelight, Chopin at his most melancholy. The flame of the candle hypnotised me. I wanted to enter it and be consumed by its energy. I leaned forward and put my bare arm right into it. Here was a bit of drama to liven up a party! - mind you, I didn't do it for that reason - in my emotional state I had
~~~

quite forgotten I was actually *at* a party. Everyone was screaming and grasping at me. Some drunken medical students decided they knew how to handle me, and were accepted by my friends as experts. These youths dragged me out and began slapping me across the face. And then it changed to something else - no longer just a matter of getting a woman out of hysterics but the boozy excitement of beating a woman up. I tried to run away from them, out of the house along the seaside terrace. They chased after me, still beating me. In the end, half conscious, I was brought back inside by a few of the older women.

> Fated as she is to be the passive prey of man, the girl asserts her right to liberty even to the extent of undergoing pain and disgust.
> Simone de Beauvoir (*The Second Sex*)

Such was the episode that caused my departure from Ireland. A young woman burnt, badly knocked about in the dark, and attempting to throw herself into the sea, while nobody at the party was quite sure of what went on. I was taken to hospital for the burns. People all over Dublin began to talk. It was scandalous... Blame the woman, remove the woman.

PART TWO

7

HORNCHURCH

I went out of Ireland to London and worked for eighteen months in a fortnightly repertory company, at Hornchurch in Essex.

I got the job from an ad in *The Stage*: they wanted a student. I went to be interviewed by the Artistic Director, Stuart Burge, at his house at Maida Vale. He told me I would be temporary Assistant Stage Manager (in a few months to become full-time) and would be playing parts now and then. If satisfactory, I would be made the official ASM. Being ignorant of the structures of the English Theatre, I did not realize what good fortune had come my way. I lived in my mother's Pimlico flat and earned £1 a week. My mother was relieved that I was off her hands; I was a problem, hanging around the place, while she had her full-time work as a junior doctor at the Coulsdon mental hospital. She paid for my monthly tube-ticket, which meant I had free access to travel on any tube-line. The £1 was left to me to spend it as I wished.

If my young American critic at Shannon [see Chapter 1] meant that I lacked political education or an understanding of how the social fabrics of life are held together within an unjust society, I am forced to agree with her that in my younger days that was certainly the case. My idealism was such that I really believed that the theatre's power to open and extend the imagination would somehow make a concrete change in society, that this could be achieved through the audience's reflection upon the issues raised in a stage-play and through the catharsis arising from the shock-effects of certain dramatic situations. But the theatre as I was now experiencing it could never have this effect because it seemed to be a total mirror of the worst aspects of the contemporary status quo. Its structure and the prevalent attitudes of many of its practitioners affirmed a dreary life of getting a house, settling down, obeying a respectable dress-code, accepting an internal hierarchy in which the height of anyone's ambition was to become a West End star working (within a halo of false glamour) for one or other of the very few established managements. Of course many of us resisted this: we were not sympathetic to the stereotypes of casting, the leading men and ladies, the ingénues, the character-roles, and so forth; we hated the standard artificiality of the West End accent, the conveyor-belt training in RADA, the suppression of working-class or "regional" actors (unless they lost their characteristics and homogenised themselves into the general home-counties miasma), the overall control exerted by a very few businessmen, the backers.

All this affected the way that we approached our roles. At Hornchurch there were idealistic actors who had trained at the Young Vic under Michel St. Denis and George Devine and who were trying to make theatre a meaningful experience. There was also the Old Guard who loved the West End and its glamour, the gossip, the parties. the social scenes -- in short, the fag-end of the Henry Irving tradition, the ceaseless attempt to accommodate theatre within the value-system of the suburban middle classes, the last years of Empire, the unspoken assertion that only the British knew how to behave.

A few examples of my struggle with them. Playful derision. As I was Irish and Ireland is full of bogs, I was naturally called Bogs. Being the most junior member of the company I accepted this badinage; but then there was the question of my dress and appearance, which brought about more personal incursions into my life, such as the leading lady feeling compelled to bring me shopping for a corset. A pink blouse was bought for my birthday and I had to display it while wearing the corset. Now they tried to get me to understand the rules of the theatre: if I wanted to get on I must play any small part as an ingénue, which was how young actresses were typed. Later on, comic or tragic *character* parts were given to those who were not classed as leading ladies or men. Timing was the all-important skill. When you see old J. Arthur Rank movies, you can see how the stock acting techniques were all fitted together. The various stereotypes were slotted into the story ready-made, whether the script seemed to suit them or not. Leading roles in particular were tacitly reshaped to accommodate themselves to the narrowly conventional style of the standard leading players. At the end of the season we did have a sort of safety valve: the last night of the panto, when we traditionally had freedom to improvise how we liked.

Stuart was himself from the Young Vic School; like the captain of a river-steamer dodging rocks and shallows, he had to navigate all the time between the expectations of the old guard and the aspirations of the new. He was not burdened with private backers; Hornchurch was a pioneer venture, a theatre subsidised by the local authority, but the local authority consisted largely of businessmen who did not look for anything too radical. He was however able to bring in some artists who were magnificently radical in their approach to theatre, Joan Plowright, for instance, and Christopher Burgess.

Some of the actors gave me encouragement in my small attempts at subversion. I played the concierge in *Private Lives* and a Welsh rural mother in an Emlyn Williams play in ways far removed from what was expected from an ingénue. I had had my first holiday abroad to Paris and had been struck by the power and arrogance of the Parisian concierge, a class which seemed to have embodied the very spirit of the French Revolution, of the tricoteuses who sat every day knitting in front of the guillotine, roaring for more heads. I had seen the concierges shuffling in well-worn filthy slippers, their clothes covered in cat hairs, the permanent fag-end stuck onto their lips; and that is how I dressed and moved for the part. This quite cut across the views of a section of actors who felt that Noel Coward's stylised comedy did not have room for coarse realism; a concierge should have been neat, tidy and clean like a receptionist in an English seaside hotel. Decorum and propriety. As for the Emlyn Williams character, I had observed that certain elderly women from the country districts were completely unaware that when they made their ample forms comfortable on a sofa they hitched their dresses up, and revealed their elasticated flannel knickers, pink and voluminous. Once again, a clash between realism and the conventional aesthetic of the English stage. Offended deputations came to Stuart, demanding that he should order me to change my interpretations; to his credit, he did nothing and let us fight it out. My refusal to comply meant that I was *not one of them*. The gravest incidents were when I would not join in the cast's singing of the National Anthem at the end of the Christmas pantomime and when, as Desdemona's lady-in-waiting in *Othello,* I decided to play her as a black woman.

I was of course a member of Equity: the theatre was a closed shop, you couldn't work without joining the union, which laid down standard wages. But I never went to any meetings or considered any other particular advantage the union might have had for me.

The theatre was still by and large governed by the traditional 19th-Century principle of dependence on private investors. But we theatre people were taught to perceive ourselves as our own community, not quite autonomous but decidedly semi-detached in relation to the main stream of society. Political parties had no influence on us as a community; the only one that had ever tried to make use of the theatre and to value it as a political entity was the Communist Party with its radical input here and there, Unity Theatre, youth groups in cities like Manchester and so on. Apart from that our function seemed to be to provide a yardstick of style for those middle classes which did not really aspire to the upper classes but delighted to view their foibles, the luxury of their homes, clubs and hotels, their servants (a play of smart modern life was not a proper play unless there was a butler in it), their fashions, hairstyles, restaurants. The theatre had its own aristocracy, the Oliviers, for example, and the powerful West End managements. We continued (in theory) to disdain the cinema, while TV was beyond the pale.

Ladies still wore hats to matinées: an item of West End smartness which was aped throughout the provinces. London, as ever, was the centre of everything. But change was in the air, a restlessness, a subterranean sense that our theatre-community really ought to be aware that World War 2 had taken place, Clement Attlee's Labour Government had taken place and maybe the stage should reflect these facts. Nonetheless, there were terrible pockets of reaction in society as a whole, which certainly affected the theatre. Homosexuals were still criminalized. John Gielgud was arrested in a public toilet; Lord Montagu and Peter Wildeblood were imprisoned for activities in a private house. The tension caused by this persecution was a regular undercurrent at Hornchurch. Christopher Burgess and David Dodimead, two gay actors in the company, were always extremely supportive of me and my little excursions into being different. The fact that I *was* different, apparently asexual (at least, I was neither glamorous nor overtly flirtatious) and a bit of a freak, appealed to them. Their lives were necessarily hidden and homosexuality was not talked about in public. Insiders knew all about it, of course, they understood the inner stories, the subversive undertones, of *The Deep Blue Sea* and *The Boy Friend*. As for race: Stuart did put on *Deep Are The Roots*, with a black actor in the lead. I don't remember any prejudice against him; but there was one nasty incident, when I was out with a group of colleagues one Sunday; a new club was opening, run by a former actress, and we had all been invited to come along and join. One of the actors (he was gay) brought a West Indian lover, who was turned away at the door. So we all walked away.

~~~o~~~

The rhythm of life for an ASM in a repertory company.
For certain plays visiting actors would be brought in. On the Saturday night at the end of the run the set would have to be struck and the new set put up to be ready by Sunday afternoon for the walk-through. If I had a part I would not have to stay up all night. I enjoyed these all-night sessions. Otherwise, we never had anything to do with the Scene Designer (a woman, as were the Electrician and the Stage Manager). On Sunday we would be sewing the curtains to fit the set. Our next job was to go looking for props all round the town, begging and borrowing. For costume plays we had to go into the West End collecting wigs from Berman's or going to Neal's for the guns. A totally self-contained world. We always went in and out of the theatre by the stage door; we never had anything to do with the audience or with our sponsors, Hornchurch Corporation. A café across the road adopted the company and did good business with sandwiches between the Saturday matinée and the evening performance. Actors are fickle, however; for some reason something happened and we all flocked somewhere else.

My routine: I left the the house at around 8am, to arrive at the theatre before 10. After the show I would get home at about 11pm. We had every other Sunday off. When a production ended and the weekend was devoted to erecting the new set, there would be a dress rehearsal on the Monday and the opening performance that night. I enjoyed this weekend work; but what it must have been like in weekly rep I can scarcely imagine. Only one or two of the big regional theatres, such as the Birmingham Rep and the Liverpool Rep, would have had similar conditions to ours. Hornchurch was considered a prestigious rep; and there was no shortage of good actors to come in from time to time.
~~~

Stuart himself was easygoing with a puckish sense of humour; he chose a carefully-balanced mix of plays -- a couple of Shakespeares, popular farces, middle-range plays newly released from the West End like *The Deep Blue Sea,* occasional starry plays (*The Lady's Not For Burning, Ring Round the Moon*). I do not know what the politics were behind the scenes of the Council, how much subsidy they allotted the theatre, or whether it made a profit. At the end of each year we had a panto which ran longer than the two weeks.

My job was varied. If I didn't have a part I would either be on the book, making sure the moves were carried out correctly in accordance with the Stage Manager's notes made at the first rehearsal; or I would be assembling the props and costume accessories. The Stage Manager was a young woman who was engaged to be married; after the wedding she was going to go to Nigeria with her husband (who was not in the theatre). The Stage Director was a young man, newly married and his wife was pregnant. She was an actress; after the birth of the baby she was sometimes called in to play a part. The Electrician was a woman; she had complete command of the lights, with a private perch on top of the lighting booth where she would ask favoured members of the cast to visit her. She was an ardent catholic and recruited proselytes by the allure of their privileged access to her lair.

I had no particular career ambitions; I just took each part as it came along and immersed myself completely in the work. Hornchurch is very close to London, and with a station on the tube, which meant that the actors continued to live in London. Only the Stage Director, the Front of House Manager and the Scenic Designer made their homes in Hornchurch. It was the first theatre in England to be subsidized by the local council, and it was also a new building. We opened the first season with a farce, *See How They Run*, famous for the number of clergymen in it and the rapidity with which they dropped their trousers.

The steady rhythm of the company was occasionally broken by the incursions of visiting actors, bringing their own particular skills, Leslie Phillips, for example, the master of farce: I had a small part as a nurse who comes in to make an announcement. I knew nothing about the art of milking laughs. But he got me a good laugh by the simple trick of casting a glance at my retreating back. He very generously explained to me how the laugh was obtained. It depended upon my first having paused slightly before my exit; and then everyone in the audience thought what a clever actress I was... I would watch in fascination during the farces: the exacting techniques of entrances, exits, double-takes and so forth, and listen to the older actors passing on these techniques to the younger ones. Our middle-of-the-road life was broken when Stuart announced that there would be two starlets joining us: a taste of the wider world of glamour. I think he had made a deal with a film company. Our young hetero male lead was very excited playing opposite one of these real film-girls. But after he had enjoyed an intimacy with her, he was not so complimentary; he told us all that her underwear was filthy. This sort of malice was very much a part of backstage gossip; as for example, the kudos obtained by one of the gay actors when he claimed to have slept with John Gielgud. He was very ungrateful; he not only bragged about it afterwards but told everybody that Gielgud's breath smelt. The other starlet eventually married a duke. They were both protegées of Stephen Ward, the osteopath who became notorious in the Profumo scandal. The future duchess was rather bossy: I remember her accosting the sluttish one with an abrupt, "Stephen wants us at his party tonight!"

I was keen to hear more of these hints of the "other life" in London clubs and the smart parties, and as an ASM I had access to the dressing rooms. I have always been a terrible snooper; I could not resist the temptation of letters left on the dressing tables... There was a West End actress in the company for a while, a deeply unhappy woman in a troubled marriage; she was having a passionate affair with one of the actors. His poetical letters to her did not somehow smooth her unhappiness away. One morning there was a bit of excitement: she had got home unacceptably late the night before, her husband had locked the door against her and turned her out... One young guest actress turned up with a aura of mystery around her, implications that she was having an affair with a very important actor -- Laurence Olivier, we all assumed... Guest actors were pleased to be at Hornchurch, gaining an opportunity to play leading roles, to be consequently noticed for it, and then maybe going on to the Stratford-on-Avon Festival.

I brought my own little ripples into the smooth flow of events, when an Irish gang descended on me. Michael Morrow, Aidan Higgins, David Reagan (who had bankrupted himself with a magazine in Dublin). The company were delighted to meet such people: a type they would not normally run into. Aidan and David were working night-shifts at Ford's of Dagenham: on their way there they would call into the café and mingle with us before the evening show. One of the gay actors fell in love with Aidan, while David fell in love with the young girls of the ballet troupe brought in for the panto. The leading lady of the current production laughed so much at one of Aidan's jokes that she fell out of her chair and toppled all over him.

Stuart liked a few bizarre Irish people about the place. At my request he gave Michael a job, to help paint the set and to play the lute in *Othello*. Michael had no accommodation, so he slept in Desdemona's bed on the stage but had to flee to protect his chastity from the overtures of the bisexual front-of-house manager.

It was easy for Stuart to get actors, and recalling the list of them I realise how many have since become household names. Wilfred Bramble, who was to star in *Steptoe & Son* on TV, a gentle chatty soul. Bernard Cribbens, who came in for one of the pantos, did a lot of film and TV work (*The Railway Children*) and played Sancho Panza in J.A.'s radio version of *Don Quixote*. Joan Plowright, who became Lady Olivier. Prunella Scales of *Fawlty Towers:* the extraordinary nervous energy that emanated from her before she made her entrance was the same sort of wound-up tension that an athlete would contain before springing off for a race. Michael Gough, Leslie Phillips, Marion Mathie (Rumpole's wife on TV, and also in J.A.'s *The Workhouse Donkey*). Lee Montague; Brewster Mason; Gwen Watford, a very private woman, played the wife in *The Deep Blue Sea.* Alfie Burke. None of them stars in those days, but the backbone of the mainstream theatre. Charles Rea. David Dodimead who went on to Stratford-on-Avon. He invited me to meet Katherine Hepburn when he and she were playing in *The Millionaress* in London, a bit embarrassing, she was strangely over-the-top, practically curtseying to show her delight at meeting me, and being extremely shy -- which might have been deliberate, a demonstration of empathy with my own shyness. Tom Chatto, married to Robert Morley's stage manager: he was an overgrown school-boy, but a bit of a softy; he was inclined to be a bit of a bully: he was the one who first called me "Bogs". One day, infuriated by him, I threw a custard pie into his face. Susan Pearson, who also wrote plays; for her first TV play (directed by Peter Potter) she kindly remembered me, and I got a part in it. Jill Melford, daughter of Jock Melford, tall with red hair, long red-painted nails; she introduced poker into the dressing room, saying as she shuffled the cards that she never lost a game. No-one ever bragged about their previous work or their future opportunities. Really it was all pretty civilized; actors on the whole are very private, and when they are at work they shed themselves of anything that would distract them *from* work.

Christopher Burgess: Christopher was different, with a great awareness of literature. My life would have been very lonely but for him; he lived in a flat in Charlotte Street and he used to invite me to visit him there, which made me feel I was really in the heart of things.

~~~o~~~

For my holidays I went to the west of Ireland again, having some embarrassing sexual adventures, and then to Paris. When I came back from Ireland, I met Tony White, a friend of Christopher's -- I enthused non-stop to him about the beauty of the West. I don't know whether it was his first introduction to Ireland; but I like to think that it was perhaps my going on and on that induced him to set up home near Oughterard in County Galway, where he founded a Wildlife Sanctuary for birds.

Christopher encouraged me not to let myself become part of the crowd and not to feel that Hornchurch was the only theatrical world. There were alternatives. Hornchurch was a job; we should simply get on with it.

I suppose I was like many young people, full of confused emotions, and a jumble of aspirations about art, music and poetry, that urgently needed to be clarified. Dublin had been a trauma; but I had been mingling there in some kind of artistic community, I had been aware of a pushing at the boundaries, a continuous struggle against the repressive state of affairs in Ireland. But in England, where was the repression? where was the artistic community? the wildness, madness and disorder, the passion and genius which I yearned for? I fell under the influence of Lorca. His work was made known to me by the stage director, who invited me to his home for breakfast one weekend after the striking of the decor. Haddock with a poached egg on top, and his enthusiasm for the Spanish poet enthused me in turn. Aidan Higgins had already introduced me to Beckett's *Murphy* and Canetti's *Auto-De-Fé*. There was another life out
~~~

there, bubbling away beneath the surface, and that was where I wanted to go. I wanted to live the rakish life, I wanted to live on the edge. If one couldn't live that way, one was dead, I felt sure of it. So I indulged in a curious kind of fatalistic passivity, just letting things slide.

I think Christopher was the only one to realise that I didn't have enough money to eat. At night, on my return to my mother's flat, I would devour great chunks of bread and butter and cook myself chips and omelettes. He would take me out between the matinée and evening performance to a rather genteel cafe and order mushrooms on toast. He introduced me to Toynbee Hall, a stronghold of the Communist Party, where I saw all those old Soviet films about collectivization of farms, problems of urban housing and so forth. He also brought me to the Phoenix Theatre Club, where they had Sunday night productions put together by actors out of work. One of these Sunday nights was *The Changeling* by Middleton and Rowley, a play of huge passion, a woman driven mad by the murder she has conceived and the treacherous betrayal of her trust. This was the sort of theatre I was looking for. It must have been the first time for years that the play had been put on. The bulk of Jacobean drama was considered crude compared to Shakespeare, over-the-top, absurd; but the night I saw *The Changeling* I picked up a definite excitement among the audience, a feeling that a gauntlet was being thrown down to the Establishment. (*The Changeling,* I believe, must have deeply affected me after I left Hornchurch. It was the first time I'd seen a play with a woman absolutely in the central role, posing a huge question of morality and principle. As I roamed around Soho, confronted by all sorts of perilous choices, I subconsciously was living out the ordeal of Middleton's heroine and striving to avoid the trap she fell into, manipulation by others and the loss of her own integrity.)

Sometimes, on my days off, I might see a matinée by Joan Littlewood's Theatre Workshop company at Stratford (East). She was very much the icon of the new guard in those years, her artistic standards impregnably based upon the reality of real people. A curious thing about my time at Hornchurch: I don't remember the audience at all. It was as though all our acting techniques served simply to press a series of buttons marked "audience response"; but from the audience as a body of individual people we were as remote as the maker of a car is from its driver. There was a great difference at Stratford East: Joan would always be there in the bar greeting her public, and kindling a warmth and sense of comradeship between actors and audience. When I left Hornchurch I went for an audition with her and was rejected. I think the fact that I had previously chosen Hornchurch instead of seeking her out for my first job in London must have been a factor. I was seen as the one of the enemy.

It was the same with George Devine's theatre at the Royal Court: she despised George and everything he stood for. Later on, when I was at the Court I began to understand why.

I had no consciousness of how actors lived when out of work; who paid the rent, for example? There was, in those years, a small amount of unemployment money available when a person "signed on". It was only when we were preparing one of the pantos and I got into conversation with a couple of women who were brought in to do the sewing that I began to have some inkling of the world of work and no work. One of them told me about her regular piece-work, she sewed at home and each separate item was paid for; it was therefore up to her how hard she worked, and she had to work hard because of her children, in fact she worked all round the clock.

Sunk into my passive inertia, I had in the end to be given a little push by Stuart, moving me out and on.

(Stuart was later to direct me in J.A.'s first TV play, *Soldier Soldier*; I was in another of his TV productions, *The Power and the Glory*, with Sam Wanamaker. Stuart also directed J.A.'s *The Workhouse Donkey* at Chichester, *Serjeant Musgrave's Dance* in New York, and the Granada TV version of *Musgrave*. Both of us owe him a great deal.)

8

UPS AND DOWNS: & J.A.

So I was accordingly out of work. Two things to do: try to find an agent, and sign on at a workshop to improve my skills.

My name was put down at a whole lot of tatty little agencies. Before visiting them, I would change into my one good pair of shoes and leave my wornout sandals in a brown paper bag with the playwright Bernard Kops and his wife Erica, who kept a little bookstall on the corner of a side street near Cambridge Circus. I would then go scurrying up and down warrens of cubbyhole offices in Charing Cross Road. The only work I got from any of them was a photo-shoot for a pin-up in (I think) the magazine *Reveille,* aimed at young soldiers; the photographer had me perched on my mother's coffee-table, dressed in a towel with a couple of golf balls between my thighs; I never saw the picture, but I was told it was displayed in the publisher's window in Fleet Street with the caption, "Margaretta loves ball-games." I was never paid for it and I was such an innocent as to be totally unaware of the double-entendre when he posed me.

There was nothing tatty about the dance-workshop I went to, Lotte Berk's in a side street off the Edgware Road. To my surprise, when I arrived there, I found John Beckett, who had left Dublin and now earned a crust playing the piano. Some of us knew already that his uncle Sam had given up writing novels and had turned to the theatre: word was getting out about the underground success of *Waiting for Godot* in Paris. John gave me a script of the play, translated from the French; he asked me my opinion of it and would it work in the English-language theatre? (This was presumably before Peter Hall bought it for his production at the Arts Theatre.) I am quite pleased in retrospect that my comments were spot on, for did I not tell John that it would surely work very well, being "a lively vaudeville-style piece, very theatrical, with short episodes and brisk dialogue"?

Later on, in 1955, I joined Valerie Hovenden's theatre club in her tiny theatre off St. Martin's Lane, which she had made out of the top floor of a warehouse and dedicated to forgotten classics. I was playing the lead in Garrick's comedy *The Seraglio* (the role he had written for Peg Woffington) when I first met J.A., a young architect just down from Edinburgh, hoping to make his fame and fortune in the London Theatre. He was there with a friend of mine - Tom Austin, an Irish architect - whom I had invited to see the show. There was a newspaper strike which had cut off all advertisements for the play, and they were the only two in the audience. The plot dealt with an Irish woman who had been captured and enslaved for the Sultan's harem. She won the heart of the Sultan and caused him to reform the court by abolishing the harem. (Historical query: was this the first play to equate Irish women with sexual emancipation?) I was a plump, feisty, gorgeous creature in emerald green Turkish trousers of diaphanous chiffon. The two gentlemen didn't seem at all put out that they were alone in the auditorium; and this shy dark-haired friend, wiry, thin, full of nervous energy with his bright brown eyes, said it was like being summoned to a private performance. They had had a few drinks before coming in and J.A. spoke with a strong Scottish accent. For a time I thought he was a romantic Scotsman. He offered me his new play, to read and give my comments. It seemed an auspicious sign of a fruitful relationship, and the play excited me hugely; it dealt with Arthurian legends and was eventually to be worked into our collaborative trilogy, *The Island of the Mighty*. The language and the rhythm and the genius leapt out. I should add that in those days, with no money around, young romantics were always looking for young, starving genius. The only problem with the play was that he had somehow left out the plot.

We didn't really meet again for another year.

Meanwhile, an actor told me there was a vacancy in a company playing in Wheathampstead near St. Albans; she had had to leave suddenly and I might be able to fill her place. When I arrived there, I found it was a touring fitup and I realized why she had left. It turned out that the company had no money. It was run by a determined middle-aged woman whose leading-man partner had abandoned her at a railway station as they were catching a train: he made sure she had got into the carriage in front of him and then he disappeared. We slept in the hall, which belonged to the Women's Institute, in wicker theatrical baskets. The only other member of the company was a 15-year old boy who had attached himself at the previous venue and tagged along. He slept on the stage wrapped in old curtains. We raided the WI food cupboard and she cooked potatoes, onions and tinned mince. Wheathampstead had become a middle-class home-counties suburb: presumably in the old days there would have been a rural population delighted to have had a touring company, but our only audience was a couple who owned a fish-and-chip café across the road. They had given us a free meal in return for complimentary tickets. There was no more than a skeleton of a script: the plot was conventional melodrama, a respectable woman confronted by her long-lost illegitimate son. This must have been the last old-style fitup in the south of England... She had a certain magnificent presence on the stage. I can't remember what part I played, but I suppose, because I was the only other member of the cast, my role was to reveal the lady's secret. When it was over, she turned to me in her rather Edith Evans style and said she was surprised: she hadn't realized what a sense of comedy I had. I actually enjoyed improvising the part. Fortunately, I had put aside money for my fare back to London. I felt like a rat deserting them: I lied and said I had been offered a part in Dublin.

Pam Scott, who was now in London, was working at Bertram Mills Circus, and told me how to get a Christmas job there; we were selling programmes along with half of the out-of-work actors in England. Ronald Fraser was one of them. It was very democratic; at the circus there was no special greenroom for the performers; we all mixed in together, really famous individuals like Coco the clown, high-wire and trapeze and all sorts of other artistes from all over the world. For the first time in my life I found myself roped into social agitation, when Pam Scott got me and others to go down amongst the animals, observe their conditions, and complain about their treatment and training. In the end, not surprisingly, access to the animals was forbidden us ... The Queen came one night for her annual visit. The only time she laughed was when the baby elephant fell off its mother's back and hurt itself ... I had got into a muddle with the National Insurance, was pursued by two officials, and in a panic burnt my stamp book. So I fled from the welfare state with the money I had saved from my wages at the circus, I hitched around Spain and immersed myself in Lorca.

I was no sooner back again, in London, in my mother's flat, when an unfortunate bit of mis-timing on my part got me thrown out and homeless: Mother returned one afternoon with her lover to find me in her bed with a Soho poet

I had picked up the previous night. I lived on and off the streets, dossing in people's flats until they were fed up with my penniless state and terminated the relationship. Fortunately, before things became too drastic, I found a job with a company taking a third-rate sensational melodrama through huge empty provincial theatres, a type of show that had all but disappeared from the live stage, already overtaken by TV. In those days there were no cheap soft-porn films but there was a trickle of companies touring would-be shocking sex plays with perfunctory social moralizing built into the script. This particular specimen was called *Creep Shadow Creep*: a story of how young virgins were kidnapped for a black mass and accompanying orgies. I played a prostitute, sordid but moral: even though I was down on my luck I refused to take on work in the orgy. I used to get a great laugh saying "Not bloody likely!" as I propped-up a lamp-post like Lili Marlene, and surveyed the sinister clergyman with scornful disgust. My first experience of the North of England: run-down cities like Manchester, Bolton, Hull, meeting a quite different breed of English person. In Manchester I couldn't find digs and was sleeping rough; a policeman brought me to an elderly "knocker-up"* who gave me lodging for the week and then passed me on to his friend in Bolton, which was the next town on the tour. The friend ran a small cinema and lived in a blissfully incestuous relationship with his niece. Another niece spent her time knitting babyclothes for her next child by a married lorry driver; as soon as these babies popped out they were adopted and she never turned a hair.

*An old trade of the industrial north, still to be found here and there in the 1950s: in the days when people were often too poor to afford clocks, they depended on a knock on their door every morning to fetch them out of bed in time to get to work.

Theatrical digs: a whole world of its own, known only to theatre folk. Actors are given a list by management on arrival in any small town in England. In Howarth (of the Brontës) I stayed with a landlady who was full of stories about Branwell and the local pub, a couple of doors down the street, where he used to drink. He sometimes, she said, would sleep it off in this very house. The room that she rented me belonged to her "gentleman-actor"; he had made his permanent home with her when he wasn't touring. It gave me an insight into the actor's life: not a trace of him in the small sparse room; did he take all his possessions with him wherever he went? -- he must have been elderly, as he'd stayed with her for years, no family, nothing except this monk-like cell.

In Hull, a small terrace house, a very friendly family. We all sat round the kitchen table while the head of the family, now retired, regaled me with stories of his life on a whaling-ship. During the Russian revolution they had berthed in Archangel; only the ordinary sailors were allowed ashore, not the officers. His pride when he said that: the one time in his life when the hierarchy had been broken down and he and his mates were men of privilege. These fragments of history, which I had only read about in books, made touring in England fascinating.

When the tour finished, back to London once more. At least I had some money: they did pay us. So two members of the cast and I rented a couple of rooms in a Hampstead progressive school, Burgess Hill, where several actors' children were educated. We hoped that in the end they might give us a job teaching drama or something; somehow we thought (if they were progressive) it would be like some sort of commune. But in fact the place was broke and made money renting out rooms. The girl I was sharing with left to go home; I moved in with Harold, dancer and choreographer, who was constantly frustrated, picking up the odd sailor or waiter, and always being abandoned. Some nights he would mysteriously disappear; he would come back the next morning shaking his head and saying, "I hate it, I hate it, I'm not going to let them do it to me any more." He got a job washing-up in the kitchen of the Festival Hall; and would bring me back food and luncheon vouchers.

I was lucky to get some film work, under the very classy direction of Laurence Olivier. *The Prince and the Showgirl*, starring Marilyn Monroe as well as Olivier himself. I should be eternally grateful to her and her sense of perfection which got us all two days extra work and enabled me to both pay the rent and eat. A scene that was supposed to be shot in one day, in the upshot took three. She was to ride in an open carriage with Olivier through the crowd. She had her caravan on the set, and every now and then -- while we all waited for the scene to begin -- the caravan door would open, out would pop her mop of blonde hair, she would blow a kiss to Olivier, and then pop in again and we would not see her for another few hours. Olivier would smile gallantly each time and give her his own encouraging wave; but after the second day the strain was clearly visible on his face. There was no doubt about it, however: when she finally appeared, we in the crowd went mad with authentic enthusiasm, we had waited so long. We were indeed a *genuine crowd,* having undergone our own

Stanislavski method. In my poverty I ratted again, a scab. Some of the personnel of the crowd scenes were Equity members, with a little bit of individual "acting" to do, as opposed to just *being there* like the non-union extras. A very grand couple, very actorish in fur coats, found out that the Equity members were getting lower rates than the extras; they told us we were to go on strike and walk out. This was not official, our absence would have not been noticed, and in fact I was getting the higher rate as an extra. I kept mum. In any case, Equity had played dirty with our wages for *Creep Shadow Creep*, where the contracts were changed after we signed them, so that we got no rehearsal pay. When we rang the union to complain, they wouldn't take any action ... So I stayed with the film.

The money meant another couple of weeks for Harold & me to stay in Burgess Hill; when it ran out I was homeless again, walking the streets in the hope of bumping into a friend with a roof to doss under. Walking the streets meant popping in and out of the pubs in Soho; ensconced in the French Pub, I found Pam Scott with a new gentleman friend, Hector, a middle-aged bachelor who had inherited property and drew his income from it. He had bought a dilapidated house in Redcliffe Square, Earls Court, as an investment which he was going to do up. In the meanwhile, I could sleep in the first-storey flat on the kitchen floor for a £1 a week. There were two other Pam Scott waifs in the flat, Vida Lestrange from Dublin (the intense young German in love with Pam; he wanted to be an orchestral conductor but worked in electronics), and an artist and hat-maker, Jocelyn Bradell (who later moved to Ireland and made a name for herself as a poet). Hector and Pam lived in a flat in Chelsea Cloisters, where they took in stray dogs and cats, and where Pam taught me the lessons of survival, living on nothing, the art of being a scavenger. We would go out down the corridors of the Cloisters, examining people's bins and picking out food and cast-offs. The building was half a hotel and half a residential condo in the American style; it had a high turnover and fridges were always being emptied and cupboards cleaned out.

One of the residents was Sir Matthew Smith, the artist; Hector suggested I should go and ask him if he wanted a model. I knocked on his door and he said "yes". So I would go to his studio in South Kensington, opposite the Albert Hall, where he would pay me ten shillings an hour to draw my breasts. Hanging on the wall was his portrait of Sir Henry Irving, painted when Irving was old and Sir Matthew was young. He gave me one very valuable lesson, he had learned it in France as a youth in the studio of Matisse: the only time to drink champagne is in the morning. He seemed to be fascinated by our binning. He laughed when he told me that one day he had left a shopping bag of groceries for a few minutes outside his door; he came out to fetch it in and it had gone. He was half-apologetic about his knighthood, saying that its only benefit was to help him attain a decent table in a restaurant. He was a shrunken little fellow, sitting there quiet and self-contained at his sketchbook. I think he felt a bit left behind by the new breed of painter who seemed rudely to disregard his tradition of post-impressionism; the fashionable men were the likes of Francis Bacon, and such powerful Americans as Jackson Pollock. Later on, when I told him I was pregnant and about to be married, he seemed rather disappointed and cautioned me against it. He died a couple of years later.

One night in the autumn of 1956, I was scurrying along Charing Cross Road in the pouring rain after rehearsal at the Hovenden club (*The Revenge of Bussy d'Ambois*, by Chapman), when there in front of me I saw a pair of bright wild eyes behind spectacles; the rain dripping off his hat, it was J.A. back from his parents in Barnsley, having gone home to recover from an appendix operation and subsequent complications. The complications came on because the beautiful blonde Highland lass with whom he was in love let him know there was no future for her in a relationship with a writer; she felt excluded from the depths of his imagination. (In fact she had already run off and wedded a one-eyed Greek smuggler and was happily engaged with him selling antiques and bric-a-brac in Kensington Church Street.)

Truth to tell I had never met such a creature before; half of him was soused in the worst kind of north-of-England provincialism straight out of a J.B.Priestley Bradford comedy. He flatly dismissed continental modernism in literature -- Beckett, Ionesco, Canetti and so forth -- his life was tightly regimented; he worked in an architect's office and earned a salary (not a wage); during the working week he must have ten hours sleep a night, he must have regular meals, he must wear his grandmother's thick knitted socks, he must wear heavy shoes, he must wear thick vests and baggy underwear, he was C of E and attended Sunday Morning Prayer. He wore striped schoolboy pyjamas -- the same ones he had worn to school -- he had short hair, voted Tory and walked on flat splayed feet. But the other half of him, the croaking cracked voice singing his northern ballads, and his coal-mining songs and sea-shanties, opened up to me a wider world and a different England of primitive rituals, which I had glimpsed when I was on tour but had not been able to set into context.

It was the contradiction between J.A.'s two selves that fascinated me; behind the eyes there was this exuberance of encyclopaedian imagination, the torrent of words, the unselfconscious delight in sharing them with me -- he made me laugh. Most important of all, he expounded the principles and origins of poetry as set out in Robert Graves's *The White Goddess*, where the Female was the centrepoint of all creativity and energy; another dimension, an ancient buried belly rumbling away in a pounding rhythm to open up forgotten caverns. But that night he was extremely distressed: he saw his inspiration receding, his well of imagination drying up; his worst fear was that he would become like Tennyson in his old age, a impotent windbag recycling old legends. He could not see how to move out of the limbo of dislocation he had fallen into. Here he was in London, at the age of 26, stuck in a career of utilitarian architecture which interested him less and less (factory renovations along the Great West Road, industrial estates in Cumberland, eternal working-drawings and phone calls to clerks-of-works from an office in Belgravia): where was the space that he yearned for in the theatre? Worst of all, he was still a virgin: impasse. The only freedom, the only way out of his tomb was to be relieved of his virginity. My god, the prospect of this would-be genius withering away in front of me was too much! Was I to be responsible for the perpetuation of the tedious and restricted theatre I had already experienced, was the great dramatic tradition to be totally given over to those terrible greenroom police at Hornchurch, shallow and soulless, their only purpose in life to preserve the professional proprieties? Were we not upon a great cusp? I thought of Gordon Craig and Isidora Duncan battling against all the conventions, I thought of Shaw denouncing Irving who sold out the theatre for a knighthood.

So I told J.A. I would relieve him of the burden of his virginity on certain terms: he had to write a play set in modern times with a part for me. We struck the bargain: under a mulberry bush in early November in an Earls Court garden, a mild moist night with the smell of the dew on the fallen leaves. So at once he began work on *The Waters of Babylon*, with the character of Bathsheba destined for me. And then *The Observer* announced a competition for new plays, with a contemporary setting, for George Devine's newly founded English Stage Company at the Royal Court.

My next theatre experience was with a touring company; the play was *We're No Angels*, a sentimental comedy, translated from the French of Albert Husson, about three golden-hearted convicts on the run from Devil's Island, and the tour encompassed mental hospitals, prisons, and army camps. A memorable moment: one of the actors was astonished to meet his ex-boss (a building contractor), now an inmate of one of gaols we visited. This boss had said to him when they parted, "I don't know why I have this feeling: I don't know when or where, but I know we will meet again." The army camps were very varied and competitive in their hospitality. The exception was an American base, where we expected great warmth and luxury but received nothing, not even a cup of tea, and their slot machines only took US currency. In the British camps we were sometimes entertained by the serjeants' mess, where they always wanted us to tell them how much jollier they were than officers' messes elsewhere. In one outfit the entertainments officer turned out to be an Australian who bragged that he had broken down the usual snooty class barriers of the poms. A Royal Artillery unit in North Wales was very strange: a full regimental dinner with the officers, all the silver out on the table, and an astonishing atmosphere of demoralised boredom, stuck up there in the rain-sodden mountains with nothing to do but count sheep on the hillsides and test-fire the weaponry if and when the ranges were clear of cloud. I affected an Irish republican zeal and suggested to a boozily flirtatious captain that perhaps he could let me have a few guns for the cause. He was highly delighted and told me I could take as many as I could carry away, showing me a long line of howitzers, each one the size of a small horsebox. I told J.A. about this little exchange: he says it had a profound impact on the later germination of his *Serjeant Musgrave's Dance.*

~~~o~~~

Halfway through the tour I found out I was pregnant. I wrote to J.A., who replied that he was entranced and excited.

Our arrangement I thought would be suitable and fair. He would live with me for two years so he could baby-sit the child while I worked in the theatre each evening. He should also take some financial responsibility for the child's
~~~

needs. But once I came back from the tour, his attitude changed. (1) He would give me £50 that he had in his post office book. (2) He could not live with me because his father occasionally came to London for business trips and it would upset him. Pam and Hector were rather shocked by this meagre offer. J.A. was earning £12 a week at the time as an architectural assistant. Hector had a string of ex-mistresses around London. He had done the honourable thing by them, giving one of them a house in Oakley Street, where she looked after a child of his by another mistress. So he was well able to advise me on the appropriate terms for a lover to pay.

I returned to J.A. to bargain. He then put forward marriage as a solution; he had been thinking seriously about it, he felt it was unjust for his child to be deprived of the right to bear the unmodified Arden coat of arms -- a bastard would have to have a white band across it. I had never seen this coat of arms or even heard of it, but I did see that it would be very unjust for me to deprive the child of its right. Back I went for advice. The notion of marriage to such a man was absolutely abhorrent. His exterior as he went through his hours and days in total self-absorption was that of a pedant with an arid and barren life-style and none of the gregariousness and openness of the Irish whom I met. He was a dull little Yorkshireman. And as a permanent mate -- ! Truth to tell in plain English, he was my sexual client. Courtesans did not marry their clients unless it was a really good deal. The day-to-day bread-and-butter J.A. did not attract me. He didn't understand about anyone living in different circumstances to himself: that's to say, no money. His only experience of people with no money was from Edinburgh, where students at times ran short but could in the end go home to their parents or have some sent. He never questioned me about why I lived on the floor of a kitchen or about why I wasn't living with my mother. We never spoke about anything personal. I knew nothing about his life at home. We were too wrapped up in our ideas of the theatre, his sense (and mine) that he was a genius; but genius or not, marriage was not what I wanted.

Hector sat me down and put it bluntly. I should accept the offer, and if after three years it didn't work out, he would pay for me to have a divorce. In those days, the early fifties, my prospects were pretty dire -- they didn't need to spell it out -- as an unmarried mum with no visible means of support and no backing. And money would be guaranteed for a divorce. Pam had been married and divorced and knew all about it. This was pretty sensible of them. Stray adults were one thing, strays with babies quite another.

So with that safety-net behind me I went back. An extraordinary thing then happened. J.A. agreed to my terms and we both felt amazingly happy and filled with love for each other.

J.A.'s mother (extreme left) with friends at teachers' training college.

J.A.'s mother in the 1960s, Yorkshire.

J.A.'s ten Arden aunts.

J.A.'s Arden grandparents, eight of his aunts, and his father.

J.A. with his father and grandfather.

9

MOTHERS

4 foot 11 inches, Lancashire, methodist, large family, her father had died young (the delayed consequences of having attended an anti-Boer-War Rally where he had been hit by a stone, which the family thought shortened his life -- or else he had caught cold at the rally: it had been very wet). She was the middle child, the only one of her sisters to have given birth. She had married the sole brother of ten sisters, her father-in-law became senile, her mother-in-law ruled the household with three daughters, a pair of twins and an invalid, all unmarried.

J.A.'s mother had been a primary-school teacher and was controlled by Miss Turner the head teacher. When she first arrived in Barnsley she lived with Miss Turner, sharing her bed. She had seemed a schoolgirl herself in those days, being so small and wearing her hair in a plait down her back; the parents indeed complained about her because they said she didn't look like a proper teacher. She hated teaching. Marriage for her meant being in charge of a small terraced house in Barnsley, an image that might have come from a child's picture-book. Her husband was head of the household, her values were non-conformist Victorian (later mixed with her husband's Edwardian anglicanism), embedded since birth, middle-class values, everything geared to the Barnsley lifestyle, good solid well-established shops in Leeds such as Marshall & Snelgrove.

This tiny woman was dominated, trained and conditioned into an uncongenial daily routine. Her justification and liberation, she hoped, would be the domination, training and conditioning of her son's wife. That is what she thought she was supposed to do. The structural order and hierarchical arrangement of the British way of life was to be imposed on me. I wonder how far she really understood what she was doing?

My existence must have been as much of a shock to her as hers was to me. How was she to begin? Ah, of course -- reminiscences of World War 2: the

Citizens' Advice Bureau where she had worked, refusing a medal for recognition of her service because she had had such a terrible time with red tape and the political intrigue of local government, people using the war for their own advancement. She felt the authorities were such hypocrites, that to accept the medal on their recommendation would only be colluding with the hypocrisy.

And then she came out with it. "Well, Margaretta, there are very nice unmarried-mother homes for girls like you. I dealt with lots of girls like you in World War 2." I stared back fascinated: her plump little legs struggling to be free from her sober grey costume, the white coiffured hair sitting like a cream bun on her head, plump little hands, a single stone in a ring on her little finger.

My own mother (reappearing into my life) had appeared confident that *she* would know how to deal with her.

Opening salvo, from *his* mother. "I've known lots of nice Jews from Leeds."

The doctor, from London, was not going to allow herself to be categorised with Leeds clothing-Jews. "Now Nancy, doesn't she look well, she hardly shows at all."

Nancy was determined that she wasn't going to allow any south-of-England person to undermine her moral certainties. It was as though a Cromwellian suddenly found herself in a close relationship with a Cavalier family. "It was a terrible shock to all of us up North, wasn't it, Charles?"

A pause whilst Charles adjusted his false teeth. "Well, John, your mother and I were most upset." Clipped Yorkshire accent.

("She has very protruberant eyes," commented Nancy to J.A. afterwards, referring to me.)

"And what about the children, Margaretta? *We* didn't get married until we had saved for a house and then we could only afford one child, he was a very large baby and the doctor told me not to have any more, I think modern parents are very selfish." She became confused, unsure of her point of attack: would it be the Irishness, the catholicism, or the actress, or the Jew? Instead, for her final salvo, inheritance and status. "You, of course, will not be Mrs Arden. I am Mrs Arden. You will be Mrs John."

There was no agreed battlefield. My world did not depend on being called Mrs Arden or Mrs John. I said nothing. Now that that was made clear, she cheered up: she had made her point, her status was secure. I said nothing. She eased herself into a narrative of her good domestic management and her twice-a-week cleaning-woman, Mrs Griffiths, a miner's wife. My mother and I could hardly believe our ears. Her first lesson to me: washing day. The laborious methods of work -- the distrust of machines -- to do the work well, do it by hand. "I boil my washing, then I put it in a tub and then we work the posher, taking it alternatively, then it goes into the mangle; two rinses, Margaretta, then the hanging out; Mrs Griffiths and I are quite exhausted at the end of the day. Tuesday, the airing, folding it all up. Wednesday, ironing the washing. Thursday, mending the washing, darning socks. The grates to be blacked. Saturday we have a joint, Sunday cold meat, Monday cold meat again. The larder and cellar whitewashed." Year in year out, the polishing, the family portraits, the family silver. Front door steps to be cleaned and scrubbed -- visions of women having their heads sliced off by passing lorries in their zeal for cleanliness-next-to-godliness. Spring-cleaning once a year: everything gets trundled out.

Now my own class reared itself inside me. My metropolitan standards, egged on by my mother. "A provincial low-income terraced house," she whispered to me, once we were alone. "Those people hang their washing in the kitchen." The Arden family heritage meant nothing to me, I had no such heritage. Nancy saw that I was not impressed; so she saved her ammunition for a later stage in the battle, when J.A. and I spent Christmas at his old home in Barnsley. All was then displayed to me -- Charles getting out the fragile Georgian porridge bowl, the christening mugs, cutlery never used, just polished and hidden away, the family portraits, stern gentlemen, provincial worthies staring down from the wall. This was their history: the lineage of all the Ardens, dating back to the Anglo-Saxon Earls of Warwick, who lost their lands at the Norman Conquest, and then lost them again at the Reformation, laid out in front of me with a hint that J.A. and I would one day inherit it. Or not quite. "*You* will not get any of these, Margaretta. If John were to die in an aeroplane crash, these portraits and silver would be for your eldest son. You will never have them. "She looked at me; there could be no response. "And if your eldest son dies," she went on, "you will not get them. They will go to the next one. And if all your children die, you will not get them: they go to Philip, J.A.'s cousin." She repeated these words like a child that had been made to learn them by heart. The old lady, *her* mother-in-law, must have fed her the speech when she was brought as a bride to the Arden household in Beverley; she had swallowed all this nonsense, hook, line and sinker. I looked at the three of them, sitting bolt upright among their possessions. So this was their England, and I was the threat of its destruction -- not so much destruction as bypass. She pushed steadily on blindly, the daughter of old John Bull: no pause, no respite -- no -- no --

She turned on her son: "Your fingernails need cutting, you need new socks. I'll send some down to you. Do cut your hair, I hate men with long hair. Go to the tailor and get a new jacket. Daddy will pay, you need a new one."

How it came about that the warring female warriors had finally come to the heart of the battle, I do not remember, but the bugle for her retreat was my words: "He is not your little boy any more, he is mine." Tight-lipped, she withdrew. There was no more for her to do except to lurk in the shadows and come out for swift attacks. It was over. No more could be said. The son sat, the father sat, without comment.

I still had the battle to free myself from Dr D. She had closely attached herself to me and J.A. because of our need for her hospital-wise expertise at the time of the birth and death of our first son. Two years before, she had thrown me out from her flat. When we got married and we were waiting for our own flat in Ladbroke Grove, she offered us hers, which was now largely unused by her. I advised J.A. not to accept, but he overrode me (being rather naive and trusting). About three weeks before the baby was to be born, she stormed in and told us to get out. She was an old experienced hand in manipulation and routing rivals, but I think she had never considered the full implications of marriage. Her own mother-in-law had long been dead, there were sisters-in-law certainly, inquisitive catlike permanent watchers and critics, but no real rival. Here though was a rival mother, Nancy Arden. Dr D. felt she was faced with a conventional and stable stronghold, a trinity, the very symbol of Christianity. There was to be no room for her. So in my vulnerable state, physical and mental, when I came out of hospital and waited for my baby's death, she looked after me tenderly, washing my blood-stained vagina, the most intimate area that I gave to my mother whilst the double pain, death and marriage, caused her to pour out her own pain. Hour after hour as I lay in bed listening to her story about my father's neglect of her whilst she was giving birth, leading on to her thoughts about my new mother-in-law, every word of Nancy's dissected and analysed: her rejection of me and by implication of her.

The in-laws came one weekend for their son's play, *The Waters of Babylon,* a Sunday night performance at the Royal Court. Nancy sitting on the bed-settee, first putting newspapers underneath her, legs slightly splayed, her broad little bum spreading, "Well, Margaretta, how long is it going to live?" A shocked pause. My mother was delighted: here was the open evidence. That was the end. My mother now could with justice attach herself to me; we were now in league against this petrified way of life, the Arden values, the British racism which is always ready to spring out and bite and sting.

Now that my mother had insinuated herself into my life and got a foot into my home, it seemed I had become her dependent accessory. She rammed it home day and night with her stories and analysis. Items which I borrowed she would insistently come for in the middle of the night. Our gentle relationship disintegrated: she was out to suffocate me and strangle me.

When I threatened to call the police (the night of the chamois-leather row) she did in fact take herself off; from then on I was free of both mothers. Polluted and shattered, I stayed indoors beating my drum and sobbing, only leaving myself a little space to go down to the hospital. The son, or son-in-law (J.A.), producer of wealth in this capitalized industrial country, was unaware of and therefore untouched by the subterranean quagmire that I had been left with. My mother's parting shot: "You imagine yourself the Virgin Mother!"

10

PAIN

The fairy story of young married life had come to an end when I woke up in hospital, after a Caesarian, looking for my baby, only to be told he had spina-bifida combined with anencephaly, and would not survive. For years I had been warned that I had been living in a dream, I was a blanked-out person -- as indeed I was, trying to grasp some sense of reality, and here it was, confronting me starkly with my total ignorance, my total inability how to handle such a complex problem. Who was to look after the child? -- his spine was open at the back, his head swollen with water and only half his brain there. The hospital said it was my responsibility to take him home. We lived in a tiny flat; my husband had begun to work at home, I had a career in the theatre, I had no medical knowledge or training. They did not bring the baby to me: it was discussed as if I had left something undesirable in the cloakroom. My mother argued with them, insisting it was their responsibility. I was not equipped to judge the circumstances. Decisions had to be made then and there. I was pulled this way and that.

My mother battled long and hard with the authorities. To begin with, he was sent to a childrens' hospital in Carshalton, quite a distance from London, and hard to get to unless one had a car. My mother drove us down to visit him. We found him in an enormous ward with children of all ages. The bleakness and feeling of neglect and indifference by the staff made us realize he had been farmed out to die -- which of course he had. The message was clear. If I would not look after him the only alternative was this reality, forsaken babies dumped on a rubbish heap. We took him out of there and my mother managed to have him admitted into a babies' unit at Fulham where I could visit him. Each afternoon I walked from Ladbroke Road through Holland Park on to the Earls Court Road, then along the road to the hospital. The nurse would coo over him in the cot with me. I would hold his little finger and he would grasp my finger. She never left me alone with him. His head enlarged, the blue veins protruding through the porcelain skin, he looked like a Goya painting of the Infant King. The presence of the nurse and her bright and breezy manner paralyzed me into a robot. I never asked her to let me hold him and she never volunteered. In hindsight it must have been as painful for the nurse as for the new mother, both of them knowing that this baby's life is so short. To break the barrier of normality might have led to a breakdown on my part that she would not want; it would take too much time, take her valuable time away from looking after healthy babies. So I remained externally frozen, his little finger holding mine. A form of communication passed between us, secret and precious. Was this once again make-believe on my part, or did we truly connect?

One evening the phone rang: it was the hospital: he had died. A terrible feeling like a gut being pulled out of me or a thin nerve: the separation had finally come. He was eight weeks old.

Throughout this period I was caught up in role playing -- the young mother pleading for special preference in the funeral arrangements -- I went to the priest asking if he could be cremated because of his deformity. But no matter how badly mutilated the body may be, cremation was not allowed by the Catholic Church. I think I had gone to that priest hoping for some comfort, some healing words, some recognition of my loss and suffering, nothing. As I put my request we could have been talking about the cutting of the grass, he was so brusque. And that was that.

Then the interview with the undertaker. A white coffin, he said. That sounded good, but when I saw it I was distressed. It was not the simple straightforward pure covering I had imagined but sheer kitsch with its pleats and furbelows. We saw my son laid out in the morgue, so beautiful, so distant so secretive. "Isn't he lovely?", cooed my mother.

Then the funeral. We had to wait outside the church in the chilly November air of a dark gloomy day, because there was another funeral. He was to be buried in the infants' common grave. He would be happier, I told myself, with all the other children, it would be cheaper as well, and that was that. I have no recollection of the burial. It has all been blocked out.

My mother became very professional, attending the autopsy; she seemed pleased that she could go to that as a medical person.

I had told no one except for a few friends who were around at that time. So my son Gwalchmei Francis was truly a hidden spirit.

11

COLLABORATION AND PITFALLS

Many plays have more than one writer and this is generally acceptable in the theatre, that collaborative place. But for critics and academics there seems to be a difficulty: it is much easier for them to categorize a single personality behind a particular text. Confronted by *married collaboration,* a husband and wife working together creatively, they are quite defeated. A wife (as opposed to a straight or gay lover) is expected to serve the playwright-spouse as an unwaged, invisible typist or secretary or manager or comforter, while the critic is left free himself to be the real lover and pursuer and owner of the man-of-talent. If he finds (and it always is a *he*) that his playwright has discovered a different way of making love or is wearing a different kind of nightwear, or prefers the shower to the bath when the critic was hoping tenderly to sponge him down in deep warm water, then at once he is filled with alarm, turning to resentment, turning to sheer vindictiveness.

In my case, working with J.A., there was an additional aspect of misunderstanding: political. There seems even today to be a prevalent view that somehow I mysteriously flew into his creative life and hauled him down the boggy road of Irish nationalism, so destroying the pure essence of his English talent, turning him into some kind of crude propagandist. Even in the 1960s, before we'd written anything about Ireland, a certain critic made a most revealing remark, a speculation upon our pillow talk. He was shocked that our childrens' play, *The Royal Pardon*, had a policeman as its villain; he seemed to assume that this irresponsible and unwholesome feature was my bedtime inspiration. Similarly, *Muggins is a Martyr*, produced in 1968 by J.A. and myself and the Cartoon Archetypical Slogan Theatre (CAST), all in collaboration, aroused a vicious attack on J.A. personally for having anything to do with such an unintelligent project, and, by implication, such worthless associates. (The play was a parable of a cockney family café taken over by gangsters under the direction of 'Mr Big', an American; it clearly referred to the collapse of the integrity of Harold Wilson's Labour government under pressure from corporate imperialism.)

ENGLISH
STAGE
COMPANY

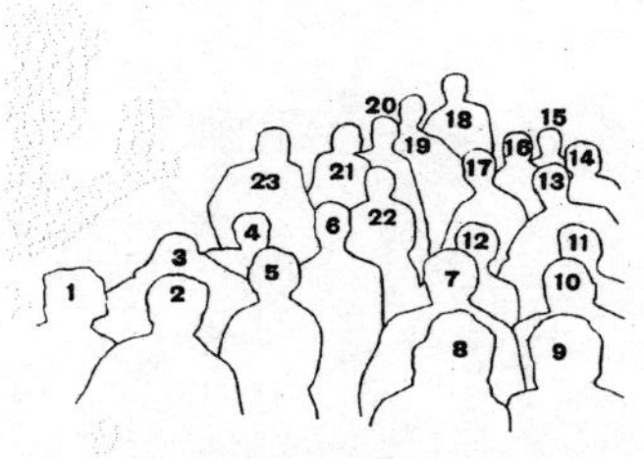

Looking like a pyramid by a notably prolific circus family: writers, actors and directors from the Royal Court, sitting for a photograph and standing for the programme opposite . . . (1) Joan Plowright. (2) Anna Manahan and (3) Jacqueline Hussey, both in Live Like Pigs. *(4) John Osborne. (5) Frances Cuka. (6) Tony Richardson, associate artistic director of the English Stage Company. (7) George Devine, the artistic director of the Company. (8) Mary Ure. (9) Alan Tagg, designing* Live Like Pigs. *(10) A. L. Lloyd, setting the ballads. (11) Alan Dobie,* in Live Like Pigs. *(12) Alex Jacobs and (13) Tom Maschler, compiling the Christmas pantomime. (14) Miriam Brickman, assistant to George Devine. (15) N. F. Simpson. (16) William Gaskill, director. (17) Michael Hastings. (18) Robert Shaw,* in Live Like Pigs. *(19) Anthony Page, co-directing it. (20) John Arden, the author, and (21) his actress wife Margaretta D'Arcy. (22) John Dexter, directing* Chicken Soup with Barley. *(23) Wilfrid Lawson.*

TO THE BOX OFFICE MANAGER,
ROYAL COURT THEATRE, SLOANE SQ., S.W.1

This coupon entitles the bearer to tickets for Live Like Pigs *at the price-reductions below. It is valid for the whole run of the play, opening September 30. It should be presented at the box office in person,* or *filled in and posted with a cheque or postal order made payable to the Royal Court Theatre.*

Four 16s. tickets for 48s. ☐ **Two 16s. tickets for 26s.** ☐
Four 11s. tickets for 33s. ☐ **Two 11s. tickets for 18s.** ☐
Four 7s. 6d. tickets for 22s. 6d. ☐ **Two 7s. 6d. tickets for 12s.** ☐
Four 5s. tickets for 15s. ☐ **Two 5s. tickets for 8s.** ☐

Date required..

Name and address to which tickets should be sent, if necessary:

....

....

Royal Court Group Photograph, London 1958.

After the 1969 explosion of civil-rights agitation in the north of Ireland, the paranoia of the British establishment became fully exposed: anything contrary to official policy on Irish issues must be muffled, repressed, obliterated, mocked. We got our first hint of this when a provincial theatre company wanted to put on *The Hero Rises Up,* our ballad opera about Lord Nelson, and demanded some cuts in the script. Almost the same cuts were made by BBC Radio in their broadcast version of the play. In each case references to the Irish rebellion of 1798 were blue-pencilled. We stopped the BBC's cuts, and we refused permission for the stage production: the start of the myth that I was the hard one and J.A. the soft one who would never have made a fuss if he'd been left on his own. Martin Esslin, head of BBC drama, did not forget the episode, and later on laid it down that he would only accept plays that were "genuine Arden". The attacks became full-frontal when the 7:84 production of our Anglo-Irish melodrama *The Ballygombeen Bequest* was sued for libel. This coincided with our strike against the Royal Shakespeare Company for their refusal to hold a full company meeting to discover why the work on *The Island of the Mighty* had lost the run of itself. A columnist in *The Times* suggested that I might be in the IRA, a smear emanating from the plaintiff of the *Ballygombeen* libel action who had described me as a Republican "henchwoman". From then on, in almost every mention of J.A. that connected him or his plays with Ireland, my name cropped up as a baneful influence, and subsequent theatre-studies tended to concentrate entirely upon what were perceived as his earlier uncontaminated writings.

1957: The Royal Court accepted *The Waters of Babylon* as a Sunday night production. I had just given birth so I couldn't play Bathsheba. The director was Graham Evans who had directed me in a play at Hornchurch. J.A. was then able to give up work at the office because he became a reader of scripts at the Court.

1958: George Devine's plan for the Court was to have a company of actors and a team of playwrights who would work together. Initially there was a young actors' group containing four men (David Buck, David Andrews, Johnny Seka, Peter Birrell) and two women (Tamara Hinchco and myself). Associated playwrights were John McGrath, Donald Howarth, J.A., and someone else whose name escapes me. J.A.'s *Live Like Pigs* was to be put on as a full-scale production. Our group would feed into the productions, providing understudies and small parts. Some of the Royal Court board thought we were like the devils from hell dragging the theatre down to our own low level. I remember Ivor Brown writing in the *Observer* to the effect that he had heard a dreadful rumour, so dreadful it could hardly be true, that there were young actors who went in at the front of the theatre and not by the stage door; some of them had even discarded putting on make-up.

The group used to give play-readings of the untried work of young playwrights. I remember one such, set in a spacecraft. Harold Pinter and myself were a married couple somehow locked into this vehicle. The play went on so long that we never finished reading it; and so for evermore Pinter and I remain suspended in outer space. I wonder about the effect on the playwright of our failure to get to the end of his script? Was *his* imagination left hanging in space with Pinter and myself and the various other characters? Another little play was *Top Deck*, devised for our improvisation by J.A., a story of the lopsided relationship between an English bus conductress and an African-American serviceman. It was later made into a low-budget half-hour film, directed by Tamara Hinchco and David Andrews, with the main parts acted by myself and Jimmy Anderson (one of the cast of the Living Theatre's *The Brig*, then playing in London). The bus-driver in the film was initially Michael Caine; in the middle of shooting he was whisked away to Hollywood ... Several years afterwards, *Top Deck* was mentioned by the British Film Institute as being the first British film in which the story was seen from the point of view of a black character.

There was a hope that the Court's Sunday night plays would become a focus for stringent dialectical debate on the nature of theatre. The gauntlet was thrown down by Ken Tynan and Elaine Dundy when they attended a play by Stuart Holroyd: this was to be the great showdown. On one side were the transcendental mystics, Holroyd, Colin Wilson (and, strangely, Michael Hastings, who somehow got cast into this role and put under ideological suspicion for years to come). On the other side, the rigorous New Left, Christopher Logue, Tynan & Dundy, with Doris Lessing following up the rear. There was heckling during the performance, and then at the end of it Tynan & Dundy stamping out past the other side all lined up in the foyer -- someone shouted, "We'll smash you!" In the pub next door there was a great buzz, the adrenalin was up, the pub divided into embattled factions: this was real! the beginning of the awakening of the dormant intellectualism of the anti-intellectual British, this was Sartre and Camus, the Paris Cafés, "Les Deux Magots," etc. -- well, it all fizzled out into the usual bread and brown gravy of leftish debate in England, social welfare, housing and education, nationalised industry.

There was one bit of fun: Keith Johnstone and Ann Jellicoe decided to make an Aristophanic Sunday-night show of rough theatre attacking the critics for their ignorant treatment of some of the Court plays -- Keith's own play (*Brixham Regatta*) and J.A.'s *Live Like Pigs* in particular. The theatre's electrician walked out, angrily asserting that this was not what theatre was all about and he'd have no part of it. The show went on regardless, it was savagely attacked, no great armies lined up to defend the Jellicoe-Johnstone faction, even Tynan in his review just treated it as another messy venture and refused to see it as any sort of breakthrough either in form or content.

The Royal Court was a focus for the soft left and disillusioned ex-communists, "Ban the Bomb," and so forth, entryism into the Labour Party, and then the Committee of 100 (which we joined; it was formed by Bertrand Russell, a list of 100 names announcing their willingness to commit civil disobedience against nuclear weapons). The war of independence in Algeria and the French atrocities were also a hot issue, as were the fag-end of the Mau Mau rebellion in Kenya and the British atrocities. Traditional communists were struggling to emerge from the débâcle of the Soviet invasion of Hungary. The leftish strategy was to get the Labour Party in opposition to embrace unilateral disarmament and to separate from the Special Relationship with the USA. (It had been considered vital to prevent Hugh Gaitskell, a firm believer in multilateral disarmament, from securing the leadership of the party. He'd secured it nonetheless.) The house of the writer Anne Piper (next door to George Devine's, on the riverfront at Hammersmith) became the hub of much of the plotting. Great excitement, one Sunday; we were all invited to lunch there and were allotted conversational roles to keep the energy flowing while Anne got her star guest, Henry Kissinger*, into serious talk with Benn Levy MP (a committed unilateralist and a playwright). It was hoped that Kissinger might be persuaded to influence the Democrat opposition in Washington to abandon the nuclear policy of Mutually Assured Destruction (MAD). Jules Feiffer, the radical American cartoonist, was also at the lunch; he had a satirical play on in London at the time. For a fleeting moment we felt we were right in there changing the geopolitics and bringing to birth a better world. With that vision we had no fear of civil disobedience, sitting down in Whitehall, breaking the ban on Trafalgar Square demonstrations, and being part of a world-wide movement.

* At that time Kissinger was a liberal academic, the up-and-coming geopolitical theorist, head-hunted by the Democrats.

Outside the theatre George had instigated workshops for the playwrights and they were carried on at Anne Piper's. In these workshops new styles of writing and staging were explored; ideas were developed through improvisation. Quite a number of writers and actors turned up, and it was delightful to be at work in Anne's informal family house with her three children popping in and out, as well as her husband, David, curator of the National Portrait Gallery. This gave rise to some snarky remarks here and there -- John Whiting, writing in *Encore,* referred to a "malicious rumour" going round that Royal Court playwrights met for weekly drama classes with their half-finished plays; what a strange and bizarre idea.

In *Live Like Pigs* I played Rosie. George Devine and Anthony Page were co-directors; George pulled out because Alan Webb pulled out of *Major Barbara* and George had to step in to his role. The play was a theatrical disaster. Poor Anna Manahan, auditioning for the role of Rachel, got so excited that she fell off the stage and broke her ankle. Anthony was jubilant: it showed the authenticity of her feelings. Wilfred Lawson had a drink problem and had to have a minder. He also hated playwrights' wives and he and I had to play together as father and daughter. As my own father became verbally abusive when he had drink taken, acting with Wilfred was home-from-home. He used to sit on my knee whilst we waited for our scenes. He was as light as a feather, muttering to himself, "They're all acting away like buggery." Wilfred had been heralded to be one of the great actors; something happened in his career whereby he lost confidence. Robert Shaw played opposite me as Blackmouth, the lost sheep; we had a scene in which he tried to soften me up so that he might return to the fold. Only once did the scene really work to my satisfaction. Acting is so subject to the unpredictable, the perfect timing (when it happens) is almost accidental; most of the audience don't even notice it. I was pleased when Michael Redgrave came to the theatre one night and left a message for me saying how much he had appreciated my performance; it must have been on the one good night. Rachel Roberts had been a possibility for Anna's part; I felt a bit embarrassed when she was full of good things to say about me, knowing she had been rejected.

The Royal Court did give us some security, and a feeling of family. But it was the sort of family where the beloved son or daughter, if they ceased to be a viable economic unit, would be cast out. Just so, had my mother cast out *me* ... Should I blame Tony Richardson for the change of atmosphere at the Court? He came back from America during the rehearsals of *Live Like Pigs*, looked in, groaned, and muttered "student Lorca". George had to be taken in hand; the court was losing money; the board was getting worried; the actors' group had to go, so eventually the playwrights' group went too; Ken Tynan, the crucial critic of the day, dismissed *Live Like Pigs* (as did most of his colleagues). To try and spark a bit of controversy, there was a public discussion about the play one Sunday afternoon, a feeble event, where old-communist playwright Alison McCleod accepted the general consensus that it was an attack on the welfare state -- I remember her standing up and pathetically declaring that all she could think about was "the poor child" in the middle of the sordid scene. The play's run was shortened; Ronald Duncan, a member of the board was heard to say, "This is exactly the sort of play I told the board the Court ought not to be doing." His dislike of the Arden style was presumably based on the fact that he himself wrote verse-drama; he must have thought J.A.'s doggerel ballads were a travesty of real poetry.

To save the Court, Vivien Leigh was booked into the next production, a Feydeau farce, *Look after Lulu,* directed by Richardson, and a new manager came in. Half the secretarial staff were sacked. We fled London to Petertavy on the edge of Dartmoor, to lick our wounds. J.A. still had one play to write for the Court, *Serjeant Musgrave's Dance*, which Lindsay Anderson directed in 1959. That did no better; and we moved to Bristol, where J.A. took up a position as writer-in-residence at the university drama department, the first of its kind in the country. We now had one child, Finn, and I was soon to expect another. J.A. wrote *The Happy Haven* for the university theatre, with a couple of scenes by me. When it transferred to the Royal Court, George was ill, and Peter O'Toole conspicuously walked out of the first night in a state of visible boredom. The play was taken off after only two weeks. That was the end of Arden at the Court.

Indeed, the board seems to have vowed "no Arden ever again!" The story went round that *Serjeant Musgrave's Dance* was the last straw; it had nearly collapsed the Court by financially crippling it. At least, that's what George kept telling John Osborne: he was too kind to tell J.A. George *was* a kind person and really felt a responsibility for forgotten playwrights -- I remember him recounting to us how he had just come back from the West Country where he had gone looking for John Masefield, then in his eighties, and living in obscurity. Who ever thought of Masefield in 1959? Yet he had been well-praised for his plays before the first world war, and J.A. had read them with considerable excitement. Moreover, George sought out Seán O'Casey, as a gesture of support when O'Casey's *The Drums of Father Ned* fell foul of the Archbishop of Dublin. He produced *Cock-a-Doodle-Dandy* at the Court. (Also in support of O'Casey, Beckett had withdrawn *his* plays from Dublin. Beckett and George were close friends, George having acted in and directed more than one of his plays.)

I was lucky, in that my way of life had got me used to rejection. I had been thrown out of Dublin, thrown out of work, thrown out of my mother's flat, I had experienced homelessness: J.A. had not, his life had been secure, home, school, the army, the university.

When he was working at Bristol, we could find no accommodation in the city that would accept young children, so we ended up twenty miles away in a ground-floor flat in the old vicarage of Brent Knoll. We didn't have a car and direct public transport was inadequate. Because I wasn't on the spot I couldn't pick up work in Bristol, and, anyway, I had no childcare. Brent Knoll was in the main a traditional farming community. When I used to go out, pushing Finn in his pram, I would get into conversation with the old women. They were really warm and friendly. I began to think, if I could not go to the work, why not create the work where I was? I was pregnant, which naturally inclined me to thoughts of birth. The baby was due around Christmas time (1960), so why not a nativity play? So began our alternative theatre, with *The Business of Good Government*, put on in the church next door with the neighbours in the cast. We rehearsed in our flat, so there was no baby-sitting problem. By now we had had a lot of experience, learning from the Royal Court, the actors' group, the playwrights' group, the science of drama analysis as taught by George Devine, Bill Gaskill, Tony Page and particularly Lindsay Anderson (during his work on *Musgrave*). The joy of doing-it-yourself was that we were free of boards and theatre politics, we did not have to worry about an audience, and we met like-minded people in the play itself. *The Business of Good Government* was an innovation for us: we created a complete environmental production, for a specific venue, a specific cast, a specific audience, and we all knew the story.

In hindsight, the next year seems unbelievable. How could two rational people live the way we did? The job at Bristol had come to an end, we were wondering where we should go next. Our third son Adam was born in December, a couple of days after the nativity play. Our first son Gwalchmei had died at eight weeks; it now looked as if Adam would go the same way. He turned out to have pyloric-stenosis, a faulty gene inherited from me. He was operated on in the Taunton hospital, the operation did not work and he had to have another. We were distraught. I was breast-feeding, so I went into the hospital to be with him when he recovered. Finn was taken care of by friends. The long wait, while I constantly had to express milk only to see it vomited up again, made me desperate; the more desperate I became, the less milk I could produce. Not only was my body producing dying children but now it was even refusing to give sustenance to one of them that might live. Adam did recover, but his ordeal had brought all the trauma of Gwalchmei back to me; I was not in a fit state to deal with the problem of new accommodation. J.A. himself was shattered by the failure and humiliation of *The Happy Haven*. His parents, now retired, would have liked us to be near them and used to send him adverts for cheap properties in Yorkshire. He had a little nest-egg of £600. (When he was four he had gone to a little nursery school run by a Mrs Dobson. At her death she left a small legacy to each of her first batch of pupils.) So off he went to look at a cottage which was going for a couple of hundred in Kirkbymoorside; it just needed some repairs and renovations; as a trained architect he could draw plans and give them to a builder; the whole job would not take more than a month. In the meantime, we would rent.

J.A.'s father found a farmer's widow, a Mrs Husband, who wanted to share her house and have some companionship. She lived in the hamlet of Full Sutton, near York. We didn't really want to live in her lap, using her kitchen and living-room. So she gave us a couple of attic rooms and her tiny scullery. This meant that we had to eat outside. Half a mile away, and visible from the top of the house, was an American missile base, the implications of which did not strike us until we had moved in. Well, we stayed and stayed, J.A. stayed in bed all day in a state of collapse and depression, I walked the roads all day with the children to give him peace, he never did the plans. It was absurd. In the middle of winter we ate breakfast out of doors in our overcoats, clearing snow off the table. I accepted this. I too must have been in deep depression. There we would have stagnated to this day if it hadn't been for the Americans and their bloody weapons. What must have aggravated our depression was the sight of the missile-launchers being erected and pointing eastward every time there was a crisis, and at *that* time there was almost continual crisis. Kennedy and Kruschev were in standoff mode at the Berlin borders -- later in the year the East Germans built the Wall -- in news programmes on Mrs Husband's TV we saw convoys of NATO troops assembling along the West German autobahns, waiting to have a war. We also saw militarist pundits such as Hermann Kahn assuring us that a nuclear war could probably be actually *won.* For the first time we heard the bland and deceptive phrase "collateral damage".

There was of course activity against the bomb: we belonged to a group in York which organised a sitdown to expose a secret bunker constructed to house government in the post-nuclear-disaster age. The whereabouts of these top secret installations had been made known by "The Spies for Peace", conscientious and courageous people like Michael Randle and Alan Lovell, the film maker. Harold Macmillan's government was furious and kept on denying everything. (Today in 2004 the archives of the period are being published, and everything we said then has turned out to be true.) The Committee of 100 organised a big civil disobedience action in Trafalgar Square. The government tried to put an end to the Committee by arresting all those members who lived in or near London. They were to be bound over to keep the peace, and most of them refused. Arnold Wesker, Christopher Logue, and Robert Bolt were among those who refused and were put into jail, or rather a special internment camp. This did not stop the demo, as at least half of the Committee lived outside London. J.A. travelled up there to take part, while I stayed behind to look after the babies; I decided to do my own local bit of civil disobedience. Leaving Adam with a neighbour and carrying Finn on the back of my bike, I cycled to the missile base through the prohibited area to hand in a letter to the commander, asking him to examine his conscience as to the morality of weapons of mass destruction. He took the letter from me and I came home. J.A. and hundreds of others got arrested in London, and next day it was in all the newspapers. The postwoman was in a flurry of excitement when she delivered a telegram from J.A. informing me of his arrest. We didn't know what this small community felt about the base, we didn't go round the village to ask. We had a distant but polite relationship with the people there. But then the crunch came, like a kick up the arse to get us moving: one evening, after dark to save embarrassment, a policeman called to say that the American commander wanted me charged with inciting him to desert. The penalty was 20 years. The poor village bobby, straight out of *Heartbeat,* looked at us with puzzled kindness. We had to receive him outside in the cold, for we had no sitting-room. He held in front of him my letter to the commander, perplexed. J.A. was a Yorkshire man like himself, the wife could be taken for a foreigner, but even so -- 20 years to please those Yankees! He said, "Well, you could take this letter both ways. I'll take it *this* way and report back 'No Incitement'." But a couple of days later Mrs Husband apologetically asked us to make alternative arrangements and to leave as soon as possible; she offered us some excuse relating to her family.

We put an ad. into our weekly bible, *The New Statesman*, asking for somewhere to live. A reply came from a Dr MacWilliam from the north of Ireland: he had a small island of eight acres for sale, in a lake in the west of Ireland. He thought it would be ideal for a literary couple with children. The writer David Garnett had lived there, which *we* thought a good omen. Our friend Tom Austin in Dublin arranged the purchase for us, for £400, which was exactly what J.A. had left of Mrs Dobson's nest-egg. As for the cottage in Kirkbymoorside, it was as though it had never been ... So once again, my talent for getting myself shunted out: this time it wasn't family but the US Air Force. Both of us were now labelled in the unfathomable archives of the state as politically questionable, with presumably a special mark against *me*, a woman of "undetermined status".

So we settled in, on Loch Corrib in County Galway, half a mile from the mainland. No electricity, water in abundance, no traffic for the children to be run over by, lots of space for them to scamper around (within a year, three of them), land to grow vegetables, and just a little wooden shack to live in; we learnt how to row a boat and had a couple of bicycles on the mainland to convey us into the nearest town, Oughterard, five miles away. There we were to have our paradise, solitary splendour in pursuit of literature, whilst the world raged around us. In a way the island was a compromise, simply because it *was* an island, for I had vehemently rejected anything to do with Ireland: I felt so hurt and betrayed by the experiences of my teens. I now realize I was looking at my own country from a disgusted "Dublin intellectual" perspective, which was much the same thing as an English perspective -- a theocratic state, an archaic IRA, a compliant subservient peasantry -- altogether a picture of the worst kind of rural backwardness.

We could ignore the world; but the world would not so easily be ignored.

We were without daily newspapers, radio or TV, but our minds were filling up with ideas from our contacts in the Committee of 100 and such magazines as *Freedom, Anarchy* and *Encore.* We read our way into a different world, a real world of change, a different way of organizing, different values (not solely based on bums-on-seats). We read analyses of Sex-and-Violence, Workers' Control, Deinstitutionalisation, the New Cinema, Adventure Playgrounds, the Ideology of Prisons, Direct Action, "Housing, Squatters, Do-it-yourself," and "What Does Anarchism Mean?" ... all this was the germination of the Kirkbymoorside Entertainment of 1963 which was to open the doors and windows so we could breathe -- children were not a burden but a joy to be integrated into our lives -- and of course J.A. was nervous of change and yet without it how was he to evolve? He wrote a poem about his state: --

The Lobster Pot.

Who can tell how the lobster got
Into the lobster pot?
When he went in he did not doubt
There was a passage out.
There was not.

Internally we became ready for change, but it was the external that produced it and brought us to Kirkbymoorside. The old cottage we abandoned had not been forgotten by the officials of the North Riding of Yorkshire. One day a letter arrived, a warning that if J.A. was not going to do something about the dilapidated building (which was encroaching its dilapidation upon neighbouring property), the council would take action, bring J.A. to court, compel him to demolish and leave him liable for costs and damages to the adjoining householder. Money was coming in now with commissions for *The Workhouse Donkey*, royalties for *Serjeant Musgrave's Dance,* fees for a TV play *Wet Fish* and for a film-script (eventually aborted) about Ned Kelly. So J.A. went off to Kirkby, and by Christmas 1962 the cottage was habitable. My father had died and we were in Dublin for his funeral in the worst winter for decades. Loch Corrib had frozen over. Jacob, our third son, had been born in the Galway Regional Hospital in July: we transported the three children to Kirkby and a new stage of a new life began. I had to put an ultimatum to J.A. -- "You move on or you move out." He moved on. And the following appeared in *Encore*: --

[abridged]

AN APPEAL BY JOHN ARDEN

Living as he does in Kirkbymoorside, a small Yorkshire country town ... From which the Railway has been removed: in which there is neither theatre nor cinema: nor indeed much industry (save for a small Glider factory and a Brickworks): near which the principal Sign of our Times is the alarming, unearthly, impossibly beautiful and probably totally unnecessary Early Warning Station on Fylingdale Moor ...

And where the population in general, deprived of their old social entertainments such as ...
A German Band
A dancing Bear
An annual Goose-Fair
The arrival of a daily Train at the Railway Station
(all remembered with grave nostalgia by the older inhabitants) ...
resort to no fewer than five distinct sectarian Churches of a Sunday, thereby splitting into exclusive fragments a community already sufficiently fragmented by the Cruelty of the Twentieth Centory and the Affluence of the South ...

JOHN ARDEN
has conceived the idea of establishing
A FREE PUBLIC ENTERTAINMENT
in his house.
To take place at intervals between the fifteenth of August and the fifteenth of September.
MR. ARDEN has been indirectly described by MR. WESKER as a Paralysed Liberal
If anybody wishes to assist him to overcome this paralysis, which he is inclined to admit

MR. ARDEN ... would be inordinately grateful for suggestions or offers of assistance for the furtherance of this small project.

No specific form of entertainment is at present envisaged but it is hoped that ... the forces of Anarchy, Excitement ... in the most apparently sad persons shall be given release...

COME TO KIRKBYMOORSIDE AND HELP ARDEN TO SPEND HIS MONEY LIKE WATER

A host of writers, film-makers, poets, and musicians turned up to overcome the paralysis, e.g. Henry Livings, Stan Barstow, Jon Silkin, Roger McGough, Brian Patten, Alfred Bradley, Piers Paul Read, Bert Howarth (later a founder-member of Welfare State), Jane Percival, Michael Hastings, Alan Lovell, Terry Randle, David Naden, Charles Lewsen, Tamara Hinchco, David Andrews, Roger Smith, Peter Redgrove, Patrick Nuttgens, Clem Beer, Valerie Beer, John Lane (later the director of the Beaford Arts Centre) ...

~~~o~~~

It is not easy to maintain a partnership, at least if it is to be an equal partnership. On the island, we had been living at a rate of £4 a week, which J.A.'s agent Warren Tute sent him from the royalties. That money was J.A.'s, even from *The Business of Good Government* royalties, for he had not put my name on the script and when the play went for publication I never considered the consequences of the omission. It took me some time to shift my perception in this matter of claiming ownership: it only really happened when, one day in 1966, Warren Tute called to our house in Muswell Hill to tell J.A. there were ten thousand pounds due to him in royalties, but it was all gone! -- squandered by Warren himself, whose agency was now bankrupt. The realization hit me that all those years J.A. had in fact been earning money but hadn't taken any responsibility to find out *what* he was earning, we had lived in a fool's paradise, as much my fault as his for taking no notice of money, juggling our own domestic creativity, *Ars Longa Vita Brevis* or *The Royal Pardon* -- domestic in the sense that they were part of our life together whilst his plays for the mainstream theatre were outside that sphere, which does not mean that I was not involved in those ventures: J.A.'s work pattern was to write a bit and then read it to me, I would comment, we would have discussions and he would rewrite.
~~~

It was different when we collaborated; then the plot, the venue, how it was to be staged and where, would all be my input. For his mainstream work (e.g. *The Workhouse Donkey* or *Left-Handed Liberty*) I was a dutiful helper as expected of a wife, and perceived as such; if I had gone away and a new wife had appeared, the perception of her would have been exactly the same. A playwright's wife was supposed to serve him as he served the theatre, and both of them were expendable. We had thought we were different but when I saw how we had been allowing an agent to lavish our money on inaugurating production companies, trying to get into the film industry and its concomitant lifestyle, playing some scam about the Bahamas and tax-free zones, wining and dining there with the likes of ex-queen Soraya of Persia (we had tasted a bit of that in New York when he brought us over to set up a musical about Lord Nelson, he did include me in the partnership then, he perhaps regretted it afterwards, J.A. and I pulled out), I understood that J.A. was just like all those other artists who are dependent on their agents to fix contracts and make big plans; only too often they experience the same sort of rip-off. From then on my attitude changed towards J.A. and his mainstream: I could no longer regard it as our primary activity.

As the sixties speeded along, it became clear that J.A. would never be a business person and I had no interest in business. It became clear that nothing was as straightforward as the amateurism of the Committee of 100 had made it seem. There was now a proliferation of forces on the left following the slow disintegration of the Communist Party. Trotskyism flourished under many different names -- the International Socialists, the Socialist Labour League, the International Marxist Group -- all of them centralised parties who wanted to co-opt the practitioners of the arts. When we worked on *Muggins is a Martyr* at Unity Theatre, Roland Muldoon of CAST, with whom we had made the initial contact, saw the play as an opportunity to take over Unity (hitherto controlled by the Communist Party). He had always wanted to run a theatre of his own -- which he was eventually to obtain with the Hackney Empire. J.A. and I were not in the loop; we were still amateurs just putting on plays. We were too individualistic to be useful in a party. New radical ideas were flaring up, fuelled by the student revolts all over Europe and the USA, and particularly by the 1968 Paris uprising. Revolutionary arts, film, posters, agitprop theatre, brought in by émigré artists from Germany and France: the centre of gravity was shifting. But it was not long before the new movement began to be absorbed into the colour-schemes of chameleon capitalism. This was done through funding, the Arts Council setting company against company, inhibiting political theatre in the name of "artistic excellence" and stopping its money. I remember Edward Heath at that time denouncing capitalism's Unacceptable Face, and reflecting that he meant that there was somewhere an *acceptable* face ...

As for the mainstream theatre, its structure and intention was now being used to maintain imperial interests and corporate capitalism, as we found out from the response to our strike against the RSC at the Aldwych: our last major play in London, *The Island of the Mighty*. We could not think why management was so adamant against a simple meeting for the overall benefit of the production. When our request was refused we briefly secured the backing of Equity through our membership of the Equity-affiliated Society of Irish Playwrights, and (no less briefly) the backing of the theatre technicians' union, a piece of workers' solidarity unprecedented in theatre history. It was too much for the cultural controllers, the implications were too frightening: the RSC was a heavily-subsidised outfit loaded with national prestige. It is now apparent that they saw our small but crucial dispute as an early stage in the wider battle between unions, management, boards of directors and indeed government, which was to engulf Britain in the 70s and 80s, culminating in Margaret Thatcher's onslaught on the NUM. Whereas we believed that artists had a right to take responsibility for their own work, their imagination and integrity, because without it we are all dead and withered.

The gap between my political consciousness in London and what I found on annual visits to the island was too wide; it was becoming unbearable.

1969: one day in Oughterard I opened *The Connacht Tribune* and read of a meeting of small farmers to establish a local Land League, in protest against the laying-out of a new golf course by a consortium of local hoteliers and business people. The small farmers were desperate for land, they felt that the Land Commission should have made the golf-course site available for agriculture, and they foresaw a general takeover by "the men with the long purse", squeezing them out of farming altogether. They likened it to the notorious estate-clearances of the 19th century, the bleeding of the land, the bleeding of the people, compelling so many to emigrate. I went to visit Tom Joyce, the chairperson of the new Land League, a dignified elderly gentleman: he himself had no land

and had spent his life working in England on building sites. He saw the independent Irish state, the 26 counties, as being no different from Ireland under the British, as far as "the people of no property" were concerned. He opened my eyes to the spirit of resistance that had always been there subterraneously and was now slowly awakening.

I made an agitprop film, *The Unfulfilled Dream.* I went about with my camera and people showed me rat-infested schools and damp cottages without electricity or running water. I heard of the dirty tricks employed by business people to acquire land, and I specifically heard of the eviction of Mrs Fahy. (All this experience went into *The Ballygombeen Bequest.*) In London I had supported council tenants in their rent-&-rates strike against the Tory-dominated LCC. I now understood that the Irish small farmers were fighting the same fight. But it was only when we went to India (at the end of '69) to study the Ghandhi movement that Ireland's position in the world became clear to me. All the more so when I brushed up against the revolutionary Naxalites and we all got arrested as suspected Chinese spies. We were deported from the State of Assam, under police escort in the middle of the flooding of the Brahmaputra combined with an earthquake ... Economically Ireland was still a colonial country and belonged to the Third World, although culturally part of the First World.

Shortly after our return from India, we moved into a small cottage in Corrandulla on the mainland, ten miles from Galway city. One day there was a knock on the door. A uniformed Garda and a plain-clothes detective. Our names had been given as an alibi by a respected academic, a socialist historian with whom we had spent a pleasant afternoon in town picking his brains about the labour movement in Ireland and absorbing material for *The Non-Stop Connolly Show.* We had said good-bye to him on Galway railway station, the evening train to Dublin. When he arrived at his flat, he discovered the dead body of a young friend, a republican socialist, murdered. And also tortured; he was hanging by his thumbs. The assassins were never found ... In left-wing circles it was seriously believed that a "special unit" of the Garda Siochána was responsible, leaving a stark message that the state would not tolerate Ireland becoming another Cuba. Cathal Goulding of the (Official) Sinn Fein had already told *The Irish Times* that the only way forward was to follow the Cuban model. There can be no doubt that this notion terrified both Dublin and Westminster, especially when seen against the turmoil in the North. Internment, 1971; Bloody Sunday and the burning of the British embassy, 1972. Clearly conditions in Ireland were closer to what I had seen in India than to anything in Britain. In Britain, however, the real Irish struggle was hidden: politicians and media alike laying emphasis only upon "terrorism" and religious sectarianism.

Out of these Irish politics came a series of collaborative plays covering aspects of "Anglo-Irish" history, 1830 - 1972. *The Ballygombeen Bequest* was first read in public in Galway at the University Theatre Festival in 1972, as a contribution to the campaign against Mrs Fahy's eviction. Later it was produced by the students of St Mary's & St Joseph's teachers' training college in Belfast: we attended the first night while a gunbattle raged in the Falls Road outside. The 7:84 production opened at the Edinburgh Festival and toured in the UK. It was followed by the six-part *Non-Stop Connolly Show,* which we put on at Liberty Hall in Dublin (Easter 1975) and took on tour to Belfast, Downpatrick, Newry and Galway. Readings were given in London and New York. *Vandaleur's Folly* was another 7:84 production, touring in the UK and Ireland in 1978. In 1984 it was turned into a radio play, *The Manchester Enthusiasts*, for the BBC, and for RTE as *The Ralahine Experiment.*

In the 1970s I started the Corrandulla Arts and Entertainment, showing films, making films, presenting play-readings, making an agitprop play about the piped water, all given in our cottage. Then followed the Galway Theatre Workshop, with a number of partly-improvised rough-theatre plays.** I devised a spin-off of the Workshop, *A Pinprick of History*, for the London public, at the Ambience Almost-Free Theatre in 1977.

** *Arden & D'Arcy, Plays:One*, Methuen, 1991.

12

CORRANDULLA & GALWAY 1975/76

Diary Excerpts
(from the first days of the Galway Theatre Workshop)

Tuesday 4 Nov 1975
J.A. got letter from Indiana for a week re Bi-Centennial of the Declaration of Independence. Took Neuss on the bike to crossroads. Poured all day, cleared up in time for us to go to Galway for workshop. We were standing at crossroads hitching a lift when suddenly a bus loomed up. It was half an hour late. The lights didn't work in lecture room we normally used, so we went to Aula Max., a fancy Victorian Grand Hall, a few dram. soc. students turned up, atmosphere quite relaxed. Afterwards we went to Ann Slattery's for a chat. Pat, Des and their wives were there. Next week they will bring resumé of their lives.

Wednesday 5 Nov 1975
Felt dead after last night, couldn't understand why, watched Ava Gardner in afternoon. Theme: man has a beautiful cultivated rose in his garden, why shouldn't he appreciate rose in garden and look at wild flowers outside garden? His rose leaves him at the end, withers.

Thursday 6 Nov 1975
Really warm today, Herrema kidnapping still going on, Franco still alive. King Hassan with 350,000 is preparing to cross over into the Sahara today. He will not lead them in as he has work to do in the capital. If Spanish soldiers fire on them they are not to retaliate, they must give food to the soldiers in the name of Allah. Official Sinn Féin are going to take their seats in local councils. Rees says he will release all detainees by Xmas; special status for political prisoners will stop.

Friday 7 Nov 1975
Herrema released at 10pm. Eddie Gallagher and Marion Coyle gave themselves up after Eddie Gallagher got ill, cramp in the neck, no dramatics. The news broke in *Seven Days.* John Hume congratulated the govt., then John

Taylor. The Convention ended today; the loyalists have sent their plan to Westminster: no deal with the SDLP. Shootings still go on between Provos and Officials. Had long talk about the 4th play of *The Non-Stop Connolly Show.* Still dissatisfied with opening, no humour, my mind is gagged. Washed floor after TV; went to bed 3am.

Saturday 8 Nov 1975

Herrema remarkably self-possessed and relaxed on TV; had been in a Nazi concentration camp. Mrs Herrema very relaxed and easy with newsmen. J.A. had breakthrough on play: Gompers more a figure of fun. Time is getting on; still no real progress. J.A. got letter from John Joyce who was in *The Ballygombeen,* wondering what was happening to the Connolly play. Cheered us up considerably, but still despondent. Realized that this is the first time since coming back from India that I can think. Situation is confused and yet issues are clear. Lovely day; walked up to Corrandulla. Then round the back road. Had a drink at Fahy's miserable pub, no-one there, empty glasses all over the place, smell of stale beer and Guinness.

Sunday 9 Nov 1975

Cold and grey. J.A. walked up to get newspapers. Congrats all round for Govt. By-election is on Wednesday. Read Edith Sitwell's book on English eccentrics. Really tired and stodgy. Amusing film about Wall Street. Am looking for inspiration; can't find any.

Monday 10 Nov 1975

Newspapers full of by-election. Got letter from Mother; she is back in her house in Cork.

Tuesday 11 Nov 1975

Got bus into Galway; v cold. Met group, smaller, 10 people. Ann Slattery ill. Laura looked in. Everyone told their story. 2 of the students call themselves ultra-conservative radicals. Pat seemed upset by their opinions. The rest of the students had no idea what they wanted to do.

Wednesday 12 Nov 1975

By-election today. Francis Stagg still alive. ICTU has given support to Crown strike but workers still on picket line.

Thursday 13 Nov 1975
Fine Gael won the by-election by 3000 votes. Massive victory. The Independent got 1500, Fianna Fáil lost by 8%. Ceasefire between Provos and Officials. Rees says all internees out by Xmas. Has closed down incident centre manned by Provos. Finn still in bed, Jacob not too good. Have been reading a book about Ulster Fiction, writer said catholic countries had least suicide numbers; not borne out by statistics in this country. Have got going quite well with the play.

Friday 14 Nov 1975
Very poor TV. Except for good programmes by *Seven Days.* A possibility of oil refinery in Dublin Bay. Lemass had tried one back in the 30s but was blocked by major oil companies because plans had been too well publicized. Hence the secrecy now. The objectors were not given a chance. Eoghan Harris really went to town in favour. Éamon Smullen was the only political party spokesman (Official Sinn Féin) for the oil refinery.

Saturday 15 Nov 1975
Had thoughts to go to Galway but changed my mind. Couldn't get eggs. Felt relieved that at last we got a bag of potatoes from Matty Lynch. Boys were difficult. We have banned their smoking. Continuous struggle on *Late Late Show* over divorce. Fr. Fergal O'Gorman said he would like the church & state to get out of marriage legislation and occupy themselves with protecting children. Woman from Galway opposing divorce. Abstractions. But the economic insecurity of women, the real position of women -- if there was divorce -- was not discussed. Last week there had been an article in the *Irish Times* saying the result of divorce in America had meant that the 30/40 age-group of women who married early and got divorced had not remarried. The ex-husbands had married younger women. Rather dismal picture for mature women, when they are supposed to have reached their most sexual awareness, that there should be no men around except one-night stands. This problem has not been discussed at all by the pro-divorce.

Sunday 16 Nov 1975
Angela McNamara on TV, "ordinary middle-class woman": at least she has been highlighting the problem. She says that loneliness is the chief problem in this country. Seán looked in last night. It is the loneliness that he finds most difficult in Cork. Good show, big film, of TV Royal Variety Performance in the

evening, rousing patriotic end. Have not seen this kind of chauvinism before. Vera Lynn, Dad's Army, Harry Secombe, all singing "London Pride", "There'll Always Be An England". Last Sunday there was an Equity meeting in London. Right wing failed. Enormous propaganda in newspapers against the left wing yet they were able to defeat right wing by small vote. March today by WRP (Workers' Revolutionary Party) to demand investigation of Police Raid on their premises. A kidnapping in Wood Green area of a Greek Cypriot girl. She was released today after ten days captivity. No word in press about it as police thought the media might scare the kidnappers and panic them to kill the girl like the Black Panther case or the wife of *The News of the World* who was minced up in a pig-food grinder.

~~~o~~~

Thursday 1 Jan 1976, New Year's Day
Poured. Johnny Keaney came round, grumbled about Farmers' Dole. Des Hogan called, asked about books and bodhrán. He had visited Tom Kilroy who said he was only eating one meal a day, he was so broke. Have decided to give up cigarettes; they are costing £350 a year. Des Johnson called yesterday. We must begin working on the union play. Des H. gave us some names of people who might be interested. This year is not going to be good.

1) The Burgess court case: he is claiming maximum damages.
2) The production of the 4th Connolly play for The Almost Free. It is going to be a very difficult task.
3) Realization that I am blacklisted in main subsidized theatres.
4) Too many enemies amongst people I have worked with.
5) I have a sore finger because I had bitten a cuticule to the quick, so it is difficult to write.

~~~o~~~

Tuesday 6 Jan 1976
Went to Galway; had to get a lawyer to witness our oath about the case vis-à-vis Burgess. This lawyer, we were told afterwards, had interests in the Fahy cottage. He did not betray that he knew us except to ask if we knew Burgess. Smoked three cigarettes. When I smoke now, it is an absolute experience, my

mind and body relaxes. I make a separate world for a few minutes. Have taken to sniffing nail polish, very delightful. The effect of not smoking so much is not very agreeable. I worry much more, going over again and again details of my life, finding new entrances to open. It is a bit like acupunture in reverse: as soon as I am free of one needle, I stick another in. Haven't got contract from Ed Berman. Paola wrote from Turin today: no one there wants to publish *Ballygombeen Bequest.* I am middle-aged and in terms of getting anywhere I am back to zero. I have placed myself in a situation where there is no potential. Seán came round to say Scullys were organizing an event at the hall. He is doing a six-minute sketch. There is no doubt about it: it is harder to break into rural theatricals than into Broadway. My depression never seems to lift.

The threat to burn out the itinerants by some residents in Rahoon, exasperated by the rumour that a woman was keeping a thoroughbred mare on the 5th floor of the flats. This must be the medical officer of health's daughter-in-law. He has to be attacked because there are rats the size of cats in Mervue & he will do nothing about it. He claims not to know anything about it.

Ten protestants in the North were shot last night as they were coming home from work. Their minibus was ambushed. The men were told to get out & asked their names. There was one catholic; he was told to walk away. The rest were machine-gunned down. Rivers of blood and personal property strewn on the road, it was 2 miles from where catholics had been machine-gunned in their homes. 20% of the North will be unemployed next year. Rolls Royce closing down.

Wednesday 7 Jan 1976
Got a letter from Tallaght Theatre Group in response to my letter in *The Irish Times* about relationship between playwrights and amateur groups. Started working on third section of the American play. Smoked 4 cigarettes yesterday. I should not read my diary out to J.A. as he seems to get disturbed if I show my morale is slipping. It was a beautiful morning but is now drizzling. Neuss went to school after big shouting match; got Finn up and out of the house with the others to go to Galway.

~~~o~~~
~~~

Monday, 12 Jan 1976
We had a fruitful discussion with Des J. and Seán about sketches for the Union play for WUI (of which lecturers are members). Made a brief scenario. My letter in *The Irish Times* got two replies: the one from drama group in Tallaght, and another from someone in Listowel who is involved in Writers' Week, also involved in a conference in Dundalk about community theatre. Photo of Kilroy in *Sunday Press.* He begins a Writers' Workshop on Sat. Not a word to us. Had two lapses in the cig. withdrawal on Friday. Great row with Adam, who pinched a packet of cigs from my pocket. Every day since Xmas it has been mild, dark and wet. Mary Ellen Staunton said she thought it was the end of the world. The British Government has sent the SAS into Armagh. Big debate in Parliament. On the *Late Late Show* Tim Pat Coogan and Conor Cruise O'Brien went for each other. Tim Pat says Brits must withdraw, Conor that if they do there will be a bloodbath and terrible civil war.

J.A. has accused me of not commenting on events. Should I in a diary or is it too difficult? As it is, by writing in simple sentences there is some sort of clarity. My political opinions on paper would take too much time.

Des Johnson implied that I do not understand the people, so I am incapable of judging their mentality. This is such an old accusation, first raised by John McManus, whose policy was to take each stage of a political strategy without ever giving overall plan in case it prejudices his case, but I would say that that was stalinism; a little bit of knowledge at a time prevents other opinions. 116,000 out of work now. Seán Newell said he couldn't see any indication of any unrest amongst the unemployed because of redundancy money and the dole; but I would have thought cancer rates, drunkenness, gambling, were *some* symptoms of alienation. Seán N. has a job at Digital; there is a union there, ITGWU. He can do as much overtime as he likes. He earned £8 on Saturday and likes it very much. After abortive start, 3rd part of American play has begun again.

Still can't get over my depression. Of course the very long holidays that the kids have don't help. They constantly complain about living here, Finn spends most of his time in bed, then gets up and watches the TV. He is nearly 17. Neuss, when he doesn't get what he wants, screams like a 2-year old, Jacob is the only one who is constantly busy doing his drawing and painting. Adam spends most of his time out of the house chatting to the neighbours.

~~~o~~~

Wednesday 14 Jan 1976
Invitation for Sinn Féin Ard Fheis yesterday. Contract from Ed Berman, also letter from Albert (solicitor) warning us of bankruptcy if Burgess proceeds against us.

~~~o~~~

Tuesday 27 Jan 1976
J.A. had a good gloom today. We bought 20 cigs, budget day is tomorrow. £880 million has got to be found. Frank Stagg is dying; his case is going to the Human Rights Court. Geoffrey and mother involved in Wakefield jail. Éamon S. wants us to do play for Cuba. It also looks as if Arts Council is going to give us a grant for the workshop. WUI section of college has confirmed that we do a piece for their social. Which direction should the union go? democracy for the uni.? political awareness? We must write a speech for the radical voice.

Went to Dublin last weekend, stayed with Pat Cobey who might be setting up a women's theatre group and has asked me to help her. She has found a friend available for raising human consciousness and might get money for them.

Crown strike has had a victory from Labour Court which says management is wrong, they must reinstate shop steward.

Bríd and Helen came round, Saturday. Helen wants an abortion. Rang up Wilma Ivimey, who is going to help her. Bríd is going to London with her. Might help us against Burgess.

Finished 2-thirds of 3rd play. It has snowed a bit; frosty nights; sun in the daytime. 2 of the kids at home with flu.

We are doubting the quality of our work more and more. Letter from W. Germany: don't want the Connolly play.

Saw Mary Manning. Is going to write to the O'Malley brothers in Boston, asking them can they help us? They know Paul O'Dwyer who is going to stand for the New York elections.

J.A. feels that he is getting more and more entangled in Irish Affairs which are so alien to him. Maria still writes loving letters to him which should warm him. Our depression gets worse; I don't know why.

The poet John Birtwhistle met us in Galway for a few hours, he is young and told us of his discomfort in his caravan at Carna, he sprained his ankle and had to hop over walls and stony paths to get to the well. He is writing a big epic poem on his stay there. Laura called Sunday evening; she has set up her etching workshop and got an apprentice from Cork to help her. The Arts Council has given her money. Tom Kilroy has his writers' course; has not contacted us. They had a big do for the opening. We were not invited. (Nell McCafferty, when I met her in Dublin, tried to involve me in a philosophical discussion on the meaning of lovers and pain.)

~~~o~~~

Thursday 12 Feb 1976
Frank Stagg is dead -- 61 days on hunger strike -- early hours of this morning in Wakefield Jail. Geoffrey is medical head of that area. Mother has been at W. They are accessories of murder.

~~~o~~~

Thursday 26 Feb 1976
First session of workshop. Free improvisation for images.
Scourging, crucifixion, resurrection, death, drowning man, boat full of men beating the drowning man away with their paddles. Frankenstein. Dracula. Cannibalism. Drunken TD. IRA man asking for bail. Workers asking for support. Accusations of being an agitator. Blind man being tormented by assailants. Students protesting against unfair treatment by lecturer, mad lecturer has overall power. Guards beating up people, kicking, nailing, throwing dirt.

Discussion. Difficulty of having a common theme till we know each other better. Students asked about love theme.

Next week impro. story-telling, boy/girl situation.

Stories from our workshop

(1) Young man doubts the existence of God, has nothing in common with his family, hardly feels any love for them; found that out when he went to college and sent them a postcard home from America, asking for books: couldn't write the word "love". Doesn't like sport, prefers books, opera, plays; has a friend who is a priest. Prefers to think of himself as ultra-conservative, mainly in reaction against left-wing atmosphere in College. Does not believe in rules: only obeys them because they happen to coincide with his own ideas. Ambition to get out of the country as soon as possible and make a lot of money. Does commerce in college; comes from Limerick.

(2) Young man from Ballinasloe; comes from large family; his mother fell ill when he was young, went to hospital and died several years later. Wanted to go to Art College but was too late for a place. Went to college for a year and hopes to go to Art School.

Agitprop play on Crown strike

We are doing play because the events of the strike show that underneath it there is a fundamental attack on Trade Unionism by American Monopoly Capitalism.

Facts: company given grants,
No clause in contract to honour normal labour procedures,
No warning when they leave,
Machinery belongs to Irish State.
One third of total Govt. money goes on foreign debt.
They borrow money from abroad, pay 2-fifths of total Govt. income on interest, then give borrowed money to foreign companies to invest.
Demands: --
Honour normal Trade Union procedure,
Refund the grant if they pull out before a certain time -- 15 years?,
Govt. take over machinery if they pull out,
Books open to Govt. & TU for inspection.

University play: why a trade union for academics?
Pilgrim's Progress
possible effects.
mass scene random images -- strobe lighting
3-6 min. film of students attending lectures.
lecturers giving them. Tape-recordings, sounds of lecturers droning on. Students chatter; ends with murder game. Lights up. Lecturer beside body. All point at him; he denies it, asserts his innocence, has only come in at that moment. Sudden change to laughter at him; fingers pointing.

student climbing ladders: primary school, secondary school, university.
teachers praise him, he is clever, he will get somewhere, he will go places
single voice reaffirmed by crowd.
Intro (maybe photo) Socrates, Galileo, Marx.

Larkin bursts through with Red Flag, slogans. Establishment of Labour Party, water Larkin down, reduce him to a stamp -- which is put on letter and circulated round audience.

Hierarchal system of seating at all faculty meetings & union meetings.
Irish Universities were set up by the British to make an administrative middle class. Influence of Catholic church, to make a business class. Catholic church philosophers: man is a fallen creature who strives to regain favour with God.

Professor on ladder: six lecturers kiss his backside.
I appoint six of you now to be my assistants because in five years' time I will want two of you to be my lecturers. Now set about to satisfy me. Prof makes ludicrous speech, all agree with him, then one is dubious & kicked out.
Lecturer asks, what must I do to be saved?

Prof says kiss my arse.

Well, we shall all have enough evil before we come to our journey's end.

Who are you?
I am professor at UCG.

What are you doing?
I am having a leak.
What are you leaking?
A secret doc. What kind of secret document?
A very secret doc.
Tell us the secret, is it a rise of salary? is it a new uni?

Dissertation
History of European unis.
Socrates: duty to question. Corrupting youth; put to death.
Galileo: challenged preconceived idea on a basis of observation; had to retreat.
Marx: challenged man's position in relation to nature; all history is struggle based on class struggle.

Neighbours' Voices

(from a collection of interviews, recorded in the 1970s.)

Kathleen

My friend over thirty years in Corrandulla. Her mother's father was a seanchai and RTE taped his stories. His mother before him was a seanchai too. Kathleen carries the tradition.

At the time I began to walk it was exactly one hundred and thirty-eight years from the battle of 1798. And that was when my great-great grandfather was supposed to have come here from Ulster: and he remained here just because he didn't have a ha'penny. He needed the ha'penny to cross the river-ferry on the main Galway road - but as he didn't have one, he just had to stay. And he must be a romantic - so he fell in love with a girl near this river: and they married - so that's how we stayed here ever since... I suppose I've always had a turbulent nature - with this United Irishman goading me!

I was 5 to 6 years of age when I went to school, and I liked my first teacher okay. But I'm afraid the second one had been away a few times for treatment for her nerves. She told me to say poetry. She called me up one morning before all the school and asked me to say this poetry. She praised me to the highest and she said how well I recited the poetry, and said how good I was. And then she told me to repeat it. She said, "How come that you didn't say that poetry as well the second time as you did the first time? Now say it a third time." When I said it the third time, she even claimed that I was worse than the second time. She told me I was just getting worse and worse, and going to the bad, until in the end I wasn't able to say it at all.

I would like to say something about the landlord, you know. The English landlord, he was so far removed from his tenants. I think the only thing they knew about him was that he was sexually-motivated like any ginger-tom. You can be sure today, if you find any scabs among us, it's dissembled from the wild oats that the landlord sowed. Oh, they got rid of the landlord, yes. *I* can't tell you, although my father did remember seeing all the noise - and they stormed the bastille, sort of thing, you know! Yes, he was thrown out - he just had to get out. He walked around like a baby, you know - oh yes, he was thrown out - he was just like what you call a pauper - I think he died in the County Home! The landlord he evicted his mother from the Castle, you know. I don't know where she went. Why should the people worry, especially the people he put out? *They* weren't worried about the landlord's mother, do you think they were, being as they were that kind?

They let the people starve: and then they gave them a real good starving - first, let them really have it, have their feeling of starving: and then they opened the mill, and they gave them a great feed. This is true, they did give them a big feed of Indian meal and some kind of soup. Of course the people were so hungry they ate such a monstrosity of a feed, that they made for the Curate - and the Curate lived back the road here, you know, the brewery - and they knew they were dying, they wanted Absolution from the Curate; but half of them never reached the Curate - they were dead, they were dead all along the road - along this road here from the mill down: and they were making for the priest to get Absolution after the feed, they died after the big feed they got from the landlord.

One day the Parish Priest was caught hunting for hares on the estate, and of course the landlord cautioned him and threatened him. The Priest told him that he wouldn't have to worry, that whilst there was one of that family, the Blakes, in Cregg Castle, there would never again be a hare on their estate. And then he told the Blakes more things they wouldn't like to hear. They would never like to think that the Castle would be without a Blake: and he said that while there were Blakes in Cregg Castle their slumber would be disturbed, the rooks would see to that. He said too, that the Castle will be there and it won't have any of you, and the last one will leave in the dark of the night... And I lived to see that in 1947 when Mrs Blake left... She was supposed to leave in the afternoon: but the taxi never arrived until after dark for her. That's true. And the following day two hares were seen going back the road and up the avenue gate. This is true.

Shall I tell you a fairy story, even though I don't believe it? There was a big rock in front of the Castle, it's not there any more - but it was a kind of a landmark - a big, big, huge stone. And anyway this particular person, a friend of mine, a relative of mine, was working there with some other girl, and there was a continuous knocking on the back door, and after a while she went out. She went over to the door, and sure there was nobody there. And she got kind of weary of it, and she went down from the back into the front of the Castle: and she was standing near this big stone I'm telling you about now. The policemen from the police-station there, they were guarding: and they were just going off duty. the sergeant and two policemen. They walked down the avenue, anyway, and they passed this relative of mine, and they said, "Oh, come away quickly, come with us, come with us." And she said, "Why?" And they said, "Oh, but you must come with us!" Anyway, she walked down the avenue: and when they came to the gatehouse, they said to her, "Now, you go in there." And she remained there until her husband came home. And she said, "What's the meaning of this?" And they said, "Well, while you were standing by that rock in front of the Castle, there was a form standing behind you with a headless thing!" There was something without a head standing behind her! Do you believe that? You would not. Why would you believe it?

~~~o~~~

Nelly

Another Corrandulla neighbour. She died a few years ago, aged over ninety. "Folklore medicine" is now becoming widely recognized and is no longer regarded as mere superstition. A child born after the death of its father has the gift to cure fungal disease, the "thrush".

I had the cure because I didn't see my father, like.

And how did you know you had the cure?
Mother knew it. I suppose she seen ones before me having it. There was two up there now, they were twins.

And when did you cure the first person?
'Tis years ago. When I was going to school they used to come into the school, hundreds of them with babies.

And what used you do to them?
Blow into their mouth and like while you'd be saying, "Name of the Father,
~~~

and of the Son, and of the Holy Ghost, Amen." When you'd have that said - then three times then for three days - Monday, Thursday and Saturday - there wouldn't be a bit on them.

What did you think as a child, being able to cure people? Did you think it strange?
I did. Too strange. And a lot of people thought it very strange, because I mean they'd go to the doctor, and they won't get cured, and they'd get stuff like to rub o'their mouths and no more. And they'd go into the hospital then and they might be six months in there, and they wouldn't be all right, only 'twould take that length of time. They'd get all right though in some months to come, but they'd suffer.

Is it painful?
Oh 'tis terrible. Couldn't eat or drink or anything.

What happens to their mouths?
Massive corruption and lumps and it goes back here in the throat, and down. It goes down the chest there. And they do suffer terrible with it. And people don't know what it is like until it is well into them. Many a one had them and they thought they were finished - they didn't know what it was on them. And when they found out, they'd come here, and they'd be all right. No matter how bad, they'd get all right the third time.

And how many people have you cured?
Thousands. I know since I was going to school now, and that years ago, that I was curing them. 'Tisn't known what came to me, and 'tisn't known what I went to when I was young. I cycled up to *Athenry,* if you don't mind! - to a case. 'Tisn't known forever what I cured.

Have any doctors come down to find out how you cure them?
No.

Do doctors send patients to you?
No. They bring them to the doctor, and the doctor keeps them going like, gives them stuff, they go out again, and they get stuff again: no good, no good, worse and worse the child is getting. J--- Mac back there, he had a little girl, she wasn't

resting day or night, he had the doctor three or four times. Many's the one had the doctor, hundreds of them. They didn't know what it was, you see. And he was as sure he said as he was living the child would die. He said he didn't want to come into the house at all. The child was morning noon and night roaring, roaring, roaring in the cot. Someone told him and he came over to me. And there wasn't a bit on her the third time. The third time he came in here, J--- Mac, he lives back there on the side of the road, don't you know - well, he said he couldn't believe it, and how the child got out - there wasn't a bit on her.

How did they hear about you?
Well, d'ya see it goes from one to one, and sure thousands of tinkers, it isn't known what tinkers - tinkers we used to call them - itinerants. Whatever they'd like to give you, like: but you cannot charge. They said if you did, you'd lose the cure.

And have they always given you something?
Every one. Some of them gives a few pound.

What did you do with all the money?
(*Laughs*)

...'tis wonderful too. Isn't it? G--- down there in D----, he was very bad, and he was too, it was Dr K--- was there at the time, and he was going to Dr K--- and he could do nothing for him. He was three weeks or four weeks going to Dr K--- and he gave up hope at the latter end, he told him to go to the hospital, he couldn't do no more for him. Someone told him about me: and we were making hay up in the field and he came back the boreen this day, we didn't know what was bringing him back, and he told the story and I done it for him in the hay; he sat down in the butt of the cock of hay and I done it for him and he came again the third time and I done it for him and there wasn't a bit on him. The mother was sure he was finished. The doctor had ordered him into the hospital and he wasn't able to walk, he was that weak. He's down there yet, living and married, in D----, below the post-office there.

And it gives you great satisfaction thinking of all the people you've cured, does it?
Yea. No matter who 'twould be I'd cure them anyway.

~~~o~~~
~~~

A Deserted Wife

I have always been a fighter: I had to fight: I was left with thirteen children on my own in the wilds of Connemara: and I had to fight to get through. My parents were farmers. I met my husband locally, he was a local person. Let's say, he was a gentleman-farmer. He left me exactly eleven years ago.

My husband has roughly three or four thousand acres of land, he has most of it sold to the forestry: and the last fight I had on my hands was the forestry came, and bought a farm which they were not entitled to buy because I had children: and they bought it without me knowing anything at all about it. So, I fought back; and I had to buy the farm back from them for one of my children.

As far as I know, the only thing I do know and I certainly do know: that if a woman is prepared to sit down and let the whole walls of the world drop around her, she will be allowed to do it by the Irish government! They do not give one tinker's curse for her or her children: and it is a man's world, that's truth.

A lot of people didn't like me fighting all these years: but that doesn't worry me very much. Well, you have to fight for it. If you don't fight for it, you don't get. I mean, I have seen so much injustice, I have seen it everywhere. There is nothing but injustice, you know; and it's always the poor persons that shouldn't be hurt that are hurt.

~~~o~~~

Ann

A Traveller, whom I have known since the late 1960s, when she was, as she says, "in the side of the road." Even today she still misses the old life.

I was in a caravan on a site for a while. Before that I was in the side of the road. This was something I always wanted, to go into a house.

When they moved us into the house - I mean, it was fine for us for the first week, but they completely forgot all about us then - and it meant we weren't able to cope with the house ourselves, because we didn't know anything about what to do for a house. I mean, the Travellers' houses get dirty because they
~~~

don't know, they're not used to keeping the place tidy so it takes them years. A caravan's a small thing - you don't have chairs and you don't have tables in a caravan... So many rooms that we're not used to them, and so much dust flying around, and it takes a lot of getting used to. We'd to get our bits and pieces ourselves - you're inclined to pile up too much in a house, and every bit you get you bring into it, when all round it takes less to furnish a house than we're aware of. You put junk in more than furniture. If we had the help from social workers or somebody that was voluntary, they'd help us and say, "Well, you don't need this and you don't need that," and show us how to put up curtains, and what to do to be sure and make it a good house, and Travellers be able to settle in it quickly.

I think that the neighbours you usually go in beside, at the beginning, they don't want to know you. And they're afraid of getting involved, and they're terrified of us, and we're terrified of them - just in case, you know. Whatever it is, anyway, it'll have to be the settled community that'll have to come out first. You can imagine a Traveller going up and knocking at the door and saying, "Will you come into my house and have a cup of tea, or will I go to yours?"! I can imagine what the answer would be the first time. After all the settled people are well organized at having evenings, and a crowd of them getting together. I'm sure they could take the call to inviting one Traveller at a time anyway, to their evening meetings, or their morning cup of coffee, or whatever it is - and it would help the Traveller more, to be able to cope with the settled life.

There's the settled people does the talk for you, which is very bad: they should give the Travellers a chance for to have their own say, and let *them* think about it besides the committee making up the Travellers' minds. I remember the day that a lot of Travelling people walked on the march, and felt very embarrassed themselves! Now it might be a good thing they marched, and maybe a bad thing, I don't know. But it was the first time the Travellers came out. But it was something they were talked into they should, and were all for it when they weren't marching, and when they started the march then they wanted to back out of it. They just didn't want to continue, because embarrassment was there. And just to keep them, give them courage, one or two of the old committee walked with them, and then didn't back them up with their husbands, which is very bad.

I've just watched other people, how their houses is, and take a guess whether they're doing the right thing. I watch at sitting-rooms or kitchens - if I get my chance, I go into them, if somebody's decent enough to invite me in - and I watch what they hang on the walls. If I get something like it, I hang it there and see how it works out. It's the same with my garden: I keep watching at other gardens. The only thing is, I don't know the names of things, don't know when to set them down and that sort of thing; which is very sad, because you see other gardens coming up so well. You say, "Why can't I have a garden like that?" and you put down things and nothing ever comes up, so it doesn't... It's probably the wrong time of year when we put them down.

The children gets very little help. They go to school and that. But when the children get home, they've work to do. A lot of the parents tells the teachers that they can't help them, so if they could keep them in half an hour after the school and help them with their homework... It ends up by the children doing their fulltime going to school, and they're not able to read. Then the committee come along and they have the cry of that they're helping the teenagers, to read, and to cook, and this sort of thing... where they could have it all done before they started as teenagers! They could have the child going into a trade or a job or something. They're not helping them enough by any means. It's not just a question of saying, "Oh they're doing fine," but they should have somebody calling at least once a week, or twice a week, to the houses that the Travellers are living, and see how they really do - they'd certainly get a great change with that!

~~~o~~~

Angela

She has had many jobs since her days in the jeans factory, including being a legal assistant, and an organizer of cultural exchanges between Ireland and Russia.

I am now working in a jeans factory, owned by an American company. There is a lack of communication in the factory between staff and management. There was two meetings where the girls went in and complained about the hot water being too hot, and the cold water too cold... just trivial things: and all the complaints were posted on the board. As they were being set right they
~~~

were ticked off. But there was nothing of any *effect* done - I mean, if you go in and say, "Why were these things not done, and what are you going to do about it?", they can just say, "Oh the union signed this agreement with us..." So we go back to the union, and the union don't have any answer - they just say, "Well, we'll get back to you on it." So there's very little that can be done. Solidarity among the workers is lacking.

I was amazed at how the union handled the agreement. And it disturbed me to think that there was somebody there supposed to be supporting the workers, and instead they just turned their back on them - and presumably support the management.

At the first meeting we had about the union agreement, they just read out the whole agreement - which is about twenty pages - and he read it out word for word, and everybody had a copy. When I tried to ask questions, and put things to him, he just said, "Well, you'll have to see the local secretary of the union," and then he said, "Now let's get on to the elections for shop-steward." When the elections were over - this one took about an hour - that was the end. Nobody could seee that any good was going to come of it. There were girls getting up and walking out in the middle of the meeting, they were just fed up: and even if they did ask questions, he wouldn't be able to answer.

When some of the girls were fired they weren't given any excuse - some of them were told it was because they had too many days off, and what they call "unexcused absence" - which was anything above two hours without a medical certificate, or else prior permission from the foreman. It was the day of the holidays at five-to-five, they were called into the office. They bring you in and they tell you that you've been fired: but if you don't want a black mark on your employment record, you can sign a form to say you've resigned. Now at least one girl fell for this, signed the form - so, okay - she got a reference from the company and you know, maybe she's got a better chance of getting herself a job - but to think that the company can do this...

Oh everybody said it was terrible, and how awful... But it was the days of the holidays, and two weeks later it was all forgotten, and they'd taken on new girls. There was definitely something corrupt in the system, and I'd like to find out what it is. If we don't get a meeting with the union, or hear something within this week, I'm going to take off to the union some day, and demand to see the secretary - if necessary go to his house or something! Because I don't think it's fair we should be just left sitting there with this agreement, which is absolutely useless to us!

I could take it to the newspapers, or there's a group in Dublin who are rank-and-file members of the Irish Transport Union, and they started to publish a paper called *New Liberty.* I have a few copies of that: and I think I will write to them and perhaps they could publish something in the paper.

A lot of the women are demoralised. It's the whole attitude, you're like a - just a - piece of machinery at times, you're timed and you're being watched, you have to produce. Like, the engineers come round with clocks, and they watch you, watch what you're doing and see what you're doing wrong - and "Why can't you do it and go faster?" and - oh, they're very polite, most of them, but I was once told that my machine was capable of going very fast, and that I should be able to keep up to it!

There is a certain amount of pressure on everybody, even if they're putting it on themselves, you know. I've seen two girls in tears - just that they felt the strain and the pressure too much, and they just broke down and cried at their machines.

I am trying to push myself: and then suddenly everything starts going wrong - needles breaking, threads break, and - you know - !

The company says to us, "Oh you'll reach the target!", and so they keep pushing and pushing themselves - and then they look to the union for support. I think it's disgraceful to think that any union would sign to those conditions. They brought over some films of machinists in America, and they brought in the different sections to watch the women at their jobs. We were brought in, we saw the girl on the film, and saw that it took her twice as long to do the job as we were allowed. We were told the film was in slow-motion! So the idea of showing us the films to let us see that it could be done was a complete washout. Because either they said they were taking it in slow-motion, or fast-motion, or something was wrong, and the layout was completely different in the factory in America to what we have to work in here!

As a shop-steward I'd have to ask permission to have a meeting in the factory. It means asking the foreman or personnel manager - really the only way would be to call a meeting, you know, some evening after work in somebody's house.

The only other union experience I've had was in the other company - the shirt-factory that went bankrupt and decided to close down. The union was involved and when I asked if there was any way there could be a public enquiry into it, to find out exactly where the money had gone, it was all hushed up. There were assessors in at the time checking the books, because the company was claiming inability to pay on the national wage agreement - that report was never published, and the whole thing was done so quietly!

It was an Irish firm with Irish shareholders. There was meetings, and this union secretary came up and said, "Now there's no need to worry, girls..." Oh, insurance cards hadn't been stamped; and tax hadn't been paid; and he said, "Don't worry. You'll get credit-stamps from the government, and you'll be able to collect your pay-related benefits..." But nothing about saving our jobs, which is supposed to be - you know - one of the union priorities. "And when the new company takes over, you'll be 99% guaranteed to get your jobs back..." And so the girls were quite happy to accept that. I could go up and say, "Well, this isn't right: and where does the money go? This money's somewhere in the company, the shareholders aren't broke. Why are they pulling out?" And they said, "It's all right... We'll go and find out..." And then the union secretary'd come and say, "All right, girls..." And everybody was calm again! I got my job in the new company: but many didn't.

The Irish want the European Common Market, which cuts down on their export costs: they have cheap labour, higher profit margins - tax-free, money for the asking! Lots of foreign industries come in on some kind of agreement with either the Industrial Development Authority or the union. This jeans-manufacturing company has sixty factories throughout the world. It's been going for sixty years and they do have a lot of factories - in Italy, Spain, Portugal, Scotland, Africa - you know, the lower-paid countries.

~~~o~~~
~~~

A Young Housewife

The last time I met her she was working with Travellers on a horticultural project.

I found in the tenants' association that it was very hard to work: because the people already in the tenants' association, they were fighting on petty issues, they were more inclined to fight against the itinerants than against the corporation.

Another thing about the tenants' association, which I find very weird, was that they weren't willing to go by the majority of the people - they felt that, "Well, if I'm in a tenants' association, I'll do what I want myself: but I won't go out and fight." Say, if there was a strike called: and the people wanted to go on strike: if the members on the tenants' association didn't feel they wanted to go on a strike, they wouldn't. And they wouldn't feel obliged to resign, or anything. We felt, myself and another mate of mine that was on the tenants' association, that it was an important thing to fight for. But I find throughout this city that tenants' associations are the same - and I think when I look at them that they are a very bad thing for the tenants - the ordinary tenants - because they mislead them. They don't give any proper guidance, and they don't give any advice. I think they should be able to advise every tenant when they move into an estate like this: but they don't: they confuse more than anything else. It's almost as if they were employed by the corporation against the tenants.

Sixty percent of the people here are unemployed. There's no facilities for young toddlers, because the playgrounds are all wide open: and the small children have to play with the big children: which is a bad idea, because the bigger children get rowdy and that. The mother needs to be at ease when she lets the small children out, that they're not going to go on the road or anything - you cannot have that ease here. And the tenants are not willing to do anything for themselves. I suggested to the tenants' association we set up a basketball court, or a tennis court, for the teenagers in the area: and maybe start an adventure playground. A few other friends of mine on the tenants' association felt this might be a good thing. But we were outvoted.

The corporation decided to increase our rents, and also to back-date them to last July - that was '76 - the tenants didn't want that at all. So one of the tenants decided to call a meeting about the rent, to get something done about it. We decided we should ask the chairman of the tenants' asscoiation to call a general meeting of the tenants to take some action. So they called a general meeting. At the general meeting twenty-eight people decided to picket the corporation, to get their back-dated rent squashed, and to get the increase lowered, because we felt they were too excessive, and that the majority of people couldn't afford them. The tenants' association was not willing to do this: because they felt it was too militant. They felt that negotiations were the only thing possible. We knew ourself from past experience that negotiations were futile with the corporation: because when the tenants' association go to the corporation, the corporation ignore them - and they don't negotiate with the working-class person, you know.

So a few days later, old members of the tenants' association pretended that the meeting was null and void - and that we should not have been co-opted onto the tenants' association committee. So that's when it all started: we formed our own group - about twelve people - and we worked to get a *right* tenants' association here. There was a meeting called to elect a new committee, and I was elected with a few other people.

Where I come from in the country, I didn't go to church or anything like that. And people in the area, although they thought it was awful for somebody not to go to church and not to believe in the catholic church, they still weren't too hostile to me. They were still friendly with me, and talked to me, and didn't keep it against me. But here it's different, if you're not part of the normal, you're out: and you're ostracized for it, you know. They don't want the neighbours to have anything more than themselves - they feel bad if somebody's getting something cheaper than they are. They say, "What's wrong, he shouldn't be getting that? I've got to report that, or do something about that!"

I think they're democratic in the European sense of the word - because a European democracy to me is a farce! Any democracy really is farce, because it's not democratic - in fact it's democratic for the businessman - but the right of the working-person and the poor person is never heard anyway. And something about here in Ireland, you know whatever party it is, they never do anything for the poor, the working-class people. It *seems* that they're doing something for the working-class people when they bring in their budgets and concession: but it's nothing.

I know myself, if you don't go to the corporation roaring and shouting, you won't get anything done. When you go down to the corporation, you have to literally scream your face off to get anything done! It's terrible to have to do that. I know, when I was getting this flat, I had to - my husband was working at night, and *I* had to go to ask them for it. I went for three months, and I was very polite and patient... and I said to myself, "This is completely negative." Eventually I had to go in every day and just get really cross with them every single day - and eventually - after two months of that - we got a flat.

~~~o~~~

Mary
She is now one of Ireland's leading blues-singers and lives in Bray, County Wicklow.

I was a crazy mixed-up kid in Galway city: and I went around slashing my wrists. They got me into the Regional Hospital: and there is this shrink and he starts on me. He thought suicide was a crime - it was a crime in Ireland to do such things - and that I would either have to go to Ballinasloe Mental Hospital or go into a reformatory. Didn't want to go back to school, though; didn't want to work; you know, I didn't want to do anything - I just wanted to be free to live, you know, in my own way. My friends at the time were a lot older. I wanted to do a lot of things - all of the kids wanted to - smoking drugs and stuff. So I got put into Ballinasloe for five weeks; and they said I was just depressed and that I'd be all right. So they let me out. Oh 'twas terrible, it was a nightmare! It was terrible, just that the rooms were big, and the doors were so big, and the big big bolts on the doors - and I was in with about twenty crude old women. They used to get dressed-up every Wednesday and every Friday because they were visiting-days, waiting for their families to come - they had been doing that for years, some of them - and no-one would ever come - and they were just left there to die. They'd their relations, but no-one ever came or cared about them. And they used to fight for the newspaper on Sundays; they used to roll up the pages and smoke them; they'd no visitors to bring them cigarettes; they'd give you anything for a cigarette! I remember, I was smoking at
~~~

the time: my visitors would bring me cigarettes, and they'd be just plaguing me for cigarettes, it was unbelievable! They used to smoke newspaper, they used to fight about it, oh it was horrid!

I met some people in the town which were in the Baha'i faith, so I became a Baha'i after a few months. Most of the people were into decent things, you know, so I learnt a lot from them. I was more into the people than the religion. My mother knew for a long time: and she was afraid to tell anyone because she thought the people would kill me, or something. I stayed with them a long time, maybe two years. They think that Baha'illah is the return of Christ, and that God just sees fit to send a prophet about every two thousand years. Baha'illah is the major prophet for this day and age, Christ was the last major prophet, Mohammed was another one. They recognize and embrace all religions: and they're into world-religion and world-government... No, they weren't into drugs. I was truly into a leading a double life at the time, I suppose, because I was still into smoking dope... an awful lot of dope...

~~~o~~~

Cindy

An American. She lives in the countryside outside Galway. She was one of the founders of La Léche. She educated all her children at home, she and her husband have made themselves self-sufficient in food and energy, she went to university and got a degree. When I rang her recently, she told me that she had just been listening to the Gerry Ryan Show, and the breast-feeding debate was still going on with the same prejudices as a quarter-century ago - "should mothers breast-feed in public?" - one woman listener rang in and said "Definitely not! Breast-feeding in public is as disgusting as lap-dancing."

The biggest thing I suppose that happened to me, that wouldn't have happened back home, was after I had the baby; when I wanted to breast-feed her in a café in town, I was asked not to. That wouldn't have happened in America: they're very tolerant of that sort of thing. I was astounded at that: I felt that really it was unforgiveable ignorance. When it first happened, I passed it off as an isolated incident - perhaps one or two people might feel that way... But it happened two or three times: I wrote a letter in to Gay Byrne's radio programme complaining about it: I was so upset about it. I wanted to do some-
~~~

thing, try and change people's attitudes. I thought this was the best thing to do, because so many people listen to Gay Byrne, and think of him as the next thing to God. So I wrote the letter and he read it out: and got a lot of response. He kept it one or two weeks. People would write in every day! Most of them agreed with me that you should feel free to feed your baby wherever you want to: and that it isn't something that should be hidden away. But some people wrote in and said that it should be relegated to back rooms, privacy in your bedroom, or whatever... That was probably the most significant thing that happened to me since I came here.

I made good friends with our landlady, who lived next door. I go and visit her in the evening, and occasionally a friend of hers would call in and visit. We'd sit around and have a chat and a cup of tea. You really begin to notice all the little games they play with each other. People that have been friends for twenty-five years, and still they wouldn't be open or honest, they'd still be comparing themselves, and ranking the women on how good a wife and mother they were by how good a dinner they cooked, and how much washing was on the line, and things like that.

A neighbour woman would stop in for a cup of tea: and our landlady'd bustle around and make a fuss about giving her a proper cup of tea and sandwiches just so. The minute the woman was out the door, she'd say how she couldn't bear to have her visit, she couldn't stand it. But all the time she was there, she would put on a good show for her. I felt that so much of this woman's life was just a show for the neighbours: and I felt that the neighbours were doing a lot of the same thing as well. If they'd come round, the conversation would be about keeping your houses just so. She'd talk about how she couldn't stand digging up the garden - yet she'd do it because it looks nice for the neighbours. So much of what she did was just "how would it look, what would people say?" I find this really exasperating, this attitude of orienting your whole life to what other people think of you: and never really dealing with real aspects of existence. We put a cat-door in the door for our cat to come in and out: and she didn't like that because it looked awful from the street. The practicality of it was so obvious, and she couldn't understand that -- it was only how it looked, you know?

13

LONDON 1978.

The Winter of Discontent, an election hovering for the next year, with the Tories gaining more and more popularity, a feeling amongst the left that they should not rock the boat and give advantages to the right (yet they still wanted to retain credibility, hence benefits organized to support the Liverpool dockers); as for the Irish situation with the prisoners on the blanket and all the smaller industrial disputes -- hold back! was the cry. The early months of 1978 found us running around London trying to find someone to put on the Irish plays, also clearing up after the libel case over 7:84 and *The Ballygombeen Bequest.* The Half Moon theatre had its benefit for the dockers; we agreed to give a couple of scenes from *The Non-Stop Connolly Show* -- the scene where James Connolly is in jail (arrested for a street-demonstration) and Keir Hardie visits him, and the other one of Jim Larkin going to the TUC for support for the Dublin workers in the Great Lockout. Pam Brighton wanted to reverse the scenes, ending with the visit of Keir Hardie. She didn't offer any explanation: I guess, now, that she didn't want the main dramatic emphasis to be on the inadequacy of the TUC bureaucracy, and she did want the more positive attitude of Hardie (on behalf of the Brit. Labour Party) to round off the excerpt, as well as the sentimental image of the brave man in jail. We refused to reverse the scenes. Then Colm Meaney wouldn't go on unless they *were* reversed; I told him J.A. would read Connolly instead. He went on. Anyway, the audience loved it. The gap between us and the theatre was widening. also the gap between myself and England.

Also I was pregnant, having gone off the pill because of the scares. I felt exhausted and depressed, and decided to have an abortion. This would have been my eighth pregnancy. Because of my seventh pregnancy (in Galway), a baby girl that died inside me, I felt I couldn't cope.

Dead Foetus

The pain seeps as through a filter
into the sponges of hope.
Even though the bands were to be removed

it is not the bands holding her together,
the inner one curled tight
not chewing her thumb.
She is unaware
the placenta has shrunk.
Dried skin and bones
like a shaven rat:
only the teeth yellowish
grin through the
wizened face.

Invitation to Greece to see production of *Serjeant Musgrave* in Thessalonika. Combined with an invitation to a writers' conference in Athens, organized by the Greek Writers' Union; we discovered at the opening reception that the union was still controlled by right-wingers who had supported the colonels' junta, and they were now excluding homosexuals. What was to be done? Each visiting foreign writer -- they were all male -- had prepared a contribution; they said their speeches couldn't be changed. I had prepared my own contribution (J.A. had had to return to London,), but I offered to change it and I did change it. Storm. Conference broke up in fury. The foreign writers kept well clear of me. But some of the Greeks surrounded me and thanked me for having had the courage to mention the unmentionable; and afterwards in the street a writer who ran a bookshop, and who had been excluded, approached me to thank me on behalf of himself and his excluded colleagues. On a conference-organized trip to the ruins of Mycenae, the coach went back to Athens without me. An English writer was one of the party; he had told them I was in the other coach. Frightening experience.

A reading of *Ballygombeen Bequest* (renamed *The Little Gray Home in the West*) in the Súgán pub-theatre. Stephen Rae, John Joyce and Roger Sloman read their original parts; I was in hospital. When I came out, went to New York to stay with Pat Cobey, trying to get support for prisoners on the blanket; not much success. Back in Corrandulla; finished *Vandaleur's Folly.* 7:84 put it on. My going to jail in the North of Ireland ended 1978: a terrible year. Bankruptcy too.

The Theatre Writers' Union was set up (after our strike at RSC); myself and J.A. were members.

* * * * * *

Diary Excerpts

Sunday 1 Jan 1978

Came home from Cherry Potter's at 4pm. Trafalgar Sq. littered with glass, ambulances in a cordoned area, cars hooting, men jumping in front of them. Wishing a happy new year; or a battlefield. Cherry with her hand on her husband's thigh as he leapt forward in the traffic. Parsees are a declining tribe now, not more than 60,000 scattered throughout the world: 4 - 6,000 in England. No wonder he looks forward to the future to forget the time of Alexander the Great. A truly terrible driver and yet he is a psychologist.

Went to the Súgán pub-theatre with Finn, no one there we knew. Full of Irish sensible girls with sensible shoes and sensible clothes, a bodhrán player, accordion and bones -- lively music. The proprietor Gerry O'Neill talking in loud voice about Michael Collins's old house, with his arm around a guest.

A bomb went off in Mayfair; two Syrians killed.

Monday 2 Jan 1978, Bank Holiday

Wrote a few notes on *The Pinprick of History*. Could it have worked better? The main failure was the lack of work done on the Historical Dialectical Association. J.A. in abstract is not interested in relationship of audience and actor versus the play, says he cannot understand concept of stretching barriers of the mind. Read Des Hogan's play: good use of names in building up atmosphere. RTE turned it down.

Tuesday 3 Jan 1978

Went to see Jackie Kaye and her new son Noel, named after Noel Jenkinson, a friend of hers, a Republican who'd died in prison: she worked in Gordon's Distillery; the white-collar workers were in dispute for more money; if they got it, the other workers would benefit as well. They go in every day during the dispute and then leave. She told us about the assembly line of bottles which they could take off the line and swig. The smell ruins everything else. They get 5p off every bottle of gin they buy. If it was increased to 10p, the management thinks it would encourage drink. Got a letter from Pat Cobey and also Tish Dace. They are coming Sunday. Tish thinks she may have found a director for

Connolly (play 4) in New York. Saw Stuart Burge; He's depressed because of very poor houses for Kilroy's Matt Talbot play. Also 7:84. Trendy Grant asked about doing *NSCS* for two consecutive nights. The theatre is wrong. Asked about doing *Vandaleur's Folly.* Rang Methuen; talked to Geoffrey Strachan; didn't have a clue what was going on about the libel case. Think *BB* may be published in summer. Paperback of J.A.'s plays will be out in the spring. Worked putting interviews in order, *Neighbours' Voices* [see Chapter 12]. Some of them read well. Putting on weight, feeling uncomfortable.

Thursday 5 Jan 1978
Went to Half Moon theatre company. Pam Brighton back from Canada. Narrow Street, empty building, no lights on. Wrong door opened; other door rehearsal room. They are short of two in play. Go to pub; young man, thick cockney accent, on about community theatre. Half Moon jammed into corner. Bangladalesh tightly-knit community. Only white people left for Half Moon are ex-fascists. "Yes, I suppose we are a bit evangelical ... It is difficult to get shop stewards over 40 ... How adaptable are you with changing material? Do you put content first? or other considerations?" The important thing is to have the play put on. I am extremely bored with political righteousness of the collectives: it is like a giant turtle sprawling on my back, gripping round my shoulders. Planning to go to Galway to campaign against EEC referendum in Eyre Sq. I must be bonkers to plan so much for three days. Following up clues. PLO man shot in London. Cold and bright. To speculate about next year.

The fortune-teller said I would have a long life and die amongst friends. Spent £5 going again. Temptress; should I? The last time knocking on the door.

Eileen Murphy and Terry Doherty. He didn't want to be thrown into such wildness with his blue smock and bookshop. Much better with IMG dolly. The disturbance and passsion of Ireland is too extreme; second generation.

I hear that John O'Mahony (Republican prisoner) is out of gaol; when he came into Corrib Hotel everyone shook his hand and said welcome back. He now has a job painting the school in Ennistymon. He can't get his property because it would mean evicting a garda. Conor O'Cleary said that when he heard Treasa speaking Irish in the *Pinprick* he must learn Irish.

Went to negotiation meeting at Steve Gooch's. David Edgar, George, David Halliwell, Olwen Wymark. Taggart gave me a lift; everything went off very peacefully for a change. Greg there as well. Had drink in pub afterwards. Steve Gooch's girl friend was at *Pinprick of History*; found it confusing. Gooch narky. His girl friend had noticed his name in the play and had understood it well enough to think I had made an attack on Gooch's socialism. Had a bit of an argument about Bernard Levin. Gooch said it was trivial that I had based a play on his article in *The Times* (where he wrote Ireland should be towed into Atlantic and cut adrift, with all the Irish aboard except for C. C. O'Brien). Defended Tom Stoppard and his ability to make in-jokes in his play to a section of the audience. The liberal humanist university type; the rest of the audience would be impressed by his cleverness. David Halliwell attacked him. Brief discussion of usefulness of theatre. Gooch said it was because people were hooked; David Halliwell said people had to develop thick hides. Olwen said it was more painful for her to write now that she was accepted; she set her own high standards. When she was a copy-typist it didn't matter. It is very painful for Mary O'Malley, who has had one success with *Once a Catholic.*

Friday 6 Jan 1978
Went to delegate meeting at Pam Gems's. David Lan, Linda, George, Greg, J.A., Barbara Creagh, Pam Gems, Caryl Churchill & hubby came along to discuss legality of the blacking of TWU by TUC. Have to be careful to avoid libel. Greg had recommendations for next general meeting on 22nd. Rules of procedure, said my motion on Ireland & David Edgar's motions were illegal because of wording. Linda thought the interim agreement was illegal because only 7-and-a-half was on it. We left. It was later found that she had been reading the wrong motion which had been rejected by the assembly. Anyway the £125 Arts Council money doesn't apply to me because I live in Ireland. Saw Tim and Treasa. Tim said the main topic of conversation in Dublin was had we crawled over the apology to Burgess, or were we right? Eamon McCann thought we did the right thing. Other topic was Conor Cruise's appointment to the *Observer*. Met Gerry O'Neill, owner of the Súgán. Knows Galway well, was educated in Limerick, has written a play about the Súgán, was friendly and courteous. The first time talking to people who had bothered to read our work. Tim and I talked about Republican movement. He thought people were not interested. E.Mc. thinking of joining the Provos. Mary Holland po-faced. Had a word with Tim and Treasa about women's plays. John Quinn has joined

Pirate Jenny. Paddy Scully directed. When Treasa had gone for an interview they asked her how many marches had she been on? she said one, but she fainted before she got to Trafalgar Sq.

There is a fishing co-op on Inismaan. Tim impressed and was very encouraged by the co-op; they hope to build a harbour and have sailings to Rosmuc linking up the co-ops in the Gaeltacht area. Also there is a man there making perfume from flowers. A sculptor, John Delaney from Galway. Left at 2am for home.

Sat 7 Jan 1978
J.A. began typing *Ballygombeen* rewrites following libel settlement. Taggart called round, a member of TWU, he had found some spelling mistakes and clumsy wording by Edgar. An American; we had a little chat about himself. He has had a previous wife. They both come from America. She was a school teacher; both interested in the theatre. He went to college here and after college went round organizing community youth conferences at universities, LSE, etc. Did all the community projects start from them? They would hold two-day conferences; he said the food was bad, they then began buying carrots, potatoes, etc., for stews. He began writing plays in '75. His first one was a lunch-time performance in the Little Theatre. An American friend told him about TWU.

Sunday 8 Jan 1978
PLO man was a friend of David Holden & he was an agent for British Intellengence in an extreme Palestinian group; they found out and shot him.

Went to Ally Pally for the meeting against the Stadium. Interesting study of how a well-organized pressure group works. All sorts of rhetoric about the people's voice being heard, how the govt. is trying to take away rights. Very democratic format: everyone can talk except when someone is debating a motion. In the end no politics. Power to the people, says the Liberal. J.A. thinks it is really a pact between Haringey councillors in tussle against GLC; cutting Cutler down to size. The Stadium could be a tactic to get the electorate interested and involved in Parliamentary procedure. No-one there from any of the left parties to warn the people of the impracticability of these politicians getting adequate funds for the Palace. Rossi said £20 million would be needed. I certainly got the impression amongst the solid middle-class audience that they are aware they are the heirs of the Cromwellian revolution. An Irish woman got up to speak, to question the Conservative woman councillor's statement about her colleagues being behind her. She asked for the names of her colleagues; when no name was mentioned, she said, "None of them are on your side at all." She had rung a councillor up anyway, and he'd said he was not interested in hearing the views of anyone who was not English. At this the audience began to bleat and get restive.

On the news that evening a West Indian leader spoke out against Judge Neill McKinnon's summing-up and remarks in the recent race relations case against the National Front man John Kingsley. The W. Indian said the immigrant communities would not be able to trust the courts and adminstrations of justice.

Later on, on the news, a ploughing religious service brought back from the middle ages. "God Bless the Plough", piped the choristers.

My speculation about the immigrant ethnic groups rising up and refusing to pay homage to the British way of life may be coming true, the great democratic tradition may come true. Certainly at the Oval & ICA those English people who regard themselves as aware and socially-centered behave as your petty-bourgeois middle class. F,-them.

J.A. rang Stuart; we are seeing him for lunch Thursday. We will try to sell *BB* and *Vandaleur.*

There is no doubt about it: J.A. thinks he is very clever and all-seeing about priest-ridden countries elsewhere except when it is portrayed on his own national TV station. Then he just thinks it's quaint. Priests blessing ploughs.

Taoiseach Jack Lynch on the news calling for a British withdrawal. Is this genuine, or a sophisticated political move to out-manoeuvre the provos now that they are at their weakest? Put it once more on the long finger whilst we all go to sleep for another fifty years? Predictably British Govt. responded by squealing. 6 Unionists break off talks with Govt. on devolution, Paisley joins

Airey Neave, says it was sweet music to terrorists. Also Lynch calls for an amnesty for Republican prisoners.

Suffering is back according to *Sunday Telegraph*, happiness comes in waves, troughs, and one will always come out of them. Comfort for the back-to-the-wall mentality for the besieged right-wingers who have fortressed themselves in their houses with their firearms like the whites in Rhodesia.

Olwyn Wymark gets asked by Britches to write plays for them.

Can I have everything? The mark of greatness is knowing what one wants.

A thought for the Vandaleur play. The American girl should have entanglement with Vandaleur; involvements between the wife, the young man, the hunchback. The liberation of the emotions, but of course forgetting the responsibilities. There is no responsibility for emotional entanglements; only financial resp., the middle classes' value. Death to them. My hatred of men and of our society, a hatred that would be extinguished only when I am dead, said Courbet. Am I allowed to express such emotions or only must I disguise them in a play? What would creepy George and Linda say?

Every woman has a right to love and be loved, said Angela McNamara in the *Sunday Press* to one woman who wrote in to complain that she had loved, but he had rejected it after accepting it: A.McN. told her "you are the joy giver."

I shall carry my diary about with me to take down bon-mots; very bad at reconstructing dialogue. Jerry O'Neill said one must be an observer, even though my master plan is to have a play about revolution coinciding with revolution.

Monday 9 Jan 1978
Tish Dace arrived. Purple & pink, straight hair parted in the middle, spectacles, dark brown boots. She's had no sleep for two nights. She said a lot was going on in New York of an experimental nature, very personal. She described one show. They come into the dark, told not to touch any of the lights, then a beam of light projected, then other lights come up. Then a uni-cyclist came

on, maybe three they couldn't tell. It lasted half an hour, then darkness again, then they had to make their own way out again. A good childrens' play about a little boy who is playing with a doll, it turns out to be his sister. Baraka (who used to be LeRoi Jones) is now a maoist, seems to be the only marxist playwright in New York.

Tuesday 10 Jan 1978
Papers still go on about irresponsibility of Lynch. I read Mary Holland in the *New Statesman*. Provos are getting tired of maintaining struggle but not dead. Saw David Hare's TV play. The national lie. In New York Tish's friends are all leaving Star War messages on their recording machines. Is this an indication of infantile behaviour because they have no control over their own articles and newspapers? She saw *Wild Oats.* I put a suggestion that in all probability Wolfe Tone had been in the play, before 1798. At the same time as London audiences are laughing, hundreds of Republican prisoners are rotting in British gaols. Still anger on TV about Judge McKinnon's remarks. 80 coloured barristers will boycott the courts.

Wednesday 11 Jan 1978
Sleet, snow. Somebody rang me who had been to *The Pinprick of History*, asking me to go to Naples. He comes on Saturday. Composed Padraig's speech for the *Ballygombeen*; used a quote from the proclamation 1916.

Floating diary-entry, 10 or 11 Jan 1978
Went to negotiating committee at Jeremy's. Edgar wants us to make concessions on RSC & Nat. Theatre contracts. I think it is v. dangerous and rather similar to wage agreements whereby better-paid workers have to level off with lower-paid workers instead of other way round, i.e. that lower-paid workers' wages go up. Had drink with David Halliwell, Steve Gooch, Andy Carr. Bitching about Charles Marowitz. He had sacked Steve Gooch because he was a communist; he didn't like commies. He told Halliwell that he (Marowitz) wasn't political. Gooch comes from East Anglia; talked about his grand-uncle who was blind in one eye, an expert snooker player and always voted Labour. He used to ask Steve, "Do you still vote Labour?" Jeremy has two families: one in Wales and one in London. "I am an anarchist," he told George: thus the two families. George very protective about his partner Annie who had flu. Talked about tactics. Would we get what we wanted by standing out?

Note (2004)
One of our main demands was for playwrights to control their own work and their rewrites; David Edgar rejected that out of hand. George thought that conceding anything in the beginning was bad; we should stand up solid. The negotiations dragged on.

Thursday 12 Jan 1978
Had talk with Tish about directors. She seemed to have accepted the role of the director without question. Saw Stuart; he is commissioning *Vandaleur.* N.F.Simpson was there. He took *Ballygombeen* away to read; we explained that we wanted a quick production. Irony is that one of Goodman, Derrick solicitors is on the board (they were against us in libel action). Stuart meets him at meetings. Don't know if they will do it.

~~~o~~~

Sunday 15 Jan 1978
Went to see Jackie and Roland to return the cuttings. Bloody-Sunday March split. Troops Out to have one from Shepherd's Bush, The Provos from Speakers' Corner. Talked a bit about the renewal of the bombing campaign. Jackie said she thought Provos had done Birmingham; talked a bit about the left; they felt left is using the Irish situation to build up support -- this was when Ken Livingstone became Ireland's friend.

~~~o~~~

Sat 21 Jan 1978
The two Italians came in the morning to talk about me going to Naples. It will depend on their teacher in Naples. Geoffrey Reeves had been there last year for ten days but they had not been prepared for him so they didn't do any practical work. I said I would have to come for three months. Naples is very left. There is a communist mayor. They spoke about the poverty and black market. Also cholera. They find it very difficult to get to know the English people because they have to work in the evenings. Their English school is £97 for two months. Met Tish to go to an Edward Bond play, *The Bundle.* A rewrite of *The Narrow Road to the North.* Very professionally executed. Saw Edward in the pub and asked him about the picket for Grunwick. He said, "another

lecture." Left after the 1st act because I wanted to go home and watch Melvyn Bragg's programme on TV. Am not on the same wavelength as Tish, who took copious notes all through the play. Thought the style of production wasn't finished enough, thought it should have been possible to have the boats running off instead of the actors having to get out and push the boat off.

Sunday 22 Jan 1978
Had General Assembly at The Theatre Upstairs. Edgar had tidied up his motion and had his coup. George Byatt was not elected. Neither was Greg. Greg's motion on reaffirming mandate laid down by the Assembly at the Warehouse meeting. That mandate was no negotiations. Edgar, Gooch & Jeremy Brooks savagely attacked him. So the hatch was brought down, all dissent thrown out, Cherry and I resigned. So all the English & 2 Americans, imperialists, reign supreme to negotiate the TWU contracts. There is no doubt they will get slightly better conditions but not the best. The Writers' Guild though is the big rival and hardly likely to get the TWU women. My motion on Grunwick didn't have a quorum; only about five people left in room. The majority of TWU not interested in political motions. To say that there is something stirring in me toward a deep hatred of England is putting it mildly. No-one mentioned the Human Rights Court at Strasbourg. Yesterday we had a small demo at Chelsea Barracks, giving out leaflets attacking the SAS. A bit of aggro from a few passers-by, which the police protected us from. Went to see Jackie and Roland afterwards

Monday 23 Jan 1978
Delegate meeting decided to have Grunwick picket on 3 Feb. George a bit stroppy, is setting up a writers' co-op. for readings of plays at the Roundhouse. Is not really useful for me and J.A. I said I wanted all Arden's plays read. Horror all round, especially from George. Said J.A. had to come along to co-op meetings. Accused J.A. of being established writer. George didn't like the idea of *names* on the picket line; he really has quite a nasty undertone; he is jealous except of those whom he helps. Remnant of his years in the BBC? Had interesting chat with David Halliwell, Andy Carr and Jeremy Brooks; they said they all wanted the British to withdraw from N. Ireland but didn't agree with political motions put into trade unions. Jeremy said that Peter Nichols had wanted to join the union but because of my political motions wouldn't.

Court at Strasbourg found Britain not guilty of torture. Great crowing in British press. Was at International Tribunal meeting at the LSE last Tuesday. Jerry Lawless was there, no-one directly wants to call for British Withdrawal, it would alienate the Labour Movement. People like Cyril Cusack don't want prejudgement on verdict. The whole trial is a mass of contradictions. Sponsors must not be offended. A broad front to influence Labour Movement. Also extraordinary that the CP and Official Sinn Féin line is the same, against Brit Withdrawal. Opinions from Conor Cruise O'Brien in *Irish Times*, Thursday: "the 20% of the Irish people who want Britain on its knees are emotionally retarded and backward, we must be friends with Britain; also, most people in Dublin are imperially orientated; Wolfe Tone & Casement were imperialists at heart." Conor is basing his findings on Fr McGreil's book. The occasion for these outpourings was the Ewart Biggs memorial lecture.

Tuesday 24 Jan 1978
Demo outside Downing St. for Thursday cancelled because of Strasbourg report.

Went to a Provo meeting; Shane Connaughton there. "The blood-debt must be paid in blood!", said the Indian Workers' Association, and a West Indian group. Both, it turned out, from the same maoist party.

~~~o~~~

Friday/Saturday/Sunday 27, 28, 29 Jan 1978
To Manchester for the Socialist Feminist Conference. The black women in the anti-racist workshop, Iranian women, and Irish Women Against War, were the most militant. Women's Aid not really analyzing where they were going. 1000 women attended conference; it poured all the time. Great emphasis on non-structure of the feminist movement. Had a talk with a radical feminist who said her group was being pushed out of the movement; there is a centralized newspaper and all articles go through an editorial board, so presumably that means her articles were being rejected..

Fascism and the NF. Stayed with a young woman, a drop-out from LSE. A young man let us in; the previous day he had been to an anti-fascist march and had been arrested and charged with assaulting a policeman. He is an epilep-
~~~

tic, his photo was in all the local papers; they hadn't wanted to give him bail. Talked to someone from High Wycombe. She said the National Front was very strong there. It is a conservative stronghold. I asked the other women about their areas and the NF and they seem to be everywhere. Had an interesting conversation on the way back in the coach with a young woman who is going to take up supply-teaching. She had spent a year in Florence teaching English to business men. She was very excited about the pace there. The big communist rallies and festivals everywhere. The communists have their own clubs and medical services for their members. She told me about a mental hospital she had visited outside Florence where the patients had an assembly-type organization. Everyone would come and talk about the programme and what was best to carry out. They had assemblies every morning in the wards. The doctors were very much in the background. She was taking courses in creative writing at the City Lit Institute; they are given exercises on conversations they have heard & people they have observed & small incidents.

Monday 30 Jan 1978
Went to a delegate meeting; not much business because no-one had collected the mail. George B. having his meeting on his co-op in his house at Romford St. Asked with a bullying grin if J.A. would be there.

David Aukin wanted to see the script of the *Ballygombeen.* Had thought it was one of the best of the Irish plays. Anyway we will have further discussion on the project mentioned -- the idea of a quest, with all of us involved. Do not think we have same ideas on improvised play. They didn't like *The Pinprick of History.* No time for discussion. Returned home in time to see David Edgar's *Destiny* on TV. Was interesting with good sense of imperialist past in India but too microsopic in the Midlands. Local parties seemed to be very isolated from main political parties. The candidate in *Bill Brand* was handled better.

Tuesday 31 Jan 1978
Went to see Foco Novo. Rang up John Hoyland in the morning to find out why he had resigned from this company. He said it was because they were shifting the emphasis of where they played, which meant different types of plays not specifically geared to the working class. It had really been Roland Reece and Bernard Pomerance that had set it up. Also Roland had made contact with

Welsh miners for *Saltley Gates.* Saw Roland and David Aukin; David Weeks (small 'tache and Sherlock Holmes deer-stalker on his head, very clean flesh). Talked of our problem of alienation with England. Not satisfactory, as Roland said.

~~~o~~~

Thursday 2 Feb 1978
Cathy Itzin came in the evening, told her we wouldn't participate in her book about British theatre by giving her an interview, as I considered myself Irish and must be treated as such. In the course of the evening she did reveal that she was not in favour of a United Ireland unless it was socialist. How she deceives herself. Anyway, she listened with wide open-mindedness, but I know she is going to be as bitchy as hell.

Friday 3 Feb 1978
Went to Grunwick for our one-day writers' solidarity with the strike. Ten of us turned up: Maureen Duffy, Bridget Brophy, Colin Spencer, for the Writers' Guild; they wore badges saying, "Writers' Guild affilated to the TUC". George made a few bitchy remarks about TWU going to take WG over. Nicholas Wright turned up, Steve Gooch made bitchy remarks to him on not being a member of TWU. No David Mercer. Linda, David Lan, Steve Gooch, Paul Thompson. I thought the police were expecting a more unusual sort of demonstration. We stood in the cold for a couple of hours. The scabs' minibus came through with grinning women. I was really cold.

In the afternoon went to the Receiver's office with Michael Henshaw. Michael was really strung up, looking like an ardent socialist from the thirties, scarf swung round his neck, plimsolls on, an anorak under his arm. The taxi let us off at the wrong place; had to walk back to Holborn, waited in anteroom, two other women there looked like mother and daughter; were they winding up their collapsed business too? A parody of a secretary, blond hair, straight line for a mouth, sweet erect head and clipped voice. "The boot is on the other foot," she said when she found out we were waiting for Mr. Boot not for the other gentleman. Mr. Boot came in, young, efficient, bespectacled. No sermons; which is what Michael had said might happen. It wasn't necessary to sign massive papers, as the High Court had dealt with it all in the sum-
~~~

mer. Questioned about the car. It was stolen. Did I report it to the police? I couldn't remember. The history of the car, stolen by squatters from Brixton, Hilary picking up tickets for parking offences all over London; she is now in Holloway. Anyway it all passed over and that was that. The shares they will sell, and there will be hardly anything over. They are just as careless as any one else is over the relation to capital and interest.

The two events today were ritualized theatre. All appearances, no reality.

~~~o~~~

Saturday 5 Feb 1978
Went off to Hornsey to photo short extracts from Kate O'Brien and Edna O'Brien, to use in my intended *Neighbours' Voices* book. Poured all day. Unpleasant assistants. No charge for machine.

Sunday 6 Feb 1978
Tish ill. She read *Neighbours' Voices* interviews & liked them. Don Foley and Des Hogan came round in the evening. Des's book untidy in its folder; Des has a superstition about not looking after his manuscripts. He wrote the whole book in six weeks, it is 400 pages. Full of accurate images. He said he discovered falsehood about the supposition that women had intuition. He realized intuition was a masculine quality. Don is occupied with a friend, writing a play about Yeats, O'Casey & O'Donovan Rossa. It begins with a dying man and everyone crowding round to buy the rights of the story. Don very obtuse about saying he wanted a United Ireland. He kept on about history preventing change. They both felt freer in London. Des about the damaged Irish people over here after the damage they had received in Ireland. Both of them generalizing like mad, like characters from James Joyce.

Monday 7 Feb 1978
Went to Bruce Castle Museum to look up newspapers. Found the Muswell Hill murder; Feb 1896. Fowler & Millsom; quite a lot of coverage. Must go to Colindale to read the rest. Then looked up 1882; found out in a house in Soho there was a meeting between American Fenians and the Nihilists. A delegate from Moscow said how much he admired the British Administration and hoped to model Russia on it after the Revolution. The delegate from the Fenians was
~~~

from O'Donovan Rossa branch in New York. In another part of the paper, a debate about "Home Rule without loosening bonds of Imperalism." It was lost by 20, very poorly attended, the delegates were Irish MPs.

~~~o~~~

Thursday 17 Feb 1978

Have had a bad cold since last week. J.A. went to Galway, Thursday. On Saturday, after Tish had her bath, no more hot water: the pipes are frozen. Tish left Tuesday morning. She is in love with her friend, but the friend has spent all Tish's money. Tish had paid her salary into the bank and the friend (who only gets 25 dollars a month for her reviews) had cashed the lot. Tish only gets 5 dollars a review from the *Village Voice*. She said a lot of actors working off-Broadway are living off their fathers. Tuesday night, went to the Irish women's meeting, forgot to bring an extra reel for film, so couldn't show the film. Felt so full of embarrassment after that, I couldn't hear what women were saying. These meetings are a bit frustrating as we didn't really talk about the situation. Peculiar non-activity. Should one push oneself forward or not, when I do I feel there is a bit of hostility? Would I have liked to go to Edinburgh conference? Everyone said they couldn't go, and quite unobtrusively two, without upsetting any ripples, said they would go. Quite devious. Mairéad Corrigan is organizing a march in Dublin against Provos' Kevin St. offices on Sat. In her press statement she wants the RUC back on the streets.

Anne O'Connor, an Irish actor, came to see me, don't know what to make of her. Des rang, said his radio play had been accepted by the BBC; also the National may do his play that was done at the Abbey. Don hasn't found work. Should I state now that I have very little interest in the theatre? but what am I going to do, I am really redundant? Middle-aged, no skills, no wonder I am always getting pregnant. I feel constantly frustrated and hemmed-in by the rules governing language.

There is always this challenge (which does seem more exciting), the confrontation of the body against nature. The last struggle in death, childbirth, breathing: exciting.

Wilma was rather bitchy when I mentioned the group of Irish women. She
~~~

spoke about this anarchist who had labelled Albert as the "Ivimey Group". The father of that girl who was murdered in Greece is in touch with Albert: he was the one who gave her the anarchist contacts.

There is a mouse in the kitchen; must have come in because of the cold. We never get mice in the kitchen as a rule.

The school teacher in Kirkbymoorside gave me a moment of recollected joy: when he conducted his choir, he *drew* the song out of them.

14

BELFAST 1978

Diary Excerpts

7:84 were putting on Vandaleur's Folly *in Belfast at the Queen's University Festival. J.A. and I were invited by Edna Longley of the English Department to each read a paper. "Do a double-act," she said. I went to Belfast a few days in advance.*

Tuesday 21 Nov 1978
Arrived at Belfast, York Road Station. Nobody to meet me on arrival. Hung around a bit. Large young woman with spectacles dragging small child came into station. She introduced herself as Angela Wilcox from the English department. She asked me how I would like Belfast, assuming this was my first visit. I told her I had been many times with plays into Republican areas. She is a single parent. Said how marvellous the staff had been over the birth of her daughter. Trouble remembering which B&B it was that I was booked into. Found right B&B: minute room. Went to day-nursery to leave Angela's daughter, then on to meet Mrs Longley at English Department. She wasn't in room. We waited, she came, we had coffee. Talked about the vitality of Irish literature. Angela attacked Lyric Theatre for putting on local plays; she mentioned David Mercer as the playwright they should be putting on. She attacked Patrick Galvin's play *Do It For Love.* I defended it because it had been very popular and also pleased both sides. We talked about the function of an audience. I referred to Socrates. She mentioned to Mrs Longley about the community play they were rehearsing in the Shankill Rd. I said I would like to go. We went to the Students' Union. I met the organiser, he said it wasn't necessary to have a card. We agreed to meet Thursday night to see her play. She mentioned that she hadn't noticed much censorship when I said that the reason why she hadn't known about my previous work was because it hadn't been in the papers. I asked Mrs Longley if I could attend some of her lectures. She said I could go to her tutorial with 3rd year students on D.H.Lawrence. Found out from Angela where the Dalys were.

Went to James Daly's office; Miriam Daly was coming out the door. We went in, had a cup of coffee. I said I wanted some leaflets to hand out about the H-Blocks at the play. We talked about the makeup of the students at James's philosophy lectures: there had been several army officers. It was the only catholic department: a concession to the minority, a bit like the black dept. in an American university. We drove off to the *Republican News* office. Went across the road, was introduced to Tom Hartley.

Girls there talking about one of the lads who had been picked up. It was his own fault: he had been warned to stay away. He had come back to see his girl friend. The march on Sunday had been banned. Tom H. was getting out a press statement condemning the banning

We went into an inner room & talked. He said that the plays we had previously brought up to Belfast (with the Galway Theatre Workshop, *The Mongrel Fox* and *Mary's Name*) were too "modern" for their audience. I talked about Women's Lib. He said his wife was French and had agreed that no women's questions had been raised at the Ard Fheis. He said that the women in the movement were equal to men. I said that one of the reasons why Women's Lib found such difficulty in identifying with the Republican movement was because the Rep. movt. never emphasised women's role. He said, yes it might appear that they were spawning a monster for the future. He said that political education was very difficult when all the energies were concentrated on the war. He said that the Irish people could never give up the struggle because there had been too much suffering. We discussed the father's role in relation to children and I agreed to meet his wife on the following Sat.

He said he hadn't too many leaflets because of the raid. He himself was waiting on bail for IRA membership that carries a ten year sentence. He gave me some leaflets. I caught a black taxi outside to centre of the city; it was 10p. It was raining. Desperate to go to toilet. Went into big dept. store, told there was one in the middle of the road.

Had to go through barriers. The UDR women talking about spaghetti sauce. No-one looked at leaflets. Walked back to B&B, no hot water, very cold in room, lay down for a bit. Then went out to Students' Union, saw play *Zone* advertised, decided to find out where it was. Asked around. Was sent over to main building to porter's office, very helpful. Rang up to find it was cancelled. He said it was very bad to mislead the public. Returned to SU. Found our cast still wandering about. Paul said hello to me. Anne O'Connor passed me on the stairs. They had very white faces. Installed myself on top of stairs to give out leaflets. The leaflet had a picture of Tom Clarke on top of a man in H-block. On the other side, Tom Clarke's speech at his trial. Some people thought the leaflet was the programme. The Just Books people came along: I agreed to meet after the show. Angela Wilcox came and took a leaflet. At about 8.10 three students approached me and asked who I was. I said I had written the play and was handing out leaflets to show the continuity of the play. They said they had received complaints about the leaflets; I said no one had complained to me. They said people going down to the bar had been offended. I said most people at that time were going to the play. They said it wasn't allowed without union permission. They had responsibility for 4000 students if there were a bomb scare. I said it wouldn't be the Provos, it would have to be loyalists. If they were worried, wouldn't it be better to go and see the loyalists, find out if they intended to bomb the premises. I said it was blackmail to be intimidated in the SU. They asked me to leave, I said no; they said they would throw me out, I said no. They said they would stop the play; I said go ahead. One of them said he agreed with me over the Freedom of Speech, the other said I must ask permission from the exec. committee. I said, who are they? One of them said he was on the committee & would raise it there; I said I would ask them, at what time did they meet? Nine o'clock, Thursday; I must show them the leaflet and write in my request. Some people passed & I gave them leaflets. They told me not to. I said if there were any signs of violence I would stop.

I returned to the B&B. There were several young men in the TV lounge. I watched an American serial about a candidate whose girl friend had died because of an abortion. The news leaked out & he lost the election. His wife had let slip to her family who were very hostile to him. After his defeat, he cheered up and said he was going to fight for abortion. Some of the lads went upstairs and returned with hot-water bottles which they clutched to their stomachs. The next programme was two Czech plays by Havel. A posh flat, two very smart people and their guest with his wife. The couple were saying how well they managed their life in every way, food, drink, from America, a new and exciting fresh approach to sex. Why wasn't the young man writing his book? why was he spending all his time in the café with undesirable friends? why was he working in such a lowly job? was it fun? The guest kept on saying there was no other job; he didn't want to improve; his wife then said he must go. They burst into tears and said don't go. Watched a bit of 2nd play, young man in a brewery where he worked, talking to the manager, who kept on plying him with drink which he had to get rid of. Had to go to the theatre. John McGuffin there with his wife, said hello. Met the Just Books people, went to SU-bar for a drink and then back to one of the young women's flat. Discovered that she was from a prod background; so was he. He had called his children by Irish names, in the spirit of '68. He wondered if they would regret it. The girl didn't like the Provo bombing, so she wouldn't support them. I tried to put it to them that they must work against the Brit. Govt.; arranged to meet his group at the book shop tomorrow at 2pm. He said that there were lots of young people could do video tapes for instance. They could save their money to buy them. He had found the play too fast. The actors had gabbled their lines. He had seen *Non-Stop Connolly Show* at Queen's, had loved it. I'd put stickers in the UN exhibition; also one in Ladies' loo, it was still there when I got back. Also in bookshop. Had put some in boat and on train. Went to bed.

~~~o~~~

Wednesday 22 Nov 1978.
Breakfast in cramped dining room, hard-boiled eggs, lots of middle-aged northeners, very cold house. Popped out to get newspaper; a woman said hello to me on my way back. Sat in lounge to read paper. Had a walk round before going to Edna Longley's English Dept., couldn't find it, had to ask several students, one of them English doing sociology. She wasn't in her room, I waited, looked through her bookshelves, found a book of poems by Michael Longley: one about his father having fought in World War 1, and also an Orangeman. Read some essays from *The Bell,* an editorial from Peadar O Donnell complaining about not getting into America because of pressure from GB.

Five students came; they discussed *Sons and Lovers* and *Women in Love*. One young man, small 'tache, round face, bright eyes, seems more open than the others, defends Morel. The other seems to shy away from the implications of the role of Paul and mother. They get very cosy when they agree Lawrence should be cut; then one of the girls backtracks and says she enjoys the long descriptive passages. They seem to think the sex scenes are too ornate and
~~~

rather corny, especially the simile about a cathedral. Mrs Longley asks about social implications. Yes, there are social implications. Women's vote, the trend of the people from the rural areas to go to the cities.

I run out of cigarettes; wonder if I can bum one off the girl beside me. I don't utter a word. When it is over I stand near the fire, I am still cold and comment on the thriftiness of the Belfast Landlady. Mrs Longley thinks it is a criticism of the hospitality. She rings up a hotel: there is a room for me tomorrow; tonight I can stay in the students' hostel where it is warm. We have a discussion about the North. She admits the classes are too large. There is no education about the implications of a united Ireland. I show her the review from the *Irish Times* of the poetry-reading at Trinity College. Michael Longley was late because of the train; John Hewitt couldn't make it. Mrs Longley cracks a joke about the Freedom Fighters having delayed the train. The review comments that when M.L. had read his poem, he fell asleep while Paul Muldoon read his poetry. She said Michael had been very tired. She said that Michael had spoken about the North at a school do. I said the protestants must take responsibility about the oppression of the catholics. She mentioned Abercorn bombing atrocity; she then invited me to a poetry-reading tomorrow at the Ulster Museum. M.L. is an organizer on the NI Arts Council. She gives me the report. It is raining; I am late for Just Books, she doesn't know where the Markets are. I go up to the hotel. She stops me on the way to discuss arrangements for Friday. I felt like killing myself at the oppression I feel: the H-Blocks & my feeling of isolation in Belfast, am I alone a defender of free speech? she is the protestant, that should be her job. Fortunately the students had allowed reason to win and not blackmail. The hotel has strong reinforcements; the security man stops me, checks me, the gate is lifted. More security at the main door. The person inside is not there to open the door; a couple of us are waiting outside in the rain. The people inside can't get out, because she is not there. She eventually comes; I grab the keys and go up, leave my bag, and walk to Winetavern St.

About 8 in room upstairs, over the bookshop which is also a coffee house; they hire it out to groups for meetings. I stated that the only position in Belfast at the moment must be complete rejection of British Rule. Even if that might imply support for the Provos. Asked them what their attitude was to be over the banned march. They said they didn't like the idea of being used by the Provos who would make them march behind them. They said they supported political status for all prisoners; which meant they did not have to face the implications of BG attitude on the Provos. They were all men. Two of them turned out to be actors: one a Scottish lad, the other a catholic -- didn't believe in a party. I felt all the time the confusion and also alienation that the Provos had caused. The effort in getting a disciplined movement with changing leadership. I asked them how many young people had radically changed their backgrounds since '69? Any of those who had, seemed to have left. These young people had no Republican backgrounds. The Scottish actor defended homosexuals, an attitude which makes for complications in the NI situation as the Provos are against homosexuals. We didn't get very far.

Raining. We left the bookshop to go to car park for their van; they were going to the play. The car park was locked. We walked back to one of their houses in a neutral area. A crowd of yelling youths in the centre waving flags. Bearded man asked what was going on. Aftermath of a football match.

Went to house for meal, a 2 up-and-down. Went back with one of them to the hotel for leaflets. Went to Students' Union; people already drifting into play. Stood outside handing out leaflets. The organizer came along, said you must not hand out leaflets; I told him that I was seeking permission, he left me alone.

Thursday 23 Nov 1978
9am. In morning got up early worrying about making statement on why I had to give out leaflets. Went up 3rd floor, asked where the exc. committee met. The door was pointed out to me. Knocked on the door; young man sitting at desk, he was the president. Showed my leaflet, pointed out the connection between 1831 and Tom Clarke. Went on about standing up to blackmail. Did not want to make controversy or violence, etc., he said it was OK. Felt minor victory for Free Speech. Felt emotionally drained afterwards.

After handing out leaflets went back to hotel. The lights in my bedroom not working, rang manager for repairs, he came, repaired the lights. Ordered whiskey and ginger ale. Watched TV. Had bath; glorious hot water. Had a nap. Went out again in rain to SU. Met them after play; we went to the pub, talked, stood out in street, and talked. Arranged that Gerard and Andrew should pick me up at the hotel tomorrow and we should visit the Arts Council and Lyric Theatre. The TV lounge in the hotel was closed because of the bombing.

Friday 24 Nov 1978
Felt I was getting trapped into the Northern situation about H-Blocks; got my stickers out, and wrote "HB" on more of them. Decided to write on wall of the museum. Take a picture down and write. Tossed a coin to decide if I should do it. Coin turns up right side. Pouring again. Met Gerard, went to Arts Council; Gerard had project to tour the North, wanted a community tour. Frank said he would have to organize it himself, dealing with each area.

Afterwards went across road and bought 2 markers, one black, one red. I went into museum, had a bag-search. Attendants very pleasant. 4th-floor modern section: a table laid out with food and drink. Paid 75p to get in. Examined walls. Gerard had said it was better to do it during the poetry reading.

I was arrested for this Mural Happening. I wrote about it, and about my subsequent gaol experiences, in Tell Them Everything *(Pluto Press, 1981).*

15

LONDON 1981

Diary Excerpt

30 March 1981

Had lunch with Richard Imison and Ronnie Mason to discuss commission for *Whose Is The Kingdom?*. Richard's daughter is married to head civil servant of the prisons. In N. I., Republican prisoners will go on hunger strike later in spring. Got drunk, went to Peggy's, signed *Manchester Enthusiasts* contract. Tim not finished reading *State of Shock* script.

16

MADRID 1987

Diary Excerpts

[moth and dates of month]

Thursday

Went to the Marabella area the wrong way. Found ourselves in dark streets behind the Gran Via; prostitutes, male and female; pimps. J.A. frightened as he was carrying all his money. Found the "protest café", no music, no protest songs; one old white-haired woman in cafe. Went to bar in square. Found a poster advertising Feminist Theatre. The Tourist Office: found a snooty young woman, said she didn't know of it. Just a group who had come together, not real theatre. The Minister of Culture had recognized them. Their name was not on the bottom of the poster. At the hotel we asked the manager, he looked up his book on What's On: it was there, performance at 10.30. Went by Metro, working-class area. We had to wait outside, the doorman was allowing some in but not us. The restaurant opposite full of lively young people. We had to eat or leave. So we had an ice-cream in the square. The theatre shabby, a young bearded man on his own reading an 18th-century printed book, the theatre less than half full, quite a few young women, typical progressive audience. Proscenium arch. Curtains. Set representing sterility, white tiles, a table, two chairs, a mirror, a bed. A butcher's knife hanging off a nail.

Man and woman enter, sit at a table eating. The man in control, steadily eating. The woman encircling him. They make love. Next scene, similar; without knife, cloth or bed. A woman with an apron ironing. The man restless, trying to attract her attention, wants to make love, she won't. He knocks her about. He kills the first woman, 2nd woman kills him by poison. A section of the audience cheered when the man put a knife into the woman. At the curtain-call the man dominates, the woman carries on *her* role at the curtain call.

~~~o~~~
~~~

Saturday

The tour of Segovia and Avila. Went to the office. All the coaches there. Luggage, sellers. Our guide has yellow braces, thin; an injury to his back makes one shoulder higher than the other. His trousers pulled up so an enermous ball bulges through. Intellectual, very sharp with an American computer-programmed family. Father bald with a Jose Ferrer look, acquisitive desire for information. The guide shouted at the whole family: round blond wife, two blond daughters, one with round spectacles similar to father. "Yesterday you asked the same questions; I answered you time and time again." The American couldn't hear. His face crumbling inside, his family stand solid behind him. The guide's authority was challenged because the father couldn't hear or understand the guide's English. Later, outside the Palace, the father asked how many rooms, "150," said the guide: honour was restored. The father had stood his ground. The mother, as she was getting on the coach, said, "We will be camping next year." "No flashes please, if you use flash you will be expelled." Someone used a flash. The guard, bearded, in blue, jolly, hurried amongst us to find out who it was.

17

FRANCE 1992

Diary Excerpts

Invited to a theatre festival/conference at Dijon.

Thursday & Friday 27/28 May 1992

Caught plane for Paris. Half-hour delay. Dinner on plane. Morning was spent trying to book an hotel. Also left message for Armand Rapoport (poet, painter, school-teacher, whom we'd met in 1972 when he invited us to a French writers' conf. against censorship). Arriving at Orly Airport, pouring with rain, got metro to Pigalle, lashing, water gushing inside pavements, got to hotel, as soon as we arrived Armand rang, said he would be over in 20 minutes. No shower in rooms. Armand and Eva (Swedish) arrived, went out to cafe, stopped raining. Eva interesting, she is a painter and works on a switchboard; Armand changed schools, he is depressed. His film producer who was backing him has disappeared & gone bankrupt because of property speculation. His son works for the UN in Mongolia. Finn had made a film on the nomads, we all drank beer, Finn had a Crocque Monsieur, strange -- just sliced bread lightly toasted. We all left, inviting Armand to Dijon. We went up to Monmartre. An American woman touting for customers, to draw us she spoke with us. J.A. tired. Finn with sore heels because he had just bought some new shoes, then he got drunk and went on about no shower. Returned to hotel & bed. The new Canary Wharf has gone bust, the workers on building site were told that's that. They had never experienced such a situation. This morning had breakfast, Algerians, no smile on woman's face as she served us, went out to find a hotel for when we return, found one, walked around; Finn noticed transvestites. Pigalle sordid, got train, it was meant to get us in at 20 hrs; was one hour late.

Countryside like home counties, no vineyards, the hills came. At Dijon was met by Solange, Michel and Judy: they run a theatre company, Michel a playwright, had a meal & discussion; they became interested in Ireland after Flann O'Brien & Tom Murphy play, old CPs, lost now. Using theatre to give direction. I went on in my usual boring way. They want to lead, Judy lives in immigrant area. There is loadsa-dough now in French Theatre. Went to hotel; jolly Afro-French man runs it. Washed my hair.

J.A. rang Armand who might come Sunday. Philippe and Gwyneth turned up at the theatre in the University for the Marivaux play. Foyer packed but we were brought into the theatre, it was full then we waited half an hour. Play good: gymnastics & precision from the seven actors, empty and drab set. About sexual politics, 2 controllers, 2 young women, 2 zombies, one older man, some clever effects with actors. At least it was just actors & director -- no scenery -- the director was precise. It was so hot I walked out to write this. There is a bar & a piano bar. The audience, students. Philippe is translating Howard Barker's plays, theatre is booming in France. Tomorrow I must speak on the panel.

Saturday & Sunday 29/30 May 1992
Yesterday had Irish debate, it was terrible; seven men on platform, more women in the audience. I made no effective intervention. Buffet, lots of meat. Rain and more rain; bought an umbrella. Then dinner. Buffet. More and more meat. More rain and thunder & lightning; inside more noise & electric shorts. *Hamlet* version: Philippe leaves; can't take it. Returns to tell us a coach leaves for town; we scramble over railings at back of raised benches, nearly breaking our limbs. Released, we laugh in the coach. The driver thinks the play is terrible: an actor masturbating and trying to shoot himself. *Hamlet?* and noise everywhere. We go to café then. Solange, Maurice and others have left as well. Upstairs we worry about Solange because she is trying to please. We go to Irish pub. A pupil of Martin O'Connor's is to play there (M.O'C., famous accordion player; lives in Annaghdown, nr. Corrandulla).

We walk home. Friday night a young woman was molested by men. Gwyneth and I are walking, two cars come along filled with men blowing and honking, nearly falling out of their cars.

Talked with Maurice, he is bitter about French C.P, & then his interpretation of IRA & Sinn Fein is reflection of his own experience. Equating IRA with Moscow, difficult. Argues that creative writers by being allowed to present themselves do not have to reveal their sources, they are not scrutinized as severely as academics, and can be just as manipulative if we do not know where they are coming from. To write is a technical skill and can hide the real mind. The audience should share with us their own experience of the written word and how it has helped them. Maurice Goldring does not say where *he* is coming from.

The Cameroon manager of the hotel is a student of International Religion. He talks about International Law. European Law. One Law: EEC overrides National Law. That is why EEC. In France non-nationals like himself do not have vote. Maastrecht Treaty states everyone must have vote, so he will have one.

Art is not a reality of reflection but a reflection of reality. Art is not a reflection of reality but a reality of reflection.

Monday 31 May 1992
Conference at Dijon: incompatible.

We paid a brief visit to the once vigorous manufacturing town of Le Creusot, now a tourist place (bars full of pictures of ancient railway engines) and quite smart. We lunched there with members of the local theatre company who had been at the Dijon conference. We wanted to gain an insight (for our Eleanor Marx radio play) into the experience of Freddy, K.Marx's son, who went to Le Creusot in its heyday to absorb engineering skills. Afterwards we travelled to the pilgrimage town of Paray-le-Monial, a complete contrast, ancient churches and religious depositories.

Thursday 3 June 1992
The Danes have said NO to the referendum.

A cycle-ride in the balmy countryside. Good lecture from enthusiastic Paray-le-Monial historian on the scandal of the church in France tearing down the local churches and building triumphalist churches in many of the villages. The people refused to allow some churches to be pulled down because of graveyards, like at Imber (where the British military took over a village for its training, but had to spare the church): so they are still there but closed.

Saturday 7 June 1992
Paris. Had dinner with Armand & Eva. Her daughter popped in looking like Sinéad O'Connor; she is into coincidences; she is at the University of Rouen, lives in a house no. 72, the year of her birth; the bridge is called Matilda, which

is her name. The Street is Jeanne D'Arc. Sinéad O'Connor is going to play Jeanne D'Arc. Armand had just received a letter from Anna Taylor who has to act in her own play because two actors walked out. Lamb and melon for dinner; lovely strawberry flan. Felt tired all day, the weather heavy, no sun. Found a launderette and washed all our clothes; popped into bookshop, found new Jenny Marx book, not very detailed.

Sunday 8 June 1992
We went to flea market, then the Pompidou Centre, and now waiting in total confusion in the Luxembourg Gardens waiting for Philippe and Gwyneth, who are to meet Armand, who is waiting in the Pastrol Cafe outside the gardens. Where are we to be to join everyone up? -- we are all to go to a Chinese dinner. Armand knows a good one, and so do they. Which fountain? the one in the garden or the one outside on the traffic island? The bell rings quarter-past seven and we sit. It is faintly chilly, overcast. Philippe and Gwyneth live a block away. Tomorrow we have lunch with the ex-stalinist Maurice Goldring. Bought a mixture of English newspapers. *The Independent* had an article on the Irish referendum, Bertie Ahern saying the Irish will say yes. Delors has been on TV. Ireland gets more lolly from EC than any other country. Had a dream last night that Ireland said NO. A kid has just fallen into the round pond.

PART THREE

18

CORRANDULLA & GALWAY 1982

Diary Excerpts
Monday 28 June 1982
Back to Galway on Thursday, big surprise: the Arts Council have authorized my financial grant as a member of Aosdána, the Cnuas [see Chapter 19], to arrive in July, thereafter every three months. J.A.'s book (first novel) arrived from Methuen, big celebrations, a packet of cigarettes. *Phaedra* on TV: Melina Mercouri, she was magnificent once she began to be rejected.

Tuesday 29 June 1982
My Cnuas arrived this morning.

~~~o~~~

Thursday 8 July 1982
In Galway, woke at 5.30 am. Can't make up my mind what suits me: quiet stagnation in Corrandulla to get my mind rested, or the effort of leaving to go to Galway then back again? Ridiculous. Haven't told anyone about the Cnuas yet, too many bitter comments. I'm learning, don't lead with my chin. Mary said wisely in Dunnes, "You don't need the job now." Set up Galway Women in Entertainment with 1st workshop, on *Phaedra:* all the classic marks of today's women, guilt, destructiveness, revenge -- compare it to Deirdre & Grainne. Usual sneers from Gene Kerrigan in *Magill* about state artists stuffing themselves at Dublin Castle for Joyce the rejected artist, etc. My money separates me from everyone now. National unemployment. John Carroll of ICTU getting up and says, "We are not allowing imports." Got SIP newsletter.
~~~

19

AOSDÁNA

Aosdána is an Irish word that means the "Gifted People". It is also the name of a partly-independent body set up to represent, and to aid, artists in Ireland. The members are self-elected, and are there in recognition of their "artistic achievement and distinction." It is a "fellowship of honour", according to Anthony Cronin, architect of the scheme, in 1981. "There is much more to it than just the Cnuas payments," he wrote. *Cnuas* is an Irish word that means a "handful of nuts". Cronin in those days was cultural adviser and speech-writer to Taoiseach Charles J. Haughey. He believed that "the art of the dispossessed is seldom great, precisely because it *is* the art of the dispossessed," that this was the normal state of the arts in Ireland, and that if artists as a social group were to be represented, then a kingdom must be provided for them, "and it must be worth coming into." The result was a very male kingdom: 89 men and 7 women made up the original membership. I was one of the seven.

I gradually came to see that this was not the sort of kingdom to fulfil Cronin's expressed ideal, that "the remedy [for the cultural starvation of large numbers of people] is not to change the mode of comunication; it is to change society." The Aosdána did indeed change things, but scarcely as I had hoped. By 1986 I found myself forced into active opposition. Individual artists were now formally designated *the national heritage*. The government obviously hoped that the *heritage* gimmick would lead the nation away from its malcontent despondency to find grace and inspiration at the feet of the new gurus. I myself, as a member of Aosdána, found this new church to be as hierarchical, patriarchal, authoritarian, secretive and class-based as any of the old ones. To ask questions in its assembly about how its affairs were conducted by its executive committee, was to provoke a backlash of witch-hunting, heresy-denunciation and character-assassination as ferocious as a mediaeval inquisition or a Macarthyite tribunal. Which was all of a piece with the contemporaneous criminalization of Dublin street-musicians, buskers and part-time traders; with the withdrawal of funds from popular festivals; and with the overall clamping-down on any spontaneous or improvisational show of spirit.

Freedom of Speech and Freedom of Information were becoming a Prohibited Area.

The individual with awkward questions was seen as a *misfit*, a *crank*, a pariah whom all must shun.

I decided that bureaucracy cannot strangle you if you stand up against it.

I remembered, from my recent visit to Nicaragua, how the poet Fr. Ernesto Cardenal had said to UNESCO: --

> A society's culture depends on the opportunity that its members have to develop their knowledge and capabilities: without this opportunity there cannot be a democratization of culture -- there can be no culture or democracy.

Could we say that culture and democracy had anything to do with the Arts Council/Aosdána complex? The majority of Aosdána members clearly showed, when they voted against my motions calling for democratization of the assembly, that they do not consider Freedom of Speech, Freedom of Information, and Freedom from Unwieldy Bureaucracy, to be a serious priority.

I made a public statement: --

> I am a 52-year-old playwright, mother and grandmother, and I am going to sit outside the Arts Council Offices in Merrion Square, Dublin, from 3 pm April 21st 1986, for two months, if I have the stamina. I appeal to all those who feel as oppressed as I do by the ever-increasing restrictive bureaucracy of the arts administration in Ireland to come together and collectively create a cultural event that will expose the dead corpse and let free the living spirit !
> OPEN ART TO OPEN PEOPLE.

I put out around the town a series of posters in a couple of designs (one of them by Gerard McLaughlin, and the other by a popular newspaper political cartoonist who wanted to remain anonymous); I sat on the doorstep for the two months; a film was made of the event with the help of Dave Hyndman of Northern Visons, Gerard McLaughlin and Michael Quinn, entitled *Circus Exposé of the New Cultural Church*; it was later shown at various festivals. The

PO-FACED PROTEST . . . Playwright Margaretta D'Arcy displays an unusual form of head covering during her protest outside the Arts Council offices in Dublin. Ms. D'Arcy will end her nine-week vigil on June 20 with a party on the steps of the building. She is protesting against the "secretive nature of Toscairi, the executive body of Aosdana.
Picture: FRANK MILLER.

Circus Exposé

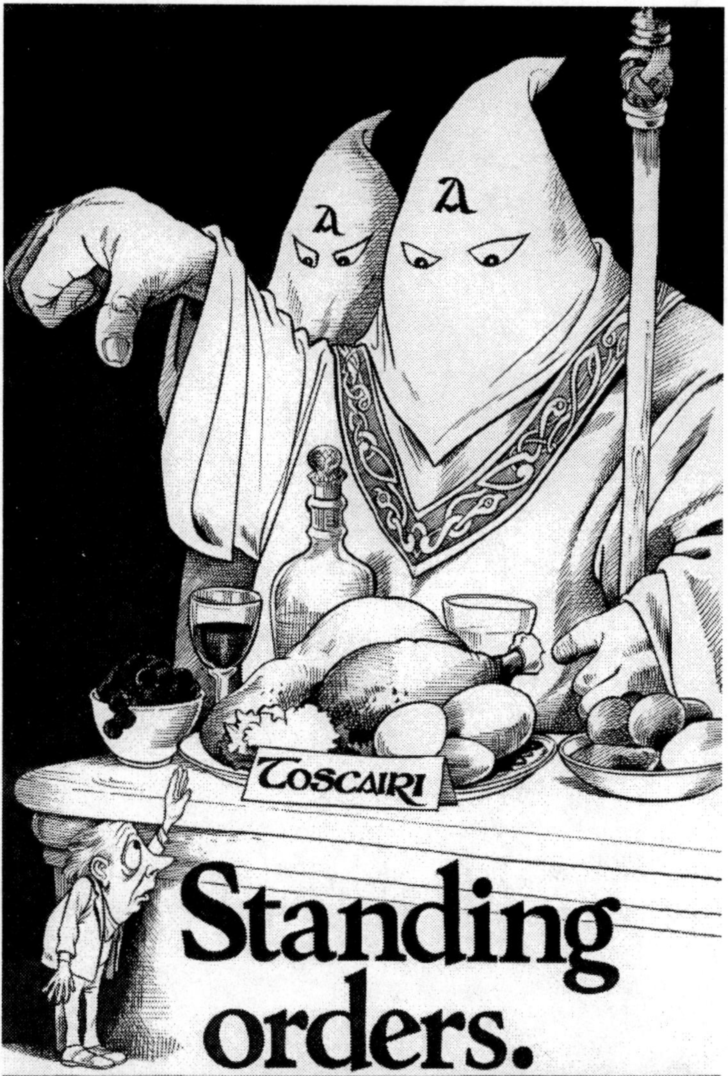

Aosdána manifesto poster.

Aosdána manifesto poster.

Pirate queen making waves
City pirate station offering abortion advice still on air
GALWAY BUCCANEERS
Defiant women pirates take to the air
Galway's pirate women
A vivid, earthy account of how a group of women run a unique pirate radio in an upstairs bedroom of a Galway terraced house.
Pirate station goes off air after 'act of conscience' protest
IT'S MORE THAN JUST THE UNLICENSED TRANSMITTER THIS TIME MARGARETTA, - THE CHINESE WANT TO EXTRADITE YOU FOR ESPIONAGE
Pirate station to go back on air despite threat of £20,000 fine
by Declan Tierney
PIRATE IN STORMY WATERS

Collage; Radio.

"dispossessed" flocked to the doorstep. Instead of asking me why I was there, they saw it as a forum for their own expression.

The whole experience brought home to me the need for a new and flexible means of communication. Ironically, most of the people who flocked had been men, but the most stringently dispossessed were clearly women: therefore any new flexibility must first favour women. Upon my return to Galway, I set up Womens' Scéal Radio, which evolved into Radio Pirate-Woman. I compiled a book about it, *Galway's Pirate Women, a Global Trawl* (Women's Pirate Press, 1996).

The results of my two months' alfresco manifestation: --

1) It is no longer mandatory to find seconders for all motions for debate at Aosdána's assembly.
2) The public may attend Aosdána's annual assembly.
3) There are many more women members.

20

GREENHAM COMMON WOMEN'S PEACE CAMP

The word Greenham has become part of the English language as a symbol of women's resistance; in the last decade of the 20th century it entered the mainstream of fiction, to say nothing of TV-scripts and films. In 1981 the USAF announced that they would operate their cruise missiles from the old RAF air base on Greenham Common near Newbury, each missile carrying a warhead with the equivalent explosive power of 16 Hiroshimas. The missiles were designed to land in eastern Europe. A small group of women and men marched from Wales with a protest to the commander at the base. His refusal to see them led to 18 years of struggle, at the end of which the Americans had left, the cruise was removed and the land returned to the Newbury District Council for the benefit of the people.

Newbury is in Berkshire in the heart of the Home Counties, tranquil Jane Austen country infused with her middle-class womanly values, next door to Oxfordshire, Hampshire and Wiltshire, a district also full of ancient sacred sites, Avebury, Silbury, Stonehenge, with a history going back to the very beginnings of human society upon the island. However, in the middle of this rich and beautiful countryside we were surrounded by every kind of horror designed to destroy life. Greenham Common, Aldermaston, Burghfield, Porton Down -- missiles with nuclear warheads (cruise and Trident), atomic weapons research and manufacture, chemical and biological warfare research and manufacture -- to say nothing of world-wide sales: if Saddam Hussein had weapons of mass destruction, where did he get the know-how? Greenham was born out of Thatcher, an alternative to the neo-liberal market forces.

The women at Greenham Common instinctively rejected the inherent irrationality of the scientific rationale.

I was involved with Greenham off and on throughout the 18 years. During that time the following manifesto was issued by the women of the Peace Camp.

* * * * * *

SUMMONS & INDICTMENT

Let all persons attend before the women of the world and hear: --

that the USAF and Cruise missiles being in occupation of common land without the consent of the people, the people do recover possession of the common land which is theirs by ancient right and which has been misappropriated for the purpose of siting weapons of mass destruction, and that the military forces do stop all preparation for genocide and nuclear war.

We are women who have taken responsibility for preventing the nuclear destruction of life on earth by accident or war involving nuclear weapons. We have been living at the Women's Peace Camp which by the commitment and work of hundreds of thousands of women from all over the world has kept a constant presence at Greenham Common since September the 5th, 1981, to protest and oppose the deployment of nuclear weapons, and in particular cruise missiles, at Greenham.

We have done this on our own authority as women working for peace.

The government and military forces' wargames are playing with our lives and our future.

Nuclear War is contrary to British Law (Genocide Act 1969) and International Laws, including the Hague Convention, the Geneva Convention, the Genocide Convention, the Nuremberg Protocols and the Charter of the United Nations.

8,000 women have been arrested, 1,000 women have been imprisoned, 270 women have been strip-searched, for obstructing the passage* of military vehicles, for walking on the common inside the base's perimeter or for cutting doors into or taking down the fence and barbed wire to permit free access to the common, as is our ancient right.

**The cruise missile was meant to be secret. It was regularly brought out of the base in the dead of night, and driven to Salisbury Plain, where firing exercises would continue for a week. Then the convoy would come back to Greenham.*

* * * * * *

When I first heard about it, I didn't feel an evangelical urge to join the protest at Greenham. I had been prejudiced against the women's movement by certain experiences in the late '60s and '70s. I went to a separatist women's meeting at

Essex University in 1968 during the student strike (part of the anarchic student movement of the time), where the emphasis was primarily on the discrimination faced by women in academia. Graduate women complained that they could not pursue their careers because they had no childcare. And later on, with the development and institutionalisation of the Women's Liberation movement, the same attitudes and demands were carried through to the exclusion of issues of race, imperialism, national-liberation struggles and (in those early days) lesbianism. I say "exclusion", meaning that the issues would be raised in workshop; but at the final plenary they would mysteriously have been dropped by the self-proclaimed leaders of "a non-leadership situation", all in such a sisterhood touchy-touchy-feely way that we'd erupt with frustrated anger; the platform looked so hurt (often bursting into tears) that other sisters would round on us as violent, abusive, disruptive, trashers of women, destroyers of the women's movement.

In Ireland in the 1970s the women's movement was split, on the one hand Republican women, concerned with the British military occupation in the north, and on the other, the liberal social agenda under the leadership of such Fine-Gael party women as Monica Barnes, with a standard run of feminist demands, contraception, equal pay, job opportunities, childcare -- pretty similar to Britain, apart from contraception.

In the extremely nasty & vicious northern war, many of my friends, Miriam Daly for example, were brutally murdered. The north of Ireland didn't concern the Greenham campaigners or CND at all. When I came out of Armagh gaol in 1980, I concentrated my energies and my emotions on the campaign for prisoners' political status, which culminated in the hunger strike. Also there had been the harassment of my sons by the British police during my imprisonments. Adam was stopped by the Special Patrol Group at least fifteen times -- each time as he came out of school. Jacob had been picked up; they had stamped on his feet in the police cell saying, "Your mother is in the IRA." Neuss had had a torch bashed into his face when he was out with friends late at night. Finn was caught-up in a debacle outside a club: a policeman claimed to have heard him say, "I'll get the shooters." This was a time when the police made a great business of putting down juvenile crime; "Sus-laws" attacked blacks; and the Prevention of Terrorism Act assailed the Irish; London was a police state. The only one of us not picked up was J.A.:

instead a Ronald Hayman did a hatchet job on him for the BBC, implying he was a traitor. We had no time to pursue all these avenues of injustice; we wrote letters to the *Guardian* about our sons; they were not published. Greenham seemed to me to be largely an affair of British women unwilling to be blown up by foreigners' bombs, a viewpoint reinforced by the apparent smug complacency of Tony Benn in Hyde Park denouncing American missiles coming onto British soil, but not denouncing the British army in Ireland. Greenham indeed was all about women, but the superficial glow, emanating from Greenham and illuminating women as somehow more caring, nurturing & loving than men ("symbolic candles that represented the conscience of humanity"), had not been applied to the women in Armagh gaol, who were merely perceived as aiding and abetting terrorists -- nothing to do with feminism.

Armagh had changed my experience of women, their strength & commitment, their negotiating skills. In the end we were able to force the IRA to respect women and give us equal status with the men on the blanket. From one section of British women, the lesbians, there did emerge overt support for the prisoners in Armagh -- one marginalized group saluting another -- many of them came over to Belfast to offer solidarity during our trials.

The liberal press was full of appreciative articles about Greenham, which made me all the more sceptical in view of its general silence over the denial of human rights toward the Irish, not only in Ireland but also in Britain -- the Birmingham Six, the Guildford Four ... Nonetheless, in spite of my misgivings, I *was* part of the women's movement; and now I was a member of Aosdána, with a pension, so I had the money to set up Galway Women's Entertainment, and we were trying to organize Women's Scéal Radio. I could afford to go to Greenham to find out for myself and eventually to broadcast what I found. I was also able to buy a camcorder.

Anyway, my friend Esta, my erstwhile compañera & sister-activist at getting the Troops Out Of Ireland, standing in the street in Haringey seeking signatures whilst the middle class bayed "Murderers!" and the working class flocked to sign -- it was *their* sons who were "the ham in the sandwich between those murderous Irish; let them cut their own throats, let them slaughter each other," -- Esta and I were to go down to Greenham together.

New Year 1983 and Esta had just learnt to drive. She had bought herself an old banger. It was pouring with rain and no sooner had we started than the windscreen wipers fell off. There we were on the motorway, the cars speeding by, we couldn't stop. A bit of a calamity, and dangerous -- peering through the nearly opaque window we had to guess how close was the car in front of us. We did manage to get into the slow lane. The hostility of cars as they cursed us to pass over into the next lane, sheer hatred & frustration, enveloped us; we did make it to a slip-off; we couldn't go back, we had to go on, we travelled on the secondary roads, until finally in the dark we arrived at Greenham Common. The rain had left off. We found there was a camp meeting taking place, hundreds of women sitting in a circle. All about us, hidden in the glades & ferns, small clumps of women sitting round fires, candles flickering, not interested in going to the meeting. Other women, newly arrived like us, wandering vaguely; yet others, well organized with camping gear, setting up their camp.

An almighty intense discussion going on: the agenda was "behaviour in the camp", as though the camp was already well-ordered (with only a few aberrations), a model progressive boarding school. Several well-seasoned headmistress types were standing in the middle of the group arguing the case for appointing spokespersons for the press, PROs to deal with inquiries or visitors, and running candidates for the election in Tory strongholds. The question they posed: was Greenham to be a serious statement on getting rid of nuclear weapons or would it merely give ammunition to the Tory tabloids with a libertarian free-for-all, drugs, drink, up-front sexual behaviour and the trashing of women? It was essential for the media to get a clear-cut, positive message

The headmistresses were outnumbered by young women fleeing from these very strictures on their private lives -- "This is our home -- why should we put an act on for visitors? it would be a lie -- we are free women -- we are liberating the world and making a free world -- we will not be hypocrites pretending a lifestyle we don't support!", fierce ferocious women lying back in each others' arms.

Young women in search of their "herstory", and their own hidden powers, were finding a vivid and personal connection with this countryside, and a whole new language from the writings of Mary Daly, e.g: *Gyn/Ecology: the Metaethics of Radical Feminism,* or *Beyond God the Father,* opening up a whole new world for women, together with a whole new language: "The Third Passage. Gyn/Ecology: Spinning New Time/Space. Spooking: Exorcism, Escape and Enspiriting Process. Sparking: the Fire of Female Friendship. Spinning: Cosmic Tapestries, etc., etc." This feminist theologian was the first to discover the historical centrality of the 16th/17th-century genocidal witch-hunts in the analysis of women's oppression. A 17th-century witch was shot by soldiers at Greenham, with a silver bullet for fear of her magic powers (they had seen her apparently walking on water); this tale awakened the imagination & a sense of continuity of history when 20th-century women came to Greenham to oppose a new generation of genocidal militarists. Old forgotten pagan rites and images -- webs, snakes, mirrors, fire and moonlight -- inspired some women, frightened the burghers of Newbury and fed the frenzy of the tabloid press. Memory may be buried deep but can be reactivated.

Greenham worked because women went off in small groups with women compatible to themselves, hence all the different camps at the different air-base gates. Indeed the growth of the camps resembled the organization of the nation-state. Yellow Gate, at the main gate, the capital; resources, donations and the first stop for visitors. Then Orange Gate and others, provincial cities; then smaller ones, villages, little settlements. The Greenham perimeter was nine miles round, so some of the settlements were four-and-a-half miles from the main gate and no transport. It differed from a nation-state in that there was no central government. Each gate had its own ethos. If you disagreed you moved on to another one. In the early days there were weekly meetings to distribute the donations; no questions were asked, you took what you wanted, invitations, news, etc. The incredible work that consistently went on just to keep the camp going, the fight for the right to receive mail, the right to vote, the right to sign on, the right to draw water; and as well, daily evictions many times a day and at night too.

Before 1986 I was a day-tripper like thousands of others, paying fleeting visits or making an occasional overnight stay at the big gatherings, observing the changes. It was only when deciding to commit myself to a few months did I begin to understand the uniqueness of the camp & the complexity of political and social pressures, some of them expected, some quite unexpected. We knew we were a threat to the government and the apparatus of state, but none of us had realized just *how much* of a threat the opposition believed us to be.

In order to protect myself from becoming too entangled in the internal politics of the camp and all the disparate motivations, I decided to be both observer & participant in NVDA (Non-Violent Direct Action) against the military, with my own agenda to make Greenham women as vocal against the British occupation of the north of Ireland as they were against the American occupation of Britain. As well, as a playwright, I was working with J.A. on *Whose is the Kingdom?*, nine plays for BBC radio; this very lengthy work involved a great deal of research, in particular the rivalry between the Goddess-religion and Imperial Christianity, and how the latter solved the problem by ruthlessly subsuming the former -- & what better place to study it than Greenham, where women were already immersed in their searchings for the ancient matriarchies?

* * * * * *

A Chronology, with Diary Excerpts

September 1986: Maria Lamburn and I came to Greenham (Yellow Gate), to stay there for a while -- I was committing myself for at least three months, while Maria was not sure how long she would stay. We intended to work on a section of our projected opera, to deal with the story of the Greenham Witch, and we hoped some of the women would help with it and take part in it.

I tried to keep a diary, not very consistently, the entries not always properly dated. I include some of them here, in no particular order, to give a flavour of what Greenham was like for a newcomer who didn't know anybody.

~~~o~~~

The first morning of our stay we got up and went to the circle of women around the fire. No-one spoke. There was a kettle beside the fire. It was empty. There were plastic water containers nearby. They were empty.
First problem for the newcomer: --

> Q: Where does the water come from?
> *One of the women at the fire points across the road.*
> A: Over there.
> *We go over there, can't see anything. We come back.*
> Q: We can't find tap?
~~~

A: There is no tap. It's from the mains.
Q: How do we get water from the mains?
A: It's in Gladys [*the vehicle, a converted ambulance*].
We go to Gladys but what are we looking for? Carol comes out of Gladys.
C: What are you doing?
One woman then brings tools. But we don't know how to operate them.
A: You have to have a yellow knob.
Q: Where is it?
A: It's in Gladys.
Carol stops us messing about.
Q: Where is the yellow knob?
C: Somewhere. I thought you knew about the water, you're such a know-all.

M.D'A as "weapons inspector" on Shannon Airport anti-war demo, 2002, with Mary Kelly and J.A..

We are nervous in our tent; heavy gales on Monday night blew the other benders down. Trying to pin down heavy plastic in the wind! -- like the sails of a ship.

My tent is in wrong direction; has blown down once already. The bailiffs came twice. First time, no sooner were we back in place when they came again. Mary said they had been as many as seven times once. When there are only a few women they come more often, to weaken us.

Last night the outer cover of my tent blew off & indeed the tent fell down.

Long supply lorries came into base. Chemicals are flown in then brought out to a dump. The women sit round the fire to observe. Carol told to get in touch with Cruisewatch on her CB radio -- cannot make a connection. Newspapers all full of Cruisewatch and their tactics of spectacular ambush (by the men), an escalation which cannot be maintained. No bailiffs yet. Am wearing Finola's grey and white sweater.

Cruisewatch was an outside action-group, men and women mixed.

~~~o~~~

Our first serious misunderstanding: --

Just had a set-to with Hazel about the rats & washing up. There was only a little water left. I put it into the pot to heat up. Holly says, "Leave some for women." I say. "There is none left. It's important to wash up because of the rats." Hazel says, "I've lived here for five years and no-one has been taken ill because of the rats. They live all around. Rats in the country are healthy," etc. Holly doesn't want to get water because of the bailiffs. I say, "That's fine with me," & walk off. This romanticism about the base as a "rural area"... It bears out everything Sarah H. was talking about, no sense of revolution: what's gone on in the past is the best way. The confusion surrounding a person's relationship with animals is in a way a death wish, a desire for the extermination of our species. Primitivism for its own sake. Had a word with Hazel about the rat controversy. She was not generous. The contradictions: --
~~~

Such women won't stop convoy in case there is an accident & a man gets injured.

They won't take precautions about rats' urine causing poison because (in their experience) it hasn't happened.

Sarah has actual experience of a man who died from rat urine: it got into his kidneys.

There is a woman from the camp in hospital with kidney infection.

They do not tell other women about the rats & the importance of rinsing the rim of the cup with boiling water. Holly's father says, "I don't mind rats."

The English virtue of loving & caring for animals more than humans & certainly more than women.

In spite of my grumbles, the women who stay are amazing, because of their endurance. They have no other life.

Lorna going on about rats so also Julie, saying I was patronizing towards rats. Has Greenham Common has reverted back to what it always used to be? A place for High Toryism, very English, where the strongest survive & the weakest go to the wall?

At last one of the women came up and told us about the (unspoken) rules of the camp.

When one arrives one has to edge oneself in; as Janet says, wait for a woman to talk to you. Your answer has to be reverential & passive whilst the words of feminism, woman-power, etc., are constantly repeated. You are then ignored whilst the regulars talk in low tones about themselves. If you are sufficiently confident to relax, you may pick up a few words, to understand they are talking about actions or court cases or women in jail. No information is publicly shared. Hazel has a radio; she doesn't come in the morning with the latest news -- her listening is personal. The newcomer is expected to do a lot of work like gathering wood, fetching water. Cooking food can also be private. As the day draws on, if one comes to the surface & tries to in any way become a lively person, then the ganging up.

Hazel told a funny story of how they had once entered the base & had a picnic on the runway, with table-cloth, flowers in a vase, tea-set, all glued down. The squaddies were running towards them as they were eating -- delicate manners, passing the cucumber sandwiches, asking the MoD police if they wanted any. When they were arrested, Hazel christened herself Militant-Uprising-in-Worthing. This was taken down by the Woman PC who asked if it was all one word. Hazel said no, it was hyphenated. Then later they said, "This is a false name. If you don't tell us your real name, we'll send you to another police station." She said, could she think about it? & sat there: & then told her real name.

Hazel was beaten by soldiers at Jade Gate, with Jean. The base had turned off the lights & soldiers came with boards to beat the women up. Then the MoD arrived with an ambulance to pick up the beaten women. That's how Yellow Gate came to hear of it. Sarah helped to purify Jade Gate with water, putting stones round the trees. Hazel has never spoken of the experience. Hazel never speaks about herself.

The Friends' House at Newbury was set up for Greenham Women & a couple employed there. The wife ran across the road to warn about the convoy & was killed. The women wouldn't talk to the husband. Another girl murdered whilst hitching to Greenham. Jane Hay lives at Orange Gate; she said that Verity went mad because she didn't have her drugs. She rolled in the mud. Denise rolled in the fire wearing only white cotton.

Message from CND: Polaris is abroad! sighted at Scotch Corner, on its way to Burghfield where it is loaded up with warheads. The warheads are repaired there. Research at Aldermaston. Chemicals dumped at Welford. Chemicals inside Greenham since Maggie Thatcher lifted restrictions.

Bailiffs came just after bulk of women left for court.

Maria left: we were not getting on with the opera. The whole idea (in these surroundings) was ill-conceived.

~~~o~~~

It is colder today, with a few short heavy showers. Gathered sticks of gorse. No bailiffs yet. The birds are giving their evening song; a young woman on a horse carrying a whippet passed by smiling. This morning a car driven by a young bearded man who waved & smiled. I find when visitors come I do not want to greet them at first.

Hazel back from jail. More women today. Erika & I dragged wood into hiding, to save it from the bailiffs. Discussion about who would go to Burghfield, to watch. The brown van at Orange belongs to camp. The sun is going down now. There was frost this morning.

Went for stroll & saw hangars open. Returned with Sarah H.; she thinks the convoy may come out before the weekend action. It is difficult to believe there are 3000 men & families in there.

Eileen came round saying that an American from the base told her the cruise was coming out on Monday. He goes to the pub & he has previously given out correct info; he also wanted the cruise video for his boss. That was strange. Eileen thinks he could be a plant & they could be coming out on Friday. They have been working on the hangar.

Money-meeting last night. Allison again puts in for petrol money. The running of the camp is over £400 a week -- fares for direct action, sleeping bags, new waterproof jackets, membership of AA, etc. Julie an efficient secretary for the meeting; it is all put in the book for all to see. The Welsh women have gone back.

The cruise came out at midnight; we missed it. Sarah Hipperson was still up & called the others. When I came to Yellow Gate, they told me the support vehicles had also left. I heard a lot of engines revving when I slept. We sang.
~~~

Donna arrived; she had been knocked unconscious by the police when the cruise returned; her neurons were damaged & her arm was numb. She had made fly-posters attacking 1807 (the number of the policeman who threw her to the ground). 3 of them went and made a hole in the fence & later on were to enter the base & fly-post.

Milly the dog was run over during the rush hour. She was taken to the vet. Women recounted the cruelty of men who stopped but didn't help. Another weapon against men. Lorna was nearly hit by a vehicle, a lorry that swerved towards her. Sarah said she thought all this was preparing the culture of war at home, war in the countryside, the acceptability that there will be casualties amongst those who oppose war. Borne out by a John Mortimer screenplay on TV, where a Greenham woman stands in front of a vehicle & gets killed.

Mary just out of Holloway; was there 28 days, she shared dormitory with 8 others, then 6. Mainly Asians & Carribbeans on drug charges; some Europeans, Danish, French. One Jamaican charged with shop-lifting; a very rich woman gave her half the price of the goods.

The women were saying the police are v. rough. A rumour that women were handcuffed. Sarah said when she was being arrested, "If you hold my arm like that you'll break it." The cop said, "That's what we're supposed to do."

Rebecca has been moved to Holloway.

The Police Bill is being enacted on Jan the 1st. Something like the PTA. Pandora from Orange Gate found letter from MoD about soldiers leaving convoy to grab women and pin them against the wall. Annette from Portsmouth is followed everywhere round her home town by the Special Branch, believes that zapping is increasing at Green Gate. The camp is much bigger.

~~~o~~~

I had been at Yellow Gate for about a month and had not taken part in any actions, even though women were getting arrested and were being sent to gaol. It was
~~~

extremely difficult to know what was going on. I went away for a weekend ...

> Esta drove me to Greenham, it is wet. Beth came to tell me that the cruise had arrived back at 4.30 this morning. They had been arrested & the magistrates had tried to curtail bail with a condition that they did not trespass on Salisbury Plain. He couldn't do that, as trespassing is not a serious enough charge. Rebecca in Newbury police station awaiting a vacancy in one of the gaols, she has got 21 days. The gaols are full. Strange development. Must get info.

The new Police Bill allowed prisoners to serve their sentences in police stations. Newbury was the worst. The blankets smelled of urine. In the cells that had toilets in them, the toilets were blocked. Rebecca was later moved to Reading (police station, not a proper gaol) where the cells were better.

> There are 18 women in camp; we have fewer now & the tents are dispersed. Green Gate is now open. Yesterday the bailiffs did not come. The others were in court, in Oxford & Newbury. Julie's case was dismissed; there was no evidence. Donna was fined.
>
> Miriam turned up yesterday, trailing her blankets round her shoulders, then returned later trailing her tent. She was griping about Katrina not allowing her to do direct action with her, while she did allow Janet who had not been at Greenham so long.
>
> **Katrina & her clique, her principles:**
>
> 1) You can only do direct action with women you know and trust.
> 2) It can only evolve & new women come in by tests of trust.
> 3) Power develops by constantly doing actions.
>
> **My views on Katrina's principles:**
>
> 4) Getting other women to do action but not letting them into inner circle makes them feel inadequate & resentful so they are not helped.
> 5) Thus the clique gets stronger & there is more concentration on it.
> 7) Women are not confident in themselves when they arrive.

8) There must be a learning process.
9) But you must learn from your own experience: no-one can teach you.

This is a women's camp & runs itself, there cannot be routine & it is more like the flexibility in the trenches or in units like the SAS. Women come & go: unique.

Inside Greenham, do some of the women want to feel they are the only ones carrying on the struggle? Yet that woman who owns Milly lives outside in her house and is sympathetic. Very little interest in the surrounding areas, or contacts made, by the constant regular women, just like a contemplative order. They glory in their outcast role. No-one aligns themselves with the state, not even with the Labour Party. No food left today in camp & I am hungry. I could cook, but that means making my way to the fire through all the other women sitting there. (This is why some of us go to Green Gate.)

~~~o~~~

Food topics.

The evening meals are now supplied by support groups from Ascot, Windsor, Reading & Newbury. A smart utility van drove up; out jumped ladies -- curry, lasagna, chili, nuts, mince pies, v. good. It happens every winter, till it gets light enough to cook. My worry is over now about starving.

The food run: 20 women involved & men. Menu: beans, rice, vegan cottage pie, apple pie, chocolate crispie biscuits, cauliflower au gratin, red cabbage, parsnips, baked potatoes, some other beans, another dessert.

Meals on Wheels again: nut roast, lentils, mashed potatoes, tarts -- a feast! The group extends as far as High Wycombe; Katrina doesn't know much about them; they are referred to as the Dinner Ladies.

Last night Sarah Hipperson told me that the Common in the end rejects women. She was going on about the lack of humanity & generosity that is in the camp, sparked off by Katrina not allowing the bacon-&-egg flan to remain in the camp; which meant that Carol would have nothing to eat,
~~~

as she eats meat & only eats meat, as a protest. Carol came out of Gladys saying she only loves missiles not vegans or lesbians. Sarah explained that Carol had no food.

Carol spoke to me about her sausages & the problem: if she cooked her sausages on the grill & animal fat fell into the fire she would be in trouble with the vegetarians & the vegans. In fact food works out quite well if we all eat vegan.

~~~o~~~

My own decision to go to Green Gate was because Yellow Gate was getting too big, and I found the politics of the women there incompatible with mine -- about food and animals, and over the Irish situation. There was a general failure to understand the causes of national liberation struggle.

Had a set-to with Lorna over Libya. Two Greenham women had been invited to attend an International Anti-Imperialist conference in Libya; the way Lorna told me the story was as follows: -- "It was the most frightening experience I'd ever had & I'm not easily frightened; it was scary. We were in fear of our lives. In the end we were thrown out. It was a conference of terrorists, IRA, PLO, Sandinistas, Kurds, etc. I had to really look at myself to find out if I was not racist, as they were all brown & black except for us, we were the only two women there unaccompanied by men. There were 600 people and only 28 other women (who were all with male groups); there was a British delegation, Spartacists from the British Collective. Bits of paper were handed out with words on them, it was half-way to being a religious revivalist convention. Col. Ghaddafi came in escorted by these women wearing lipstick & high-heel shoes with rifles on their shoulders. They lined the walls; the doors were closed. Ghaddafi asked us all to stand for one minute for the death of the Colombian leader. We didn't; we sat. We also sat for Ghaddafi's ovation: believe me, it was the bravest thing I have ever done. We were ignored, no-one took any notice of us. We didn't go to any more of the conference; we wanted to see Tripoli, so we went into the city. When we returned, the Deputy Foreign Minister was there & asked us why we hadn't attended the conference. We then got a minder, but we gave him
~~~

the slip. The conference ended on Wednesday. The Foreign Minister said the conference was over & told us the plane we should catch. The others were asked to stay until Friday. They had been taken to military bases; we hadn't." I questioned the story. At no time were threats given to them, nor did they ask to address the conference on their non-violent philosophy, which they could have done -- especially as I had made a video with them on the work at Greenham and had shots of Lorna at Welford (where the women had taken action to ground a plane that was being sent out to bomb Libya, one of the reasons why they had been invited). Whether they ever gave the video to Ghaddafi, or in disgust left it behind, I will never know. But I am sure if they not been so high minded they could have shown it and so perhaps changed the course of history by the persuasiveness of non-violent direct action ... Anyway, even questioning the story brought on outrage from the other women: I was accused of attacking her, I was put in the same league as all those terrorists, IRA, PLO, etc. When I asked her for her definition of the word "terrorists", she said that all armies were terrorists. Years later when in charge of letters in *Peace News** she refused to publish Yellow Gate's letters because Yellow Gate women were "terrorists".

* *See correspondence quoted, below.*

A rat scuttled past looking for food. Lorna & Sarah B. (who are twenty) reminiscing about when they were teenagers & mad about pop stars: Sarah lying to her mother when she was 14, saying she was staying the night with a friend but really going off to a party where her favorite pop star was supposed to be turning up. Hazel back last night. Water carriers full this morning. Carol looks after the money & the CB, so has central role. She slagged me off to Esta, "Is that woman there with her video?" What Lorna didn't like (re Libya) is my asking her why she hadn't spoken up publicly. Their sureness that they are right; they are not interested in hearing why they may not be. They maintain that to argue is male. They are young, they are bossy, they are like their mothers, they are Cromwell's heirs, they are the inheritors of imperialism, they are protecting their land for themselves. They say they are non-violent only because they don't control the guns. They are children brought up under an ideology of counter-terrorism (Maggie Thatcher); so all national liberation struggles are the same as NATO. Vegans and vegetarians, if the the rest of the world copied them would there be no wars? -- just collect the dole, escape to the sun for a rest -- they are fed, clothed and heated, they are the goddesses of today, all women come to worship at their shrine, place their offerings, stay awhile in silence, then leave in the morning. The post brings more offerings. These vestal virgins keep watch, everything that goes in they see, everything that comes out they see, as they watch by the fire in the mud. Carol with all her plugs tied round her waist, she watches & invents her own words as she listens to the radio.

Three days later:

Big bust-up again; with Katrina, over my Indian experience and gaol there. She began accusing me of being manipulative and using male arguments. She brought up Lorna's distress over my questioning of the Libyan conference. She accused me of being violent -- as had the other women -- there is still deep antagonism there.

~~~o~~~

It all got to be too much. There were two very jolly young Americans there, Dara and Phelene, equally pissed-off. We decided to move to Green Gate and were joined by Lonie and Allison. Green Gate evolved into a story-telling gate. Dara and Phelene had come to London as members of a group studying British culture. They had skived off to join Greenham. (What better place to discover British culture?) Their stories were like every movie one ever saw about wealthy, dysfunctional families in the States ...

Dara & Phelene both have women relatives who are multi-millionaires. Dara's Aunt Dot wants to be buried with her money; she owns most of the oilfields of Alaska. Dara's father designs nuclear submarines. Her parents' marriage began to disintegrate, so her mother went off to a therapist (who had been married eight times) and was the head of the Psychology Department at some university. In the course of his therapy, he started an affair with Dara's mother and settled into the family with his own current wife, creating a ménage-à-quatre. The children wanted to kill him. He's an alcoholic, he broke his wife's arm because he thought she was a hooker, he became the family's gaoler. Children, husband and grandmother not allowed upstairs. Children must be nude, together
~~~

with the adults ... Phelene's father owns an enormous multi-national food company. A very Italian family. He makes his own pasta and cooks Sunday dinner. Phelene was a coke-dealer at school ... Lonie's father is Swiss. The family is v. nationalistic and would not accept her mother, who is English. The mother gets depressed and has returned to England. Lonie gets left behind and has been wandering abroad since she was 13. Before she came to Greenham, she was living in toilets. She feels more secure here ... Allison (aged 17) comes from the north of England. Her father is housing inspector for the council; breeds birds, has a parrot in the kitchen that makes a noise like a telephone, 2 rabbits, a goldfish and a dog. She told her parents she was coming to Greenham because she was absolutely committed to getting rid of nuclear weapons. They are all committed evangelical Christians.

We were joined by others who had felt excluded at Yellow Gate; we set up our own village.

Carmen, another American, slept with half of the judiciary in Kentucky when she worked at the courts for a year with prisoners; she was drunk most of the time ... Julie goes on a cycling trip: on her return from Ireland, she was pulled in at Fishguard under the Prevention of Terrorism Act for wearing an Ann Francis T-shirt. (Ann Francis, a vicar's wife, the first Greenham woman to be sentenced to gaol -- six months.) They held her until the train pulled out. At a youth hostel they wouldn't let her stay because she had an address at Greenham. The court had made her have the Greenham address.

When Sarah Hipperson was here, a letter of solidarity came to the camp from Nepal: a soldier, we think in a Gurkha regiment. Sarah enjoyed the letter & said it passed the time. Do women here get bored, wanting tension like the British army in the base, gang up on each other? An American soldier raped a woman and assaulted a woman; he is on trial & was let out on bail.

I was now beginning to get the hang of Greenham and to understand where Katrina's principles were coming from. At Green Gate we now had our own little "trust-group".

We did three pieces of direct action.

1) Putting woman-symbols (made from potatoes) on fence: this is a criminal offence.
2) Putting tinfoil on fence: this is a criminal offence.
3) Putting out false information about Kinnock coming to the base. (This was to suggest that the Labour Party might be about to adopt a policy of removing the cruise missiles.)

Dara liked talking to the soldiers and was able to tell me a lot about their attitude.

One squaddy who was sympathetic told Dara he admired the women, and his colonel had him taken off duty. They can choose to go to Greenham and are paid £30 extra a day.

The base inside is enlarging itself: more buildings.

Woke up to frost. Heard Dana going to make fire, her feet passing my tent sounded like the army. An awful lot of noise, the soldiers crying like wolves in the dark. Went round fence with Dara to make woman-symbols out of potatoes & failed. The soldiers hate being at Greenham; they have to leave their homes, regiments & regular jobs, to guard the base. This one: his fire had gone out when he arrived on guard duty. During the day they are not allowed fires, he is married 4 months; his wife is in the RAF. They are not allowed to talk to us or take tea or food from us in case it's poisoned. Katrina the witch has made her point.

Soldiers also told Dara:

1) They noticed poster; no one would talk to policeman 1807. They were forbidden to read posters.
2) Soldiers are drafted in (different story from the other soldier) and are bored when they come to Greenham.
3) Women's direct action livens things up for them.

Soldiers encourage women to take action, and then report them to MoD. They use women's actions to break their boring routine.

The hangars are open at both ends. I could hear the engines revving-up inside. American airmen in different uniforms coming & going. It is important to keep one's mind fixed on the base & the reality of the weapons and what they can do. The whole base is built over what used to be a lake & the runway is constantly cracking.

Talk with Dara about growth of Greenham causing breakdown of law and order. More and more bylaws passed which are broken, fines which are allowed to accumulate. Women given short sentences. Women being put into police cells as there is no room in gaols.

In spite of all the laws we remain. And women come. Scottish, Welsh, Irish, American, Norwegian, Dutch, Swedish, French, Japanese. I am fascinated by the the Dinner Ladies: very decent straight women, many of them Quakers. They must have had a background of voluntary war work. They do not mind us not appreciating what they do for us. Protestant ethics, the deed is sufficient. They are efficient, quiet, capable.

The laws have been changed constantly. In the begining it was not an offence to go into the base: women could use the launderette. Now there are more & more laws. The Newbury Council have taken over the land of Greenham. They swapped a patch to the MoD.

The contractor in charge of the fencing was measuring today, watched by the MoD; they must be widening the gap between the inner and outer fences. The soldiers have blacked their faces.

~~~o~~~

Yesterday evening, went to Yellow Gate. Donna & Holly gone to London. Small camp, everyone friendly. Cutting the fence doesn't bother the soldiers but breaks their base discipline down. Bailiffs came yesterday. At Green Gate, Allison screamed at them; then they in turn roughed us up.
~~~

Greenham Common landscape with soldiers.

At Yellow Gate, Gladys' brake stuck; the bailiffs helped to push it off & were friendly. There is a pet blackbird & a dormouse -- long tail, huge ears, bright eyes. A lot of air activity last night. A young man was hanging round Yellow Gate, he wanted to leap into the base & be a hero because there was an audience to watch him. Hazel & Janet standing still like witches, seeing him out of the area. Jane Powell (whom Sarah H. does not trust) was the other woman beaten up with Hazel.

Allison went into Welford base, which is all-American, with Lynette, Sara & Sara's dog. They were there for 2 - 3 hours. Americans came up & asked them to get into truck; they refused. They walked out free. Set up camp outside. Women's camps at Aldermaston, Salisbury, Burghfield. Snowball-actions once every three months. Menwith Cruisewatch camp. Food-runs. CND.

We think cruise is coming back; there is a lot of activity at silos.

I said to Katrina that it had been a very nice quiet day. This upset Katrina because she feels that there has to be action all the time. She was also, I think, disturbed by how easy it was for the three to post up the fly-bills, that they had mingled quite naturally with the people inside the base & had not been challenged; the timing is all important. Afterwards they all said how good it had been, how it made them feel better.

I don't know why Katrina was "disturbed". Perhaps she thought it was wrong to be inside the base without confrontation. Visitors to the camp were frequent and not necessarily appreciated by everyone.

Yesterday was interesting (I went to Yellow Gate). 4 male visitors. Then a catholic priest from Liverpool with 49 of his flock. A large hairy American with car. 4 gangly older men. Richard, who works at night as nurse in mentally-handicapped childrens' hospital; he brought us lots of info, his CND magazine from Sutton about zapping, info about the American Ploughshare prisoners, some of whom have sentences of 12 years. The women here object to Richard the most: he was the one who came by public transport; he talked the most, made the loudest presence & was resented. In fact of all the men he came with the most information; he produced his banner, "GOD SAVE US FROM OURSELVES."

Dewsbury women came to stay at Blue Gate. Jolly women, they'd had a sponsored walk and raised the money for their van & food. Bruce Kent stopped off with a carrier bag full of chocolates, after-dinner mints & a cheque.

A lot of visitors. Party from Ruskin College. 2 American women spoke about Seneca (a women's camp) which is near where they live. One of them told me about fundamentalist bible group that says nuclear war is all in the Bible, the Apocalypse. The evangelist Falwell preaches this.

An Israeli journalist is here about the arrests.

Wages for Housework (the Kings Cross collective) came for the day, black women, handicapped women, lesbian women, women from Bristol. It was like a great gathering where the Greenham Common Tribe recognized the spontaneity, strength & organization. Food was produced, the fire widened, Katrina even came with me to help me carry a settle back. Donna snipped the sweet bag for me. Elizabeth from Violet Gate is sculpting a "cultural manifesto totem."

Sarah Hipperson had already spoken about Selma James of Wages for Housework; she said the group is very committed and well-centred.

Sarah often comes into the diary:

Sarah Hipperson, the Scottish woman (59), a strong catholic mother of 4 boys & one daughter, is very interesting. She went on hunger strike for a month whilst she was on remand. She sat with prisoners during meal times, just taking water. She lost two and a half stone; she also raised a cross during the Malvina/Falklands victory march -- she is a genuine catholic. She was once dragged from her tent to the police station. She is quite amazing: she has stood up at Mass & challenged the priest. She has a great quality of discerning what is right & wrong; with the directness of her Glasgow voice there is no room for confusion.

My tent blew down in the night. Gentle hands put it up whilst I slept inside; they bathed me in a light like the fairies. I was talking to Sarah Hipperson about all the really strong women, wonderful women, who came to the camp: all had had children. The camp is a secular convent; we are the virgins of life.

Eileen came to tell us that Reagan had broken the SALT treaty by adding one extra cruise. Went for walk, returned by fence because we saw a truck revving up outside Green Gate (suspicious). Tried to take short cut, failed. Great valleys of water & swamps. When we got back we found Beth & Katrina worried. Spud spoke about Xmas: bad time at Greenham; women got drunk. Sarah Hipperson said Hallowe'en wasn't good either; she had been unhappy & felt that women coming didn't understand the spirit; were racing around & then there was a feeling of witch-hunting. Last night hid the wood so bailiffs wouldn't get it.

A problem arises when women come to Greenham who don't know what they want but feel they must do something spectacular & there is not a sufficient nucleus here to influence them. Cutting the fence is criminal damage, very serious, so women should not give their address as Greenham unless they really are staying, because we then have to deal with the arrival of warrants for women no longer present, involving unnecessary police raids and harassment.

~~~o~~~

Differences were beginning to emerge. I can now see that this was the beginning of the Split: --

A visitor from Haslemere (member of CND) told me that condemnation of the rape at Molesworth was debated by CND as an emergency resolution. The resolution was defeated. Pat Arrowsmith opposed closure of Molesworth. Women got very emotional & held banners, the Haslemere woman thought it was wrong that the rape should have had an emergency debate, she didn't think that Molesworth camp had a collective responsibility towards rape, which she regarded as personal. Also an anti-racist motion was dropped when Bruce Kent said there was no racism in CND.
~~~

Sunday 7 December, 1986: a important meeting: --

Wet. We hang around waiting for the meeting, at least 30 women. We sit in large circle round the fire. In my opinion the meeting began too boldly, Indra being thrown into the middle of it. Beth had told Indra that only the pure and strong were acceptable at Greenham. Indra has worked with men in actions ...

The divisions that had emerged at Greenham concerned the role of Cruisewatch, the mixed men-and-women outside action-group: Lynette Edwell a leading organizer. (At the same time, Greenham Women Everywhere had opened an office in London with a co-ordinating committee.) The December 7th meeting was called to discuss these questions. Katrina Howse brought up the Molesworth outrage -- in the mixed men-and-women peace camp at Molesworth air base, with some women from Greenham, one of the women had been raped. Katrina felt CND -- sponsors of Molesworth -- should, at their AGM, acknowledge and condemn the rape.

Katrina, Beth, Hazel felt that Sarah H. had not been supportive enough, that women who worked with men betrayed women when it came to believing a man against a woman. 13 women from Greenham went to Molesworth to support the raped woman. One of them pulled a bender down & slogans were painted. The Greenham women were accused of violent acts. Katrina came out and said she would not work with heterosexual women. Sarah's arm had been injured & she had left the camp for 6 weeks. Hazel felt that Sarah, when she came to the fire, had not listened to Hazel's account of the Greenham women's action at Molesworth. Letters had been sent. It was very messy.

Katrina went on to speak strongly against Cruisewatch having any status within the Greenham Common women's peace camp. Said she was withdrawing from any relationship with Cruisewatch; she and Beth Junor would begin their own outside actions on Salisbury Plain against the military. She believed that a woman-only peace camp could survive at Greenham; but to bring Cruisewatch men into our counsels, with equal rights of debate and decision, would destroy everything. Molesworth was a warning. She also said women should be actually at the Greenham camp to help practically and actively, instead of vicariously attempting to direct policy from Cruisewatch or Greenham Women Everywhere ...

The meeting spun out. Katrina gave an emotional outburst that she was a witch and she was being witch-hunted & burnt. Some women said Katrina was too strong & intimidated women. What about women coming to the base? women have been exiled & don't want to come. Allison said women at the base should be grateful & appreciate the food that supporters bring & not send it back. At Greenham (one woman had said) they didn't want non-vegan food & so on.

The meeting broke down amidst acrimony. The start of the split; the start of the targeting of Katrina as a "disruptive element". There was to be no further meeting of women from all the gates until the final meeting on 26 July 1987 when the camp finally split over events at the Moscow Peace Conference.

Help was now arriving from the Kings Cross Women's Centre in London, women who came regularly to offer material and physical assistance: to look after the camp when so many were in court or prison, and when evictions took place every day, sometimes 2 or 3 times a day. Wilmette Brown (of the Kings Cross Centre) became the first black woman elected to the CND executive, where she gave support to Katrina's demand about Molesworth.

~~~o~~~

Katrina now says she is a witch. She has a spiteful sense of humour, quite open about how she has to stack food away to survive. Her eyes slant & glitter. Her poster for the weekend has witches' faces just like hers.

Katrina is making herself a religion. Some women believe in the Goddess; & Katrina is her. Milly the dog is all right, no bones broken. Hazel & Jane think it is the healing power of the Goddess. Is there an ideological difference between the christians & the goddess-worshippers? Is it defined yet? Are only goddess-worshippers acceptable? These are questions which have not been clarified at the discussion. I returned to where I'm living, Green Gate, and we discussed these matters. What is a witch?

Had talk with Sarah H. about not tilting from centre. Katrina is looking for centre and Sarah might be pushing her off-course. Katrina uses pain to traumatize herself: this is dangerous & may be where witches come from.
~~~

Carol fears Katrina & believes that she meddles in black magic. There is fear of Katrina around, but that is only because Katrina is positive as to where she stands & uses the weakness of women to overpower them. Lorna is a little acolyte but does not believe in the goddess. Jane said to Katrina, "Good morning, Goddess." Katrina smiled & said, "You are coming to recognize that?" Jane said, "No." There are games & fantasies being played out. Sarah H. looked old & worn; she is going to London until Wednesday.

Julie came Monday night & said that Rebecca & Katrina were called Goddess. There were 6 goddesses. Julie was nearly initiated, because she loves the moon: "The moon is my weakness." So women are initiated? and it becomes an honour. They tried to initiate Miriam in a ceremony at the full moon but she was frightened.

~~~o~~~

A chronological diary-account of the mass-action which changed me from an observer into a Greenham Woman. The Ant Action: it was created by Sarah Hipperson. Women cut the fence of the air base. We went through in file, carrying "garden candles", a march like a column of ants, not recognizing any obstacle. About 100 of us got arrested.

Thursday 11 December 1986
Beth came by, returning from Salisbury Plain, calling outside the tent. She came in a car with two women, who brought wood & dry blankets. The noise, Beth said, is the cruise in the base communicating with the cruise on the plain. The noise is evil. We hear it on the plain and that's how it is tracked down: the high-pitched buzz going through our brain. There is a lot of activity, one cruise inside the base, the other out. That is new. They are trying to avoid taking them out so they won't be seen. But they can be heard. What does it do to our brain? My head reels with the buzz.

Sarah H. & Georgina come by in the evening. Helen Johns too. Food-run not so good as on previous night, as more people to feed. Already we as a group have become fixed. In the beginning I found it difficult to plug into Sarah.
~~~

The visit was about the convoy which was expected back. Allison & I were to go to Indigo Gate. I went back to sleep there till midnight, then we walked to Yellow Gate. Frost. Clear night. Many new women at Yellow Gate, drinking hot wine & brandy. Sarah was going to signal with torch on the side of the road. We lined the road. Some women in the bushes. We waited for the police cars & vans. Heard vans arrive & we heard a line of them. Before that a red car had gone up & down; we waited & waited; hushly deathly silence; the moon; waiting for the roar and the lights of the convoy. Miriam (who suffers from epilepsy) was beside me swaying closer to the kerb; I kept pulling her back. Then the lights, the noise, motor-bikes, cars, the convoy! Military colour with cloth flags, like Dracula's coffin: very very weird. Sarah was told to put out her torch. Lights flashing in the bushes; the cops picking up women, throwing them down, rolling them over, as the convoy trundled past. It was over. We went back to Yellow Gate, women bruised & sore. We returned to Green Gate, to await bailiffs & supply vehicles.

Friday 12 December 1986
Elizabeth came round to warn us about the bailiffs & we were all in bed. It was was a clear sharp frost. We had everything cleared before they came. I asked what union they were in. I raced to Yellow Gate in time for the return of supply vehicles. Made a chain, stopped them, we were held back, then we released them. More chains. The cops' nerves stretching as the vehicles stopped, Miriam falling under one. We made for the cars, running, and stopping each one. Janet arrested. We hung around; then back to Green Gate with Helen J. and Evelyn, with water.

Stewed apples with cream. It is raining; I mess up tent; can't find pole. More women arriving for the big event, the mass gathering to mark the anniversary of the arrival of cruise. Workshops, ending with a mass action. Great white campers. Efficient women setting up camp. We feel small & fragile & disorganized.

Visitors: 2 retired teachers, Elizabeth & Victoria, Cambridge. One English Litt., the other Classics. Victoria recites Greek verse. Elizabeth recites her poems & dreams: one a haunted ballroom, the other a Kafka one in church, changing shapes, pink dolls turn to pink beads. Then an examination of the influence of Greek thought. We sing & play; me on the tin whistle, then the recorder.

A group doing video for Channel 4 get a lift to Orange Gate. Sarah there with plans for mass trespass. On to Indigo then back to Green. On Thursday night we stopped cars leaving base.

Saturday 13 December 1986
Woke early. Hear women talking. They have put a new lot of squaddies in. These ones are rougher. Allison, after convoy, very upset, talks to them for three hours; then 4 women go to shout. Squaddies hurl rocks. Yesterday they were shouting abuse: "Slags, lesbians!" What is my attitude about verbal abuse? From the women, it does escalate violence; they do it all the harder on the other side. Helen J. going on about CND & Labour. Sarah H. on top of the world to get her Ant March going. Annette from Portsmouth to make her roundabout blockade. Indigo to make free expression of music. The squaddies call me Whiskey Woman. Apart from that, we are hungry, now that we won't be getting food-run. Too many women for a food-run. Instead, each gate has been given £10 to buy food: we gave it to Louie who squirrelled it away with her herbs and lost it. She & Phelene moon about holding hands, Louie with a startled look on her face as if any moment she will break out. "I am very sorry," she said. "I know, but I did help in cleaning up the camp."

"You look a real Greenham Woman," said the 2 teachers to me. "It's the assortment of garments & the smell," I reply. Loney ("I am a vegan," she constantly says) went out for a piss to find a group of Liverpool women stumbling along the fence for Blue Gate. Muddy. They had a stove, made tea for us. One woman had cancer. Her son is awaiting trial for a snowball action (i.e. mass fence-snipping) at some other military base. Go to Blue Gate. More Liverpool women came down by coach; are going back at 4pm; wonderful old ones. Newbury women arrive to do play. We have strung up the banners. They do the play. We join in ring-a-ring-of-roses, then they read out a speech. Go back to Yellow Gate: tail end of workshop. We meet about blockade at roundabout. Allison says she feels strong. Dora & Phelene leave camp and go back to join their group in London: the end of their course, and so back to America … Good group rituals to bring workshop to a close. Rituals is the in-word. The police have blocked entrance. Women decorate the base. We go to blockade.

Police have women penned-in. Allison drives van, stops, it blocks road; we all cheer. Back to Yellow Gate. All camp women there have been arrested for blocking Yellow Gate off. There is confusion.

Talk to Janet & Orange Gate about plans that must go on still. Women released. Sarah gathers group. We go off to do mass trespass: the Ant March. Miss turning; meet Mary Millington; go back. ("The Women's Army is Marching!" ... or Angela Brazil?) There is frost & a full moon. We wait for Sarah, who finally goes off to cut fence. Sarah gets arrested. Women go to fence; there is a hole; we scramble through. Some jump over barbed wire. I crawl through. We all march along, and then run, in line ahead. Soldiers run to intercept. "Halt or I'll shoot!" -- but I run on. Squaddie arrests me. We all get taken to process room. Long wait. After 6 hours those of us left are to go to Newbury. Louie, Mani and I are not given bail, so will stay in Newbury till Monday. Only one telephone line at base, so it takes ages. We are given tea. Put into paddy wagon, each in a cell. Newbury: more waiting. Sunday the 14th., at 10 am, go into cell, locked up, no heat. 11 am, cell unlocked, and we are given bail. Sarah & Esta there in car, also Donna. Go to Friends' House for wash & tea. Back to Green Gate to say goodbye, on to Yellow Gate. Finola there. Say goodbye: back to Friends', more tea. Jane Graham there. Phone J.A. All is well. Back to London, en route to Ireland. Bath, bed.

~~~o~~~

This was my first arrest at Greenham; four months later I described the subsequent court proceedings in the letter reproduced below. It was published in Irish papers and the English-based Irish Post, *but ignored by the other English papers to which I sent it. I received a lot of support. J.A. got an anonymous letter (British stamp) asking him if his wife was a "Lesbian pervert like ...* [a list of well-known contemporary women, concluding with the name of the late Countess Markievicz]. "

* * * * * *

Letter to the Press

Galway 3 April 87. To the The Irish Times *and other papers.*

'Human rights' now seems to be an obsessive priority with the leaders of the Western
~~~

World. Let me recount my recent experience in the magistrates' court at Newbury, Berkshire, and the denial of human rights to the hundreds of women charged with civil disobedience at the Greenham Common peace camp.

On 13 December 1986 I was arrested with nearly 100 other women for entering the Cruise-Missile base at Greenham. I attended my trial at Newbury court on 19 March 1987. I observed (and indeed suffered) the following anomalies in the procedure of justice.

Defendants were not allowed to question the Ministry of Defence Police as to where exactly they were in "the prohibited area" when they were arrested. The magistrates ruled such questions "irrelevant". When defendants asked if this was because of the Official Secrets Act, that question too was ruled "irrelevant". Defendants wished their cases adjourned so that they could seek legal advice as to the legal status of the bylaws under which they were arrested -- these bylaws having been specially brought in to deal with the Greenham Peace Camp. This was refused. Women who insisted on making statements from the dock questioning the morality of the laws protecting nuclear weapons were threatened with contempt of court. But when they ignored this threat, they were not charged with contempt but forcibly removed from the dock and thrown out of the courtroom by the police, and the court was cleared. Dates on which arrests were made did not tally with the prosecution evidence. This should have resulted in the dropping of charges; but the court ignored it. Women in court who drew attention to this were brutally evicted from the premises.

When women are convicted and fined, no effort is made by the authorities to collect the fines on the dates given: months, even years, can go past, and then the women are suddenly arrested and imprisoned for non-payment. The length of such imprisonment seems to bear no relation to the amount of the fine. In addition to gaol sentences, women who refuse to pay their fines are prohibited from entering certain counties of the UK for specified periods -- a device amounting to internal exile, and regarded with horror when it takes place in the Soviet Union.

In my own case I was subjected to the following phenomena: --

On the charge sheet there were no specific charges and the date of arrest did not tally with that given by the chief witness for the prosecution.

In my defence, I began by saying that the laws under which I was charged had been "abused for the political and military interests of government" and that as an Irish citizen I was aware of a long history of such abuse of the British law ...

As soon as I came to that point my statement was torn out of my hands by the police.

When women demanded that I be allowed to continue, I was forcibly removed from the dock and sentenced to seven days' imprisonment. I did not hear the court find me guilty of trespass (with which I was charged), nor did I hear them give me time to pay a fine -- which is normal, 28 days being the regular condition.

I was told that I would serve my time in Newbury Police Station, which is quite unsuitable for convicted prisoners -- no sheets on the uncovered foam-mattress, no light except artificial light, no exercise facilities, and no copies of prison-rules available.

I had not expected prison and had no change of clothes or toilet articles, and none were given me.

Imprisonment in a Police Station seems to be a legal grey-area: relatives and friends cannot find out from the authorities where you are serving your sentence, and there seems no machinery for providing this information. When I constantly questioned my legal situation in the Police Station, I was moved -- after two nights -- to Holloway Gaol. In Holloway, I was knocked down and dragged off to solitary confinement because I said I wished to attend Sunday worship at both the Catholic and Anglican services. I had been told that other prisoners were allowed to do this: but, in my case, it appeared I had to declare myself as belonging to a specific religious sect.

These abuses against the Greenham Common women have been going on with increasing intensity over the past three-and-a-half years. Because they are now considered "normal practice", they are no longer considered newsworthy by the British media. Greenham Common women, because of our constancy and non-violent determination to get rid of weapons of mass destruction, are dangerous to the governments of Thatcher and Reagan: our human rights, therefore, are irrelevant.

During the 48 hours I was in Holloway, I was strip-searched twice.

* * * * * *

Spring/summer 1987:

I had returned to Greenham a few weeks previously, for the court case described above.

* * * * * *

Monday 16 March 1987

Bailiffs came 3.40pm. No bailiffs Sunday. Beth & Katrina had seven charges dropped. They tried to give them bail conditions: failed. Lin active with computers. The Hacking Guide to computers, to break into MoD's computers. Inside the base, more bunkers (not the posh ones), offices, dormitories, officers' bedrooms with carpets and old furniture. There is an "art bunker". There was a lot going on, a TU disarmament conference, Trident replacing conventional nuclear weapons. When jobs are lost, workers come to listen for an alternative. BBC came last week about Gorbachev's talks which are now off. Sarah Hipperson not well, Rebecca badly hurt when the last convoy came out; they are coming out once a fortnight, they are behind with their tests. The army marched off today.

Tuesday 17 March 1987

Had a word with Beth about video as a historical record of details. The forecast said it was going to get cold & windy. Will convoy leave tomorrow? Now in the base they sound reveille & in the evening play 'The Stars & Stripes' on a cracked tape. They must all stand to attention. The civilians who go into the discos are thrown out if they get drunk; then they hang around us. On Sat. night a drunken man wanted to stay by the fire to get warm, then he pissed on Katrina's garden. Sunday: lots of mods and mopeds. "Rusty Old Faggot!" they roared at me when I went to my tent to get the video in case there was trouble. They went to the gate, had their photos taken, then left. Yesterday a Mrs Brooks came, a clairvoyant animal-healer. She said we would all be gone in 6 months, but the camp would remain. Water cannon would be used. In a couple of weeks I would fall ill & go to jail. She was looking for a homosexual who had murdered a child. She blamed murders on homosexuals. She was middle-aged, lower middle-class, well-dressed with her husband staying in the car. She had gone to a writers' workshop where (she said) they were recruiting lesbians to go to Greenham, did we know? She said she was married 40 years & it took her 38 years to stand up to her husband. Her sister was a lesbian. Her brothers had been killed in the war.

A fellow from Wales came by to ask questions about nationalism. Donna carried the argument with him. Louie back from Hamburg Women's Fair (which has its own pub). Got two new sweaters on Sat. Finola left for bus & left two blankets, one pink, one blue, so now I am warm at night. Sheila, from Canada: when she told her born-again sister that she was a lesbian, the sister threw her out. The sister says, "You will see Christ & be saved." Lindsay swears at the women, eats toast, drinks tea. The women are stopping the convoy. There is Sara, the obsessional photographer from New York who is coming to marry Rebecca. Personal & political all mixed up like an Irish stew. She photographed Donna when she was unconscious, knocked out, after the convoy came out.

There is food now in the pram. Yesterday there was none. We hovered round it, talking about food & also waiting for the bailiffs who didn't come till the afternoon. US planes flying into the base with their mail. Lin had a friend from prison come to visit her. A woman came with a black man offering to help. An old married couple, the wife a refugee. Women come, women go. Food-run: there was meat in the stew Sat. night. Last night vegan and vegetarian. Allison now vegetarian. Her father's parrot is dead. So many women going to gaol.

~~~o~~~

Wednesday 22 July 1987
In London; where J.A. and I came for script-conferences on *Whose is the Kingdom?* with Ronnie Mason at the BBC. Went by tube to Holborn to meet Sarah Hipperson. Station under repair: only one escalator, no stairs, thousands jammed in, waiting to get on escalator. Pouring with rain. Met Sarah, went to High Court in the Strand to hear the Newbury bylaw litigation. Lots of politics. John Buggs, Ian Lee (longtime peace activists), putting in their cases. *Mandatus* -- i.e. for the judges to decide whether the bylaw cases come to the High Court or are dealt with by magistrates. Beverley, the lawyer, bright-eyed like a wren, dark, nervous energy, good, explaining -- do the Greenham women (Georgina Smith & Jean Hutchinson) want an adjournment? because Ian Lee wants one and John Buggs is trying to attach himself to Ian Lee via the Greenham Women's case. Anyway, no-one wants John Buggs. It's like a railway station at holiday time, people willing to get into any train to take them somewhere -- they were intending to go Bournemouth but Southend will have to do.
~~~

Sarah tells me the camp is now split. She has just come home from Moscow and tells me the background. There is to be a meeting at Greenham on Sunday.

* * * * * *

July 1987: I now found myself caught up in the internal politics of Greenham, and was to be a bit-player in an unexpected internecine conflict. (As well as myself, the hapless J.A. was unwittingly dragged in.) Once the Intermediate Nuclear Forces agreement (INF) between Reagan & Gorbachev had been projected, leading to the eventual dismantlement & removal of the cruise, ideological war broke out between different factions of the peace movement over the future of the Greenham campaign. Already Sarah Hipperson was being looked at with suspicion, after she and Wilmette Brown had shamed CND into pulling out of the "International Year of Peace" because of the involvement of pro-nuclear groups. Katrina Howse, together with Wilmette, led a number of us to make a demonstration at the CND's AGM, where discussion of the Molesworth rape had been refused the previous year. Wilmette and Katrina were now personae-non-gratae with CND, Cruisewatch and Greenham Women Everywhere.

The ideological incompatibilities had come to a head in Moscow at the Women's Global Peace Conference. Greenham Women Everywhere and Cruisewatch were invited, but they did not pass on the invitation to the women at Yellow Gate. The latter wrote directly to Mrs Gorbachev, who sent them tickets. During the conference, Sarah Hipperson, Katrina Howse and Beth Junor, from Yellow Gate, challenged the implication that Greenham women were a Communist front and all their work had been in the interests of the Soviet bloc. They asserted instead that both superpowers (US & USSR) formed a nuclear-armed, racist club to dominate the non-aligned world and that *all* nuclear weapons had to go.

* * * * * *

Sunday 26 July 1987
All was so clear today at the Greenham meeting. The lynch mob, as Wilmette said. Is the CP behind it all? Stirring the shit, using women's jealousy of Wilmette,

using racism to destroy Kings Cross Women's entry into Greenham -- after all, on the outside, Kings Cross is the best organized group apart from the CP. For years the CP has been trying to claim Greenham, and now it's losing it. CP's methods very murky. They tried to hijack our workshops in Moscow. Before going to Moscow, Sarah & the others told the Camden women (Greenham Women Everywhere) they should not talk about Greenham now, because they don't *go* to Greenham. The determination of the CP to take control in Moscow. Sarah has come out of the (political) closet, very painful for those around her.

* * * * * *

July 1987 (cont.)**:** The Communist Party's *Morning Star* had published a glowing report on the conference without mentioning the non-aligned position of Yellow Gate. Sarah, Katrina and Beth were allowed no right-of-reply, so Yellow Gate responded with a picket on the editorial office. The management called in the police and had us removed. The following night, the Yellow Gate camp was raided by the MoD police with sniffer-dogs. Sarah's bi-carbonate of soda was taken away, and they seized papers from all the women's tents and bags. A notebook of mine, with portions of my diary and the outline of the opera, was taken. I suspect this unprecedented raid was in response to somebody's anonymous phone-call, doubtless accusing us of drugs and unspecified subversion. As I wrote later, in *Awkward Corners* (Methuen 1988): --

> The MoD police had obviously read the *Morning Star* piece; and were now confirmed in their opinion that Greenham women are KGB agents. A day or two later, when the cruise went out, for the first time ever four arrested women were handcuffed, on the ground, their faces pressed into the road, and then dragged face-down to the police vehicles. They were dragged face-down out of the vehicles and thrust into the cells at Newbury Police Staion. One of the women thus mistreated lost consciousness. The four were later released without being charged. I was thrown down ... in what I can only describe as a foul-tackle from the Rugby field. I sustained badly-bruised ribs and a lacerated arm which then went septic; one of my legs was also heavily bruised.

September 1987: a statement was issued from Blue, Woad, Orange and Green Gates at Greenham, and published in the *Morning Star*, asking for all donations to be made payable to Greenham Women Are Everywhere, instead of to the

Greenham Women's Peace Camp, and announcing that "a bitter dispute has erupted between a small group of women at Yellow Gate and the rest of the camp. These women are refusing all dialogue, forcing us to conclude that any further attempts at rational communication are futile. They are allied with Wages for Housework Campaign [emanating from the Kings Cross Women's Centre] whose standards and aims they have come to accept." Yellow Gate was also accused of "tactics of intimidation and verbal abuse." This statement led to a spew of insidious propaganda through mainstream and alternative media. *The Guardian, The New Statesman, Sanity, Time Out,* and *City Limits* all carried apparently objective, but thoroughly slanted, accounts of the Greenham controversy, and in 1992 *Peace News* capped it all by refusing to take a classified ad from Yellow Gate, because the women there were not considered non-violent. Sarah and Katrina were alleged to be puppet "leaders" of Yellow Gate under the ideological orders of Wilmette, as laid down by Wages for Housework.

(The Wages for Housework Campaign had come into collision with the regular women's movement as far back as the early '70s over the question of the unwaged work done by women as mothers and carers, very much the big taboo subject at the time. Wages for Housework wouldn't shut up. Their slogan was "Welfare not Warfare." Their incessant reiteration that the value of women's unwaged work was crucial to the economy was to be heard at every feminist meeting, and was of course anathema to the Labour Party and Communist Party. 30 years later, Rosie Boycott, a founder of *Spare Rib*, admitted that mistakes were made: "I cringe with shame," she wrote in the *Sunday Times*, [7 Dec '03]. "There was one issue we all ignored: children ... As I witness women agonise over motherhood, I wish we had done more. And I am not alone. Ursula Owen, who co-founded Virago press, says, 'We wanted women to have a choice but what we created was a notion that careers were everything. We didn't make motherhood the primary concern it needed to be.'")

* * * * * *

Thursday 26 November 1987

Have they started internment again in N. Ireland? 40 arrested. The Extradition Act will be passed in Dail Eireann but with modifications. Still the British Government complains at that "dilution". Stella came Wednesday with Granada

TV: her case against the MoD. Joan had been strip-searched to her knickers & bra but did not take a case

Got this manuscript back from the police yesterday: Writers' Guild worked hard to make them hand it over. Kings Cross women came down in force. Had up-front row about giving water. On Tuesday Helen Johns came for use of water pipe; this was refused. (She is setting up her own camp in opposition to Yellow Gate, across the road into the base. She asked me for water and I gave it to her. Debate: should we give water to HJ? I say, "Whoever asks for a drink of water, I will give it as a human right." "Would you give water to MoD police?" I say. "Yes, it is a basic right." They say, "What about black people's rights?" They rabbit on.

* * * * * *

1988: Aftermath of the INF Agreement and the complete separation of gates. Helen Johns and other women left Greenham to set up a similar peace camp outside the electronic listening station at Menwith in Yorkshire; later on, Angie Zelter (also a Greenham veteran) founded Trident Ploughshares as the British chapter of the U.S. Ploughshares movement which takes non-violent direct action against nuclear installations and weaponry. The original vision of Yellow Gate remained firm: --

1) to get rid of nuclear weapons,
2) to restore the common to the people.

I published my analysis of the post-Moscow faction-fight in "Power to the Sisters", an essay in the book by myself and J.A., *Awkward Corners*. The result was an attempt by a group of women to suppress the book; they initiated legal proceedings against me. To quote parts of the beginning of the essay in question: --

> "I want the names of those women who blockaded the *Morning Star*, I want Sarah Hipperson to expel herself from Greenham ... We have access to computer files: so we can investigate everyone at Greenham." When this phone-message [from Lynette Edwell] was relayed to us, my blood ran cold: *I* was one of the women who had *picketed* the *Morning Star*. Now it was being referred to as a blockade (there was also an accusation that it was a CIA-led operation!), and our backgrounds were being "investigated".

I had already warned the publishers, Methuen Ltd., that they really should check "Power to the Sisters" because of the sensitivity of its content. They sent the text to their lawyer who clearly did not think that an assertion of the non-alignment of Greenham women could actually be a serious matter. He wrote back and said, in effect, "Oh no, there is nothing libellous in it, it's just women squabbling amongst each other. It's all absolutely trivial." So the book was printed and sent off to reviewers. One review copy went to the *Morning Star.* Janie Hulme of that journal announced to Methuen that she was going to sue me for libel. I said to Methuen, "Your lawyer maintained there's no case for libel; we should ignore her." So they ignored her. And then, an hour before the book was due to appear in the bookshops, five other women (associated with the opposite faction at Greenham) suddenly shot up saying, "We're suing for libel, and we are going to the High Court; we have the money, we're getting an injunction." Methuen withdrew the book.

Their lawyer wanted "Power to the Sisters" to be removed from the book. J.A. refused to go along with this unprincipled sell-out. I came to the conclusion that the lawyer was no good for us; we demanded a second opinion, someone who might understand the political undertow. So Methuen found David Hooper; he had been involved in the defence of *Spycatcher*, the book of MI5 revelations which Thatcher had tried and failed to suppress. He suspected that our adversaries were politically careerist women who knew exactly what they were doing -- i.e. censorship by stealth -- and recommended we call their bluff, ignore their threatened injunction and fight them in the courts. Whereat they began to cry, "Oh we don't want to suppress the book, we believe so much in freedom of speech." In the end we went ahead and published, with a small disclaimer inserted in each volume, accepting that there was a genuine difference of opinion ...

The consequence of the media attacks on Yellow Gate and Kings Cross was a heavy dossier of press cuttings which were used at later dates to question the women's integrity and good faith. Kings Cross Women's Centre had grants cut by the Camden Council, and Katrina was named in *The Sun* as "Britain's biggest scrounger". When she took her (successful) libel case against the paper, and another one against *The Star*, she discovered the defendants' lawyers were using the dossier as evidence. It was similarly used in the attempt to suppress *Awkward Corners* and was one of the reasons for our first lawyer's decision not to contest the case but to withdraw the article. And no doubt it was also used when Sarah was temporarily banned by the courts from Greenham; and when the Treasury, in order to recoup its legal costs, threatened to deprive her of her house.

* * * * * *

Letter from Katrina Howse

[abridged]

Yellow Gate. [no date]

> Dear Margaretta,
> The libel case stands like this, on July 31st after I had spent 2 solid weeks with my documents & had sent them the list of documents, they send me a letter offering an apology (brief one). No costs ... I'm NOT going to negotiate for my costs at this stage. I might later. When I didn't hear from them I assumed that was it. So I'm carrying on. The next stage is witness statements. Could you do one for me? ... General ideas I had were, how hard you had worked as a writer, how long, how little back. The same with your political work & work at the Camp. With whatever statements you want to make. Would John Arden do a statement for me as well, about the Artist's Role in Society? Or whatever you both agree!

* * * * * *

1987 onward: After the split, Yellow Gate had become smaller and more cohesive; it was less disruptive for me (and other women) to occupy part of our time making videos and radio tapes. Beth and I would bring our recorders and tin whistles when we went out on actions; we would play Mozart and folk tunes whilst we waited for the military.

During most of the internal tensions I kept a diary. I can't remember the number of times I got arrested, a lot of the charges were dropped; 2 of them put me in gaol, while some got as far as the court but were then not implemented. At other times I was arrested but no charges. Re-reading the diaries, I see so clearly how the actions, court-cases, gaol, were as much part of one's life there as the ordinary events of life outside; they were simply the work. But the tensions inside our peace-camp home, the rows etc., those I recorded because it was not helpful to the health of the camp to express my thoughts overtly at that time.

* * * * * *

Diary Excerpts, Letters and Court-case Summaries 1988, '89, '91 & '92

1988. *Aftermath of IFN Agreement. Yellow Gate on its own and boycotted by the Greenham Women Everywhere Network: no more free food-runs from local well-wishers.*

Wednesday 1 June 1988
Sarah came, Laura & her son Logan (aged 10) came. Allison flushed from having been let out at Woad Gate, she & Spud had been splodging & Spud's loaded balloon had gone smack into the 20-year old MoD policeman all down half his body from his head down; he had to change his clothes; Spud offered to put his clothes into the laundry with hers. He declined. "You'd rather I went to Holloway for 2 weeks?" He turned his head away. Janet came back from Cornwall at about 8am. She was sleeping. Katrina & Beth went to look up records.

Reagan & Gorbi have signed. Katrina full of hate because Jenny Silver Moon & Jenny Donkey arrived to camp at Green Gate. "I hate them, they come to upset me." Beth & I try to console her, "Paint murals, put your hate into your murals & hang them on the trees."

At the weekend lots of visitors come to Woad, Blue & Green. I passed them at Green. One of them came down to the Sanctuary when Jean was there.

The Sanctuary. Yoko Ono donated money to enable the women to buy a piece of land on Greenham Common which was offered to them by a sympathetic resident. It was used as a place of refuge where the women could be safe from bailiffs and the MoD police. Katrina eventually became a trustee of the Sanctuary, which led to her gaining Commoners' Rights, which in turn led to the Newbury District Council returning the land to the people (after her constant legal challenges, and after the failure by the MoD to buy out the Rights of all the Commoners).

"You are very violent," this woman told Jean. Jean has gone to hospital; she has been bleeding; she is on a Cambridge diet & is losing weight. Mary Millington, who works in a self-health group, asks her anxiously, "Is this what you want? You are a strong woman; you don't need to lose it."

Pat, & Sam her child, strolled into Yellow Gate as if Pat owned it. "I was here in '83 for six months." She went over to Gladys (our old ambulance) to get bedding. "Is there a tent?" She sits by the fire. "Anyone got tobacco?" Laura gives her some. "My head is in a whirl." She doesn't want to know. She eats. Sam wastes food. She does no work. She goes off in a sulk the next morning. Laura gives her a lift to Blue Gate, where she had left the push chair.

Young women getting out of cars in summer white dresses: "Good Lord, are you still here?"

Sarah recognizes that her energy must not go on hating the women at the other gates. Beth soothes Katrina. Read *Sanity*; confident, pushing more & more goods for readers to buy. Nuke Watch meetings, busy busy.

Last night when Katrina & Beth came back we were sitting round the fire. Laura & Logan: Logan said a boy in class 14 called him a hippy, they were playing disco music, the boy turns round & says "Logan, do the hippy dance." "They call me hippy when I go to school: I have holes in my trousers." Laura said Hippy was scrawled on a door of her house because the occupants looked like hippies. The teacher in class 14 is a lesbian, she has been to Greenham. Logan became a hero when the theatre group for children came to the school, because Laura was involved. Logan is very pale & thin. He is learning the tin whistle.

A story.

> A long barrow was dug up. Inside it an old woman with her buried items. The old farmer put her skeleton inside his garage. One day a traveller came & he gave him one of the old woman's fingers. Some time later the farmer's finger got grangrene & fell off. He put the fallen finger into the place of the old woman's missing finger. Then he saw the old woman peering through the window, in fear he returned her skeleton to her burial ground.

Thursday 2 June 88
Cases. Georgina in court to help Ellie's fence case. Ellie got conditional discharge & is appealing. Barbara Cohen helped her. Big blow-up when one of the women came back from Newbury. Two others hadn't helped her over marketing; they left her standing there, with a shout of "I am not your servant." Tensions about money, donations, relationships between Sanctuary & Yellow Gate. Jenny Silver Moon & Jenny Donkey (from Green Gate) stalked through whilst we were having dinner. "Hello," they kept saying. We didn't reply. Katrina said, "We don't have to say hello." Later it turned out they were doing an action, going into the base, turfed out at Main Gate by MoD, & now they peered around for attention.

Sarah was a snazzy dresser when young: only six and a half stone, new look, sky-blue coat, navy-blue pumps, navy cloche & short black hair. Red mouth. Her sister was a beauty: *she* wasn't thought to be too forward and all mouth. Discussed opera with Katrina & Beth. Commissioned banner from Katrina. Can't believe it really; must make invoice out for her. Discussed future action: Imber village taken over by army in 1943; villagers forced to sell, but promised they could return. Army renegued on its promise & then Americans came. *Newbury Weekly* full of Russians coming into base; because of illegality of buildings, all building has stopped. There is nowhere for Russians to stay. Am going in for Allison's case who will be sent down tomorrow.

State of play: others all busy now. Cruisewatch will hand in symbolic letter to all bases on Sunday. Young woman came round to inform us.

Discussed Joan Winfield's meeting on Sunday at Newbury. She is an aborigine on tour of England to highlight situation of her people in Australia and is coming to Newbury tonight, invited by Lynette Edwell. I suggested letter of regret for Joan for not coming, as a compromise -- Sarah wants to go but Katrina fears there will be confrontations with other gates and Cruisewatch. Isobel & her three children came for workshop but one of them ill; such pale fragile children. Laura wants to move closer to camp. We drove to village to see memorial church where Stanley Spencer murals are. Strange coming into old village: do they know or care about base? Illusion of such certainty of continuity, such a gap, are they all blind? there were council houses, and a Dallas-style building reached by a lighted driveway. We drove up; no lights or life. Must be a club of some kind. Yellow Gate are constantly working; the others just jump in & out & so campaign-emphasis weakens & trivialises. No real politics. The lack of reality in England amongst controlling class. Do they know the damage they do to themselves & others? To ask awkward questions unravels the reality of laws. Bylaws themselves an unreality, a lack of responsibility for development.

Friday 3 June 88
Show trial in Newbury Court. 2 women accused of cutting fence. They weren't there when it was cut. Motives for prosecution: revenge & loss of face against 2 committed women. The collective action of the women has made explicit the illegality of the base, this is now exposed. The raison-d'être, to defend death, has been nullified. So they have to cook up evidence, the courts collaborate in this. Same as Birmingham 6. Ways of robbing land, brute force, ways of martial law. Ways of getting land back, exposing laws, not obeying laws, civil disobedience. Remove the definition of good behaviour to expose the brutality & corruption in maintaining order. Not to be frightened of the punishment.

Downpour. Had chat about Janet. As a Swede she can't live in England, but has to have her visa renewed each year. Beth found a convenient marriage for her which would last 4 years but she wanted permanence. Katrina thinks that when women leave the camp it is a personal betrayal. She still feels insecure & does not really regard the Sanctuary as her home. Beth wants a house; each woman leaving is like a bad marriage. Katrina finds it hard work keeping the Sanctuary & Yellow Gate open, so does Janet. Katrina talks about hard winter. Yellow Gate is the pivot; if it collapses the women's revolution has collapsed. Katrina is keeping it alive; she says, "After 2 years it is crisis-point." That is, living here permanently; yet other women who don't live permanently do come back to other gates. Greenham is unique. Still women are around the gates. The skinheads at Blue, the partying at Orange.

Saturday 4 June 1988
Had a blazing row with Katrina, there are thunderstorms, rain storms, tensions amongst ourselves -- she told me to clear off, etc. With Laura, Logan & Abigail, went to Stanley Spencer's memorial church, on the way called into the Dallas-style (Southfork) flashy establishment, it is a private house, young woman with 2 girls came out when Abigail had gone in asking the way, friendly, easy, very

other-gates, frank slim young body in jeans. Laura fuming, her false teeth foaming, saying she was going to squat. Abigail, who has bought property, saying, "disgusting," they both puffed and fumed at every house. When we got to the church, we knocked on one of the alms-houses who had the key. The woman said it was one o'clock; Laura then demanded we be let in. Quite wonderful inside. Stanley Spencer's job as an orderly. Simple tasks. The woman came in; I chatted with her. It was Stanley Spencer's sister who built the church for her nephew who had been killed in the war & they got Spencer's pictures & put them there. The woman shares the duties with the other house; she is a cleaner; they work for nothing. We go into the village church. All army people: served in Afghanistan, Boer war, India. Adbury Park was the squire's place. Must ask more questions. Laura wanted to squat in it; Abigail wanted to ring the bells; I wanted to wring their necks. Laura drives with no hands. In afternoon, made potato cakes, we all rolled them & cooked & eat them in the tepee, rain, hot sun, then rain. By evening, glorious light: I saw a deer, rabbits, pheasants, moorhens. MoD going by in their vehicles; when they saw me, stopped until I left. 2 punks from Blue Gate embracing. When they saw me, they separated. Both had dogs. Katrina and Beth moving back on Sunday. Tidied place, went into tepee, admired Katrina's banners. She came in; we made it up. She will do me the banner. Felt happy. Katrina and Beth going to Scotland for the holiday; want to hire a car; don't want to walk or cycle.

Sunday 5 June 1988

The question of Joan & the meeting. Cruisewatch did come today with their symbolic letter. Banging on gates, they came into Sanctuary to make connection & keep in touch, as they put it. Later a friend of Yellow Gate, Rosemary Laze, single, with another woman & her two children, donated money. Changeover: Sarah & Janet here, Katrina & Beth gone. Sarah upset by letter from Barbara Cohen the solicitor. In the letter she says she could do no work until Legal Aid's money comes through; she is a professional; she has a partner who can deal with the case when she is not there, & a secretary. Decoding time: who is putting pressure on her? So Sarah worries & worries. Went though my case with Sarah.

Monday 6 June 1988

D-day. Laura, Katrina, Beth & me to Devizes for court case. Lovely day. Saw Silbury Hill & the grass. The hill itself is called the Womb of the Mother, great farming plains full of wealth, lovely old village houses. How many women from these houses were executed for witchcraft? Arrived Devizes. Portakabin crammed full of young people. Had to hang around. Used tape: discussion of nuclear weapons, all on tape. Men angry with us. 12.15 pm, case. I wouldn't stand up -- they had to accept that. Asked their names and interests: 3 women 2 men. Lunch. Back at 2, finished 3, fined £45 & £75 costs.

When we came back to camp, Katrina's appeal was there for 20 June. Decided not to appeal. Went back on fags. Laura wants to move nearer the camp or on camp. Women didn't think it right for Logan, they could put him into care -- past experience, Teresa from Kent, her child was taken by father, Sarah worked to get him back. Discussion of importance of Imber village: used by the SAS in training for West Belfast, Genocide Act, notice of responsibility for everyone against Nuclear weapons, Hiroshima, World War 1. Bylaws are wrong. Must prepare speech for Imber. Janet's exams tomorrow. Katrina & Beth happy. Had to go to expensive vegetarian restaurant, I bought cheese, marzipan, ice-cream. Thoughts: 6 women alone fighting the state, a unique cell of power, is that possible? Rang J.A.; bank holiday in Ireland

Tuesday 7 June 1988
Glorious day. Sarah cleared tepee, taking its apron off. I washed all my clothes. Janet went to Newbury for exam. Sarah not well; looks old; terrible red eruptions on her joints with rheumatism and arthritis; old wounds.

Joan Hayman. Seven children. Married to Italian catholic at 19. Husband extremely jealous. Kicked him out. Became parish councillor. Has taken part in lots of actions, imprisoned. Herself illegitimate, her mother thrown out. Joined ILP. Joan & I went to pub for beer; refused to serve us; MoD & CID there.

Janet shyly brought her wicker basket with the lid on & opened it. She showed me the wool she had dyed from the Common's nettles, bracken, ferns, yellow, light green, other greens. She is knitting a sweater. She soaked & then boiled them. All from the Common. Women gathering herbs from the Common, dying the wool, making their charms, were caught & executed, witches. Trees around me: hazel, cherry, oak, beech, hawthorn, rowan. There is a lot of rain to make the lusciousness. Allison in Holloway. Consequence of my fine: I can be picked up at any time; my freedom has gone; my freedom in England belongs to the crown. I am a hostage.

Spud has just come down to say press is going inside Greenham to observe. Sarah gone up.

Janet spoke about when she was an au-pair with upper-class family outside Newbury; 2 children; the mother had been in Ethopia; a psychologist. "Children should not be blocked, Janet." And a cleaner to clean up after them.

Had meeting with camp; tensions still unresolved. Janet wouldn't come. Spud gone to collect Allison from Holloway.

Thursday 9 June 1988
Last night it poured. I went to my tent early; later I got up for a piss; Janet was by the fire. I sat with her & tried to speak to her about the anger. It filled her, she said, in her very guts & rose up in her like a yellow rod with red flames on top. She said anger was good; she had to try to work out why she was so angry. Women got into the base & unfurled the banner; Spud & Mia got arrested; Sarah bellowed outside. Strange dreams again.

Friday 10 June 1988
Allison back from Holloway, quiet & pale, it was ok, the screws were ok, they were given lots of association. Janet's anger is still there.

Politics. Janet wants lesbian-only camp with Katrina in charge & herself as second-in-command. I would think with this new development about trustees that Katrina has enough on her plate. Also the appeal on the 20th. Janet is also in court; may go down.

All these women constantly up in court going to jail & so the tensions in camp are increased and we turn on each other.

Allison gone home; mouth all swelled up.

Sarah was single, handy, doing the emotional maintenance work at camp without the women doing it for themselves. I step in; counsel Sarah to withdraw as maintenance person, to ease tensions.

Katrina is the only one of Yellow Gate to be a trustee of the Sanctuary.

Tuesday 14 June 1988
All is resolved. Went to Imber village, got into church; Sarah, Beth, Katrina and I.

* * * * * *

Imber Village Church

from *Greenham Common Women's Peace Camp Newsletter* Sept 1988 (anon).

"Imber" is now a ghost village, which lies between Warminster and Tilshead on Salisbury Plain. On 17 December 1943 the people of Imber were evacuated from their homes, so that the United States Forces could use the area as an artillery range.

Although it is recorded in the Domesday Survey of 1086 under the name of Immerie, there had been many earlier settlements in the neighbourhood. It was an isolated community, on account of its situation -- it's in a sheltered position at the junction of 3 valleys. It was completely self-sufficent : there was a blacksmith, carrier, carpenter, undertaker, miller, cobbler, grocer, baker, the church, and an inn -- everything that a village needs to survive. Many of the cottages were thatched -- it must have been a beautiful village

When the villagers left, they were told that they would be able to return when the war was over. But this promise has not been kept. The military are still in possession in Imber village, it is now being used by the British Army. British Army Troops are being trained in house-to-house fighting there -- practice buildings of concrete blocks have been made up to look like West Belfast streets; signs saying "McBride's Upholstery" or "Fruit and Veg" have been put up on some, to make this barren construction look like a Northern Irish community.

The Cruise missile convoy from Greenham Common USAF Base also goes to Imber village to practise genocide. We think that the convoy goes to Imber village when it has live missiles/war heads on it, since it is very difficult for us to get to it, and stop its excercises, at this location. (Although we have managed to do this.)

But Imber church, nevertheless, is opened once a year, for a service which the evacuees can attend. Some of the evacuees have relations buried in the churchyard, and this is the only time in the year in which these people can visit the graves. (The graveyard is now overgrown, and untended.) Therefore the church has a wire fence round it, topped by strands of barbed wire, as well as signs to the British Army saying " Out of Bounds".

* * * * * *

Letter to Sinn Féin Newspaper

[abridged]

to An Phoblacht/Republican News, Belfast.

Galway, 5 Feb 92.

... I have personal experience of [the subconscious attitudes of certain members] of the Crown Forces rank-and-file. A few years ago I was at Yellow Gate Women's Peace Camp, Greenham Common; some of us made a non-violent protest in the nearby village of Imber, compulsorily depopulated by the British Army and now transmogrified into a mock-Irish village where troops are trained for Six Counties duties. We occupied Imber church to commemorate Mairéad Farrell's recent assassination by the SAS in Gibraltar. We had interrupted an exercise by the Royal Green Jackets; a detail from the regiment secured our arrest; and when I asked an NCO in charge why he and his men were going to Ireland, he unequivocally replied, "To kill Gerry Adams." I told him that I hoped he would stand over his statement in court.

He should have appeared as a prosecution witness; but amazingly, when the case did come to court, he was the one soldier of those involved who was absent from the proceedings, and all the others denied all knowledge of him.

Yours etc., Margaretta D'Arcy

* * * * * *

Thursday 16 June 1988
In Sanctuary. Yesterday Sarah went off for her holidays. Jean, Janet & myself. Heat wave. Joan came down to visit in the afternoon. Her eldest son has been made bankrupt because of the big bang in the city; he lost about £250,000; he had invested in shares to give money to Scientologists. He was a computer analyst & earned £1500 a week; his wife ditto. There was a lot of publicity in the papers about it. He bought 2 autographed books by L. Ron Hubbard for £37 each; his finances are now in the receiver's hands; his house will have to be sold; his children taken away from a scientology private school. Money meeting. Joan & Jean. New system: every woman is supposed to put in a fiver. Joan didn't have it. Beth rigid, so Joan left. Beth rigid because she feels Joan doesn't take responsibility for camp. Jane, an American with flowers in her hair, back from Central America, intruded into us from Blue Gate. She used to be at Yellow Gate, sat down, said it was a social call & not interested in

rift. Then the commercial proposition: she had come back with slides from Gautemala to show round the countryside; any money will pay her expenses; & she wanted to have a show with us. So she had to barter, saying, "OK I do want to know what I can do." Janet said she was very bright, real travelling rep in Venture Capitalism.

Katrina went to solicitor about Evelyn. Sarah was upset on returning from Imber village. She'd hurt her head on Landrover while being pushed into it after her arrest; but Beth insisted she telephone press, saying she was tired too as she hadn't rested on Monday. There is no allowance made for women over 60 at all. There is inconsistency over most policies. Each woman when she comes should be told that she has to pay something towards her keep. Joan on the other hand used to get dole from camp; has never wondered how the camp is in her absence.

Georgina sits alone outside Emerald Gate & camps in rectory at Blue Gate. Very strange, the complexities each woman is prepared to embrace to assert her identity & independence. Not coming down on revolutionary side.

Without Katrina, would Yellow Gate Greenham collapse? Her input with such ferocity gives her energy.

Joan, by not taking responsibility, does not know of the daily outrages committed by the other gates. The recent one, the effort to remove Katrina as trustee, is highly illegal.

Jean is back, her womb cleansed, disappointed by not going to Imber. Wanted to stay in Sanctuary yesterday. It rained all day. Sarah went to Newbury to do shopping. Sian & Ruth came down with wood. The removal of the Kings Cross Women's grants means that they have to work harder -- 3 days for a jumble sale & £15 gathered.

The Measuring/Valuing of women's unwaged work to be included in the GNP, is in a bill going to the House of Commons.

The maintenance of the Kings X centre, Camden still refers women to it despite cuts of grants.

* * * * * *

Court Case Summary

from *Greenham Common Women's Peace Camp Newsletter* Sept 1988 (anon).

1) **19, 20, 21, 25 & 26 July 1988**

DPP v Hutchinson & Smith.

Greenham Common Bylaws Case.

In the five-day hearing, the lawyers of Georgina Smith (Beverley Lang & Barbara Cohen) and Jean Hutchinson, who represented herself, worked to refute the submissions made in appeal from the Ministry of Defence.

Present Status.

Awaiting the judgement in the High Court, due in October.

2) **5, 6 & 7 October 1987**

The Fence Case.

On the 18th June 1987, straight from the Bylaws Case in the Crown Court, we cut down 16 sections of fence. In the Magistrates' Court in Newbury, there was tough and legally doubtful treatment from Stipendary Magistrate Voelker. This included the banning of Sarah Hipperson and Georgina Smith -- so we appealed.

Present Status.

Awaiting Appeal in the Crown Court.

3) **Begun 1 March 1988**

The Restoration Case.

According to Law of Property Act 1926. By 1st March shortly after the Bylaws judgement in the Crown Court (25 Feb 1988) a decision was taken at Yellow Gate to apply for the base to be restored because we were certain the buildings and all structures are illegal. Later, Mr Roger Freeman agreed with us -- House of Commons (29 April 1988).

Present Status.

Awaiting a hearing in the County Court.

4) **First appearance: 2 August 1988. Second appearance: 5 August 1988**

Action to Preserve Commoners' Rights.

Papers served on Sec. of State and Property Services Agency (4 August 1988).

Present Status.

Two appearances before County Court judge. Awaiting Pre-trial Review, to be held in private, 29 Sep 1988.

5) **Imber Village Church Occupation.**

In the early hours of 14 June, four women from Yellow Gate occupied this deserted and desecrated church. The promise from the 1940s to return the village has never been honoured. On two counts the land is abused: for the cruise-missile Convoy, and for military training for Ireland.

Present Status.

Awaiting trial date in Magistrates' Court, Devizes.

6) **23 August 1988**

Challenge to Upper Heyford Bylaws.

Another case to join the pattern of cases. The action had involved walking on the runway, part of which, it turns out, is a right-of-way. The challenge to the Bylaws is being done by way of the existent right-of-way.

Present Status.

Adjourned in Banbury Magistrates' Court after an initial hearing, to await the Bylaws Case judgement from the High Court, due in October.

* * * * * *

1989: Various Letters.

[abridged]

Yellow Gate. 23 March 1989.

Dear Margaretta

Thank you for your letter, with information about "Time To Go"*. We've just been talking about your suggestions for "Time To Go" -- YES, we could do a good leaflet, & we've just realised that the history on the leaflet can go back to May 1985, when 200 women walked across Larkhill Artillery Range, and stopped the British Army's firing. Then, all the events and work which you've outlined. Sarah says it would be good to have an EXHIBITION -- we have good enlargements now, of our Imber Church Occupations, & she also suggests blowing up the *Irish Post* article to a big size, plus Katrina's banners? Katrina has the "Stop Strip Searches" banner, plus the "Imber Church Occupation" banner. So, we will apply for an exhibition space, and hope that, as your son says, it's not ALL stitched up already ...

Katrina and I had a very productive visit to Germany -- it was refreshing to do Workshops with women who hadn't heard all the smear-campaign stories about us. They were very receptive. Some showed an interest in the mock German village, which is being built on Salisbury Pl. not far from Imber. We met a woman who had been supporting the hunger-strikers, in the German prisons -- it was worth it all, just to make a good connection with her. One more good woman.

Then we went to Basel, Switz., for a few days -- where we discovered a Programme for a "Peace & Justice Week" which included a "Report from Greenham Common"! -- Which we discovered to be H-----, *lying!* Two Swiss women attended, with *Yellow Gate Newsletter* & Car Appeals, etc., so it was a funny quirk of fate, that we were there at that time, to find that network out!

Convoy came back in last night -- Katrina & Abigail met it inside one of the Hangars. Sarah, Helen (newly arrived from Wales), & I, resisted it at the Gate.

Lots of love, Beth.

* *"Time To Go! Show" was a conference to demand British withdrawal from Ireland.*

* * * * * *

[abridged]
Yellow Gate. 19 June 1989.

Dear Margaretta,

... a quick note to tell you the ["Time To Go"] conference went well. Although the entrance fee made sure *no* grassroot people could go. There were very good Irish people there, though; but they were very busy holding workshops and speaking. Gerry Adams, Nell McCafferty and Fr. Des Wilson spoke, amongst others. I spoke to Paul Gibbon (*Irish Post* journalist who got our Imber actions into print) and he promised further support. Lord Gifford was there, and he came up to have a short polite conversation.

All in all I found the conference a big intellectual exercise, I must say. I think it is all set up as a "pressure group" (in the sense CND call themselves a pr. gr.) and I think they are anti-action, be it violent or non-violent. Anyways, there was some interest shown for our work, and BBC Northern Ireland were there to film. I think they might send some film of Katrina's banners. The report will be sent out Thursday night (22nd), on BBC Northern Ireland, so if you can get it in Galway, keep a look out.

Yours, Janet.

* * * * * *

[abridged]
Yellow Gate. 30 June 1989.

Dear Margaretta,

... The Billy Graham "Livelink" has been held INSIDE the Base, this week -- which has created a lot of work for us, & which has, in turn, revealed just how fascist this society is. We've been arrested in a *public place* for -- holding a banner -- speaking through a megaphone -- holding sandwich boards -- chaining ourselves to railings and speaking -- remaining silent!! We are telling the "public" they are inside a nuclear concentration camp. Thanks for the *Irish Post* articles about Time to Go!, and the *Guardian* article re the police sadism -- frightening!

Looking forward to your visit & to speaking with you -- love, Beth.

* * * * * *

Yellow Gate. Monday 3 July 1989.

Dear Margaretta,

Thank you for your letters to us at Yellow Gate. They have been reassuring at this time of renewed struggle -- Janet got 28 days in prison, Jean 21, & Catherine 14. They all do half of that. Jean is out today, Janet on Friday. With Allison leaving as well as Catherine, it has put a much bigger burden on all of us at the Camp, particularly with Janet & Jean being in prison. This is a leaflet for August which we are sending out in the last month.

We are looking forward to seeing you for August. We hope to have a camp cat very soon. My trial with Spud when we had guns aimed at us is on July 21st. The struggle continues. Think of us then.

Love, Katrina.

* * * * * *

1989: *this year, before I arrived at the camp, there was a rift between Yellow Gate and Kings Cross. I inadvertently put my foot into it in a letter I wrote to the camp after a long conversation with Catherine (who had left the camp and later joined Kings Cross). Sarah wrote a reply to me, I rang her up, she put the phone down on me. But it had already been agreed that I should come to Greenham where it would be sorted out at a camp meeting. I arrived to find Sarah had gone to Japan, invited by a women's group to commemorate Hiroshima.*

Friday 4 Aug 1989

Rang Selma, she knew Sarah was in Japan because CND had rung her to get in touch with Sarah. Selma rang Isobel who's had her baby, the little girl was born with a club foot. Bee arrived. Had a long talk with her about evening meeting with Mary Millington, Spud, Katrina, about Hiroshima plans for Saturday. Helen came round with petition for Welsh language movement. Had talk about Tim and Lin in Cardiff (both keen language supporters). Janet asked me to work with her tomorrow on Irish Statement for "Time to Go!". Portsmouth women have arrived, Frances and Rosie. Rosie writes poetry. Frances is a vegetarian, going to study English literature, she writes poetry, her mother writes poetry, her grandmother writes poetry. Lisa arrived from Canada. Very hot.

Story.

Frances gives out leaflets in Portsmouth; police take her to station; her father works in the naval museum; a senior comes to him & says, "Your daughter is an activist on our list, she is not allowed in any military base; you could lose your job." Pressure is put on Frances to stop working.

While I was waiting for Sarah to return, an unexpected tragedy struck the camp.

Saturday 5 Aug 1989.
Went wooding with Bee, opened up again about problems with rigidity of camp. Bee told her life story, wealthy southern US family, mother alcoholic. Bee brought up to get married. She came to England, wants to write.

Went to Sanctuary to work on Irish Statement. Helen there. Spud came to tell Helen a friend has arrived at the gate, Janet & I continue, made salad for myself.

Jean, Laurie, Rosie came in: Jean says, "There has been a terrible accident! Helen is dead, knocked down."

We all go to the camp. The body is in the morgue at Newbury. Katrina wants us all to stay at camp. The white police horsebox that hit her (en route to charity festival) is down the road, the horses have been taken out, & are grazing on roadside. Police are there, I feel we should examine horsebox & talk to the driver. I feel we should go to the hospital & stay there beside Helen's body. We stand in circle, holding hands; then it is decided to do vigil at hospital, 7.30. Jean, Janet & I go to the hospital, they say police are in charge at the morgue and parents are coming tomorrow. We are sure they are coming today. Hospital says it is closing. I walk round to find morgue. Jean & I walk round. Police car is there. Lights on in morgue. We sit on a bench outside hospital door. Police car arrives: parents have arrived; they will see us; and we can see the body. Mother weeps when I hold her. We go to morgue; Helen is lying there, white towel on brow, no top of head, her tongue is twisted in her mouth, her eyes half-closed, her ears big, sticking out; I feel her body, it is a board. I am too frightened to touch her face. Spud and the other women have arrived; we go back to camp. I stay up till 5.30.

Sunday 6 Aug 1989
The gate is cleared. We are in mourning. No-one has yet come to sign book.

Helen aborted on the road.
That leaves Spud.
Phew ! another cry yelling from the road, couldn't catch it but the sound hit the spot
where Helen
        died.
In the morgue her face like a classical gargoyle.
The mouth opened & the tongue twisted inside,
sticking out. In death the defiance of the naughty child.
Buried with her tongue sticking out
her eyes half-closed
blue iris beneath the lid.
Hi girls! fucking lesbians.
Would Helen have stuck her tongue out at them & half-closed her eyes in contempt
so that the
        Welsh cobalt blue of her eyes
tantalizing peeped out?
Or was the face in shock? Oh why the tongue sticking out?

Bee & I go to Sanctuary for afternoon. Katrina says Isobel has arrived with Chris and children. I go to Gate. Di McDonald etc., have sent cards. I sit on vigil till 5.30 a.m. Katrina comes for a chat about protecting camp women & Yellow Gate from disintegration & takeovers now that we expect all sorts of women to come in and sign the book -- worried about Kings Cross & Catherine. We discuss boundaries. James arrives.

Monday 7 Aug 1989.
I sit most of the day. Jo and friends arrive. Jo weeps. People are arriving. It is now a proper wake. Catherine comes from London and signs book. There is an inquest; women go. Press Statement from the police that she stepped in front of horsebox and was dancing in middle of road. Bee tells press she was not in middle of road, not dancing: Bee was there, a witness. I go to Sanctuary with Bee for vigil.

Tuesday 8 Aug 1989
Abigail goes to Newbury to meet the undertakers: Helen goes to Wales. Beth

and Spud get arrested. Convoy is coming out. A python has escaped. I film convoy. Teresa arrived. Jean's friend Mary has to go home because her husband's mother has died.

Convoy. This was an entire military manoeuvre carrying the cruise missiles out of the base to practise launching them on Salisbury Plain. It took hours, we were out there all night resisting and held back by police, MoD and Thames Valley. A very tense affair with appalling destructive noise, huge vehicles, motorcycle outriders, a blaze of light. **This was why we were at Greenham** ... *This time, they were nastier than usual, they knew it was their last time because of the INF Agreement, they knew it was our work that had won.*

Wednesday 9 Aug 1989
Sarah is still in Japan. Stays there. We get a fax today, camp sends fax. Pressure on women to stay at camp. Katrina terrified when Helen died; her thoughts, "What about me? more work!" Mary bargaining her position, she is coming in December. Mary is upset. She must go to funeral; saw a dead rabbit on road; saw a baby being fed in a car.

Horse-box driver comes to us & says, "I know that you don't have much time for us; I'm sorry."
"Did you drive?"
"It doesn't matter who drove, but I did."
TV comes. Janet says, "I'll break your equipment."

~~~o~~~

Friday 11 Aug 1989.
Go to main gate. Silent vigil. Friends of Helen come. Was at vigil most of day, went wooding with Teresa who gave me a lift to London. She is an incest-survivor, makes pottery dragons to understand herself, wants to write, she stays in London with me. Rang Bee.

Saturday 12 Aug 1989
Went to London for Irish demo, "Time to Go!" Pat Arrowsmith upset because she is told we believe Helen was deliberately run down by police. She insists there is no proof. Spud got message across about women having been arrested.
~~~

Sunday 13 Aug 1989
Caught bus back to Greenham. Thunder & lightning at Greenham. Taped Lisa and Ute's account of arrests, they were threatened with PTA.

Monday 14 Aug 1989
Katrina & Beth off to meet Sarah at airport. Wet. Spanish couple came from Peace Movement. Three Germans arrived, Sunday & Monday. Linda Jones from Oxford, who has money to write book on peace women in the UK & Gautemala, wants to interview Mary, Katrina and Sarah.

Everyone quiet, must be tired, fatigue is biggest obstacle.

Ute, very German, is frightened of West German police & her studies, says Beth. British police are not like in S. Africa; she wasn't frightened and was in control, so therefore it wasn't political torture. Lisa was frightened and was tortured, psychologically. Ute feels superior to Lisa (who is a village woman), couldn't remember her name, referred to her as "the other woman".

Sarah back from Japan. Jean & I alone at Main Gate; no driver, then Spud came. Had talk with Spud about when she did sociology at school, commented on physical likeness, culture & age of women in camp. Bee returned; we went wooding. Bee confused, doesn't like rows.

Tuesday 15 Aug 1989
Walked to roundabout with Bee, who rang Guy and dictated letter to *Observer* contesting the police evidence at the inquest. Got letter from J.A. & flowers (squashed). Eviction: did Slow Movement, took half an hour. Convoy came back. Three more Portsmouth girls came. Camp fuller than it has been for some time.

Eviction. The bailiffs would come and they'd put out the fire & take the wood, and we'd have to move everything or it would be put into the "cruncher" and destroyed. During the mourning for Helen, their arrival was an act of malice. Our Slow Movement routine, carrying our possessions with grave deliberation, was a piece of passive resistance.

Sarah said that at a conference in Japan a Russian woman came up & said they had underestimated Greenham's NVDA position; in particular it's not being just an anti-American camp. Russian said they would have to look into NVDA. Sarah just had her fare paid, no hotel bills or food, the women had to pay for her.

~~~o~~~

Thursday 17 Aug 1989
Bee caught bus back to London at 7 a.m. Yesterday Helen's parents came, Janet and John. I spoke to them about Helen. Janet Thomas spoke about Welsh language & the Welsh not wanting it in schools. John Thomas spoke about a cheese factory that the Milk Board closed down & yet Britain is 60% under quota for milk. Janet Thomas said, with Welsh activists who refuse to pay the fines, they just hold them for the rest of the court sittings, in one case 26 seconds, clever.

The women went on action to Imber in evening. Thunderstorm. Isobel came with baby. Passing taxi driver abusive again. Beth went to gate to complain. Janet went in evening again. MoD fellow said "I'm here for the next 3 nights between 7pm & 7am," i.e. saying, "I will look the other way when they abuse you"; he is corrupt. So they do allow private vengeance to take place. How many others do that? Like the time Hazel & Jane were beaten with batons. Like the sectarian assassinations in the north, like Miriam Daly, Bernadette McAliskey.

The Portsmouth women are leaving today. Karin left yesterday. Henrietta stayed to do action. I have nothing to say to the women, I must listen to their angry emotions.

Janet Tavner goes off in car, returns, puts banner up at gate, "Yellow Gate women have occupied Imber church!". The cars & the MoD see it.

Where does all the mourning go? It goes into anger and scapegoating. What can I do to get out from under it? What I *do* do, is turn to my diary and scribble. I withdraw inside myself and detach myself from the camp.

Because the meeting had been postponed, there had been no discussion of the feelings of the camp about my letter. They had seen it as a deliberate interference, even a bit
~~~

of sabotage; it looked as though I was supporting Catherine leaving Greenham, and passing judgement upon the camp without hearing their side of the story. So all the time I was there, throughout the mourning for Helen and the arrangements for her funeral, I was constantly being watched; my slightest comment or action was taken as proof of my betrayal. For instance, the day after Sarah returned, I mentioned to her that I had met a local woman on the road who had shown mild support to the other gates against Yellow Gate. She was therefore on an "enemies' list" and was not to be talked to, even though she had stopped me and offered sympathy about Helen's death. Later, Sarah came out & asked me to go to the fire to talk; she accused me of "controlling" the camp. I said I would talk in the evening. I felt that this was leading up to a scapegoat situation, so I stayed at the Main Gate in silence all day. And then there had been a crisis with another Yellow Gate member; she and I had been having what I thought was a casual chat about thought control. The next day herself and a friend came to the fire, full of anger, accusing me: "You have stuck a knife in my back," and, "We are throwing it back." I lost my temper and shouted at them. Bad news. Everyone fell silent. As a protection, as an exorcism, I put my soured and vicious sarcasms into my diary: --

While she's away, Sarah has given charge of camp to Janet. Janet went off in Gladys, handing charge of camp over to her good old arthritic myrmidon …. Graham turns up (friend of Helen). Rosie saws pallets. I collect wood. I go to fire, ask Graham to go to roundabout for me to get cigs; he says he must speak to arthritic myrmidon. Myrmidon, delighting in her bureaucratic swollen-froggery, says he must wait for Janet. I walk to roundabout: abuse from lorry-drivers, noise, wind from lorry nearly knocks me under like Helen. Rain on way back. Graham still in chair. I am drenched with cold.

Conversation with Graham.
Horticulturalist. Job in play scheme in Cardiff, in peace movement. Tall blond wimp & bearded. Henrietta has extended family, new terminology meaning her parents who have adopted 5 disabled children, she has a sister & one child. They live in a farmhouse. Henrietta speaks of great sacrifice her son made by allowing her to come to Greenham, was fond of Helen. Graham said you don't have to know a person long to know them.

So there were 3 motor vehicles at camp; but I had to walk for 2 hours in pouring rain for cigs. Tuesday, I had to walk 5 miles for milk, again there were 3 motor vehicles. I said to Sarah, "Why doesn't the van pick up water?", she snapped back that that would mean a driver and more work; & yet it was the traffic on the road that killed Helen. No connection in her mind that cars kill.

They came back from occupation of Imber church, no charges, they enjoyed themselves; the church was warm & Sarah felt spiritual, saw the Russian planes in sky, coming into the base to land, blue sky, white planes: INF Agreement.

Direct actions are fun, everyone protective; because they are dealing with men.
The wily women, the ancient sex struggle.
Back at camp the objectives are not so clear.
They don't need me, so what I think is irrelevant.
They want good fodder.
Good servants don't have opinions which they voice.
We are now in the dictatorship era at Greenham.
First the democratic city-states, then dictatorship,
with an ever-increasing awareness of enemies waiting to come & take over.
The terror is maintained by the constant allusion to past pain which can come again.

I have Bee's mattress: soft like Bee. My limbs are weak, I have no energy. I hear the roaring of the traffic & somebody's hyena laugh. Somebody else has pretty laugh with Edinburgh refined mock-shocked tone. Did I write about the inner sanctum of another somebody as she bent over, the back of her dress too short & her two buttocks & cleft like two vast moons? Sarah in purple pink and elegant with her white hair tied back.

Greenham is on its feet again, new alignments. An unscrupulous woman making up to another woman who has a year off, so the first woman can go on holidays with a third woman, not caring to travel alone; so she charms no. 2 and no. 2 obediently follows her wherever she goes like a demented orphan servant. Louie called with a friend and Sarah roared off like a white mare: "That one tried to make aggro with me at Glastonbury over Evelyn Parker."

The people's army a threat
& the gentlemen of the landed aristocracy
led by Granny Grogan's granddaughter,
she of the famous notorious battles over Hare House,

screams & laughs with a nod of her white hair.
Trim figure in the new look blue
princess-style coat, her hair cropped black like Audrey Hepburn's,
steps out to challenge matrons, bring nurses out on strike.
"We're all out & will be fed
in the evening, if we're late back.
Nurses need a full belly to care for the sick:"
so, years ago, spoke Granny Grogan's granddaughter.
Now when she is in court
the slant of her head, the slight shaking of that slanted head
the tapping foot
the mouth pursed
nervous laughter comes out in a broad grin & a word rises from the gullet.
Street talk, back chat talk, savage talk to still the uneasy poking of the conscience.

There is no doubt Sarah is in control, she is in her Granny Grogan element. "I am a criminal!" She laughs & the young women laugh, she breaks the trespass laws.

In the end we did not go to do an action in honour of Helen at the FIBUA (Fighting In Built-Up Areas) village -- the naming of the victims. Too exhausted and traumatised.

Henrietta joined the South African picket because it had been denounced by the main Anti-Apartheid movement -- this was the 24hr picket outside South Africa House. "I would join those who break the law." She has dimples & uneven teeth. So many martyrs & masochists searching for action. Graham was not in a union. As individuals they like to be in small groups. The Russians are in the base. Katrina comes running in to tell Beth, they coo together, lovely, sweet. Katrina stretched out in her tent reading about Imber village. The first time for 4000 years that no-one has lived there. It was Katrina who found out about Imber. We do not talk to each other.

Last night, asked Sarah when we were having our meeting. She looked startled, I thought; said she had not forgotten but couldn't do it now. Tomorrow morning, she said. Asked Katrina. Tomorrow afternoon, she said, 2pm after court.

In court today
Spud & her support
Women, women, white-haired Sarah the wife of Abraham & divorced wife of Alan, mother of Mark, Matthew, Alistair, Jane, Martin, criminalized countless times, outcast, obscured;
now the abuser of Allison, the daughter who defied the mother on her own grounds.
"You are ungodly women."
The daughter's words flew straight into the mother's eyes.
"You are working for the military."
She responded inside, her heart
contracted & tightened, her breathing became woddled & the words making no sense came.

The religious-minded Allison has gone home to be confirmed, she told Yellow Gate they were ungodly. Sarah ungodly, being a Catholic. Allison left the camp.

Allison alone will stand.
Will it be guilty, as she wants to end it now?
One more visit to Holloway
her rights nullified & suspended like me.
Alone she will go, the last time
her chin, her steady voice as she will tell the state what's what: like the mother soul.
(Spud: no chance for her to ground herself, suffocated under & between her mother's thighs
Peeps out.
half-defiant but well incubated in her mother's heart.)

The warring factions: another cult
to take Allison back to Patriarchy
identified, genetically computerised for the Lord in confirmation.

Every day must be filled with crisis now, every day must have confrontation with the state to purge the guilt of wiping women out.

By the by, an observation.
Walking past the memorial table to put my cup (*Krasic Jizbo* cup, from Moscow) down, which had been filled with coffee. Beth had said there is

coffee in the pot. Thank you I said & picked the cup, narrow white two yellow stripes & filled to near the brim then walked over to the pram & filled it to the brim with soya milk, they're vegans here; also helped myself to two rich tea biscuits... Having emptied the *Krasic Jizbo* cup, I washed it, returned it to the wire shopping-trolley. Beth at this time had left me alone while she entered the clearing, having seen me scribbling away. She took courage & opened her wheely-bin, given by the Thameside Nuclear Free Group in happier times, got her red folder out. £40 a week business-scheme to write the history of the Scottish witches... Well: to get back to my return journey, caught by the smell of incense, I had out of the corner of my eye felt Beth's presence by the fire, wondering if she was approaching me or wondering if she was wondering at my presence. She was just waiting for the joss sticks to stay alight, then returned to the incense store. To get back once again to my return journey from the wire shopping trolley, given by a well-wisher in a different far-off time, I walked to the memorial table, bending over it, Helen's petition now in a cellophane folder & her old snap picture outside the court: she in the middle, Allison on the left, Spud on the right, smiling all smiling; Allison reluctantly, her waist belted, so; her full hips waiting for the seed.

Spud, her left hand in her pocket, red corduroy trousers;
Allison, her dark mack, one hand rigidly down, the other in her pocket;
Helen, her hand half-way up:
that much surprise,
her head tilted to one side
no hand in pocket.
Spud: the bother with her coat.
Helen with carrier bag, her mack wrapped round her belly & bloated like a pregnant woman. One foot left behind, the step in front:
a startled pose, her head & face in expectant look.
I have come to hear & listen & to understand.

I have nothing to say, no meaningful pronouncements to announce, what was in the past is past & now is now & my role is now. To understand that past was me of me & that now is now. That is all: --

the Amazonian woman sits in the hot sun by the fire.

Not a word from her lips drops
to the other woman
sitting in the shade.

Three women gone off
in the Princess
to wash clothes,
gone four hours
& the sun beats down.
A prison or a hell
created here at Yellow Gate
a silent observer
to defy the military.

Non-violent action is the centre piece
of our work
the white-haired woman will cry;

A death, crushed skull
is an excusable reason
but a word in the wrong place
another matter.
The waiting, hewing & drawing of wood, water.
To maintain others to do that task
the function of women
Is
to work for the camp
women have only one function
women have only one use
work for the camp, for the good of the camp, to maintain the camp.
the camp of six women to maintain & work for six women.

At last we were to have the meeting. I was determined to take hold of myself and work out what exactly was my role in the camp. They had been there a long time, I had not; it was not suprising that they thrust all their traumas onto me, particularly in the emotional aftermath of Helen's death. Helen was part of us; we were the bereaved family. A grieving process can contain anger, bitterness and recollection of hurts given in the past, triggered within the family by the shock of death. It is a function of the pain of reassembling ourselves after the death. It may look as though everything is about to disintegrate; but real solidarity will recover and grow anew.

I am not a member of Yellow Gate, only an occasional visitor alongside many others. My contribution is not for me to evaluate but for the permanent ones. What visitor would have the arrogance to rearrange the fixtures & relationships within the home? That is for the house itself to say. Likewise the visitor is not bound by the fixtures of the last home when visiting the next. This time it is extraordinary, because outside the house the woman dies & others come to claim her for their own, the house itself changes to receive others not of the house, so we are all in different changes to receive, be one & then wait on the sideline to be called, our role a multiple one of different shades; now it is over, we go back to what we were. But then different alignments, older & perennial even as the base itself changes from cruise missiles into air launches, new machinery coming in, with ladders leading up to pads, & long guns; all new. This is the action we should be doing: stopping these new guns from coming in instead of rubbing salt into old wounds. The clock has stopped at Yellow Gate whilst Granny Grogan limps along to watch for the Hares from the old dead holes. Hares are magical animals & dance in the full moon & dance in the snow in Germany. I am the watchful eye for new metal toys for the boys. First on the cereal packet & now for real: bang-bang! As soon as the Russians are out of the way, the mice begin to play, only seconds in the air & the joke is turned around again, the Russians are just visiting another base.

I am invisible & yet not invisible
but no recognition who I am.
They decide who is a person.

I am in a limbo state
I spoke to Katrina:
when can we have our talk about Kings Cross women?
Well, when can we have our talk?
When?

When you say.
She goes off, is mild, had a good night's sleep.

I said to Sarah, when can we talk?
Have you forgotten?
She said no, not now.
But sometime, I said.

I am a traveller resting here
beside the fire
unknown & yet they all used to know me.
But the anger still
remains to
bubble over
& spew out to someone else.

I am a silent menacing stranger
enemy
my tongue & voice have seized up
my brain ticks over, messages & images.

So they have come back from court. Granny Grogan stole the show as Mackenzie adviser to Spud. Allison was not there, but sent a letter of not guilty & to say she wants her fine dealt with on the 18th.

To put Allison's history into perspective
the Cromwellian dissident of freedom of conscience:
now at Greenham
totalitarian rules.
Allison her bright eyes, her stubborn chin, her closed mind, her gypsy passion, her earrings, her plated bracelets, she will be still & harsh as she faces the
magistrate.
In prison she denounced the prisoners for drug smoking & asked to be placed elsewhere.
Squealer they yelled out as she passed, yet she wept when she left the jail & wished she was back
rather than be at Greenham.

She snuggles up close to her mum on the settee in that huge panelled old house with ducks on the
walls, a garage stuck in the middle of the lawn,
She prepares her own vegan meals, or will she return to her passion of chocolate? A grin released her
dimples as she twinkles and tucks in.

Helen the crushed and squashed, Helen (her charges have been dropped) & Spud who is part of Helen, Helen part of Spud in death: they are observed by the courts. Spud's case will go ahead (her defence: to ask for commander to appear as witness), whilst Helen, who also sprayed & splashed with paint & damaged £1994 worth of MoD property, broke no law. A dead woman cannot break the law. To deserve penalty, she must be judged, so the courts too do not recognize the past, there is no past only now.

Spud, Allison, Helen in the court for painting hangars
serious charges.
Helen had sought a new type of court, in the Welsh language. A tongue not heard at Newbury
and silent today.
A horse box, four horses, festival; a show took precedence over her.
In court the uniforms of the crown
who took the language away
From Helen.
Who wiled her way to bring it back.
The uniforms of the crown
silenced her
by splitting her brains, her innards
encrusted in the road.
Marks of blood & guts.
A yellow chalk outline of her body
remains.

A launch vehicle leaves empty to return full: what is being brought into the base? Must I hurl myself in front of it when it comes back & ask why? what?

The fat runner has returned freckly & pale like an over-fed milk baby. The fat boy clutches his crotch & heaves his trousers up, puts his earphones to his ear & waddles by.

Janet in grey blue, embroidered skirt, at edge yellow, shoes yellow, hair. Spud off-white, natural white, & white laces. Katrina's hairy legs in ankle socks.

Spud now in leaf-green cotton, sheer, so golden and delicate with yellow shoes & white laces; all the shoes have changed to tennis ones, light, elegant, like Edwardian summer wear for strawberries and cream.

The women are in prime condition, sleek, not an ounce of superfluous flesh, long-legged, long-haired, blond, black & in-between, they move like gazelles in the forest delicately picking their way through the ferns.

They were all assembled; this was the meeting. I understood that I was to be the (temporary) scapegoat, that was my role.

2 p.m. a circle. The catalogue of my faults. Katrina: my thought-control, my attack on lesbians. Abigail ditto. Jean on my behaviour on London march; my attack on Yellow Gate. Sarah: softly softly approach ... An uneasy pause. I don't defend myself.

Sarah thought my letter critical of camp, was angry because of my interference. Sarah was not pleased with what was happening, felt that "Margaretta's working against the camp", making approaches to Sarah to separate *her* from camp, every woman is a resource for the camp, Sarah will not be syphoned off; will not allow social phone-calls to make her separate from the camp: that's the package, I must accept it or reject it. Sarah said she'd changed, sharpened up her thinking because women have abused her trust and friendship. She'd asked to meet me by the fire and I had put her off. My refusal changed Sarah; she thought that the way I'd handled Helen's parents was making political capital. That I made no adjustment & took no leadership from camp.

"When letter came, it was hurtful & showed lack of trust. Catherine had privilege." Women had to work harder, there was a play for me going on, undermining of the camp by Catherine who had left it: I said it was a viewpoint ... They felt I was winding them up, it was an insult to say it was a viewpoint.

Allowances were made because of fatigue, my coming here was not good. "Catherine being able to meet with you, being able to have dialogue without the camp being there: a lack of trust."

Root of poison, response to police violence against Catherine & Beth at a demo in London, police threw an iron bar at them. Beth did most of the work for legal appeal and felt that Kings Cross were only focussing on C, who was black. C had allowed Beth to be sidelined.

I talked too much. Too nervous. Went wooding.

Waste. How to recycle frustrated anger into NVDA. Must be studied.

~~~o~~~

Saturday 19 Aug 1989
J.A.'s letter arrived. Went wooding.

Sunday 20 Aug 1989
Hot. Beth told me about further plans for Imber. Decided to come back for that weekend. General camp-trouble brewing. The old nag: women who leave camp are soft wimps. Sarah wants to strengthen community. My meeting did not give them relief, the maggots are still nibbling inside the apple.

Monday 21 Aug 1989
Swedish women arrived Sát., belonging to Wicca group. I was left behind in camp with them. Canadian couple came, talked about radio. Three young men, pylon workers £ 2.75 an hr., very dangerous work. Scottish: one of them worked in Dingle, they have insurance policies on their death, his daughter will get £10,000. "We are family," they said, "Desperate." That broke the ice between me & the Swedes. Age mixture: the older Swede engaged to a 21-year old brother of the 18-year old whose mother is married to a 30-year old.

Beth & Katrina went to Humanist Day Fun Fair. Katrina said when she returned, "We really are going to the dregs."
~~~

Tuesday 22 August 1989
They returned from funeral 10-30pm on 21st. The Thomases then had them in their house & gave them food, showed Helen's paintings from school. The Thomases were beginning to understand that their daughter was serious in her politics.

At eviction time the baliffs wanted to move Helen's memorial by order; we resisted. The police were talking to the postman.

Money came. Invites from Edinburgh School of Art. Talk round the fire about community: their visions for the future of Greenham. The sapphic myrmidon announces she wants lesbians to have meetings on their own, a wily move to exclude the old crone. The old crone intones: invokes a community of women abandoning the world and bound together in dedication. I am uneasy. The old crone bringing back her past: she had wanted to be a nun, a Benedictine, but as everyone said she should be, she wouldn't be.

Wednesday 23 Aug 1989
Just had conversation about the Austin Rover car called Princess, the sapphic myrmidon flares up at my questioning the car's name. I'd asked, why a patriarchal name? Am I impugning her values? Likewise the word "bitch": all defend that word, particularly the sapphic myrmidon. She is motherless & her mother was an actress. Worked as sound engineer for the BBC World Service. She justifies everything, car that won't work: that's life. She bulldozes everything that is uneven instead of wading through. Dogmatic. Spud the same.

Even a discussion on the name of the car can be implied as a threat to Yellow Gate. All criticism now is an attack, because there is no trust. All are enemies until submission is offered.

Had there been cursing-stones here to scream abuse at,
the abusers & abused could hurl the epithets like August rain.
That custom's gone & instead the State will see the spent curses
the warring factions
brought together
against the warring state.
The warring factions

slept ate dreamt, worked & like foxes in the night
slipt into the still of darkness
& left their mark.
Now they mark each other first
before the State leaves *its* mark.

* * * * * *

1991. *Until 1999, after the departure of the cruise and the Americans from Greenham, the work of the camp was focused on getting rid of Trident, i.e. NVDA at Aldermaston & Burghfield, and following Trident on its journeys to Faslane. Court cases, jail, and continuous use of the courts to challenge the bylaws and to challenge nuclear weapons by reference to the Genocide Act and international law.*

Wednesday 11 Dec 1991
Katrina, Beth & I went into base, saw the new commander trying to hide in his swivel chair, then his lackey came out: curious incident. Katrina said it's all happening underground. The MoD woman said *her* enemy was Fat; eating chocolates, she feeds them to her fiancé. "The only enemy now is the enemy within, the law must be obeyed above all." Human rights: she does charity work. Social works alone will save the world, purge the guilt. Cold. Went to Tesco, bought tapes, then to Sanctuary. Fire & life at Green Gate. Lisa & Emma at Sanctuary. Beth cooked wonderful meal of noodles & veg; opened my whiskey; had hot toddies & so to bed, piles of bedding. Dark, frosty & cold; but had warm night.

~~~o~~~

Friday 13 Dec 1991
Hard frost below freezing. Today it may be a point above freezing. The whole of southern England is in the grip of a hard ice. The sun comes out during the day & then it's warm till 3 o'clock. Honor came Wednesday, Suzanne maybe Sat. Spud & I went into base on Wed, with video. "Who is your enemy?" "We don't think," say the MoD. Their eyes racing round their faces as they are thinking. Christmas carols wheeze out. The baby not in the crib yet. I am allowed to stop and video the crib; no-one tries to take the video away. "Excuse me, I
~~~

can handle this, sir," says young moustached USA guy. Old Bull of the MoD is being coarse, putting his hand over video; criminal damage. Turkish-Arabian night, sunset, moon; everything sparkles lit up by the camp fire.

~~~o~~~

Tuesday 17 Dec 1991
Went to Imber yesterday. Fog, mist. Lit a fire. The military began exercising. MoD came & swiped the lot of us, including tapes. All charged -- i.e. Claire, Fred, Lisa, Honor, Emma, Katrina & me. MoD made me erase bit of Imber from my tape, went to Aylesbury for meal.

~~~o~~~

Friday 20 Dec 1991
The weather milder; wet & windy; the birds race across the wind. The morning star. Heard an owl. The traffic goes on & on. There was frost last night.

Two women from Green Gate swaggered down asking for the loan of a wheelbarrow. The wheelbarrow was returned. When Beth was in the mobile she saw one of them wheeling the barrow, opened door & said it would be better if you were self-sufficient, or else ask Blue Gate for one. Katrina worried about lack of women in January; she sees this Green Gate "invasion" as the first salvo of an attempt to take control of the Sanctuary. This is reinforced by the new magazine *Flame* with its strong attack on Katrina: "The Goddess Valkyrie, the Holy War." The Holy War of course is for the Sanctuary, Mecca: who is entitled to it? A new religion is developing at the other gates -- its message is: give up the fight against the military base, pray to the goddess! the enemy is within (as with the MoD woman; *her* enemy is Fat). If the other gates do gain control of the Sanctuary, the whole question of Commoners' Rights will be muddied. Is that why the 2 wheelbarrow women are here? -- because of pending legal action by Katrina & Sarah to preserve the Rights, and establish the illegality of all the structures within the military base?

MoD & dog followed me to Yellow Gate, then two MoD on the way back. A feeling of desolation at Yellow Gate with the loss of Emma. Honor did look quite brisk. Beth & Katrina & I did baking to cheer Katrina up.

Saturday 21 Dec 1991, the Solstice
Gladys sold for £40, it will pay for the cats' anti-flu injections. Mistral & Domino, fat neutered toms who got milk & meat for the solstice, bundles of fur scratching, demanding to get out. Had magnificent feast: roast potatoes, parsnips, mashed turnips & carrots, gravy, salad. Fruit salad, apple & blackberry & marzipan flan, jam turnover, coffee, wine. I am full. Went out & put 2 wishes for women to come to Greenham for Jan & Feb. Katrina in anxious worried state, Lisa & Spud likewise. The joyriders on their motorbikes in the woods, with their legs in the air as they drive at 70mph. It is dark, moist, windy, warm like new bread.

The last witch would have visited Lisa Gray's house which was the forge. Here in the Sanctuary the witch ran wild; no church for her; a silver bullet in her brain as she danced on water.

~~~o~~~

Monday 23 Dec 1991
Sarah sent a Xmas card. Up at Green Gate they light their fires.

Trident is coming: 10,000 times more power than original Hiroshima bomb & British too. Scottish Christian CND got out a good book about it. Kinnock supports Trident.

Croatia, Serbia, Europeans slaughtering one another in the name of nationalism. USSR no more, as from yesterday, Gorbi out of a job. In Britain, 85 thousand families to be dispossessed, mortgage defaulters. Why are people evicted? -- because they lose their jobs and can't pay the mortgage. I am sitting in the middle of the wood surrounded by women discontented with each other in turn; we surround the base where those inside are discontented by us sitting here; we are discontented by them & their role. Who is content in the base but the RAF commander who will receive the Trident? It is not the American who swivels in his chair, holding on to the telephone to avoid talking to us; *his* power has been taken from him; he has nothing to do with Trident, so must go home. We are sitting & wooding, eating & sleeping in the woods surrounding the base, waiting for the Trident which is more deadly than the bombs dropped at Hiroshima.
~~~

Tuesday 24 Dec 1991
Wind died down, sun out, slight frost last night. Katrina & Beth gone to pay their visit to a Nigerian woman in Holloway. She was charged with smuggling cocaine, on arrival at Heathrow; & will be deported Jan 8. She ran a business in Lagos, her husband had taken up with another woman & she has three children. In England the proselytisers visit her: but she is already a christian.

BBC Radio 4 full of the Soviet Union. People there naive about free market. The peasants holding on to food waiting for the highest price, that is market forces: the old & poor starve. I remember reading that the workers are OK; they barter. West can move in with its efficiency, collar market. All the oldies redundant. There is an alternative way of life: NVDA. Yesterday walked to Tesco, bought cigarettes, sat on a seat outside to smoke. The English people shopping en masse, not an attractive lot. Admittedly the high wind was leaping at them, but still ... the stress. What price the Gulf War? the repossession of houses? unemployment on the increase. So many look half-starved or else unhealthily overweight, their trolleys full of breakfast cereals. Big reductions in chickens & ducks. By focussing on collapse of USSR we don't notice what's going on here. How can one feel satisfied? Provos have called a cease-fire for 72 hours so they can eat their Xmas dinner. Loyalists don't celebrate Xmas, so they have not.

The women at Green Gate drove out the man with the camper who sometimes walks inside the base. There are so many strays camping. Katrina takes the side of the man against the women at Green Gate. They are invading her space; they cause her mental suffering; she doesn't know what is going on or what they are up to. All peace forces *will* finally join in against Trident, won't they? There is no more trust: look at CND going to sit down with Chinese who shot at the students for wanting democracy. (In the end CND backed off.)

The sun is going down. There are no cruises now. There is the Sanctuary. There is no doubt that the base is there and Trident will go in, there is no doubt that CND wanted Greenham to finish, there is no doubt it is the last & only autonomous women's resistance; that is why I am here. Katrina has fought for that. The Sanctuary is important. Katrina who has been here for 9 years, to stay at the gate day after day ...

It is getting dark now & they are not back, I grumble to myself; but I do not live here. It is silent; the last witch of Greenham, was she here in the bracken? I saw a deer move. The witch would be about her business like Bina McLoughlin in Connemara, making sure that the animals were all right. The witch resisted.

~~~o~~~

Thursday 26 Dec 1991
One woman's sister committed suicide on 18 Dec. by taking an overdose of sleeping pills. The suicide was prepared for; she told them at work she was going away till Friday. So on Tuesday with a bottle of whisky & sleeping pills she began her journey across time. Friday, the police broke down her door. What kind of journey aspirin makes? the stomach bleeds; whisky can make one vomit. Someone else's brother killed himself when he was 23; she was at the university in Scotland. She came home & they told her he had been dead two months. They hadn't wanted to upset her. Now her younger brother is in a mental hospital, collapsed over grief for his brother. Her mother won't believe him: "Nonsense, it happened a long time ago." J. the German, when I went to interview her, burst into tears, *her* sister had tried to kill herself & in the end went mad. J. wept, "She is so stupid." She had always copied J. "Now," says J., "We could have been partners in our activities." O's cousin committed suicide by throwing herself under a train.

We did action in FIBUA village by writing names of children killed by plastic bullets in N.Ireland. Taken to Salisbury police station, headquarters for Wiltshire. Locked up, our shoes & scarves removed just in case we hanged ourselves. Very warm, artificial light, toilet, wash-basin. Terrible police.

* * * * * *

1991 & '92: Various Letters.

POLICE REPORT [excerpts]

To: Detective Inspector P. Townshend
From: Detective Constable V. Phillips

This report deals with criminal damage caused to forty-five headstones by three female peace campaigners [Elizabeth JUNOR, Judith WALKER and Margaretta D'ARCY, at
~~~

1545 hours, Wednesday 25 December 1991] in the mock churchyard at FIBUA village, Copehill Down, Salisbury Plain Training Area, Wiltshire ... The three accused ignored the security Officers' warning and entered the village mock churchyard, produced cans of spray paint and commenced to paint names and what appeared to be PIRA slogans on the headstones ...

~~~o~~~

From Statement by: Messrs. CS Cleanmaster, Fordingbridge, Hants., 7 January 1992.

... I was escorted by Sgt. Moorehouse to the mock church and graveyard where he showed me a number of mock gravestones daubed with black paint. I made a survey of the gravestones and found that 76 sides had been daubed with black gloss graffiti paint. I tested one stone with graffiti paint remover and found that it took me half an hour to remove the words written on the stone *(R.I.P.) Irish children killed by British troops ...*

* * * * * *

Galway, 28 Feb 92.
To: Liberty (London):

Dear Friends,

I have just received your leaflet about the NI Human Rights Assembly to be held 6th-10th April in London. I shall not be able to attend; but I would like to offer a submission which I think would fall within the scope of Commission No. 7 (Rights Secured with no Discrimination).

A comparatively small incident, which could have implications in court when it comes to sentencing. Myself and two other women from the Greenham Women's Peace Camp, Yellow Gate, are charged with criminal damage in the course of a non-violent demonstration against the British Army's training "village" on Salisbury Plain. I enclose a copy of the Crown Prosecutor's documentation. We put onto the mock gravestones the names of children killed in the North of Ireland by plastic bullets; and I added the names of three women (two of them being personal friends of mine) who have been killed -- Máire Drumm, Miriam Daly, and Mairéad Farrell (shot by SAS at Gibraltar). We also wrote "British Troops out of Ireland".

At Greenham Common we are totally opposed to violence; we never use it; and the technique of all our demonstrations is non-violent direct action as the MoD police know perfectly well. Yet the charge sheet says "PIRA slogans", a clear association of ourselves
~~~

with a specific paramilitary group, carrying the implication that only those who support the Provos can call for "Troops Out", or openly bear witness to killings by the British Army in the North of Ireland. Of course we will argue this in court, but I believe that our case has already been prejudiced. I hope that this, slight though it may seem to you, will be of some value to you.

Yours sincerely, Margaretta D'Arcy.

* * * * * *

From: Liberty (London). Original is incorrectly dated: probably 10 March 1992.

Dear Margaretta,

Thank you very much for your letter of 28th February and your submission to the Northern Ireland Human Rights assembly. Your evidence is certainly relevant and I have passed it to the co-ordinator on the Commission on the Right to a Fair Trial. I am sorry to hear about your difficulties and wish you luck at your trial. It might be a good idea to get legal advice about whether you can take a case to the European Commission, if you have not already done so.

Yours sincerely, Jane Winter.

* * * * * *

Thursday 26 Dec 1991 (cont.)

Green Gate expanding; new brand of Mother Goddess religion. Warm & moist. Gas ran out, so have to light fires. Honor washed her hair, looked better all fluffy like a persian cat. MoD out yesterday touring fence. Queen's Speech: praise for voluntary workers, people who take action. Last night after release, found service-station open, disaffected youth hanging around drinking hot drinks from slot machine. Terrible country.

A diluted landscape made into mud tracks by the military.
such beauty such green spaces
hemmed in by bylaws:
our eyes are put into boxes.
Nowhere to look
except into the eyes of
law & order officers.

Friday 27 Dec 1991
Yesterday, a beautiful day, Lisa Gray came for lunch. I walked up to Yellow Gate. At night on 26 Dec, Katrina & I went on top of silos & played recorder & tin whistle -- the Jewish folk dance. Eerie inside silo, like the pyramids. Each silo's got a narrow service-station passage. We played our tunes & it echoed. Now they say that mummies are radio-active. Today & all last night they turned the lights on in the base & worked all through the night, moving earth & making holes.

Saturday 28 Dec 1991
Beth has gone to Edinburgh & Katrina joins her this evening. Yesterday videoed Lisa Gray. Xmas! and she got a repossession order from the bank for the house. They already took the van & pictures. Curious world. Joe sitting there doing crossword puzzle from the *Daily Express,* shouting, "You borrowed the money, they have a right to take everything." His son works in Aldermaston. The Trident will come here.

Everyone has gone from the Sanctuary except Domino, Mistral & I. Janet's friend heard on Swedish radio that the fences had come down. Vehicles came into base. Will Lisa Gray tell us when the Tridents come? -- 49 of them. The Labour party wants them.

What is to be done if the press don't take statements of arrests, imprisonments? Wait it out. Beth is writing plays; Katrina makes her banners. When Green Gate came down I did go up to speak to the conservationists about the birch trees & the heath. Lisa says there is a shortage of heather; what about the birds, the lizards? Conservationists come to defend heather, Green Gate come to defend birches, bailiffs come to defend bombs, Joe to defend Trident, Yellow Gate to defend people & the earth. Young women kill themselves to defend themselves. And what does the Labour Party defend? Newbury Council owns the Common; the birds, insects, snakes, flee. The ghosts living under the silo. The witch of Greenham and the civil war.

Sunday 29 Dec 1991
The church bells peal. The birds sing, blackbirds, chaffinches, starlings, crows. The cats prowl. There is stillness on the earth. Honor is late. The fire hisses with wet wood. Women are asleep in tents; cars, vans, are idle, taking up space. Sarah's energy clings to the skeletal thistles. Jean Hutchinson's spluttering lisp-

ing laughter, & Joan Hyman in red & blue woollen jumper & trousers from Oxfam shops. Her tinkling laughter like little bells. Mary Millington, angular, walks sedately to pick up a stick, throws it down again. She works too hard for her daughter Zoe. All these women have gone & come, & still working -- & Katrina, the granddaughter of an imperialist who tried to put the Irish down in '22. Blue, woad, red, violet, orange, indigo. Elizabeth Abrahamson, squeaking like a hen laying an egg. Naomi in Nicaragua. Katrina washes & cleans the mobile home like any proud housewife peering through the lace curtains at her messy neighbours, "Irresponsible, dirty for the sake of dirtiness." So she says. I sit here, the spectator, dirty, wood-fire smoke clinging to my clothes, my eye constantly watering, waiting for Honor. The private contractors rape the earth, for what we do not know: the clanging & banging late in the evening; the vehicles rush through into the base; the war still goes on. This morning early I went to have a look, the earth is piled higher & higher so I can hardly see. It is overtime for the men, they must be in a hurry or else money is no concern, whilst others huddle in their houses with their repossession papers, too old to struggle any more. For the Englishman's house is his castle no more.

Yesterday a new-age man jumped in to entertain us. He gave Honor a bracelet. A young woman from Faslane peace camp also came. Mia & woman went to Blue Gate. Lisa got a rash, we said the doctor must see it, she has gone to Casualty.

* * * * * *

1992: *I returned to Greenham for my FIBUA trial.*

Saturday 18 Sept 1992
Americans left the base a while ago. Ceremonial taking-down of the flag. Greenham is now a ghost town, school is closed, all the shops looking derelict, the base will be formally given to the MoD. Am happy to be back, the birds, the trees, the fallen leaves, not the noise of the traffic.

~~~o~~~

Thursday 23 Sept 1992
Monday, went to Devizes. They wouldn't give me a retrial, so it goes to Crown
~~~

Court. Prosecution lied in the evidence. Beth & Judith must just have been sentenced like me. Argued but rules are rules. Taped it. Had lunch in pub; manager a Welshman; left army, settled down in Devizes; did not vote Tory. Devizes unemployment, 1300 out of 13,000: only brewery & army left. Artillery were exercising on Salisbury Plain. Boom Boom. No-one took any notice. It was like thunder.

Finola was worried because Lisa said 4 yobbos from the base came down & attacked the caravan when Katrina was in it with Beth, breaking windows. MoD did nothing, said it wasn't their business & now police in Newbury say they can't check files about this complaint. It must be wrongly numbered. The smears of *Peace News* & Lorna Richardson: "Yellow Gate is violent, Kings Cross Women trashing women, kangaroo courts." They have decided to have policy excluding Animal Liberation Front & Yellow Gate, nasty. How to counteract such crude generalizations? Odd that this policy defines itself just as we are accused of being Provos.

* * * * * *

Correspondence with *Peace News*

from *Peace News (26 Aug 92)*

(for non-violent revolution, in co-operation with War Resisters International) 26 Aug 1992.
to: Beth Junor,

Yellow Gate, Greenham Common, etc.

> We cannot accept your classified advert for the Yellow Gate newsletter. I therefore return your cheque for £13.50.
>
> Lorna Richardson (*Peace News* Promotions worker)

* * * * * *

[excerpts]
Yellow Gate, 14 Sept 1992.

> Dear *Peace News,*
>
> With reference to your curt letter of 26th August 1992 ... This is quite a statement,

which has serious implications as regards your policies on freedom of information and freedom of expression.

The Yellow Gate Greenham Common Women's Peace Camp Newsletter advocates (for example) non-violence, justice and equality worldwide, the restoration of Greenham Common, an end to censorship of all forms, anti-racism, non-alignment to any state, an end to the war in Northern Ireland; one would have thought that these were methods and aims with which you would be in agreement ... Either one believes in freedom of information and freedom of expression, or one does not ... As a newspaper purporting to be "for non-violent revolution", you are not even waiting for the state to impose its censorship, you have volunteered to do it yourself ... Another very serious issue arising from your decision is the abuse of power by those who have more resources, both to receive and impart information, over those who have less ... In fact, Lorna Richardson, your "Promotions Worker", has herself lived at Yellow Gate Greenham Common Women's Peace Camp, and is well able to describe the constant evictions and general living conditions to you ...

Yours sincerely, Beth Junor, Katrina Howse.

* * * * * *

Thursday 23 September 1992 (cont.)
Went to see Lisa in Sanctuary. Wonderful day, real heat, air balloon in base, lots of aeroplanes, asked Lisa. She had heard nothing; told me that planes can now fly over the area.

Finola will sleep in tent as the attack on caravan scared her. We imagined a gang towing caravan with Finola inside & leaving it in the middle of the road for a bit of fun. Today is Ramblers' Day: 50 of them went by at the main gate. Finola told me at length the saga of Ramblers' Day, reclaiming the land. Elderly man told Finola that MoD said they couldn't walk round the periphery & he believed MoD, and an elderly woman (who had first approached Finola) hustled him off; she said ditto. And then scarpered. They were told it was a forbidden day for them to ramble round the fence. They were having a public meeting in Cookham car park, addressed by an MP.

Newbury Journal had bit about Spud & bylaws. MoD & Crown Prosecution Service are in disagreement over bylaws at Aldermaston. CPS wants to prosecute; MoD, no. So Burghfield & Aldermaston are in with illegal bylaws, but then when silly twats like the ramblers won't even walk in their own right but allow MoD to keep them out, I give up.

Friday 24 Sept 1992
All coming in for the kill, to write the requiem of Greenham. An Academic from USA is writing a book on women's groups: "It will be for your benefit," she writes. The blond lecturer from Leeds: "I can only afford a fiver." USA vehicle went into base yesterday. Thought they'd left. More USA loading trucks going into base.

~~~o~~~

Tuesday 28 Sept 1992.
Kinnock has openly derided CND. Bruce Kent wants a new broad party. All support-vehicles are lined up at Green Gate for inspection & departure waiting for the Soviets.

* * * * * *

1992: Various Letters

[circular letter]

Yellow Gate, 8 Dec 92.

Dear Friends,

Yesterday, Katrina & Aniko, two of the women who live full time at the camp were sentanced to 28 days imprisonment at Reading Magistrates court. The case was in answer to the charge of criminal damage at Aldermaston from the August actions. They were in court with two others, & all four were found guilty & given nominal fines & costs to pay., but no compensation was awarded against them as the prosecution failed to prove the amount of damage. Katrina & Aniko were targeted due to their long records of resistance & the stipendary magistrate tried to bind them over to keep the peace for a year, which they refused to accept & so received the sentences, which they will serve WITHOUT REMISSION.

This means they will be in prison until early January & Yellow Gate needs women to cover & help hold the camp. Please try & make the time to come down, for however long you can manage. We would be grateful if you could let us know whether you can make it, so we can plan accordingly. Also letters break up the monotony of prison days
~~~

so please write or send cards to either Katrina Howse or Aniko Jones (or both) at HMP Holloway, 1X Parkhurst Rd., London, N7 ONU.

Many thanks for your support, Rosy Bremmer, Lisa Medici, Abigail Adams.

[personal PS] Dear Margaretta, didn't think you'd be able to make it over, but thought you'd like to know. XX Abigail.

* * * * * *

1992 -- 1998: I kept going back to Greenham for short stays to support the women at Yellow Gate, but was not involved in any of the actions against Aldermaston and Burghfield. Prosecutions continued all this time, as well as legal challenges brought by the women in regard to the illegalities of the military base, and subsequent similar challenges concerning Aldermaston and Burghfield. On 16 March 1998 at Reading Crown Court I attended the trial of Sarah Hipperson and Peggy Walford for cutting the Aldermaston fence. They claimed in their defence that "the production of nuclear weapons breaks international law." This brought about a hung jury. Upon retrial they were found guilty, because the judge would not admit the evidence of the international experts which had been given in the first trial.

In 1997 Radio Pirate-Woman, together with the Yellow Gate women, made an audiotape of an historic event, the official taking-down of the Greenham base perimeter fence and the restoration of the Common to the people. The Women's International News Gathering Service (USA) gave this tape the Katherine Davenport Award for "the International Story of the Year".

3 November 1999: the West Berkshire Council gave approval for a "Commemorative & Historic Site" to be built on the land that was occupied for 18 years by the Greenham Common Women's Peace Camp.

2000: The camp was officially closed.

21

LAST STAND AT THE PIT-HEAD: ARMTHORPE 1993.

Diary Excerpts

I went with J.A. to a meeting at Kings Cross, on one of our fleeting visits to London -- we had come to discuss the commissioning of our Eleanor Marx radio play for the BBC; Ronald Mason was to direct. There was a railway drivers' strike and Arthur Scargill addressed the meeting. Arthur made a rousing speech, asking for volunteers to help the women's camp in Armthorpe in support of the miners whose pits were being closed down. I decided to volunteer for the weekend, called in at the union headquarters, and off I went to Yorkshire, "representing the NUM."

Friday/Saturday 14/15 May 1993 3.14 pm. Armthorpe Colliery.
Am alone in canvas shelter, the rain just finishing off from a lashing.

The taxi driver told me I was his only fare all morning & it was now 1.30pm. Depression yes.

The caravan had been burnt out on the day the closure was announced, all the men accepted redundancy except for SWP member. A drunken man set fire to the caravan and canvas. There is a hut now. Brenda Nixon here since Jan., exhausted, a young blond attractive woman with two children; has been keeping the camp going. She treats me as an official NUM representative: embarrassing, because I'd no idea when I volunteered that that's how I'd be perceived. Maureen, from Women Against Pit Closures, was here to discuss getting money for new caravan, three men here, plus Maureen, husband and dog. Still unclear as to exact role of WAPC. Was there a definite decision to open camps? Morale is low as men did not stand side-by-side with women & women's work. Did some videoing, security guard told me to go back to outside gate. (Security guard at Holloway told me to go back outside entrance when I videoed Katrina being released.)

There is a council housing estate opp. where I sit. Though in 1993 the men got more money because of the women's camp. But no "thank-you" to the women. Brenda said '84 strike took the guts out of the men. There is enough coal for 18 months. The men, when digging it, have unwittingly dug their own grave. It is cheaper to get coal abroad. On Thursday the High Court will make their judgement on closures; 6 collieries in this area; only two are open. I am waiting for a relief to come, have not found toilet, didn't ask. Brenda has returned, asked after Aggie the relief who has not arrived. There were two phone calls for Brenda. Where has it gone wrong? TUC, Labour Party not calling for a general strike to back up popular feeling; last Oct. there were 100,000 marching against Pit Closures.

The militant Aggie came, put her on video; coal delivery man and his assistant came. In evening Aggie's mother Jean from Scotland; before that, Trudie, John and their grandson Ryan. Tommy and his son Daniel were there when I came back from collecting charger and video from Mike. June v. religious, Cof E; she had owned pubs with her husband in London, Fleet St., Brick Lane, Poplar. She remembers '26 General Strike, her father and grandfather were miners. Lively evening as men and women walk past to their night's drinking at the Pit Club. Opposite, a house full of young people, must have been a party but couldn't hear music. Joe rang Aggie's mother & Brenda rang to see if I was OK. Had tomato soup & bread, finished fudge cake which I had bought in Doncaster.

My observations, pretty angry with the world. Who is to blame?

1) NUM for not educating the miners. They only read the tabloids, which attack them.
2) Helen Johns for setting up the camp without getting the support necessary to see it through, so the few women left are exhausted as at Greenham. When it was in the media they flocked; no media now, they're gone.
3) National Fuel Distributor: why is there not a campaign to expose the consequences of its policy?

This was a farm. Village people were brought in from all over to create new industry. All that was before, erased. They claim it for their own, it is only 75 years. Now it is over; it cannot be other than a dump whilst NFD remains.

I think of Eleanor Marx & how she must have felt on the last legs of the engineering strike, betrayed; to the workers, what could she say? there was no more magic. Had she failed them by encouraging them to resist? Brought more misery on them? Gave them false hope? Why did only a few listen?

Labour power is more powerful, more deadly than any cannon? The women support the men but the men don't support the women. They don't stand side by side. Time stands still; waiting for Thursday & the High Court. The Coal Board has behaved irregularly by forestalling closures: this pit is now ruined & unworkable; a fire two weeks ago; this pit must be sacrificed for NFD. The ruthlessness of profit, productivity. They were brought in & promised eternal working life, then the reneguing of the promise.

Timex, majority women workers.

Workers in Timex factory were on strike at this time and getting a lot of support.
I am the woman sent up from London by the NUM. I am official. The London representative.
I am sole representative of the giant NUM's struggle against pit closures.
I am the sole visible presence. Absurd.
In my blood is now embedded the continuity of struggle since the late 50's. H-bomb, rent and rate strike, Vietnam, Ireland, Industrial Bill, anti-racism Bill, immigration bill, prostitutes' rights, H-Block/Armagh: I am a walking parody, the aged retainer of the World Movement struggling to use the tool to overthrow capitalism.
I wear Oxfam PC-struggle laced boots.

Trudie has 3 sets of clothes, working clothes, good clothes for celebrations, plain clothes for everyday. When she's giving out the clothes which have been collected to help the miners' children, she wears her best clothes, boosting her morale as well as theirs. June never throws anything away.

I was too late for the newspaper, it opens 5-30. To have a shit I must go to the public toilet down the road. Chocolate fudge cake always moves the bowels. Strong sun & wind outdoors. A heat glazes from the coalite -- made from imported coal. Some one always makes money from someone else being deprived of it. Aggie cried last night, wiping away her tears with hands smeared with coalite dust, tears of anger & frustration with life's cruel tricks. The bribe.

The camp was fired last week, and Mike (74) lies in bed worshipping at his dead wife's shrine. Strained muscles to save the camp and now will never get up again or walk to put his 15-hr stint in.

Life is cruel & futile for those who struggle; or is the reward an opening of the eyes, a lifting of the blackout, to see what is really there? The messenger must carry the message on, & not forget to keep the fire of anger going.

A buxom blond curly-headed postwoman, red & black bike, cheerily calls out, "Good morning! I've got some letters for you." Three big brown envelopes and hands them over. Very few cars honk, in truth not one has called to say good morning or offer flowers -- a posy with a single bloom to brighten up the camp.

Since the fire incident, fear. I was frightened last night, what with the smell of gas & thinking about Sylvia Plath; I could end up cinders in the District Trades Council hut. They wouldn't dare, Brenda says, the fire was started by an angry man kicking over the coalite brazier, old Mike was in the toilet. The man's wife was angry with him. Where was everyone else?

The day, the final day, when all the men except one took redundancy. Took the silver and closed their eyes. First the dissident, then the breakaway, and scabs. Then the military occupation, the fear, suspicion, each for themselves, the conquest. But the strategy whereby the conquest takes place, the battlefield? Jobs; what jobs? The miners' resistance? -- a tool had to be made obsolete. Solidarity, community, pride, fair exchange.

Well ... 12.52, a busy morning, Brenda came perked up by meeting in Hull last night: 20 people turned up, 5 names put on rota and money donated as well. Visitors. A *Newsline* guy popped in to deliver the paper. Australian radio. A trainee manager who left the pits. A young woman asked if I'd seen her children passing by ... When I first arrived, I noticed a definite shift in temperature after I mentioned I was at Greenham. Now they are more at ease with me, and the shit comes out about two Greenham women who wanted a women-only camp à la Greenham, no men after 10pm. Sara Lee's driver had called to deliver apple-pies from Scarborough. One of these Greenham women intercepted, took the food, and said "There is a curfew:

no men." Brenda hit the roof. Sleeping bags: 2 were missing. Brenda said the Greenham women must have borrowed them (they were returned in the end). May, a self-contained woman who slept in her van, told one Greenham woman that the other Greenham woman had pinched them; she was told she was not fit even to wash Greenham women's feet, & so on. So the two Greenham women stormed off. (I'd heard of one of the two, but I didn't really know them.)

Jane came last night about 11.30, stayed until 3am. Hadn't known I was in the hut.

Brenda is sound. She doesn't really like the Vicar coming round for Sunday Service. Mike is a troubled soul, exaggerates his stories, refuses to accept that his wife's cancer was caused by coal dust. He refuses to accept that NFD, National Fuel Distributers, do cause contamination. In fact his wife held him back, she used to go every night to the club & bingo. Mike does not drink but went with her where she would have 5 or 6 glasses. Wasn't interested in politics.

Brenda rang the "Under-5s" and gave solidarity to them, they were chuffed.

The "Under-5s": a playgroup in Finsbury Park, London, having a sit-in against closure by the council: I'd visited them.
Arthur Scargill's secretary rang; then Brenda spoke to the Scargills, Ann and Arthur. A new caravan is coming tomorrow. Brenda was pleased at having spoken to the Scargills. Dave the parish councillor called. He said it was Arthur who wanted the camps kept going till outcome of the High Court. Brenda under pressure to give up. Many women, since the acceptance of the redundancy money by the men, have been pressurized not to come, it would look as if they were attacking the men. The area branch opposed full acceptance/membership for women. The smoke is lying on the ground due to fall in pressure; there are spasms & flurries of hail, with the wind getting furious and ferocious. Then the birds sing and the sun comes out. Dave on his bike to watch Sheffield and Arsenal on TV. Reversal of roles between men and women now. Trentham women occupying pit in '84; men were working in the strike. A slow emasculation of NUM; sliding through the back door.

A visit from Nell the union secretary: --

Nell the secretary called.
The women are scabbing on the men,
the men are blaming the women
the men are scabbing on the women
Scabs, Scabs, and scabs.
Stop blaming one another
divide & rule
this is what they want. Scabs on scabs
the monster feeds off the scabs
close ranks
make unity
& march forward.
The working class have rejected her
an insult was thrown at her.

The grey car across the road. The man who lives where the grey car is parked hurls insults at us.

There is a red van parked opposite the camp, three young people inside discussing selling it to the young man who lives beside the man with the grey car. The red van has driven off now, the young man returns to his house across the road.

Neuss has to go to hospital with haemorrhoids on Tuesday.

Sunday 16th May 1993
End of play. I'm off tomorrow. Last night Aggie came on her bike; she works in an old folks' home in the mornings. She's from Torbay, a real character, pugnacious and spirited. Trudie, John, June, Tommy and Daniel went off to charge my battery at Mike's, he wants a copy of his section of the video. He has only one book to read. Community Police won't press charges against the arsonist: turning over a brazier isn't enough; he says he was helping with the caravan. Mike was in such shock, yet he gave a statement in that state; wasn't even brought to hospital.

It wasn't a party, it was drug-dealers' clients; very busy all night so also the Pit Club. There is an outside toilet next door, the woman is away "but if son comes don't use it." Smelled gas, talked about turning it off, didn't know how. John this morning showed me. Trudie with John: an older man laden down with plastic bags. Sleeping bags arrived. Minibus came, they all went off to the Timex strike rally. J.A. rang, had a chat. I got my *Observer*, the Chris Evans lookalike who sells the papers is a student of history and politics in Huddersfield University and is helping his cousin over weekends. Students all busy with exams, so they can't help. Was woken by satisfied drug customers at 4.45 am. Loud beat music.

Brenda never got back with papers, don't know if there will be any relief tomorrow. Had two Golden Delicious apples for breakfast. Left battery on all last night.

When people are down they close up, they have no more to give. Timex strike is important for them, get away from it, receive energy and hospitality then back to carry on. I think a morning shift (skeleton staff) is finishing now.

They look after me well, they are concerned for me. But if I am not right then I must ask, they have no more energy. The euphoria at the beginning that they would win, the attention, the applause, it all came to nothing in the end.

The story of the Belfast woman who withstood police torture when held in Castlereagh and refused to sign a false statement: "I knew the value of myself." The drug-dealer family at the gate of the pit equals the gin palaces of the 19th century.

I am getting as obsessed by the dirt and grime as any hereditary coal family. I am always washing my hands, feeling how tacky my hair is. The drug-dealer family: young mother, aggressive, tough and thin, the husband more bullish, 2 kids, drove away, the pushchair in the boot. She drove. They are back. Whilst they were away, many callers for them, young miners, a very posh Rolls with a snooty couple.

Masses of cyclists passing, families, one mother & daughter in pink wigs, pink and white boleros; a penny-farthing hailed me then went on his way.

4.10 pm. No caravan yet. Two caravans did go into the colliery. One St John's ambulance. The sun has gone. Flocks of birds overhead, wind, & dust from the brazier. Have used one full bag of coalite already. Swallows. House martins.

June trundled up on her bike, same red woollen stockings, slingback shoes with her toes like rose posies sticking out, she has elegant legs. She asked me about my life story, & we got on to Jews & Irish. She knew a Jewish tailor when she ran the pub in Brick Lane & liked him, he made a coat for her, Jews make money, etc. Ireland? that's nothing to do with England, even though she and a girl friend had visited Skerries for a holiday in 1947 and met two nice boys at a dance. She was very lively and gay when young, then 12 years ago she had a breakdown when her daughters left home, never to see their mother again. She was superb landlady: "Out out you're out of order, go out and come in again!"

Vicar arrived, then three old ladies on sticks, a couple with a guitar who led the singing (being a small soul of the party), a Scotsman and a little woman, then a bearded doleful young man who turned out to be the industrial chaplain. John the vicar lively, a Ken Barlow manner. After the service, chats; then blow me over, another cleric arrives: had been at GCHQ, now he is in the New Life Church. They are prowling around looking for souls for their CVs. The colliery has rented them a hall, a dark place.

June said that under Labour the public services had been fantastic: cheapest buses in the country etc.

The druggies are busy. Well-heeled middle-aged miners & their wives going to the club inside the pit gates. Bingo for a few pints. June says they are in a state of shock.

Monday 17 May 1993
It rained yesterday evening and it is still damp & dark. They emptied the Elsan this morning, 6.30. I thought they were going to remove the hut, not knowing I was inside.

The day begins at five around here; at 7 quite a few waiting for the bus to go to work. The gardens are not wonderful. Tommy didn't turn up last night;

the industrial chaplain brought some lovely victoria sponge slices. June and I scoffed the lot. Went to see Mike about key; he had perked up and was sitting writing a letter to the paper. His altar and the ashes of his wife, he won't leave his wife behind.

(A young Afro-Carribbean comes to the camp, goes up to a man says to him, "I'm a racist & I'm going to knock your head off," runs into camp, gets arrested and dragged away.)

> But what of the future? What now as the North Sea gas runs out, as oil prices soar, now the pits have gone and [the pitmen] have dispersed? The old boys outside the club told me: "We always knew this would happen; that some day they would need us and coal. But now it's too late for all that."
> from *The Guardian* (30 August 2004)

22

A MAFIA OF MAGGOTS: GATESHEAD 1991

Diary Excerpts

J.A. and I were asked to deliver speeches at a theatre seminar at Lancaster University. I prepared a paper on "playing with radio". Two women from Gateshead, Esther (who was organizing projects to uplift Tyneside) and Jerry (from a women's group, Them Wifies) were at the conference; they seemed to be excited about my ideas. Some time later I got a letter from Esther, inviting me up to Gateshead to work with Them Wifies, in the hope of setting up a women's radio there. In the end I didn't do that; instead I made a video of the anti-polltax campaign and took part in agitation against the Gulf War.

More like a hallucination than a regular diary.

Monday 7 Jan 1991

To Gateshead. Left Muswell Hill at 7 am by minicab. Cab driver didn't arrive. Discovered he was waiting in Donovan Avenue and only found the right street after phone calls; got to Victoria. Clipper bus-stop well documented, no smoking in café, no seats in Victoria. Draughty. Clipper bus comfortable, with film: *El Cid.* Confusion on whether I should get out at Gateshead. No Esther. Went on to Newcastle on Tyne, not there. Then she was there. Drove to house. Dump. Went to Jerry's for dinner.

Jerry lent me history of Gateshead. Harold & Viv live downstairs; retired railwayman; she worked at Fenwick's. They have a cosy flat, telly, video-recorder.

Can't understand heating.

Jerry came round with duvet and blanket. Watched TV: the Gulf crisis. J. said she'd contact Katherine in Sheffield about central heating. It was off. Went to library & swimming pool. Overheard a conversation in the changing-room between two local women (catholics). They talked about their trip to Lourdes and then went on to say they were relieved their two sons had joined the army -- it would be good for them and the serjeant-major would soon shape them.

The mothers in Gateshead
Hate their sons
Their hearts are as strong as stone
Encased in the deep earth
The women in Gateshead
Hate their men
& take their revenge with venom
When their men go to war
Their bellies ripped open
Their blood spilt
In the desert war.
The women of Gateshead
Hate their men
Their quiet satisfaction
That the men do not know.
The women of Gateshead
Under the earth
Are watching & waiting
To rise up
Reclaim the earth
When all the men are dead.
The women have remained silent but
Rumbling under the earth

Collected leaflets. A few mums, one dad. Everything there, reading room with newspapers, uncomfortable; no dailies, only *Morning Star.* In reference room there are the dailies. Tried to get lemon juice, failed. Eventually walked down hill; got some. The place is like West Belfast. Corner shops mainly run by Asians. What am I going to do? Use video, I guess. Everything filthy, all furniture stained, uncared-for junk. Someone had thrown it all out because they didn't want it.

~~~o~~~
~~~

Undated entry
In Gateshead the officials have grabbed and evicted those not valuable. War begins in one's back yard. Injustice begins in the family and conditioning makes it acceptable. This house is a symbol of heat and fumes going into the atmosphere to make holes to destroy us all. Thick & dirty lace curtains.

As Katherine works in environment she knows it all.

To the council offices: outside in the street, a protest against cuts. 40 faces stare out, Labour faces, what secrets lie behind their faces? (These protesting women are all survivors of the patriarchy and yet joined to it still, listening to the lineage, who came from whom: father, mother, grandfather, grandmother, daughters, sons, which father? which mother? which grandfather? grandson? A thicket of birch, bramble, ivy, holly, oak, larch.) A mounted policeman comes, the bouncers snarl, "Have you been invited by the Lord Mayor?" What, to question each councillor as they come in to ask why the cuts? So in the streets the police prowl, why leave to go to London? keep them on the hop here in the backyard.

Post-cold-war world: Moscow takes advantage of the Gulf. Cold water and troops rounding up draft dodgers.

The shop which said, "Knock next door if you want something." I knocked. A young Asian woman. "We're closing down on Monday, we're all upping out, we have other businesses and business interests, our business here declined when the school was burned down."

~~~o~~~

Sunday 13 Jan 1991
So the cover is slowly being lifted up, the convoluted confabulations of the patriarchy. M. with a brain-damaged daughter, Sarah, 13, strong as a horse, an engine that revs & roars at all hours. The husband is there, a dark gateman of the river & woe to whomever crosses the Styx alone; his stick stuck into the ground and his hand firmly placed on it. M., now with a one-legged man and his child in her belly: will he go and leave her with the mess? One daughter refuses to come to the 2-bedroomed house where she lives, preferring to stay
~~~

with dad. At least three days a week she is free without the steam of Sarah. Sarah canot be left alone with a new baby. How can M. manage her? Her will, cased in cement, will crack if she does not breathe. The problem could be solved if Sarah went to residential school five days a week, but the husband, would he agree? Already taken to court as a bad mother. "Holy Jesus, Holy Mother, my sin at nineteen, my bed I have made & must lie on it." L. locked out by her mum who is visiting gangsters in a nearby flat. Jerry is frightened of these burly men and fears L. will be beaten. Just ask the mother for the key, or go round & say enough is enough. We cannot see her suffer. I have strayed into the hornets' nest where I will not be stung but must be a bystander to let others writhe with venom. Allotments controlled by men who grow leeks for prizes & the women are at home cooking dinner. How to agitate, organize, educate?

~~~o~~~

Tuesday 15 Jan 1991
Called on Rabbi to have dialogue about the war, he supported extermination of Saddam Hussein. Went off to get paste for Susie's posters, bumped into Jerry, went into Newcastle, called at Them Wifies' office; bought leads for video.

Wednesday 16 Jan 1991
No war yet. Vivian was the one tearing my posters off. Had word with Harold, he supports war, wants IRA hanged, stubborn little man, Dad's Army facing up to bully. Likewise Vivian. "I've done my stint," she said. A man going into his house took a leaflet. Had been in the army 17 years.

> It's war in Gateshead
> He had his head in
> the boot of his car
> As he rummaged for his filled carrier bags. Excuse me, I said
> As he entered his garden path;
> Showing him the leaflet.
> It is too late for me
> I'm going I've been called up
> I was seventeen years in the army.
> Don't go
~~~

Desert, I said.
He took my leaflet
Before he closed the door.
Why didn't I say
I dont want you to die?
Would that have touched his heart
To make him want to live
Or given him on the street a
Rose that he could carry with
Him to his death?

Met a young girl; her brother was in the Royal Navy out there. The whole of Gateshead involved in giving blood for oil. Connemara men from Rosmuc. Two men digging a hole in the road. In their graves? "I'm English now," one said. "Let the blackies go; I'm English, I stay here." Inside the repair shop, met another man, older. "I saw inside the concentration camps. Have you seen that? Saddam, Hitler." It is a nightmare.

Thursday 17 Jan 1991
The war has begun. The Brits and Yanks have moved in, bombarding Iraq.

Mothers of Gateshead.
The women of Gateshead
Hate their men.

~~~o~~~

Saturday 9 Feb 1991
Went to Full Sutton for march and rally against detention of Iraqis there, about 60 of us in bus. The York group came in cars after us, frail gallant march through snow. When we reached gaol, 2 police blocking way to main door, strapping SWP young fellow pushed through, we all followed. Ancient WRP fellow nervous. When we got to the speeches, modesty and hesitancy. Young bearded member of York Trades Council got up on wall to speak. I mentioned to Hugh about Birmingham 6 who were there: they chanted out "Free the 6, free the detainees!" It was an enjoyable warm experience. Had completely forgotten & couldn't recall exactly where we lived in Full Sutton, & that episode
~~~

over 30 years ago when I rode on my bike with Finn to hand in letter to the American CO at the base, asking him to get out. The base is now the prison. Mrs Husband will be dead. There is an industrial estate, but little changed. The battery of my camcorder ran out so couldn't take the prison.

Sunday 10 Feb 1991
This morning, Harold out shovelling the snow away. When he saw me, he looked blank but angry underneath. I asked him for a loan of his shovel, he gave it to me, telling me to leave it outside his door. There was a poster gone from the top of my door. Some one had climbed up to take it down. Here I am in Gateshead, paid £250 a week for doing nothing.

Monday 11 Feb 1991
The History of Gateshead: controlled by the gentry then the Labour Party.

The politics of Gateshead revolve round the Labour Party, the fringe groups (SWP, Militant Against War, Anti-polltax) all outside the centre. The war. The weather. Fundamentally bringing extra pressure on women who already have too much.

Women are being liberated by taking part in campaigns, taking college courses, courses in balancing relationships at home. Power balance being shifted. Husband is still wage earner.

1) Women in the home, dealing with unemployment amongst the men.
2) Women in the home dealing with husbands stretching themselves.
3) Independent women. How many are there?

Connie ill, not fighting.
Lin ill, but fighting.

~~~o~~~
~~~

Wednesday 13 Feb 1991

Went to Stop-the-War meeting last night at Friends' House, murder to get there as it's cut off by motorway, at deserted Metro asked a young woman the right line, very belligerent, she later turned up at meeting selling *Militant.* SWP & Militant there. Poor turnout. Started late. Debate about smart alec with video "for channel 4." Vote: video remained. I abstained, then debate about items in newspapers about row in National Stop-the-War Committee with threatened expulsion of Trots supporting Iraq. Should local meetings be decision-making, or should it be left to steering committee in London? but then what about membership? In London only members were allowed in. Either way it can be hijacked. Reports from activities: mainly organizing little groups in workplace; then women's group concerned with building/mobilization/awareness for Int. Women's Day, very sparse on ideas. To broaden campaign, I mentioned that mothers were being encouraged to buy food for the army. Dismal lack of reality and urgency. Lots of meetings, too many; Labour Party meeting on Monday. Claire Short on TV, against war. Is Labour Party wavering about support for war? I think so: 20% oppose war, is that figure just for Labour Party or for country as a whole? More women than men in Labour Party.

Almond and Liz came round in afternoon. Almond spoke about Lesbian Mafias in Newcastle. Labour Mafia in Gateshead. Community-workers/area-project-offices mafia decides who's in or out. Their prey, working-class women, inner city, that's venture capitalism or creative enterprise. Posted a Valentine to J.A.: --

Here in Gateshead
A mafia of Maggots
let loose to
parasite the living &
turn them into bait for war. Your envelope with
your love feeling poem
Is put through my letter box, drops in the
cluttered dark mess inside the door
on top of a thousand bills, ads,
free newspapers and letters,
all for someone else who once dropped in to pass the time.
Viv and Harold live downstairs
an old couple who lived "through three world wars;
I want to hang them all,"
says Harold with Viv behind, square and bold with mottled face.

Your poem catches
my heart
pushes emotions
up through my eyes
so water drops like
waterfalls.
The sun cold & hard
outside to catch
a welling tear
& turn it into a thousand
Prisms of colour.

23

LONDON 2003

Diary

(29 August -- 4 September, written up after my return to Corrandulla)
A long weekend in London was like a journey back in time, careering round the city on buses, each journey having some reminder of episodes of my life. Finn my son lives in Curzon Road, Muswell Hill. Walk down the road and turn right and we get into Cranbourne Road where we lived from 1966, after leaving Kirkbymoorside to . An old woman had owned our house, next door another old woman from Dublin. Then next door on the other side a family moved in from Tipperary. They arrived one day wheeling their belongings. One night the young wife was huddled on the doorstep, her husband had locked her out. She wouldn't take shelter in my house for the night; I lent her a blanket and there she remained till morning. Next day everything was normal; we never referred to the incident, just our formal "good mornings", etc. An artist nearby, with two small children and a traditional wife. It was rumoured that he sexually abused children. Then an Indian family arrived to live next door; they came to our wedding anniversary and gave us a silver-plate condiment set.

The children nearby. A dysfunctional little boy led a gang raiding the neighbours' gardens. When we found out that our own boys had been involved, we brought them round to apologise to our Indian neighbours, which is how we became acquainted with them. Later on a Greek Cypriot family moved in. Jo Liebowitz lived down the road; her children the same age as ours. She was the new breed of young mother, a graduate influenced by the philosophy of collective action, sharing duties such as bringing the children to the play group. I was startled by her at first, this large woman with red hair saying "It's silly we both have to take our separate children, why don't we take it in turns?" She was married to an Israeli lecturer, Theo. She rarely left the house, stayed at the kitchen table smoking, her women friends calling. All over London these young mums were organising and setting the agenda for Women's Lib, childcare, more democracy in schools, Labour voters, working-class roots. Watchdogs on behalf of the welfare of the community, lobbying against motorways that threatened to eradicate the neighbourhood, banning the bomb. All these local mushroom groups, disparate: the Greek Cypriots wanting union with Greece, the Turks wanting separation from Greece. The Irish were not organised at that time in London or elsewhere. In Harringay we did organise after 1969: the Harringay Irish Assoc., including members of the Connolly Association. I was on the committee for a time ...

Meeting women changed my life. I would never have gone to Belfast if I hadn't met Paula in Jo's kitchen -- a single mum from Belfast lodging with Jo. When her children grew up, Jo went back to teaching. When we returned from India (1970) and found out what the newly-elected Tories were like, we got together with Jo and inserted a postcard in a newsagent asking for like-minded people to contact us to do something. That's how we got to know people in Muswell Hill; in that small corner encompassed by three streets, Rosebery Avenue, Muswell Road and Cranbourne Road, the history of 20th century radicalism unfolded. The Ivimeys brought the anarchist connection, and recollections of the Socialist Party of Great Britain. They were now in the Labour Party and resigned from it over the treachery of the party in not fighting the cuts; Cheryl and Mike had been members of the Young Communists; Paula was an artist. We had a motorcade and march: Stop the Cuts!, to Wood Green, inviting Michael Meacher MP. Pat Arrowsmith was on it, and also Mary Hopkin who had campaigned successfully for fair treatment for contract workers.

Then the Angry Brigade: Ian Purdie and Co., with all their excitement at discovering Victor Serge, the dissident Russian revolutionist. Petrol bombs were discovered in our cellar after Purdie was arrested -- how theatrical! -- Jo volunteered to get rid of them, it made me understand how close to public disorder Britain was, by all the evidence of our small area -- revolution but no clear-cut way to do it. Our house had been rented to Purdie while we were India. When we returned we found a busy little anarchists' nest. It was there I was introduced to Schlacher's Cinema Action. He was a young German émigré from the Paris uprising. He was working with London council-tenants in support of their rent-and-rates strike. I remember going to a tenants' meeting, the chairman telling us how in the '30s when there were protests over housing he brought his dead baby and threw it on the desk of the bureaucrats. Indeed Neuss's mother-in-law, when she was homeless, brought her four children into the Housing Department, refusing to leave until they were housed.

My experience of the centralized radical left is not inspiring. The International Socialists and the Socialist Labour League. John McGrath and Michael Hastings called a meeting for all of us to carry a banner on a huge march against Barbara Castle's proposed curtailment of the power of the unions -- *Writers Against Reaction*, it read, *WAR!* Where was the Irish crisis in all this? Busy and fractious: Troops Out of Ireland, the International Tribunal, each faction had its own hidden agenda, each group proclaimed that its line was the correct one. *The Non-Stop Connolly Show* was the culmination of all our experiences in that era. To withdraw from the melée once one's eyes were open to the reality of the state and the nature of the foundation of the state was impossible. One could not ignore it. Wherever we went we met the same fervour. The Vietnam war, and the attacks on communities and on unions (in America also) -- the struggle was the same. But there was no linking it all together, each faction wanting only to remove someone else and appropriate their cause.

Reform or Revolution? Get something for yourself. Like a squirrel in Highgate Wood, scramble down a tree, find a nut and bury it for your own eating.

Every section, to begin with, organised in a free manner. I remember Ken Campbell at the first Theatre Writers' Union meeting saying that if it was to be like a cricket club he would be *in.* But orthodox organization eventually held sway. The culmination of revisionism: when David Edgar told TWU that only those who could speak the language of the enemy should take part in the National Theatre/RSC negotiations. History has shown the value of *not* speaking the language of the enemy. This is where the women's movement came in: the Personal is Political, the Local is Global. A butterfly fluttering in Latin America is said to have an impact on the rest of the world. But what happens when every faction flaps its wings? At a meeting in the Roundhouse a Peruvian Maoist waved his *Little Red Book*, trying to get the English to be more global. David Mercer growled and shouted: "Shut up!"

At all these meetings I never spoke; just listened, trying to make sense of it all.

My sons (left to right) Adam, Neuss, Finn, Jacob; Muswell Hill, London 1960s.
(Photo by Roger Mayne)

J.A. and me, 1960s. (Photo by Roger Mayne).

Released from Shillong Gaol, India, 1970. (Left to right) Jacob, J.A., Adam, me, Neuss, Finn.

Adam and family. L to R: Emily, Debra, Laura, Adam, Sydney, Australia

Neuss and karen.

Neuss and Karen's children; Craig holding Jade, Zak and Danha.

~~~o~~~

When J.A. went to London this summer I decided to be consistent and keep the diary every day he was away. This was broken when I heard about Karen in hospital and decided I would have to come over to England myself; her illness frightened the life out of me and it seemed as if the bottom of my world would have to undergo a fundamental change. In London it was impossible to continue with the diary. Finn's flat was too small and I was not familiar with his computer. I arrived in London Friday morning and left Wednesday morning. The weekend was spent with Karen (now out of hospital) and Neuss and the grandchildren. It now turned out that she wouldn't hear the results of her hospital tests for *a whole month*, and this was "because of the bank holiday." In the meanwhile all our lives had to be put on hold. Two extended families: Karen herself, Neuss and their four children, Karen's mother, her three brothers and their partners and children, J.A. and me, Neuss's three brothers and partners -- not counting the staff and children at Karen's nursery school.

Weeks after I'd got back to Ireland, we did hear the results of the tests -- All Clear! But my God, what an ordeal for all of us, and I'd been so upset that I got spasms in my leg and was crippled for two further months ... I had not realized how great the strain had been until my body told me.

Monday was spent visiting J.A.'s aunt, his godmother, aged 93, living in a sheltered home outside London, barely able to walk or see; she said she was tired of life, had a sharp sarcastic Yorkshire way of expressing herself, she didn't mind at all talking freely about how much she had hated her elder sister who had been in charge of all the younger sisters, (ten girls in all, plus J.A.'s father); she rarely saw her own father or mother; he was out all the time at meetings in Beverley; he ran a wine cellar and was one of the town worthies.

Round and round London, whizzing on the tops of buses. 137 past the Roundhouse, where we had left our mark now long scrubbed out. Arnold Wesker's dream, Centre 42: he showed us around his half-finished building. We asked him if we could produce *The Hero Rises Up* there; I think we were the first to put on a play in the building. Tony Richardson coming in during rehearsals, expecting J.A. to abandon the production and fly off to Australia to rewrite his old script of *Ned Kelly*.
~~~

Wood Green where we did our first agitprop play against Maggie Thatcher's milk-cuts, Maggie Thatcher Milk-Snatcher -- the W3 route, past Alexandra Palace where I worked with the theatre professionals of the Socialist Labour League, writing and acting for their big panoramic show, *100 Years of Labour History*, culminating in everyone's children (including my own) waving little red flags to a standing ovation from the packed audience of radical trade unionists. Past King's Cross and Unity Theatre: *Muggins is a Martyr,* where Tamara Hinchco played a stripper, a straight part which was also the first mobile nude to be seen on the London stage (the puritanical committee of Unity attempted unsuccessfully to axe her). There was an open-air extension to the play, not so much street-theatre as forecourt-theatre with Peter Bowles as MC in a white panama hat. Now it was all in the past, I am a parcel in transit. St. Martin's Lane, where I used to be with Valerie Hovenden's theatre club: exactly where it was has vanished from my mind because everything is so different now in that part of town. Peggy Ramsay's agency office in an alleyway running off St Martin's Lane, proud of the fact it used to be a brothel; now they are in very posh buildings in Wardour Street. The Almost Free theatre in Rupert Street. The Oval theatre, where I had my first job of reviewing plays, for the *New Statesman*; I compared a play by Howard Brenton (at the RSC) unfavourably with the dynamism of Gay Sweatshop's "deconstruction" of the Jeremy Thorpe attempted-murder trial and with the political immediacy of *The Man on the Blanket,* an open-air Republican play at the Derry Festival. The RSC made trouble for me over this; I was removed from the arts-pages. Poor John Caute, literary editor of the *NS*, was replaced shortly afterwards ... The Aldwych where J.A. and I mounted our stage-door picket in a back lane. Places and events I have written about before; but how many more have been purged from my memory?

All over London, some sort of theatrical work in draughty school halls (the World's End, Chelsea) and untenanted apartments, Oakley Street, also Chelsea, in a house all painted white inside (to hide the shoddiness of the junk furniture) so that it had the superficial appearance of an 18th-century bijou residence for a mistress.

On our final day in the capital; our eye was caught by an exciting-looking event at Battersea Arts Centre -- an "unfinished opera" called *Tell Me The News*; I assumed it would be based on the old newspaper-theatre format, bringing the day's happenings instantly on-stage. We tried to book tickets over the telephone time after time. We couldn't get past the answering-machine which told us to try another number which in turn sent us round in a circle to the first number all over again. We assumed there was something wrong with the phone and we should go down in person for the tickets. So off we went to Battersea. At the little box-office cubby-hole we found a young man leisurely trimming his nails; he had disconnected the switchboard. It looked as though he'd sat in that posture all morning. There was nobody else there, no queue or anything, no hustle or bustle, and no tickets. He just lifted his head and casually told us, "Sold Out." (No notice to say so.) It was one of the most unwelcoming and barren fronts-of-house I had ever encountered.

I had hoped at the Battersea Arts they might have taken pity on two aged pensioners travelling all the way from North London, having spent hours (let alone money) trying to book a ticket over the phone. But the young man was not to be moved; we looked the wrong sort anyway to be attending his way-out Cool Brit experimental theatre; after all, they were the flavour of the month after the transfer of their *Jerry Springer* show to the National. These arts centres in old council buildings or churches have their own ambience of dedication. The slight swagger of the young people swinging in and out, carrying folders and notebooks and bits of paper, stopping and chatting with their friends in that familiar manner which spells total exclusion for the onlooker. This is how we must have once appeared to our elders in the purlieus of the Royal Court. At Battersea, J.A. and I were the only outsiders. In the café, two men earnestly talking, heads close together, obviously some exciting theatre project; another couple of nonchalant young men having a break. All dark and dusty on the surface; but underneath, the creativity is beating away, pushing up its shoots. We had disappeared. Even J.A., "the king in exile," according to Michael Billington. We felt like any forgotten monarch. Yugoslavia? Romania? Bulgaria? Albania? Queer Balkan names. Zog. We were the forgotten. Successful special pleading might have allowed us the luxurious feeling we were part of something; we could have sat there that evening, enjoying being in the know. But even if we had lowered ourselves to give as a reference the forthcoming revival of *Serjeant Musgrave's Dance*, getting its management to intercede on our behalf, it would not have made any difference because rehearsals for *Musgrave* down the road (in the Community Centre) had not yet begun, and in any case Billington's article was not to appear in print for several weeks.

We travelled on a succession of buses -- 134 to Tottenham Court Road, then a 24; picking up a 159; then returning on a number 4 -- it was as though we had encompassed our whole London theatrical career, passing each point in our lives. Number 4 makes a really incredible journey, a route neither of us had ever taken in its entirety. Waterloo; over the bridge, looking out down the river; Blackfriars away to the right from Ludgate Circus, the Mermaid theatre. What if we had not refused (or rather if *I* had not refused) to meet the Queen at the first night of *Left-handed Liberty?* There was a funny story going the rounds at that time: the Queen was encouraged to invite artists to a special tea party; when Arden's name cropped up, a courtier at her side said, "Not this one, ma'am, he has hair. Yes ma'am, one of those hairy ones." A shudder. Hairy ones, long hair, lice, nits, fleas, goddam it! the palace would need a complete overhaul: think of the money, ma'am, cleaners, exterminators; the press might get hold of the story, *exterminators* coming through the palace? After the debacle of Christine Keeler, the Vassal case, pests alive? NO! In short, I reared up with all my republican atavistic memories -- I *am* a Republican; never could I bend the knee to the descendant of the Famine Queen. I don't think in fact it was quite so precisely principled ... Anyway, no invitation. Bernard Miles was furious and punished us by not giving us our expenses. Anyway, no title for J.A. (I remembered Matthew Smith and the usefulness of his knighthood.) If we could have swanned in, with all the magic of a title, would we not be sitting with everyone who is anyone out there in Battersea instead of on the top of a Number 4? On reflection, though, the new breed of theatre people at the Arts Centre would certainly be republican ...

Past Aldwych and the Law Courts -- libel! aiding and abetting the IRA, a henchwoman no less of the armed struggle. Safer ground as we go through Islington, passing Caryl Churchill's residence, sitting in her house at a meeting of TWU. Kings Cross. Selma, Wilmette, and the Women's Centre (nowadays Crossroads), against the feminist careerists who lobbied with their lies and back-stabbing to get the GLC to stop the Centre's funds, until finally the premises were lost. Like a salamander from the fire, they emerged undaunted and stronger in Kentish Town (not far from the same bus route): to mount a weekly picket at Westminster during the Iraq War, holding up the mirror of shame in front of the House of Commons as the jelly-kneed Blairites skulked in and out.

Holloway Road, passing Parkhurst Road and the prison. "Filthy poseuse and exhibitionist, Greenham ! -- in she goes, not forgetting a thorough roughing-up before we send her in." When the doctor and nurse come in for my initial examination to make sure I have no vermin and I'm not a drug addict -- "Excuse me, doctor. I want my arm examined, it is very sore and also my back," having been thrown down and the mattress pulled from under me, so I'd crashed onto the cell floor. A Wexford woman, the nurse, young, timid. She'll have a look. He briskly flicked his papers at her crotch -- a curiously familiar gesture to make, to flick a professional colleague's private parts. He grinned at her. I was holding my arm out. She was too far away to examine me. Instead, she meekly gave in, turning to the doctor: "I can see nothing." O little girl, what about the brave Wexford women of 1798? Where are they when you sleep? Will they not cry out to be remembered?

The next time I was gaoled in Holloway, I decided I wasn't going to cooperate with the strip-searching. Like a pack of hounds, the screws tore my clothes off and threw me into solitary. After a day or two, naked, refusing food, I had two visitors. The first was in the Irish Catholic mode. There was a light tap-tap on the hatch in the door. A sweet small voice calls out to me. I peer through the hatch and there is a little Irish nun holding a plate of scones. She says, "I have just baked them; wouldn't you like to try one?"

"I am on hunger strike. I'm protesting against strip-searching."

"Yes I know, it's terrible. Wouldn't you like to try just one?"

I say, "No. What I would like you to do is to give your opinion about strip-searching to the authorities." She crept away.

My second visitor: Joyce-Grenfell style Anglican deacon. A big grin at the hatch. I recognized her. Just before I was put into the prison, she had organized a meeting with the Kings Cross Women, about discrimination against women who wanted to be vicars in charge of parishes, at which I had spoken. When I told her we had met at this meeting, she denied it to my face. I then launched into my speech about torture and Amnesty International's denunciation of strip-searching. She got very uppity at my attitude. She said, "You are condescending and patronizing." She slammed down the hatch.

On we buzz through my history. The Sugán where Stephen Rea read his original role in the rewritten *Ballygombeen Bequest,* also Roger Sloman & John Joyce from the old 7:84 cast. All along the Holloway Road; upstairs in pubs, readings of the *Non-stop Connolly Show,* organized by ex-actor and Labour councillor Alex Farrell -- Ken Livingstone and Jeremy Corbyn re-enacting the Freedom of Speech action in late Victorian Dundee. Connolly's words planted everywhere. The turning to Camden Town and Chalk Farm -- my books and plays published there; now all out of print, oh cruel time! but when we were young, we too felt cock-a-hoop.

In the 1980s many thought we were not much more than a pair of drifting spectres, with our compilations of episodes from our Irish plays, *The Menace of Ireland* and *The Poisoned Stream*, welcomed in German and French universities by students thirsty for information about Ireland; whereas here in the imperialist fowlers'-net, our erstwhile colleagues stayed away. One well-known director, indeed a former director of J.A.'s plays, was heard to say (when asked if he would be attending any of the 14 parts of the *Non-stop Connolly Show* at the Almost Free), "It's a difficult decision to make; I might choose one of the boring parts." At the Half Moon we were however honoured by the presence of Judith Malina of the Living Theatre, which had been booted out of Brazil. Its impact is now largely forgotten by callous up-to-speed youths unaware that their gaps in theatre-knowledge are placed there deliberately, part and parcel of the corporate New World Order (Cultural Division).

~~~o~~~

The Living Theatre had an enormous influence in its day. In my home in Galway I have been presenting "In-house Experiences" as alternatives to the events of the mainstream Galway Arts Festival. In 2003 the In-house was based on theatre, using my collection of archival, poster, radio and video material. It included a play-reading programme of radical plays from the sixties; one of them was the Living Theatre's *The Legacy of Cain*, written for Brazil, and read in conjunction with an interview in *Performance* magazine (December 1971) with Judith Malina and Julian Beck.
~~~

MALINA:

... the word "romantic." It has a lot to do with optimism, with the possibility of a happy ending or the possibility of virtue being rewarded. Now the real revolutionary problem is very closely integrated with problems of pessimism and optimism. Whether you're cheerful or not is practically the key to your potential effectiveness. It's not a question of happiness -- you can be very gloomy and at the same time have strong faith in the romantic notion that what is good and what is beautiful and what is right and what should be loved is going in the end to be stronger than the forces of evil, to prevail. When we talk about revolutionary change coming from the people and not from a group of theoreticians, when we present the idea of people being able to find and sustain the means to create a world better than the world that has been created by an élite, when we express this belief in a revolution that's not just a violent shift from one authoritarian to another authoritarian group, but really turns all that around -- then the thing we need most is that the people believe this is possible.

BECK:

... We are doing our kind of theater because we want people to be more able to feel and thus more able to take a moral position, but at the same time we're saying to people that they must not only encompass a new moral position but take some kind of action to support it.

I hadn't until then realized how much of the spirit of the Living Theatre had gone into the shaping and production of *The Non-Stop Connolly Show*, particularly the way in which we broke up that long epic into a series of short interlocking sequences which could be taken out of it and presented separately, in the street, market-places, outside churches or in small halls or public houses. Because of the political situation -- internecine assassinations within the Republican movement, to say nothing of the bombings, the British Army, and the Loyalist killers -- some of our actors cried off at the last moment before travelling into the 6 Counties. So we had to ask for members of the audiences to read scripts and fill the gap. From then on, all the rules of regular theatre were out-of-window and Loose Theatre was the only way forward. In England, too, Loose Theatre became a requisite because of the number of bomb-scares intimidating actors and managements.

Before the Living Theatre went to Brazil they played in Dublin. After the show they asked the audience to accompany them to protest against the treatment of prisoners in Mountjoy Prison. This was a novelty for Dublin, but in fact they had always asked for participation by the audience in some sort of radical act to close the gap between pretend theatre inside and real theatre outside. They also wished to inspire the audience to see state institutions as theatre -- the military, the law courts, the gaols, the churches, the hospitals -- a dehumanizing theatre based upon hierarchy and imposing acquiescent roles upon everyone who becomes involved. Hence I see the Greenham struggle as consistently including large elements of Loose Theatre.

This was brought home to me when I attended one of the United Nations educational seminars in Galway University. Dick Spring, leader of the Labour Party and Minister of Foreign Affairs, was the main speaker. He kept referring to "actors" or "active players" on the world scene. I asked, "Who's the playwright?" and was met with an embarrassed silence. My group, Women in Media & Entertainment, has consultative status at the UN (thanks to our connection with the "Women Count" international network). When I went to the 4th UN Women's Conference at Beijing in 1995, I suddenly realized Dick Spring had failed to mention the most important aspect of UN procedure at such conferences, the resolutions. These often begin with grassroots groups, as it were playwrights drafting a script, issuing leaflets on the street, collecting signatures, and so forth, with many different theatre techniques to engage the public and turn them into participants. Once engaged, the participants bring the script to wider and wider organizations and lobby-groups, local, regional, national, until finally the finished script is brought up at the UN General Assembly as the final script, where it will be voted upon. If passed -- *in theory*, the world will take it on as agreed policy, binding upon all the nations. In practice, the most powerful countries can put a stop to anyone's play in favour of their own.

To give an example: there was a resolution at Beijing, emerging from grass-root NGOs, to eliminate all Weapons of Mass Destruction. The EU (one person representing the bloc) got up and said, "This is ridiculous; it is too simplistic." But it had to be voted on. Every bloc and country voted in support of the resolution, even those countries that owned or were building their own WMD: except for the EU, the USA, and Israel, who voted against. Now here is the UN as a truly theatrical arena, *if* one understands "theatre" as meaning a "public pretence." There are two ways of looking at the final dramatic offering. They do not necessarily contradict one another:

1) Cynical. Countries with their own WMD voted for the resolution for propaganda purposes, knowing full well that it would fail.
2) Idealistic. There is a genuine worldwide movement to get governments to disarm and to use the resources of the world to feed the world. The poor countries voted for elimination of WMD, the rich countries did not.

By contrast, our resolution (brought forward by the "Women Count" network) got through: --

> ... to measure and value the unwaged work women do -- in the home, on the land, in family businesses, and in the community, including volunteer work -- for inclusion in a satellite account of the Gross Domestic Product.

If this were to be properly implemented, the vast redistribution of wealth inevitably involved would automatically eliminate WMD because no nation would be able to afford them ... The USA and the EU had to be dragged kicking and screaming to vote in favour, for otherwise they would have been labelled racist -- most of the unwaged work being done in the undeveloped world. This success opened the way for further Loose Theatre, in the shape of the Global Women's Strike which now involves, every year, women in more than seventy countries with their own theatrical manifestations on the theme of "Invest in Caring not Killing: End all Wars!".

The idea of the Global Strike, first germinated on Radio Pirate-Woman in 1998, was to call on the National Women's Council of Ireland to mark the year 2000 with a national strike of women (for the valuation of unwaged work) which could be linked up internationally. This was adopted, endorsed and enlarged by Selma James and Crossroads, and launched at the UN in the millennium year.

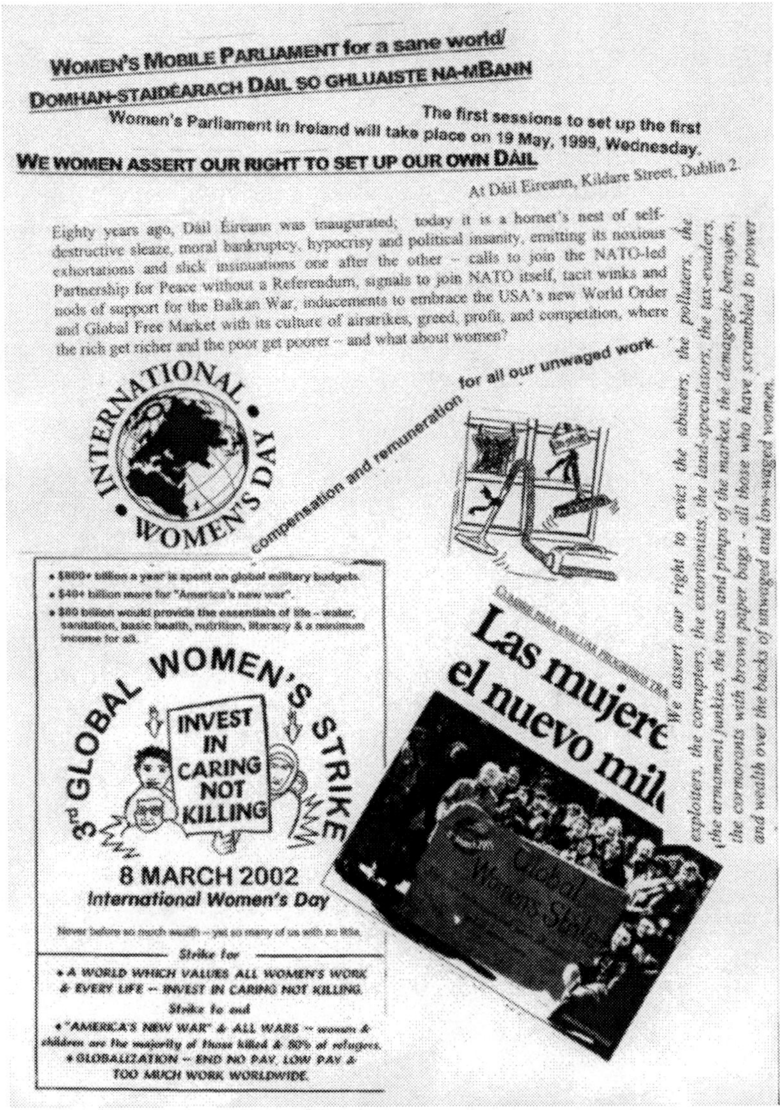

Collage; Global Women's Strike.

EPILOGUE

Journey across London on last day of my visit (Wednesday 4 Sept 2003) to catch the cross-channel bus for Galway at Victoria Coach Station. We got onto the Victoria Line tube, only to be held up at Green Park. The stoppage looked as though it might be terminal. We left the train, thinking we had plenty of time to catch a bus to the coach station from Piccadilly. We hopped onto one labelled Sloane Square, because I thought I remembered there was a bus that arrived at the coach station having gone round by Knightsbridge and Sloane Square. I also thought it would complete my London experience with a swift sight of the Royal Court. No sooner were we aboard than the conductor told us, no! it wouldn't, not his route.

We nearly got ourselves killed at the traffic lights jumping from the bus and setting off at a run all the way to the coach station. We cut down near Belgrave Square where J.A. had his first job, with Ronald Ward & Partners, architects: the firm's main claim to fame (as artists) was the Millbank Tower, and (as a business consortium) the National Farmers' Union in Knightsbridge, a disgusting neo-georgian building of plutocratic pretensions ... So no opportunity for last-minute reminiscences of acting in *Live Like Pigs* -- or understudying in *Major Barbara,* when I shared a dressing room with Vanessa Redgrave; looking into the mirror, she said gravely that she thought nothing could be worse than growing old and losing her looks.

LOOSE THEATRE INDEX

Note
Items are indexed by chapters.
Chapter 12 is subdivided [a] Diary & [b] Neighbours' Voices.
Chapter 20 is subdivided chronologically [a] 1986, [b] 1987 & [c] 1988, '91, '92.

Abbey Theatre, fire: 5.
Abrahamson, Elizabeth: 20c.
Actors' Equity trade union: 11.
Ada: 5.
Adams, Abigail: 20c.
Adams, Gerry: 20c.
Adbury Park: 20c.
Afghanistan: 1, 20c.
Africa: 2.
Aggie (at Armthorpe): 21.
Ahern, Bertie: 17.
Alaska: 20a.
Aldermaston: 20a, 20c.
Alexandra College, Dublin: 5.
Alexandra Palace: 13, 23.
Aldwych Theatre: 11, 23.
Algeria: 2, 11.
Ali: 5.
Allende, President: 4.
Allison (Greenham Woman): 20a, 20c.
Almond (at Gateshead): 22.
Ambience (Almost-Free) Theatre: 11, 12a, 23.
Amnesty International: 23.
An Phoblacht/Republican News: 14, 20c.
Anarchy: 11.

Anderson, Jimmy: 11.
Anderson, Lindsay: 11.
Andrew (in Belfast): 14.
Andrews, David: 11.
Angela (Doherty): 12b.
Angry Brigade: 23.
Aniko (Greenham Woman): 20c.
Animal Lib. Front: 20c.
Ann (Ward): 12b.
Anthea: 6.
Anouilh, Jean, Ring Round the Moon: 7.
Ant Action: 20a.
Aosdana: Introduction, 18, 19, 20a.
Apartheid & S. Africa: 5, 20c.
Arab Detainees: 22.
Arden, John (J.A.): Introduction, 2, 3, 4, 5, 6, 7, 8, 9, 10, 11, 12a, 13, 16, 17, 18, 20a, 20b, 20c, 21, 22, 23, Epilogue.
Works: --
Armstrong's Last Goodnight: 6.
Don Quixote adaptation: 7.
Left-Handed Liberty: 11, 23.
Live Like Pigs: 5, 11, Epilogue.
Ned Kelly filmscript: 11, 23.
Serjeant Musgrave's Dance: 7, 8, 11, 13, 23.
Soldier Soldier: 7.
Silence Among The Weapons: 18.
Waters Of Babylon, The: 8, 9, 11.
Wet Fish: 11.
Workhouse Donkey, The: 7, 11.
Arden, Adam, 11, 20a.
Arden, Charles (J.A.'s father): 9, 11.
Arden, Finn: 11, 12a, 17, 20a, 22, 23.
Arden, Gwalchmei Francis: 9, 10, 11.
Arden, Jacob: 3, 11, 12a, 20a.
Arden, Karen (nee Stokes): 2, 23.
Arden, Nancy, nee Layland (J.A.'s mother): 9.
Arden, Neuss: 2, 12a, 20a, 21.

Arden family in general: 9, 23.
Armagh: 2.
Armagh Gaol: 2, 14, 20a.
Armthorpe, Yorkshire: Introduction, 21.
Arrowsmith, Pat: 20a, 20c, 23.
Arts Council (Ireland): 12a, 18, 19.
Arts Council (N. Ireland): 14.
Arts Theatre: 8.
Aronson, Jack: 6.
Ard Feis (Provo. Sinn Fein): 12a.
Arthur (husband of M.D'A's aunt Esther): 5.
Asian Immigrants in UK: 2, 23.
Ascot: 20a.
Assam: 11.
Attlee, Clement: 7.
Aukin, David: 13.
Aula Maxima, Uni. Coll,, Galway: 12a.
Austin, Tom: 8, 11.
Australia: 23.
Austria (& Emperor of): 2.
Avoca School, Blackrock: 3.
Avila: 16.
Aylesbury: 20c.

Bach: 4.
Bacon, Francis: 8.
Baha'i faith: 12b.
Bailiffs: 20a, 20b.
Baka-el-Garbiya, Israel (clinic for Jews & Arabs): 2.
Ballinasloe Mental Hospital: 12b.
Baptism, 1st Communion, Confirmation & Sacraments in general: 4.
Barker, Howard: 17.
Barleycove, Co. Cork: 3.
Barnes, Monica: 20a.
Barnsley: 8, 9.
Barstow, Stan: 11.
Basel: 20c.

"Bathsheba" (in The Waters of Babylon): 8.
Battersea Arts Centre: 23.
Battersea Community Centre: 23.
Battle of the Bogside: 2.
BBC: 11, 15, 20a, 20b, 21.
BBC Northern Ireland: 20c.
BBC World Service: 20c.
Beaford Arts Centre: 11.
Beauvoir, Simone de, 6. Also, The Second Sex: 5
Beck, Julian: 23.
Bee (Greenham Woman): 20c.
Beer, Clem: 11.
Beer, Valerie: 11.
Behan, Brendan, 6. Also, The Twisting of Another Rope aka The Quare Fellow: 6.
Behan, Dominic: 6.
Beijing: 23.
Beijing, "Forbidden City": 3.
Beckett, John: 6, 8.
Beckett, Samuel: 6, 8, 11. Also, Murphy (novel): 6; Waiting for Godot: 8.
Belfast: Introduction, 14, 23.
Bell, The: 2, 5, 6.
Benn, Tony: 20a.
Bennett, Louie: 2, 3, 4, 6.
Bentley, Eric, The Playwright as Thinker: 5.
Berit Shalom: 2.
Berk, Lotte: 8.
Berman, Ed: 12a.
Berman's (wigs): 7.
Bernhardt, Sarah: 5.
Bertram Mills Circus: 8.
Beverley: 9, 23.
Bible (quotes): 5.
Billig, Arthur (M.D'A's uncle, died aged 13): 2, 3.
Billig, Barnet (M.D'A's grandfather): 2, 3.
Billig, David (M.D'A's uncle): 2, 3, 5.
Billig, Esther (M.D'A's aunt): 2, 5.
Billig, Hannah (M.D'A's aunt): 2, 3, 5.

Billig, Levi (M.D'A's uncle): 2.
Billig, Millie (M.D'A's grandmother): 2.
Billig, Mina (M.D'A's great-aunt): 2.
Billig, Rebecca (M.D'A's aunt): 2, 3.
Billig, Rossi (wife of David Billig): 5.
Birmingham 6: 20a, 22.
Bi-carbonate: 20b.
Bihar, India: 4.
Billington, Michael: 23.
Birrell, Peter: 11.
Birtwhistle, John: 12a.
Bjornson, Bjornsterne: 6.
"Blackmouth", Robert Shaw as (in Live Like Pigs): 11.
Blairites, jelly-kneed: 23.
Blake, George: 4.
Bloody Sunday etc., 1972: 11.
Blossom Time (film): 4.
Boer War: 9, 20c.
Bogarde, Dirk, & Mai Zetterling, in Point of Departure: 5.
Bolt, Robert: 11.
Bolton: 8.
Bond, Edward & The Bundle: 13.
Boot, Mr.: 13.
Bowles, Peter: 23.
Boy Friend, The (musical): 7.
Boycott, Rosie: 20b.
Bradell, Jocelyn: 8.
Brady, Mary: 5.
Bray, co Wicklow: 5, 6.
Bradley, Alfred: 3, 11.
Bramble, Wilfred (in Steptoe & Son): 7.
Brazil: 23.
Brecht, Berthold 5.
Brennan, Maeve (and family): 3.
Breffny, Brian de, Irish Family Names: 2.
Brent Knoll: 11.
Brenton, Howard: 23.

Brick Lane, London: 2, 21.
Bridget: 6.
Bristol: 11.
Brig, The (play): 11.
Brighton, Pam: 13.
British Film Institute: 11.
Broe, Irene: 6.
Brooks, Jeremy: 13.
Brooks, Louise (in Pandora's Box, film): 6.
Brontes, the: 8.
Brophy, Bridget: 13.
Brown, Ivor: 11.
Brown, Wilmette: Introduction, 20a, 20c, 23.
Browne, Dr Noel: 5, 6.
Bruce Castle Museum: 13.
Buchanan, Mr & Mrs George: 2.
Buggs, John: 20b.
Burge, Stuart: 7, 13.
Burgess, Christopher: 7.
Burgess, Commander: 12a, 13.
Burgess Hill: 8.
Burghfield: 20a, 20c.
Burke, Alfie: 7.
Buskers: 5, 19.
Butler, Hubert: 2.
Byatt, George: 13.
Bylaw litigation, Newbury: 20b, 20c.
Byrne, Gay: 12b.
Byrne, Paula: 5.

"C" (M.D'A's friend): 3.
Cabra Convent, Dublin: 3, 4.
Cable Street, London: 2, 5.
Caine, Michael: 11.
Cambridge University: 2.
Camden Council: 20b, 20c.
Camden Women: 20b.

Campbell, Diana: 6.
Campbell, Ken: 23.
Camus: 11.
Canary Wharf: 17.
Canetti: 8. Also, Auto De Fe (novel): 7.
Capon, Eric: 5.
Cardenal, Fr. Ernesto: 19.
Cardiff: 20c.
Carey, May: 6.
Carey, Denis: 6.
Carol (Greenham Woman): 20a.
Carr, Andy: 13.
Carroll, John: 18.
Carshalton (hospital): 10.
Carter, Esta: 20a.
Cartoon Archetypical Slogan Theatre: 11.
Cassandra (novel): 20c.
Cassin, Barry: 6.
Casson, Christopher: 5.
Castlereagh Interrogation Centre, Belfast: 21.
Carraroe, Connemara, Co Galway: 3.
Castle, Barbara: 23.
Catherine (Greenham Woman): 20c.
Catherine of Siena, Saint: 4.
Catholicism: 2, 3, 4, 5, 6, 11, 23.
Caute, David (John): 23.
Centre 42: 23.
Chapman, The Revenge of Bussy d'Ambois: 8.
Chatto, Tom: 7.
Chelsea Barracks: 13.
Chelsea Cloisters: 8.
Chenevix, Helen: 2, 6.
Cheryl & Mike (Muswell Hill): 23.
Chichester: 8.
Childbirth: 9.
Chris (Greenham): 20c.
Churchill, Caryl: 13, 23.

Cindy (Drew): 12b.
Citizens' Advice Bureau: 9.
City Limits: 20b.
Civil Service, Irish: 2.
Civil War (Irish): 2, 3
Claire (Greenham Woman): 20c.
Clann na Poblachta: 5.
Clarke, Austin: 6.
Clarke, Tom: 14.
"Cleanmaster" company: 20c.
CND: 20a.
CND AGM: 20b.
CND Executive: 20a.
Cnuas (Arts Council grant): 18, 19.
Cobey, Pat: 12a, 13.
Cohen, Barbara: 20c.
Cohen, Mrs: 3.
Cold War: 2, 11.
Colindale newspaper library: 13.
College of Surgeons, Dublin; 4, 6.
Collins, Paddy: 6.
Collis, Dr Robert: 3,
Committee of 100: 4, 11.
Commoners' Rights: 20c.
Communist Party: 11, 17, 20b, 23.
Conditions of Employment Bill (Ireland): 3.
Connacht Tribune: 11.
Connaughton, Shane: 13.
Connemara: 20c.
Connie (at Gateshead): 22.
Connolly Association: 23.
Convention (N. Ireland): 12a.
Convoy (Cruise Missile): 20c.
Cookham: 20c.
Coogan, Tim Pat: 12a.
Corbett, Mrs: 5.
Corbyn, Jeremy: 23.

Corrandulla, Co. Galway: 2, 3, 11, 12a, 12b, 13, 18.
Corrandulla Arts & Entertainment: 11.
Corrib, Loch, Co Galway (& island): 3, 11.
Coughlan, Dorothea: 5.
Coughlan, Maureen: 5.
Country Shop, Dublin: 3.
Coward, Noel: 5. Also, Private Lives: 7.
Coyle, Marion: 12a.
Cracow, Poland: 4.
Craig, Gordon: 8.
Creag, Barbara: 13.
Creep Shadow Creep (play): 8.
Cregg Castle, Co Galway (& Blake family): 12b.
Cribbens, Bernard (in The Railway Children; Don Quxote): 7.
Croatia: 20c.
Cronin, Anthony: 6, 19.
Crown factory strike: 12a.
Cruise O'Brien, Conor, 12a, 13. Also, The Siege: 2.
Cruise Missiles: 20a, 20b, 20c.
Cruisewatch (& men in it): 20a, 20c.
Cuba: 11, 12a.
Cusack, Ralph: 6.
Custom House, Dublin (destruction of): 2, 3.
Cuthbertson, Iain: 6.
Cypriots (Greek, Turkish) in London: 23.

Dace, Tish: 13.
Dad's Army: 12a.
Dalton, Audrey: 5.
Daly, James: 14.
Daly, Mary, Gyn/Ecology, The Metaethics of Radical Feminism: 20a.
Daly, Miriam: 14, 20a, 20c.
Daniel (at Armthorpe): 21.
Dane, Clemence, Granite: 6.
Dara (Greenham Woman): 20a.
D'Arc, Jeanne: 17.
D'Arcy, Cecil: 6.

D'Arcy, Eddie (M.D'A's uncle): 2, 3.
D'Arcy, Joseph Noel (M.D'A's father): 2, 3, 4, 5, 6, 11.
D'Arcy, Margaretta (works): --
Circus Expose of the New Cultural Church (film): 19.
Pinprick of History, A: 2, 11, 13
Tell Them Everything: 2, 14.
Agitprop etc. (D'Arcy + group authorship): --
Galway's Pirate Women, a Global Trawl: 19.
Hunting of the Mongrel Fox, The: 14.
Improvised Rough Theatre: 2.
In-House Experiences: 23.
Little Red Riding Hood & Granny Welfare: 5.
My Old Man's a Tory: 5.
Mary's Name: 14.
Muggins is a Martyr: 11, 23.
One Hundred Years of Labour History: 23.
Unfulfilled Dream, The (film): 11.
D'Arcy/Arden or Arden/D'Arcy (collaborative works): --
Ars Longa Vita Brevis: 11.
Awkward Corners (incl. "Power to the Sisters", article): 20b.
Ballygombeen Bequest, The: 2, 11, 12a, 13, 23.
Business of Good Government, The: 11.
Happy Haven, The: 11.
Hero Rises Up, The: 11, 23.
Island of the Mighty, The: 8, 11.
Manchester Enthusiasts, The, aka The Ralahine Experiment: 11, 15.
Menace Of Ireland, The: 23.
Non-Stop Connolly Show, The: 2, 4, 11, 12a, 13, 23. Also, Play 4: 12a.
Poisoned Stream, The: 23.
Royal Pardon, The: 11.
State of Shock (filmscript): 15.
Suburban Suicide, A: 21.
Top Deck (filmscript): 11.
Vandaleur's Folly: 2, 11, 13, 14.
Whose Is The Kingdom?: 2, 15, 20a, 20b
D'Arcy, Miriam (aka Marie), nee Billig (M.D'A's mother): 2, 3, 4, 5, 6, 7, 8, 9, 10, 12a.
D'Arcys (M.D'A's father's family, first names not known): 2.

D'Arcys (aristos, 18th cent): 2.
Death: --
Helen Thomas: 20c.
Mike's wife (Armthorpe): 21.
M.D'A's father: 3
M.D'A's mother: 3.
M.D'A's son Gwalchmei: 10.
Deep Are The Roots (play): 7.
Delaney, Colette: 2, 6.
Delaney, Pauline: 6.
Delors, Jacques: 17.
Demuth, Freddy (son of K. Marx): 17.
Deux Magots, Les: 11.
deValera, Eamon: 3, 5.
Devine, George: 7, 8, 11.
Devizes Court: 20c.
Dewsbury women: 20a.
Dickens, Charles: 2,
Digital (factory): 12a
Dijon: 17.
Dike, Taggart: 13.
Dillon, James: 4.
Dillon, Maeve: 4.
Divorce (Irish attitudes to): 12a.
Dobson, Mrs: 11.
Dodimead, David: 7.
Doherty, Terry: 13.
Dominican Order: 3, 4.
Donna (Greenham Woman): 20a.
Dostoievsky, Crime & Punishment: 4.
Downing Street: 13.
Downpatrick, Co. Down: 4, 11.
Drumm, Maire: 20c.
Dublin: 2, 3, 4, 5, 6, 7, 11, 23.
Dublin, bars & restaurants (the Bailey, Davy Byrne's, Jammet's, McDaid's): 5, 6.
Dukes, Ashley, The Man with a Load of Mischief: 6.
Duffy, Maureen: 13.

du Maurier, Trilby: 6.
Duncan, Isidora: 8.
Duncan, Ronald: 11.
Dundy, Elaine: 11.
Duse, Eleanor: 5.

Earls Court: 8.
Easter Rising (1916): 2.
Economic War: 3.
Edgar, David: 13, 23. Also, Destiny: 13.
Edinburgh: 8, 20c.
Edinburgh School of Art: 20c.
Edwards, Hilton: 3, 4, 6.
Edwell, Lynette: 20c.
Egypt: 6.
El Cid (film): 22.
Elizabeth II, Queen: 8, 23.
Ellie (Greenham Woman): 20c.
Emma (Greenham Woman): 20c.
Encore: 11.
"Enemies List" at Yellow Gate: 20c.
English Stage Company: 8.
Envoy: 5, 6.
Erika (Greenham Woman): 20a.
Essex University: 20a.
Esslin, Martin: 11.
European Common Market, aka EEC: 12b, 17, 23.
Evans, Graham: 11.
Extradition Act: 20b.
Eyre Square, Galway: 13.
Ewart Biggs (ambassador): 13.

Fahy, Brid: 12a.
Fahy eviction: 11.
Fahy, Mrs: 12b
Famine, the Great: 3.
Famine Queen, the (Victoria): 23.

Farrell, Alex: 23.
Farrell, Mairead: 20c.
Feiffer, Jules: 11.
Feminist Theatre, Spanish: 16.
Feydeau, Look After Lulu: 11.
Fianna Fail party: 2, 12a.
FIBUA (Fighting in Built-up Areas) mock village: 20c.
Fine Gael party: 2.
Finland: 20c.
Finnegan, Honor: 20c.
Fitzgerald, Barry (in The Quiet Man): 6.
"Fitzsean, Siobhán" & her father: 4.
Fitzwilliam St., Dublin (flat): 6.
Flame magazine: 20c.
Fleischmann, George: 6.
Flynn, Mrs: 4.
Foco Novo (theatre company): 13.
Foley, Don: 13.
Food Run (Greenham), aka Meals on Wheels, aka the Dinner Ladies: 20a, 20c.
Food, vegetarian: 20b.
Forbes-Robertson, Jean: 5.
Forrest Gump (film): 2.
France: Introduction, 17.
Frances (Greenham Woman): 20c.
Franco, Generalissimo: 12a.
Fraser, Ronald: 8.
Fred (at Greenham): 20c.:
Freedom: 11.
Freedom from Unwieldy Bureaucracy: 19.
Freedom of Information: 19.
Freedom of Speech: 14.
Freeman, Hector: 8,
Free Market in USSR: 20c.
"French Pub", the: 8.
Freud, Lucien: 6.
Frier, Michael: 6.
Friel, Brian: 6.

Friends' House, Newbury: 20a, 20c.
Fry, Christopher, The Lady's Not For Burning: 7.
Fuchs, Anneliese (& her father): 5.
Fulham (hospital): 10.
Full Sutton: 11.
Full Sutton Gaol: 22.

Gaitskell, Hugh: 11.
Gallagher, Eddie: 12a.
Galvin, Patrick, Do It For Love: 14.
Galway Arts Festival: 23.
Galway, city & county: 3, 6, 11, 18, Epilogue.
Galway corporation: 12b.
Galway Theatre Workshop: 11, 12a, 14.
Galway Women in Entertainment: 18, 20a.
Gandhi: 11.
Garda Siochana: 1, 3, 5, 6, 11.
Gardner, Ava: 6, 12a.
Garrick, The Seraglio: 8.
"Garry Ard" (house): 3, 5, 6.
Gaskill, William: 11.
Gateshead, Co. Durham: Introduction, 22.
Gate Theatre, Dublin: 3, 5.
Also plays at, Mrs Warren's Profession; The Seagull; The Recruiting Officer: 5.
Gay Sweatshop theatre conmpany: 23.
GCHQ, Cheltenham: 21.
Gems, Pam: 13.
General Strike, 1926: 21.
Genocide Act: 20c.
George and Margaret (play): 6.
Germany: 20c.
"Gerry Ryan Show" (radio): 12b.
Ghaddafi, Colonel: 20a.
Gibbon, John: 6.
Gibbon, Paul: 20c.
Gielgud, John: 7.
Gifford, Lord: 20c.

Gilbert & Sullivan: 5.
"Gladys" (converted ambulance): 20a, 20c.
Glastonbury: 20c.
Global Resistance: 2.
Global Women's Strike: 23.
Goddess: 20a.
"Gods, The": 5.
Godmother (J.A.'s): 23.
Goertz, Capt. Hermann: 3.
Goldring, Maurice: 17.
Goldsmith, Oliver: 2,
Gompers: 12a.
Gooch, Steve: 13.
Good Friday Agreement (1998): 2, 6.
Goodman Derrick (solicitors): 13.
Gorbachev: 20b, 20c.
Gough, Michael: 7.
Goulding, Cathal: 11.
Graham (at Greenham): 20c.
Graham, Billy: 20c.
Granada TV: 7.
Grandchildren (M.D'A's): 2, 23.
Granny Grogan: 20c.
Graves, Robert, The White Goddess: 8.
Gray, Joe: 20c.
Gray, Lisa: 20c.
Greece: 5, 13.
Greek Writers' Union: 13.
Green Cinema, Dublin (& Kitty's subterfuges): 4.
Greenham Common: 20a.
Greenham Common "Commemorative & Historic Site": 20c.
Greenham Common (Women's Peace Camp): Introduction, 3, 5, 20a, 20b, 20c, 21, 23.
  Newsletter: 20c.
  Gates: --
    Blue: 20a, 20c.
    Emerald: 20c.
    Green: 20a, 20c.

Jade: 20a.
Indigo: 20a.
Orange: 20a.
Yellow: Introduction, 20a, 20b, 20c.
Greenham, internal politics: 20a, 20b, 20c.
Greenham Missile Base Perimeter Fence taken down: 20c.
Greenham Split, the: 20b.
"Greenham Women Everywhere": 20b, 20c.
Greenville Rd., Blackrock, Dublin: 3.
Griffiths, Mrs: 9.
Grunwick strike: 13.
Guardian, The: 20a.
Gulf War: 22.
Guildford 4: 20a.
Gurkha regiment: 20a
Guy (Bee's partner): 20c.

"Hacking Guide": 20b.
Hackney Empire Theatre: 11.
Half Moon theatre: 13, 23.
Hall, Peter: 8.
Halligan, Maureen: 5.
Halliwell, David: 13.
Hamlet (version at Dijon): 17.
Hampstead Garden Suburb: 2,
Hanbury Street, London: 2.
Hares (& Hare House): 20c.
Hare, David: 13.
Hamburg Women's Fair: 20b.
Harold (dancer): 8.
Harold (at Gateshead): 22.
Harringay Irish Association: 23.
Harris, Eoghan: 12a.
Hartley, Isobel: 4.
Hartley, Tom: 14.
Hassan, King: 12a.
Hastings, Michael: 11, 23.

Haughey, Charles J.: 19.
Havel, Vaclav: 14.
Haworth: 8.
Hayman, Joan: 20c.
Hayman, Ronald: 20a.
Hazel (Greenham Woman): 20a, 20c.
H-Blocks (& hunger strike): 14, 15.
H-Block/Armagh prisoners: 21.
Heath, Edward: 11.
Hebrew (language): 2.
Hebrew University, Israel: 2,
Helen: 12a.
Hemingway, The Killers: 5.
Henrietta (Greenham Woman): 20c.
Henrietta St., Dublin: 2.
Henry V (film): 6.
Henry, Paul & Gladys Young: 3.
Henshaw, Michael: 13.
Hepburn, Katherine (in The Millionairess): 7
Herbert, A.P., The Water Gipsies: 5.
Heron, Hilary: 6.
Herrema, Dr.: 12a.
Herrema, Mrs: 12a.
Herzl, Theodor: 2.
Higgins, Aidan: 6, 7. Also, Langrishe Go Down: 6.
Higgins, Jill: 6.
Hinchco, Tamara: 11, 23.
Hipperson, Sarah: Introduction, 20a, 20b, 20c.
Hiroshima: 20c.
Hitler, Adolf: 2, 3, 5.
Hobson, Harold, Theatre; Theatre 2: 5.
Hogan, Des: 12a, 13.
Holden, David: 13.
Holland, Mary: 13.
Holloway Gaol: 20a, 20c, 21, 23.
Holroyd, Stuart: 11.
Homosexuality: 5, 7.

Hone, Evie: 6.
Hooper, David: 20b.
Hope, Peter: 5.
Hopkin, Mary: 23.
Hone, Rosemary (M.D'A's sister): 3, 4, 5.
Hornchurch (& Repertory Company): 5, 7, 8, 11.
Horovitz, Michael: 2.
Hovenden, Valerie: 5, 8, 23.
Howarth, Bert: 11.
Howarth, Donald: 11.
Howard, Edie: 6.
Howse, Katrina: Introduction, 20a, 20b, 20c, 21.
Hoyland, John: 13.
Hubbard, L. Ron: 20c.
Hull: 8.
Hume, John: 12a.
Hungary: 11.
Husband, Mrs: 11, 22.
Husson, Albert, We're No Angels: 8.
Hutchinson, Jean: Introduction, 20b, 20c.
Huxham, Ken: 6.
Hyndman, Dave: 19.

Ibbs, Ronald: 5.
Ibsen, Hendrik, Hedda Gabler: 5. Little Eyolf: 2.
Illsley, Stanley: 4.
Imber (deserted village): 17, 20c.
Imber church: 17, 20c.
Imison, Richard: 15.
Independent, The (London): 17.
Independent Labour Party (ILP): 20c.
India: 3, 4, 5, 11, 20c, 23.
Indiana: 12a.
Industrial Development Authority: 12b.
Inismaan (Aran Is,): 6.
Intermediate Nuclear Forces agreement (INF): 20b, 20c.
International Anti-Imperialist Conference: 20a.

International Marxist Group: 11.
International Socialists (aka Socialist Workers' Party): 11, 22, 23.
International Tribunal on Britain in Ireland: 13, 23.
International Year of the Peace: 20b.
Internment in Ireland: 11.
Invisible Woman (film): 4.
Ionesco: 8.
IRAs: 2, 3, 6, 11, 12a, 17, 20a, 20c, 23.
Iraq: 1, 22, 23.
Irish Association: 2.
Irish Arts Council: Introduction,
Irish Censorship Board & censorship in general: 3, 4.
Irish Citizen, The: 3,
Irish Congress of Trade Unions: 3, 18.
Irish Constitution: 3.
Irish Dept. of Agriculture: 3.
Irish Dept. of External Affairs: 2.
Irish Dept. of Local Government: 2.
Irish Dept. of the Environment: 2.
Irish Free State (later, Republic): 2.
Irish Housewives' Assoc.: 3.
Irish in London: 23.
Irish Land Commission: 2.
Irish (language): 2.
Irish Post, The: 20a.
Irish Republicanism: 2.
Irish Times, The: 12a, 14, 20b.
Irish Women Workers' Union: 2, 3.
Irish Women Citizens Association: 3.
Irish Women United: 3.
Irving, Henry, Sir: 7, 8.
Isobel (Newbury): 20c.
I Spy a Dark Stranger (film): 6.
Israel: 2, 5, 23.
ITGWU: 12a, 12b.
Itzin, Cathy: 13.
Ivimey, Albert: 12a, 23.

Ivimey, Wilma: 12a, 23.

James (at Greenham): 20c.
James, Selma: Introduction, 20a, 23.
Jane (Greenham Woman): 20c.
Jean (at Armthorpe): 21.
Jellicoe, Ann: 11.
Jenkins, Noel: 13.
Jenny Donkey (Greenham Woman): 20c.
Jenny Silver Moon (Greenham Woman): 20c.
Jeremy Thorpe Trial (play): 23.
Jerry (at Gateshead): 22.
Jerry Springer Show (musical): 23
Jews (in Russia, Austria, England): 2, 5, 9.
Jews (in Ireland): 3, 4.
Joan (Greenham Woman): 20c.
John (at Armthorpe): 21.
Johns, Helen: 20a.
Johnson, Des: 12a.
Johnson, Neville: 6.
Johnson, Rebecca: 20a.
Johnstone, Keith: 11. Also, Brixham Regatta: 11.
Jones, Linda: 20c.
Joyce, James: 4, 18. Also, Dubliners: 2.
Joyce, John: 12a, 13, 23.
Joyce, Tom: 11.
Judy (Dijon): 17.
Junor, Beth: 20a, 20b, 20c.
"Just Books": 14.

Kahn, Hermann: 11.
Karin (Greenham Woman): 20c.
Karpf, Anne, Surviving the Holocaust: 2,
Katherine (at Gateshead): 22.
Katherine Davenport Award: 20c.
Kavanagh, Patrick: 5, 6.
Kaye, Jackie (& Roland): 13.

Keane, J.B.: 6.
Keaney, Johnny: 12a.
Keeler, Christine: 23.
Kellett's shop, Dublin (& Irene Kellett): 3.
Kelly, Seamus: 6.
Kenya: 11.
Kennedy, J.F.: 11.
Kent, Bruce: 20a, 20c.
Keogh, Finola: 20a, 20c.
Kerrigan, Gene: 18.
Kickham, C.J.: 4.
Kilcroney, Co Wicklow: 2, 6.
Killiney, Co Dublin: 3,
Kilmacanoge, Co Wicklow: 3, 5,
Kilroy, Tom: 12a, 13. Also, Talbot's Box: 13.
King's Cross Women's Centre: Introduction, 20a, 20b, 20c,
    Loss of grant: 20b.
    as Crossroads Women's Centre: 23.
Kinnock, Neil.: 20a, 20c..
Kirkbymoorside (& Festival): 11.
Kissinger, Henry: 11.
Kyteler, Alice, of Kilkenny: 2,
Koestler, Arthur: 2.
Kops, Bernard: 2, 8.
Kops, Erics: 8.
Kosher regulations, etc.: 5.
Khruschev: 11.

Labour Party (British): 20a, 20c, 21, 22.
Labour Party (Irish): 2, 23.
La Leche: 12b.
Lamburn, Maria: 20a.
Lan, David: 13.
Lancashire: 9.
Lancaster University: 21.
Land League & Ladies' Land League (Anna & Fanny Parnell): 3.
Land League, new: 11.

Lane, John: 11.
Laragh, Co Wicklow: 3.
Larkhill Artillery Range: 20c.
Larry (cousin of Jimmy Timmons): 3.
"Late Late Show" (TV programe): 12a.
Laura & Logan (Greenham Woman & child): 20c.
Laurie (Greenham Woman): 20c.
Laverty, Maura, Tolka Row: 6.
Lawcases at Greenham (as at Sept. '88): --
    Greenham Common Bylaws case,
    Fence Case,
    Restoration Case,
    Action to Preserve Commoners' Rights,
    Imber Village Church Occupation,
    Challenge to Upper Heyford Bylaws: 20c.
Law Courts (in the Strand): 20b, 23.
Lawless, Gerry: 13.
Lawson, Wilfred: 11.
Laze, Rosemary: 20c.
League of Nations: 3.
Le Broquy, Louis: 6.
Lee, Ian: 20b.
Lee, J.J., Ireland 1912 -1985, politics & society: 2.
Leeds: 9.
Leigh, Vivien: 11.
Le Creusot: 17.
Legacy of Cain, The (play): 23.
Lemass, Seán: 12a.
Leonard, Hugh: 5
Lesbian women: 20c, 22.
Lessing, Doris: 11.
Lestrange, Vida: 6, 8.
Lever, Nora: 6.
Levy, Ben: 11.
Lewsen, Charles: 11.
Libel, threats and actions: 20b.
Liberty Hall, Dublin: 11.

Libya: 20a.
Liebowitz, Jo: 20c, 23.
Lilienblum, Moshe Leib: 2.
Limavady, Co Derry: 2.
Lin (at Gateshead): 22.
Lipmans, Eddie & Eva: 2,
Lisa (Greenham Woman, from Canada): 20c.
Little Flower Hall, Bray: 5.
Little Red Book & Maoists: 23.
Littlewood, Joan & Theatre Workshop (Stratford East): 7.
Liverpool women: 20a.
Living Art Exhibition: 6.
Living Theatre, The: 11, 23.
Livings, Henry: 11.
Livingstone, Ken; 13, 23.
Liz (at Gateshead): 22.
Lockwood, Margaret: 5.
Loftus, Paddy: 5.
Loftus, Seán Dublin Bay: 5.
Logue, Christopher: 11.
London: Introduction, 2, 9, 11, 21, 23.
London County Council: 11.
London Hospital, Whitechapel: 2.
London School of Economics: 2, 13.
London Theatre, snapshots, mid-20th cent: 5.
Long barrow (dug up): 20c.
Longfellow, Hiawatha: 4.
Longford Players (and Lord & Lady Longford): 5.
Longley, Edna (& English Dept., QUB): 14.
Longley, Michael: 14.
Longueville House, Mallow, Co Cork: 3.
Loose Theatre: Introduction, 1, 23.
Lorca, Garcia: 7, 11.
Loreto Convent, Bray, Wicklow: 5.
Louie (Greenham Woman): 20c.
Lovell, Alan: 11.
Loyalists (N.Ireland): 20c, 23.

Luxemburg Gardens: 17.
Lynch, Jack: 13.
Lynch, Matty: 12a.
Lynn, Vera: 12a.
Lyric Theatre, Belfast: 14.

"M" & daughter Sarah (at Gateshead): 22.
Maastricht Treaty & Referendum: 17.
McAliskey, Bernadette: 20c.
McAllister, Claire: 6.
Macarthyism: 19.
McAvin, Josie: 5, 6.
MacBride, Maud Gonne: 3.
MacBride, Seán: 5.
McCabe, Leo: 4.
McCafferty, Nell: 12a, 20c.
McCann, Eamon: 13.
McDonald, Di: 20c.
McGrath, John: 11, 23.
McGough, Roger: 11.
McIntyre, Gilbert: 6.
McKinnon, Judge Neill: 13.
McLaughlin, Gerard: 14, 19.
McLoughlin, Bina: 20c.
McLiammoir, Micheal: 3, 4, 6. Also, All For Hecuba; Ill-met by Moonlight: 5.
McLeod, Alison: 11.
MacManus, John: 12a.
MacMaster, Anew: 5.
Macmillan, Harold: 11.
MacMurrough, Dermot: 2.
McNamara, Angela: 12a.
McQuaid, John Charles, Archbishop of Dublin: 2, 3, 4, 5, 6, 11.
MacWeeney, Leslie: 3.
MacWilliam Dr.: 11.
Madrid: Introduction, 16.
Magill: 18.
Malina, Judith: 23.

Malvinas/Falklands: 20a.
Manahan, Anna: 6, 11.
Manchester: 8.
"Mandatus" (legal terminology): 20b.
Manning, John: 3.
Manning, Susan: 3.
Manning, Mary: 3, 6, 12a.
Marabella, Madrid: 16.
Marowitz, Charles: 13.
Martin, Colbert: 5.
Marx, Eleanor: 2, 17, 21.
Marx, Jenny: 17.
Marx, Karl: 2, 17.
Marivaux: 17.
Mary (Coughlan): 12b.
Mary Cecilia, Sister (nun): 4.
Mary Louis, Sister (nun): 4.
Mary Raymond, Mother (nun): 3, 4.
Mary Scholastica, Mother (nun); 3.
Masefield, John: 11.
Mason, Brewster: 7.
Mason, Ronald: 15, 20b, 21.
Mass: 3, 4, 5.
Mathie, Marion (in Rumpole; The Workhouse Donkey): 7.
Matilda (daughter of Eva, Paris): 17.
Mau Mau: 11.
Maureen (at Armthorpe): 21.
Mayes, Elizabeth: 6.
Meacher, Michael: 23.
Meaney, Colm: 13.
Measuring/Valuing unwaged work: 20c.
Medici, Lisa: 20c.
Medicine, mainstream v. alternative: 20b.
Meldon, Maurice, Aisling: 6.
Melford, Jill: 7.
Melford, Jock: 7.
Men on the Blanket (play at Derry Festival): 23.

Mercer, David: 13, 14.
Mercouri, Melina: 18.
Mermaid Theatre: 23.
Merrion Square, Dublin: 19.
Methuen, publishers: 13.
Mia (Greenham Woman): 20c.
Michel (Dijon): 17.
Mickiewicz, Adam: 4.
Middleton & Rowley, The Changeling: 7.
Middleton, Colin: 6.
Mike (at Armthorpe): 21.
Miles, Bernard: 23.
Miles, Glenys: 3,
Militants: 22.
Millar, Ronald, Frieda: 5.
Millington, Mary: 20a, 20c.
Miriam (Greenham Woman): 20a.
Millbank Tower: Epilogue.
Millett, Kate: 3.
Miss Merediths' School, Dublin: 3, 4, 5.
Mistral & Domino (Yellow Gate cats): 20c.
Moby Dick (film): 6.
Molesworth: 20a.
Molesworth rape, the: 20b.
Molloy, M.J., The Paddy Pedlar: 2.
Monika: 6.
Montague, John: 5, 6.
Montague, Lee: 7.
Montague, Lord: 7.
Montmartre: 17.
Moore, George, A Drama in Muslin; Sister Teresa: 4.
Morley, Robert (in The Little Hut): 5.
Morning Star, The: 20b, 22.
Morocco: 2.
Morrison, George, Mise Eire; Saoirse (films): 6.
Morrow, Michael: 6, 7.
Morrow, Bridget: 6.

Monroe, Marilyn: 8.
Moscow Peace Conference: 20a, 20b,
Mosley, Oswald: 2.
Mother and Child Bill (Ireland): 5, 6.
Mother Cat: 5.
Mother Levy's (maternity home): 2.
Motley: 3.
Mountjoy Gaol: 2, 23.
Mount Street Club, Dublin: 5.
Mozart: 4.
Mulcahy, General: 4.
Muldoon, Paul: 14.
Muldoon, Roland: 11.
Mulligan, Eileen: 5.
Murphy, Delia: 6.
Murphy, Eileen: 13.
Murphy, Tom: 17.
Muswell Hill, London: 5, 11, 22, 23.
Muswell Hill Murder: 13.

Naden, David: 11.
Naomi (Greenham Woman): 20c.
National Coal Board: 21.
National Farmers' Union offices: Epilogue.
National Front: 13.
National Fuel Distributor (NFD): 21.
"National Heritage" (i.e. Irish artists): 19.
National Theatre: 13, 23.
National Union of Mineworkers: 11, 21.
National Women's Council of Ireland: 3, 23.
Naxalites: 11.
Neal's (guns): 7.
Nellie (Fahy): 12b.
Nenagh, Tipperary: 3.
Nepal: 20a.
Newell, Seán: 12a.
Newbury: 20a, 20c.

Newbury Court: 20c.
Newbury District Council: 20a, 20c.
Newbury Weekly, The: 20c.
Newcastle upon Tyne: 22.
New Liberty (newspaper): 12b.
Newman House, Dublin: 6.
Newry, Co. Down: 11.
Newsline: 21.
New Life Church: 21.
New Statesman, The: 11, 23.
New York: 7, 11.
Nicaragua: 19, 20c.
Nichols, Peter: 13.
ni Fhatharta, Treasa: 13.
Nixon, Brenda: 21.
NVDA (Non-Violent Direct Action): 20a, 20b, 20c.
No Resting Place (film): 6.
Norman Irish: 2.
North of Ireland: Introduction, 2, 11, 13, 14, 17.
N. Ireland Human Rights Assembly: 20c.
Northern Visions: 19.
Nuns, Benedictine: 20c.
Nuttgens, Patrick: 11.

O'Brien, Edna: 13.
O'Brien, Kate: 4, 13.
O'Casey, Seán: 2, 11. Also, The Drums of Father Ned: 6; Cock-a-Doodle-Dandy: 11.
O'Connor, Anne: 13, 14.
O'Connor, Martin: 17.
O'Connor, Sinead: 17.
O'Donnell, Peadar: 2.
O'Donovan, John: 5.
O'Dwyer, Paul: 12a.
O'Faolain, Seán: 2, 4,6.
O'Flaherty, Liam, The Puritan: 4.
O'Grady, Tim: 13, 15.
O'Keefe, Paul: 14.

O'Mahony, John: 13.
O'Mahony, Nora: 5.
O'Malley bros. (Boston): 12a.
O'Malley, Mary, Once a Catholic: 13.
O'Neill, Dan: 6.
O'Neill, Gerry: 13.
O'Nolan Brian (aka Flann O'Brien, aka Myles na gCopaleen): 2, 6, 17.
O'Reilly, Jo-Jo: 6.
O'Shannon, Grania: 6.
O'Shea, Kathleen: 12b.
O'Shea, Milo: 6.
O'Toole, Peter: 11.
Oakley Street, Chelsea: 8, 23.
Observer, The: 8, 11, 13, 20c, 21.
Odessa: 2.
Olive (Newbury): 20c.
Olivier, Laurence: 7, 8.
Orly airport: 17.
Osborne, John: 11.
Otway, Miss: 6.
Oughterard, Co Galway: 11.
Oval Theatre: 23.

Page, Anthony: 11.
Paisleyites: 6.
Palestine: 2.
Paray-le-Monial: 17.
Paris: 17.
Paris Uprising, 1968: 11.
Parker, Evelyn: 20c.
Patten, Brian: 11.
Peace News: 20b, 20c.
Pearse, Patrick: 3.
Pearson, Susan: 7.
Pembroke Rd., Dublin: 3.
Percival, Jane: 11.
Performance magazine: 23.

Persian Gulf: Introduction, 1.
"Peter Pan": 3, 4.
Petertavy: 11.
Phaedra (TV version): 18.
Phelene (Greenham Woman): 20a.
Philip (J.A.'s cousin): 9.
Philippe & Gwyneth (Dijon & Paris): 17.
Phillips, Leslie: 7.
Phoenix Theatre Club: 7.
Picasso, Pablo, Desire Caught by the Tail: 5.
Pike Theatre, Dublin: 6.
Pimlico, my mother's flat: 7, 8, 9.
Pimm's shop, Dublin: 3.
Pinsker, Leon: 2,
Piper, Anne: 11.
Piper, David: 11.
Pirate Jenny (theatre company): 13.
Pirate Radio: 22.
Plowright, Joan: 7.
Poll Tax: 22.
Pollitt, Geoffrey: 12a.
Pompidou Centre: 17.
Porton Down: 20a.
Pinter, Harold: 2, 11.
PLO: 20a.
Polaris Missile: 20a.
Police (Yorkshire): 11.
Police Bill (Westminster Parlt.): 20a.
Police, Metropolitan (& Special Patrol Group); 20a.
Police, Ministry of Defence (MoD): 20a, 20b, 20c.
Police (personalities):
    Sgt. Moorehouse: 20c.
    "Old Bull": 20c.
    DC Philips: 20c.
    DI Townshend: 20c.
    No. 1807: 20a.
Pollock, Jackson: 8.

Potter, Cherry: 13.
Pottle, Pat: 4.
Power, Arthur; Doris; & son: 3.
Powerscourt House (Oliver & John, footmen): 4.
Pre-RADA: 5.
Prevention of Terrorism Act (PTA): 20a.
Pride & Prejudice (film): 4.
Priestley, J.B.: 8.
Prince and the Showgirl, The (film): 8.
"Princess" (car): 20c.
Pringle, Pat: 6.
Prison experience: 23.
Purdie, Ian: 23.
Pye, Patrick: 6.
Pylon workers, Scots: 20c.
Pyloric Stenosis: 2, 11.

Queen's Speech (Xmas '91): 20c.
Queen's University, Belfast (& Festival): 14.
Quinn, John: 13.
Quinn, Michael: 19.

Rabbi (at Gateshead): 22.
"Rachel", Anna Manahan as (in Live Like Pigs): 11.
Racism: 20b.
Radio Pirate-Woman: Introduction, 19, 20a, 20c, 23.
Rahoon, Galway: 12a, 12b.
Ramayana: 4.
Ramblers' Day: 20c.
Ramsay, Peggy: 15, 23.
Randle, Margaret: 5.
Randle, Michael: 4, 5. 11.
Randle, Terry: 11.
Rank, J. Arthur: 7.
Rapoport, Armand (& friend Eva): 17.
Rattigan, Terence: 5, 7 Also, The Deep Blue Sea: 7.
Rea, Charles: 7.

Rea, Stephen: 13, 23.
Read, Piers Paul: 11.
Reading Crown Court: 20c.
Reagan, David: 7.
Reagan, Ronald: 20a, 20c.
Redcliffe Square: 8.
Redgrave, Michael: 11.
Redgrave, Vanessa: Epilogue.
Redgrove, Peter: 11.
Reece, Roland: 13.
Rees, Merlyn: 12a.
Reeves, Geoffrey: 13.
Reid, Nano: 6.
Reveille: 8.
Rice, Elmer, The Adding Machine: 6.
Richardson, Lorna: 20a, 20c.
Richardson, Tony: 11, 23.
RIP for Irish children, graffiti on FIBUA tombstones: 20c.
Rituals: 20a.
Roberts, Rachel: 11.
Rodway, Norman: 6.
Roberts, Judith (M.D'A's sister): 2, 3, 4, 5.
Ronald Ibbs Players
& plays (Blithe Spirit, French Without Tears; Rookery Nook): 5, 6.
"Rosie", M. D'A. as (in Live Like Pigs): 11.
Rosie (Greenham Woman): 20c.
Rosmuc, Co. Galway: 22.
Roundhouse: 23.
Royal Air Force: 20a.
Royal Artillery: 8.
Royal Court Theatre: Introduction, 6, 7, 8, 11, Epilogue.
Royal Green Jackets: 20c.
Royal Shakespeare Co. (RSC): 23.
RTE: 11, 13.
Ruskin College: 20a.
Russia (& Czars of): 2, 5.
Russian/Irish cultural exchanges: 12b.

Russians (in Greenham base): 20c.
Russian woman, on NVDA: 20c.
Ruth (Greenham Woman): 20c.
Ryan (at Armthorpe): 21.

Saddam Hussein: 20a, 22.
Sahara: 12a.
Salisbury: 20c.
Salisbury Plain: 20a, 20c.
Salomon, Esther: 22.
SALT Treaty: 20a.
"Saltley Gates" play: 13.
Sanctuary, the (at Greenham): 20c.
Sanctuary Trustees: 20c.
Sanders, George (in All About Eve): 6.
Sanity: 20c.
Sartre, J-P: 6, 11.
SAS: 12a, 13, 20c.
Scales, Prunella (in Fawlty Towers): 7.
Scapegoat: 20c.
Scargill, Anne: 21.
Scargill, Arthur: 21.
Schedule of addresses and schools in M.D'A's life, 1935 - 50: 3.
Schlacher & Cinema Action: 23.
Scott, Pam: 6, 8.
"Sculptor, the": 6.
Scully, Paddy: 13.
Scylla (dog): 5.
Secombe, Harry: 12a.
See How They Run (play): 7.
Segovia: 16.
Seka, Johnny: 11.
Seneca women's camp (USA): 20a.
"Seven Days" (TV programme): 12a.
7:84 theatre company: 11, 13.
SDLP: 12a.
Serbia: 20c.

Shackleton, Roger: 6.
Shakespeare, Richard II: 5. Othello: 7.
Shankill Road, Belfast: 14.
Shannon Airport: 1, 7.
Shaw, G.B, In Good King Charles's Golden Days; Pygmalion; Saint Joan: 5. Major Barbara: 11, Epilogue.
Shaw, Robert: 11.
Sheehy, Edward: 6.
Sheehy Skeffington, Andree, Skeff, a life of Owen Sheehy Skeffington: 2,
Sheeran, Pat: 12a.
Sheridan, R.B. : 2.
Short, Claire: 22.
Sian (Greenham Woman): 20c.
Silbury Hill (Womb of the Great Mother): 20a, 20c.
Silkin, Jon: 11.
Simpson, Alan: 6.
Simpson, N.F.: 13.
Sinn Fein (Official): 11, 12a.
Sinn Fein (Provisional): 12a, 17, 20c
Sitwell, Edith: 12a.
Sladen, Verena: 5.
Slattery, Ann: 12a
Slocum, Vera: 6.
Sloman, Roger: 13, 23.
Slow Movement, at Greenham eviction: 20c.
Smith, Georgina: Introduction, 20b, 20c.
Smith, Sir Matthew: 8, 23.
Smith, Roger: 11.
Smolenskin, Peretz: 2,
Smullen, Eamon: 12a.
Smock Alley Theatre, Dublin: 5.
Snazzy dressing (Sarah's): 20c.
"Snowball Action": 20a.
Sniffer Dogs: 20b.
Socialist Feminist Conference: 13.
Socialist Labour League (aka Workers' Revolutionary Party): 11, 23.
Society of Irish Playwrights: 5, 11, 18.

Soho: 7.
Solange (Dijon): 17.
Soldiers: 8, 20a, 20b, 20c, 22, 23.
Somerville-Large family: 3.
South Africa House: 20c.
Spain: 16.
Spain, Kitty: 3, 4.
Spare Rib: 20b.
Spencer, Colin: 13.
Spencer, Stanley: 20c.
Spina-Bifida & Anencephaly: 10.
Spivack, Miss Edith: 2, 5.
Spivack, Mrs: 2.
Splodging: 20c.
Spring, Dick: 23.
Spud (Greenham Woman): 20c.
Spycatcher, attempt to suppress: 20a.
St. Denis, Michel: 7.
St Mary's & St Joseph's College, Belfast: 11.
St Paul's Cathedral: 5.
St Stephen's Green, Dublin (flat): 6.
Stacey family (Laragh): 3.
Stagg, Frank: 12a.
Stanislavsky, My Life in the Theatre: 5.
Star, The: 20b.
Starhawk: 2.
Staunton, Mary Ellen: 12a.
Stein, Gertrude, Two Plays for Children: 5.
Steinbeck: 5.
Stevenson, Melford (Judge): 2.
Stoddart, Moira: 5.
Stokes, Margaret (Karen Arden's mother): 23.
Stokes family: 23.
Stop the Cuts: 23.
Stop the (Gulf) War Committee: 22.
Strachan, Geoffrey: 13.
Strasbourg Court: 13.

Strongbow & Eva (marriage): 2.
Strindberg, The Father; The Ghost Sonata; Miss Julie: 5.
Strip-searching: 23.
Stuart, Aimee: 5.
Stuart, Francis, Iseult Stuart, & children: 3.
Students' Union (QWUB): 14.
Sugan pub theatre: 13.
Suicides: 6.
Summer of the Seventeenth Doll (play): 3.
Sun, The: 20b.
Sunday Telegraph, The: 13.
Suzanne (d. of Vivien Leigh): 5.
Suzanne (Greenham Woman): 20c.
Swift, Carolyn, Stage by Stage (memoirs); The Millstone (play): 6.
Swift, Patrick: 6.
Switzerland: 2.
Synge, Deirdre of the Sorrows: 5.6. The Tinker's Wedding: 5, 6.

Tallaght Theatre Group: 12a.
Tate Gallery: 5.
Taunton (hospital): 11.
Tavner, Janet: 20a, 20c.
Taylor, Coleridge, Hiawatha (cantata): 4.
Taylor, John: 12a.
Tell Me The News (opera): 23.
Tenants' Association: 12b.
Teresa (Greenham Woman): 20c.
Terry, Ellen: 5.
Thatcher, Margaret: 5, 11, 20a, 23.
Thameside Nuclear Free Group: 20c.
Theatre Upstairs (at Royal Court): 13.
Theatre Writers' Union: Introduction, 13, 23.
"Them Wifies": 22.
Thespian Players, Bray: 5.
Therese of Lisieux, Saint: 4.
Thessalonika: 13.
37 Theatre Club, Dublin: 6.

Thomas Aquinas, Saint: 4.
Thomas, Helen: 20c.
Thomas, Janet: 20c.
Thomas, John: 20c.
Thompson, Claire (M.D'A's sister): 2, 3, 4, 5, 6.
Thompson, Paul: 13.
Thorndike, Sybil: 5.
Thorson, Felix & his mother: 2.
"Tiger-eyes": 5, 6.
Tim & Lin (in Cardiff): 20c.
"Time To Go" conference/exhibition: 20c.
"Time To Go" demo: 20c.
Timex factory strike: 21.
Timmons, Jimmy: 3.
Toal, Maureen: 6.
Todd, Mrs: 20c.
Tolstoy, War & Peace: 4.
Toller, Ernst: 5.
Tom (Warden of Friends' Ho.): 20c.
Tommy (at Armthorpe): 21.
Tories: 13.
Tourist Office, Madrid: 16.
Toynbee Hall: 7.
Trade, Irish, with Germany: 3.
Traynor, Oscar: 2.
Treaty of Nice (& EU in general): 2, 6.
Trevor, William: 6.
Trident Missile: 20b, 20c.
"Trident Ploughshares" (resisters): 20b.
Trinity College, Dublin: 3, 5, 6, 14.
Troops Out of Ireland campaign: 13, 20a, 23.
Trudie (at Armthorpe): 21.
TUC: 13, 21.
Turner, Miss: 9.
Tute, Warren: 11.
Tweedy, Hilda: 3.
Tynan, Kenneth: 11.

"Under-5s" playgroup: 21.
UNESCO: 19.
United Irishmen: 2.
United Nations: 23.
UN 4th Women's Conference, 1995: 23.
United States of America: 11, 23.
Unity Theatre, London: 5, 7, 11, 23.
University College, Dublin: 5.
University College, Galway: 11.
Unknown Political Prisoner competition: 6.
Ulster Defence Regiment: 14.
Ulster Museum: 14.
U.S. Air Force (and bases): 8, 11, 20a, 20b, 20c.
USAF flag-lowering at Greenham: 20c.
Ute (Greenham Woman): 20c.

Vassal case: 23.
Van Druten, John, I remember Mama: 5.
Vecchi, Laura: 12a.
Victoria Coach Station: Epilogue.
Vietnam War: 23.
Vienna: 2.
Vivien (at Gateshead): 22.

Waddington, Victor: 6.
Wages for Housework: 20a.
Wajda: 4.
Wakefield Gaol: 12a.
Wales: 8, 20a.
Walford, Peggy: 20c.
Walker, Judith: 20c.
Wanamaker, Sam (in The Power & The Glory): 7.
Ward, Ronald (& Partners): Epilogue.
Ward, Stephen: 7.
War of Independence (Irish): 2, 3.
Waters, John: 3.

Watford, Gwen: 7.
Weapons-of-Mass-Destruction: 23.
Webb, Alan: 11.
Weeks, David: 13.
Welfare State (theatre company): 11.
Welford: 20a.
Welsh language movement: 20c.
Wesker, Arnold: 11, 23.
West Berkshire Council: 20c.
West of Ireland: 6, 7.
Westminster Abbey: 5.
Westminster (parliament): 12a.
Wexford women of '98: 23.
Wheathampstead: 8.
White, Tony: 7.
Whiting, John: 11.
Wicca: 20c.
Wicklow families (Parnells, Bartons, Childerses): 3.
Wicklow, Earl of, his belly-button: 6.
Wilcox, Angela: 14.
Wildeblood, Peter: 7.
Wild Oats (play): 13.
Williams, Tennessee, The Glass Menagerie: 4.
Williams, Emlyn: 7.
Wilson, Colin: 11.
Wilson, Fr. Des: 20c.
Wilson, Harold: 11.
Wilton Place, Dublin: 3,
Windsor: 20a.
Winfield, Joan: 20c.
WINGS (Women's International News-gathering Service): 20c.
Winter, Jane (Liberty): 20c.
Witch, the Greenham: 20a
Witches, Scottish: 20c.
Winter of Disocntent: 13.
Wolfit, Donald: 5.
Woolf, nee Billig (M.D'A's great-aunt): 2.

Woffington, Peg: 2, 5, 8.
Women Against Pit Closures: 21.
Women Count Network: 23.
Women Graduates Assoc. (Irish): 3.
Women in Media & Entertainment (WIME): 23.
Women's Global Peace Conference: 20b.
Women's Lib.: 14.
Women's Sceal Radio: 19, 20a.
Wordsworth, William: 2.
Workers' Revolutionary Party: 22.
Workers' Union of Ireland: 12a.
World War One: 20c.
World War Two: 2, 3, 5, 7, 9.
Wright, David: 6.
Writers Against Reaction: 23.
Writers' Guild: 13.
Wyeman, Dickie: 6.
Wymark, Olwen: 13, 20b.

X (magazine): 6.

Yeats, W.B. (& the Abbey): 6.
Yiddish (language): 2, 5.
Yiddish Theatre (London): 5.
Yoko Ono: 20c.
Yom Kippur: 5.
York Rd. Station, Belfast: 14.
York Trades Council: 22.
Young Mums in Muswell Hill: 23.
Young Vic School: 7.

Zelter, Angie: 20b.
Zionism (incl. Balfour Declaration, Lansdowne proposition, etc): 2, 5.
Zoe (d. of Mary Millington): 20c.
Zog, King: 23.
Zone (play): 14.

ISBN 141203376-4

9 781412 033763